W9-CEW-035

Roosevelt
and
Churchill

ALSO BY DAVID STAFFORD

From Anarchism to Reformism
Britain and European Resistance, 1940–1945
The Silent Game
Camp X: SOE and the American Connection
Spy Wars (with J. L. Granatstein)
Churchill and Secret Service

ROOSEVELT AND CHURCHILL

Men of Secrets

David Stafford

THE OVERLOOK PRESS

WOODSTOCK & NEW YORK

First published in the United States in 2000 by
The Overlook Press, Peter Mayer Publishers, Inc.
Lewis Hollow Road
Woodstock, New York 12498
www.overlookpress.com

Copyright © 1999 by David Stafford

All rights reserved. No part of this publication may be reproduced or
transmitted in any form or by any means, electronic or mechanical, including
photocopy, recording, or any information storage and retrieval system now known
or to be invented without permission in writing from the publisher, except by
a reviewer who wishes to quote brief passages in connection with a review
written for inclusion in a magazine, newspaper, or broadcast.

PICTURE CREDITS
1, 2, 10, 11, 12, 13: Churchill Archives Centre,
Crown Copyright; 3, 4, 5, 6, 7, 8: Franklin D. Roosevelt
Library; 9: Courtesy of Rupert Wilkinson

Library of Congress Cataloging-in-Publication Data

Stafford, David.
Roosevelt and Churchill : men of secrets / David Stafford.
p. cm.
Includes bibliographical references and index.
1. Roosevelt, Franklin D. (Franklin Delano), 1882-1945—Friends and
associates. 2. Churchill, Winston, Sir, 1874-1965—Friends and associates.
3. World War, 1939-1945—Diplomatic history. 4. World War, 1939-1945—
Secret service. 5. United States—Relations—Great Britain.
6. Great Britain—Relations—United States. 7. United States—Foreign
Relations—1933-1945. 8. Presidents—United States—Biography.
9. Prime ministers—Great Britain—Biography. I. Title.
D753 .S68 2000   941.084'092—dc21 [B]   00-055750

Manufactured in the United States of America

3 5 7 9 8 6 4 2
ISBN 1-58567-068-5

To my transatlantic family and friends

Contents

AUTHOR'S NOTE

I write this during the week that the United States Navy launched its latest and most advanced guided-missile destroyer, in Bath, Maine, naming it the USS *Winston S. Churchill* – the first time that any American ship has been named after a British figure since the war of independence over two hundred years ago. The symbolism of the ceremony, attended by a crowd of several thousand, was enriched by the fact that the vessel was personally launched by Churchill's last surviving child, Lady Soames. President Bill Clinton, announcing the decision to the British Parliament in 1995, said the choice to name it after Britain's Second World War leader was so that it could 'ride the seas as a reminder for the coming century of an indomitable man who shaped our age, who stood always for freedom.'

The tenacity of what the British like to call the 'special relationship' would have been inconceivable without the personal bond forged between Franklin D. Roosevelt and Winston Churchill during the Second World War. This has been glorified, exaggerated, mocked, derided, criticised and lamented – and not necessarily in that order – on both sides of the Atlantic over the last fifty years. Yet it endures, as the Maine ceremony so vividly demonstrates, and will surely survive well into the new millennium.

In thinking about and writing this book I have benefited greatly over many years from the work of numerous others. In particular,

I would like to mention the following friends, colleagues and others who have all helped in different ways and at different times: Paul Addison, Director of the Centre for Second World War Studies at the University of Edinburgh; Richard Aldrich; Antony Beevor; Gil Bennett, Chief Historian of the Foreign and Commonwealth Office; Mariana Berry; Laurence Blairon, Information Officer at the International Court of Justice, The Hague; Piers Brendon, Keeper of the Churchill Archive at Churchill College, Cambridge, as well as Allen Kucia, Caroline Lye and Allen Packwood; Harry Bridgman; Ronald M. Bulatoff and Carol Leadenham of the Hoover Institution at Stanford, California; Paul Cardin; Richard Clogg; Lawrence Collins; Jeremy Crang; Ralph Erskine; Michael Foot; Sir Alexander Glen; Rhodri Jeffreys-Jones; Peter Jones, Director of the Institute for Advanced Studies in the Humanities at the University of Edinburgh, who has most generously provided me with suitable accommodation and writing facilities, and whose staff, Anthea Taylor and Charis Stewart, have been indispensable; Warren Kimball; Paul Lashmar; William Leary; Andrew Lownie; James Muller; Verne Newton, Director of the Franklin D. Roosevelt Library at Hyde Park, New York, as well as Raymond Teichman, Robert Parks and other members of his staff; Hayden Peake; Mary June Pettyfer; Ken Robertson; Norman Rose; Alan Samson and Andrew Gordon at Little, Brown; Mark Seaman of the Imperial War Museum; Bradley F. Smith; Sir Peter Smithers; Robert D. Storch; Duncan Stuart, CMG, the SOE Adviser at the Foreign and Commonwealth Office; staff at the National Library of Scotland; Wesley Wark; and Rupert Wilkinson.

Friends and family contacts across the Atlantic have also nurtured the project. I have experienced the rich rewards of Anglo-American relations through my wife Jeanne, an American by birth, and in the United States have frequently enjoyed the generous hospitality of her parents, Bettye and Walt Cannizzo, who lived through the Second World War and retain vivid memories of the Roosevelt and wartime years. To them, to other members of my wife's American family, and to many American friends, I dedicate this book.

DAVID STAFFORD
Edinburgh, 20 April 1999

'If anything happened to that man I couldn't stand it. He is the truest friend; he has the furthest vision; he is the greatest man I have ever known.'

CHURCHILL ON ROOSEVELT, 1943

'One of the greatest sources of danger to us in this war is the temptation to regard as our first enemy the partner that must work with us in defeating the real enemy.'

GENERAL DWIGHT D. EISENHOWER, 1943

'There are no friendly secret services; only the secret services of friendly powers.'

TIME–HONOURED ADAGE

PROLOGUE

Franklin Delano Roosevelt and Winston Spencer Churchill sit chatting together on a bench. The American President stretches his arm along its back towards the British Prime Minister, a cigarette in its holder poised delicately between his fingers. Their body language is relaxed. Churchill, wearing a bow tie, is gripping the inevitable cigar. It seems they have just shared a joke, for each is smiling broadly at the other, like friends caught in an intimate moment by the camera.

Yet this is not some Cartier-Bresson photograph, but a bronze sculpture, and the two men, as its title reminds us, are political allies. Unveiled in 1995 in London's New Bond Street to commemorate the fiftieth anniversary of VE day, it stands a stone's throw from such icons of blue-chip taste as Asprey's, Tiffany & Co. and Cartier – and only a hundred yards or so from Brown's Hotel, where Roosevelt spent part of his honeymoon before the First World War. So popular and celebrated has Lawrence Holofcener's sculpture become that it now forms part of 'the knowledge', the arcane grasp of London's streetscape the capital's taxi-drivers need to acquire for their licence. Tourists perching on the bench to have their picture taken have rubbed Roosevelt's knee shiny with their hands.

It's a remarkable tribute to the enduring relationship between the United States and Britain forged in that last 'good war' half a century ago. Much heart-warming myth has since encrusted around this alliance. The greatest myth-maker was Churchill himself, who in his post-war history of the Second World War airbrushed Anglo-American relations of their blemishes and presented Roosevelt as an almost bosom buddy. Yet in reality Roosevelt never even visited London during the war. The city immortalised for Americans during Hitler's bombing blitz by the famous wartime photograph of St Paul's Cathedral, its dome dramatically etched against a vivid background of flames and smoke, and by the gravelly-voiced reports of Edward R. Murrow over the CBS radio network, was a stranger to the wartime journeys of the President of the United States. This was deliberate. Despite numerous appeals from Churchill, Roosevelt adamantly refused to visit him. His stand had nothing to do with the dangers of journeying to the war-ravaged capital, or the President's increasingly fragile health, factors that did not prevent him from travelling to such far-flung places as Gambia, French Morocco, Egypt, Malta and Iran – not to mention the gruelling trip to Yalta in the Soviet Crimea just weeks before his death.

London was out, Roosevelt told Churchill in December 1942, for political reasons. He did not elaborate, because there was no need. For London was not just the British capital, it was also the heart of an Empire whose territorial possessions straddled the globe, and Roosevelt's long-standing anti-colonialist views were well known to Churchill. Only weeks before, in an 'Open Letter to the People of England', *Life* magazine had spelled out what was also a widespread sentiment among ordinary Americans when it declared that they were not fighting 'to hold the British Empire together'. By visiting London, Roosevelt would have been condemned for placing himself in Churchill's imperial pocket.[1] And for all the criticisms since levelled against Roosevelt – that he failed to anticipate Pearl Harbor, that he secretly manipulated events to drag his country into the war, that he naïvely delivered Eastern Europe into Soviet hands at Yalta, that he refused to bomb Auschwitz and rescue the Jews – it's noteworthy that no one has seriously accused him of selling out to Churchill, the bulldog embodiment of the British Empire.

Ironically, though, the charge of being in Roosevelt's pocket now assails Churchill's reputation in Britain. Until his death in 1965 he was untouchable as the saviour of his nation, a living legend, 'the greatest citizen of the world of our time' in the words of Clement Attlee, the former Labour Prime Minister and Churchill's loyal lieutenant throughout the war. Chipping away at Churchill's image began with critics of his wartime strategy, and Anglo-American competition and rivalry has become a cliché of scholars. More recently, scorn has been poured on him for causing the post-war decline of Britain and the loss of Empire. Churchill's much-vaunted 'grand alliance' with the United States, it has been charged, was a self-delusory handover of power to Roosevelt, with Churchill himself as little more than Roosevelt's 'pensioner'.[2]

Such imperial fantasies may be left to the tearful nostalgia that climaxed with Britain's handover of Hong Kong to China at midnight on 30 June 1997. Churchill deserves better than that. So does Roosevelt. For all that Holofcener's portrait of the two war leaders embodies a myth, it also expresses an important truth. It is, after all, a profoundly human sculpture. Life-size, it deliberately eschews monumentalism and presents the two leaders in all their human frailty. They do not stand or sit face to face in confrontation or even debate, but instead rest companionably side by side as though watching the crowds of tourists go by – many of them American, for this is a popular window-shopping spot for transatlantic visitors. We can even sit between them and not be dwarfed or feel diminished. These are people like us.

Of course, neither in reality was a man of the people. Roosevelt belonged to the unofficial east coast aristocracy of the United States. Churchill, born in Blenheim Palace, was a blue-blooded offshoot of the Marlborough dynasty. Yet each had the ability to inspire visions of hope and optimism that spoke to ordinary people and caused thousands to weep openly when they died – Roosevelt with his radio 'fireside chats', Churchill with his powerful rhetoric and evocations of British history over the BBC. Above all, they forged a powerful personal link that bridged the Atlantic and helped win the war.

Both leaders understood the political value of the personal touch. Each worked hard to create a jovial and informal atmosphere, sending each other greetings at Christmas and birthdays, developing jokes and exchanging wisecracks, enlisting friends and family, remembering each other to their wives, sending them on official missions, and regularly meeting face to face. Their appearances before the cameras – they both had a keen appreciation of the power of the visual image – were deliberately orchestrated events aimed at influencing public opinion. But behind the scenes they also worked hard to keep on track. The miracle is not that they created a rosy wartime myth of their friendship, but that despite significant obstacles they kept two great war machines together for so long and with such effect.

It might have been otherwise. How precarious the personal pitfalls could be was made clear by Roosevelt only weeks after the European war began. Early in December 1939 Joseph P. Kennedy, his ambassador in London, travelled home for his Christmas break, took the night train to Washington and was whisked up in the White House elevator, tired and unshaven, to see Roosevelt. An exhausted-looking President was sitting up in bed pouring coffee from a thermos flask. But he was in a cordial mood. Kennedy, a notorious defeatist about Britain, gave him a gloomy view of British prospects – 'bearish', responded Roosevelt – and then they fell to talking about Britain's First Lord of the Admiralty, Winston Churchill. Why, Kennedy asked, referring to an exchange of letters initiated that September by Roosevelt, was the President carrying out a private correspondence with Churchill? The outburst this provoked took even Kennedy aback. 'I have always disliked him since the time I went to England in 1918,' replied Roosevelt, going on to recall his official visit to Britain as assistant secretary of the navy in Woodrow Wilson's administration, when he had been an official guest of the British Cabinet at a dinner at Gray's Inn Court. 'He acted like a stinker at a dinner I attended, lording it all over us . . . I'm giving him attention now because there is a strong possibility that he will become Prime Minister and I want to get my hand in now.'[3]

Kennedy, no fan of Churchill, certainly exaggerated this story. But there is little reason to doubt its essential truth. Roosevelt's soreness at Churchill went even deeper than he admitted. Churchill had snubbed him even earlier during his first tenure at the Admiralty, when he brusquely refused his request to make an official fact-finding visit to London to observe the Royal Navy at war. 'Hurrah for the Boers,' the schoolboy Roosevelt had cheered when grizzled Dutch farmers bloodied the British Empire's nose in South Africa – and held prisoner the politically ambitious young war correspondent Winston Churchill. As late as 1932, when Churchill visited the United States and sought him out, Roosevelt deliberately avoided him.

Roosevelt shared all the mixed emotions about Churchill's land felt by millions of Americans. On the one hand he was fascinated by its traditions and institutions, and rose magnificently to the occasion when King George VI and Queen Elizabeth paid their official state visit to Washington in June 1939 – the first by a reigning British monarch. But he was repelled by Britain's class-ridden society and imperial hubris. 'Too much Eton and Oxford,' he would say, invariably subjecting British visitors to the White House to ritual censure over an Empire that he saw unforgivingly through the eyes of 1776.[4] Churchill, with his family background, and especially with his robust opposition to Indian independence – which made him enemies even in Britain during the 1930s – was a supreme exemplar of the Briton that Roosevelt so heartily detested. 'Cousins' was how he usually described the British. But they were more like kinsmen of another clan than flesh and blood of the same family. During the war Roosevelt and his right-hand man Harry Hopkins devised a secret code they could use between themselves to talk about important Allied leaders. The secret names were drawn from people connected with Roosevelt's Hyde Park estate. For Churchill, the President chose that of Moses Smith, his outspoken tenant farmer since 1920. And speaking to others about Churchill, Roosevelt never entirely lost the tone of exasperated *bonhomie* and condescension that he used with all his retainers.

As for Churchill, his views about the US President were deeply ambivalent. His own mother was American – indeed, like Roosevelt, a New Yorker – and by contrast with most of his British contemporaries he warmed to things transatlantic. Some of his closest friends were Americans, and he genuinely admired the democratic spirit of the great republic. When he was elected president of the English Speaking Union in 1921, he told Clementine,

xviii   ROOSEVELT AND CHURCHILL

his wife, that friendship with America was 'the only road to tread'.[5]
Yet, well into mature middle age, he regarded Washington as a
potential threat to British interests. Scarcely more than a decade
before his celebrated high-seas meeting with Roosevelt to sign the
Atlantic Charter, he opposed the London Naval Treaty because it
gave the United States an 'almost limitless right to criticise and
interfere' in Britain's affairs.[6] He admired Roosevelt's boldness of
vision, and included him in his pantheon of great contemporaries.
Yet his conservative instincts made him wary of what the New
Deal could deliver. Churchill drew inspiration from the past,
whereas Roosevelt breathed the future.

A rich hinterland of personal and political difference thus
scarred the landscape between them. It helps neither man, nor history, to pretend otherwise. Fantasies about their personal relations,
or about Churchill's American ancestry, or about some innate
Anglo-American intimacy, paradoxically only diminish the stature
of the two men. For their true achievement lay in overcoming the
real and powerful obstacles that stood between them. Nor did
they eliminate them all, even by the end of the war. But they built
the greatest wartime alliance in history, one that endured into the
Cold War that followed.[7] And at its heart stood an intelligence
alliance that lasts to this day.

The most sensitive touchstone of trust between individuals, as well
as nations, is how far they are prepared to share their secrets.
Roosevelt and Churchill were no exception, and how much they
revealed to each other, and how, when and why they co-operated in
the secret war of intelligence provides a significant barometer of the
changing climate between them. Some twenty years after
Roosevelt's anti-Churchill outburst to Joseph Kennedy, the reading
choice of the latter's son, President John Fitzgerald Kennedy, provided a telling glimpse of their legacy. In 1961 the same *Life*
magazine that had been so critical of the British Empire placed the
British novelist Ian Fleming's James Bond novel *From Russia, With
Love*, in a top-ten list of Kennedy's favourite reading. Jacqueline
Kennedy gave a copy to the CIA director Allen Dulles, and the
James Bond cult in the United States was suddenly under way. The
blockbuster Hollywood versions that followed transformed Bond's

relationship with his fictional CIA buddy Felix Leiter into the central narrative of a Cold War soap opera.[8]

Fiction pinpointed a truth whose details were then still opaque. The world of James Bond embodied a reality about the complex web of intelligence and espionage that lay at the heart of the London–Washington political axis. As the Washington-based journalist Christopher Hitchens has said, this forms one of the most fascinating subtexts of the 'special relationship'. It also provides, in the words of the former British diplomat Robin Edmonds, a 'hidden dimension' of wartime Anglo-American relations. By the end of the war Americans and Britons were toiling side by side, breaking enemy codes and carrying out joint intelligence operations behind enemy lines around the globe.[9]

The story of wartime cloak-and-dagger agencies such as the American Office of Strategic Services (OSS), the British Special Operations Executive (SOE) and Secret Intelligence Service (SIS), and the massive codebreaking operations the two allies mounted against Germany and Japan, has often been told. Yet conspicuously absent from these accounts have been the two great war leaders themselves. This does them an injustice and distorts history. Both Churchill and Roosevelt were fascinated by the world of espionage, and each played an active and crucial part in waging secret war. The intelligence communities they built were not just machines for waging war, they gave them tools for the personal wielding of power.

Churchill was a prominent player in the creation of British intelligence operations before the First World War, and eagerly followed the exploits of his codebreakers and secret agents in the Second. 'Where are my golden eggs?' he would demand, in requesting his regular diet of top-secret files of intercepts. Sir Stewart Menzies, the head of Britain's Secret Intelligence Service from 1939 to 1952, was an almost daily visitor to his office; one of his oldest friends, 'Top' Selborne, was the minister in charge of the Special Operations Executive; and the fate of its secret agents behind enemy lines often preyed on his mind. But he could be ruthless about covert action against enemies, as demonstrated in the assassinations of SS General Reinhard Heydrich and the pro-Nazi French Admiral François Darlan, and he authorised an SOE attempt on Hitler's life. The triumphs of British intelligence owe much to his personal interest and inspiration.

By contrast, Roosevelt's role has remained more hidden. By character he was a deeply secret man, and to historians his decisions have remained opaque. 'I am a juggler,' he once said, 'and I don't let my right hand know what my left is doing . . . I am perfectly willing to mislead and tell untruths if it will help win the war.'[10] His biographers have remained astonishingly silent about his part in the intelligence war. Yet here, as with his role as commander-in-chief of the American armed forces, his apparent vagueness concealed an active leadership that made him a warlord equal to Churchill. In 1942 a British intelligence mission to Washington, bewildered by the proliferation of sister agencies in the capital, concluded that 'the only common factor in this tangled skein [is] the President himself'.[11] Without his personal interest and direction, wartime American intelligence would have taken a radically different track.

Together, both men built an alliance greater than the sum of its parts. They were not alone, of course, and the intelligence professionals on both sides were indispensable. But only Roosevelt and Churchill could break the inevitable bureaucratic logjams and map out the route ahead. It took Roosevelt's personal admiration for British intelligence to first open the doors for its experts in New York and Washington, and he took breathtakingly daring decisions before Pearl Harbor to help Churchill's shadow warriors. One of the boldest, detailed here for the first time, was to support a $10 million bribery scheme to stop General Francisco Franco from throwing in his lot with Hitler. Involving Roosevelt's close friend and intimate Henry 'the Morgue' Morgenthau, his Secretary of the Treasury, as well as a frozen bank account in the Swiss Bank Corporation in New York and the machinations of the sinuous Majorcan multi-millionaire Juan March, bankroller to General Franco, it provides a classic example of secret financial subversion during the Second World War.

Churchill knew he could count on Roosevelt. Only his impatient insistence ensured that early British codebreaking triumphs were shared with the Americans, and his frequent visits to Washington buttressed the complex task of building an effective and secure intelligence link. And it took a remarkable degree of personal trust in Roosevelt for him to clear the ground by confessing so frankly in 1942, in one of their late-night White House chats, that before Pearl Harbor his experts had been breaking American codes. 'But now,' he added, 'I've ordered them to stop.'

The alliance was the product of need and hard bargaining, not of sentiment. Roosevelt did not live to tell his side of this story. Churchill, who did, was governed by secrecy and sentiment to edit and distort it. But on both sides of the Atlantic documents now tell a fuller story. OSS and SOE papers are open to researchers, as are the vast bulk of Churchill's own intelligence files, and both his and Roosevelt's personal papers. So are documents from the 'Venona' project – decrypts of wartime cables sent to Moscow by NKVD intelligence officers in New York and Washington that have been released by the National Security Agency. In one of these decrypts a source codenamed 'deputy' reports on a meeting he attended between Roosevelt and Churchill in Washington DC when only three persons were present. The date of the meeting identifies 'deputy' as none other than Harry Hopkins, Roosevelt's closest wartime confidant and his crucial intermediary with Churchill. Living in the White House for much of the war, Hopkins has been described as 'Roosevelt's own personal foreign office', being a combination of chief of staff and national security adviser. Churchill valued him so highly that he said that if ever Hopkins was elevated to the peerage he should take the title 'Lord Root of the Matter'. But was Hopkins a controlled Soviet agent, or was some NKVD intelligence officer so desperate to ingratiate himself with Moscow that he presented a harmless conversation with Hopkins as more sinister than it was?

Even now, it is often difficult to 'read' the intelligence, and the role it played in winning the war for the Allies has often been inflated. Both on the battle front and at home intelligence agencies could get things badly wrong. One notable example directly affected Roosevelt. An early American study written about Roosevelt and Churchill is Joseph P. Lash's 1971 book, *Roosevelt and Churchill, 1939–1941: The Partnership That Saved the West*. Lash himself fell foul of the chaos, rivalries and mistakes of American intelligence. A former secretary of the radical American

Student Union and journalist, he befriended Eleanor Roosevelt in 1940 and became an important confidant and frequent visitor to Val-Kill, her cottage on the Roosevelt estate. In March 1943, by which time Lash had entered the army, they met in the Blackstone Hotel, Chicago. The Counter-Intelligence Corps (CIC) of G-2, US Army intelligence, which had already been monitoring Lash's correspondence with Eleanor, bugged the room. Discovering this, Eleanor complained to US Army Chief of Staff George C. Marshall, who immediately disbanded the CIC and kicked 'a lot of butts'. But G-2 officers continued to spread rumours about Lash and Eleanor. Confusing a tape of Lash and his mistress making love in a hotel room with that of the Blackstone Hotel encounter, they told the FBI that the First Lady and Lash had engaged in sexual intercourse. This and other fiascos led Frank Knox and Henry Stimson, Secretaries of the Navy and Army respectively, to agree that 'our intelligence services are pretty bum'.

Did the allies cease to spy on each other after Pearl Harbor, as Churchill promised Roosevelt? The answer is both yes and no, for mirrored in the fractured world of wartime Anglo-American intelligence are all the complexities, suspicions and rivalry embedded in the personal relations between Roosevelt and Churchill. For if secret intelligence is a touchstone of trust, it also provides a gauge of difference and discord, competition and conflict.

The two men sitting on that London bench were like any others in real life. They had secrets they shared. But they also possessed knowledge they withheld, because their interests were never totally the same. From 'Ultra' – the top-grade intelligence from broken German ciphers that reached him daily in special files – Churchill knew when Hitler had called off his 1940 invasion plan against Britain. But to keep the pressure on Roosevelt to get American help, he did not reveal this to the President. Different vistas for the peace ahead certainly loomed into the mind of each national leader. In Asia, Churchill's hope of restoring the British Empire clashed violently with Roosevelt's hopes for a post-colonial world, and by 1945 he was denouncing Roosevelt's intelligence chief, William J. 'Wild Bill' Donovan, as 'that dirty Donovan' for his efforts to thwart British plans. Similar intelligence clashes occurred in the Balkans and the Middle East.

'Fighting with allies' therefore had an ironic meaning for Churchill and Roosevelt. The closer they got, the more they needed to know about each other. 'No lover,' confessed Churchill after the war, 'ever studied the whims of his mistress as I did those of President Roosevelt.' And like lovers throughout the ages, he sometimes resorted to clandestine tricks.

Thus, when it seemed that Roosevelt was at political risk from the ambitions of the Pacific war hero General Douglas MacArthur, Churchill sent his own personal agent, SIS officer Gerald Wilkinson, to report to him personally on the General. Although roundly denounced at the post-war Pearl Harbor hearings by MacArthur's intelligence officer General Charles Willoughby as a British spy, Wilkinson's secret mission for Churchill has, astonishingly, remained obscure until now. Likewise, Roosevelt despatched his personal friend William Phillips to India. Ostensibly instructed to report back to Roosevelt, in reality he travelled to set up an outpost of OSS that would deliver intelligence to Washington about the growing nationalist threat to Britain's hold on its 'jewel' of Empire.

Yet such episodes only reinforce the conclusion that the strong personal link between Churchill and Roosevelt was vital to wartime Anglo-American relations. Any of the intelligence quarrels simmering beneath the surface could have exploded into open conflict had either leader behaved differently. Indo-China, flashpoint for the later Vietnam War, was an obsession for Roosevelt, who strenuously opposed efforts by General Charles de Gaulle, leader of the Free French, to regain the territory for France. This profoundly challenged plans for a secret war against the Japanese, and British and American intelligence were at loggerheads. Yet Churchill insisted that nothing on the issue, whatever its rights and wrongs, should threaten relations with Roosevelt. 'Do not,' he ordered the Foreign Office in 1944, 'raise this before the presidential election; the war will go on for a long time.' Roosevelt likewise backed off over India in deference to Churchill, refusing in the end to give his personal emissary Phillips the backing he requested.

The role of intelligence, or indeed of the wartime London–Washington link, should not be exaggerated. Codebreakers, spies and secret agents did not win the war, although they certainly helped shorten it, and the Anglo-American alliance against the Axis powers was only part of a far broader global upheaval that began with Japan's attack on China in the mid-1930s. The atomic bomb that ended the conflict in 1945 is a separate story of Anglo-American alliance and secrecy in its own right, and is not dealt with here. Neither is the reaction of Roosevelt and Churchill to the Holocaust, and what their intelligence revealed of it. On reflection, I have decided that this still unfolding story, too, is so important that it deserves separate treatment.[12]

What Churchill and Roosevelt achieved, however, was momentous. Personally, they replaced doubt and suspicion with trust and respect, and as national leaders built an intelligence alliance with many victories to its name. In the Cold War that followed, it provided the backbone of Anglo-American defence. Roosevelt was dead by then, and Churchill out of power. But it was their legacy. No wonder they still smile on that London bench.

1

⇒►◦◄═

MEN OF SECRETS

Outside CIA headquarters at Langley, Virginia, stands another bronze, life-size statue, this time of Nathan Hale, his hands bound and a noose around his neck. A graduate of Yale, he is celebrated as America's first 'patriot spy'. He was a 21-year-old captain in George Washington's Continental Army when he volunteered to spy behind British lines. Captured in New York City, he was hanged in September 1776. As he mounted the scaffold, he is reputed to have said, 'I only regret that I have but one life to lose for my country.'

Four years later Major André, spymaster to the British commander Sir Henry Clinton, suffered the same fate as Hale for negotiating with Benedict Arnold, the commander of West Point, to betray its secrets to the British. Caught when the plot was foiled, he was hanged by the Americans in October 1780.

Both spies have become legendary in the annals of Anglo-American intelligence. Yet behind each stood a spymaster usually invisible or unnoticed. American mythology long held that the New World had cast off the evil habits of the Old, not least the murky world of espionage, counter-espionage, codebreaking, deception and domestic surveillance. Yet the nation's first President, George Washington, regarded intelligence as one of his top priorities. 'The necessity of procuring good intelligence,' he told one of his secret agents, 'is apparent and need not be further urged. All that remains for me to add is that you keep the whole matter as secret as possible. For upon secrecy, success depends . . .'[1] Most of his successors took the same view. When William Casey, Director of Central Intelligence under President Ronald Reagan, declared that his first predecessor was none other than George Washington, he was uttering an awkward but undeniable truth about the traditions of the White House.

As for the British, its leaders have always relied on secret services to obtain intelligence about foreign powers and keep tabs on dissidents at home. The Victorian years of peace and prosperity made this less important. But for both America and Britain the end of the nineteenth century was a turning-point. The defeat of the Spanish Empire in the war of 1898 meant that the United States was now a world power, while the rise of the Kaiser's Germany posed a threat to a Britain already under pressure from Irish nationalism and domestic radicalism. The Americans created an Office of Naval Intelligence, and in 1909 the British, in total secrecy, established the Secret Service Bureau for both espionage and counter-espionage.

Roosevelt and Churchill, then both young and aspiring politicians, absorbed the spirit of these years. The intensity of their partnership during the Second World War often obscures the fact that in many respects they were an ill-assorted pair. Paradoxically, each defied his national stereotype. Churchill, the nostalgic Victorian wedded to the glories of Empire, was emotional, direct and transparent, with a lifelong predilection for the company of self-made men. Roosevelt, the New World Democrat, had the manners of an English gentleman, and behind the surface bonhomie was impenetrable, enigmatic, secretive and machiavellian. Churchill carefully wrote down his thoughts and instructions. Roosevelt was deliberately informal, often giving inconsistent verbal orders. Churchill described him as 'a charming country gentleman whose business methods are almost non-existent'.

Yet they had much in common. Each was an ambitious high-flyer who lived and breathed politics, and each courageously overcame severe handicaps: Roosevelt a crippling attack of polio, Churchill a debilitating childhood stammer and lifelong bouts of depression. Both leaned heavily on their wives. Eleanor became her husband's political eyes and ears, Clementine provided the emotional rock on which Churchill stood. Each, too, was accused of being a turncoat and evoked bitter political enmity. The patrician Roosevelt who brought in the New Deal was loathed by Republicans, while many British Tories never forgave Churchill's early radicalism or his maverick behaviour after he returned to the Conservative fold. Echoes of these controversies still have potency on both sides of the Atlantic.

They shared another thing in common. From their knowledge of the world and experience of politics they knew what intelligence could deliver. Neither lacked courage to use the levers of office, and intelligence was a useful source of power and influence. Combined with their personal vision and imagination, it delivered important rewards. Roosevelt has been described as a 'genius of the unexpected, maestro of the improvisational, [and] artist of the dramatic [whose] mind danced across the scene where his legs would not carry him'.[2] Churchill was similarly agile – 'his mind once seized of an idea works with enormous velocity around it', noted the British journalist A. G. Gardiner, a rare and early admirer, on the eve of the First World War, '[it] intensifies it, enlarges it, makes it shadow the whole sky'.[3]

By nature, Roosevelt liked secrets. An only child with a powerful mother, he needed them. A lifelong reader of spy novels, as a student at Harvard he constructed his own secret cipher for recording special confidences in his personal diary. One such entry translated into 'E. is an angel'. It referred to his cousin Eleanor, the favourite niece of President Teddy Roosevelt, and he married her soon after. But his first encounter with the official world of intelligence came as Assistant Secretary of the Navy under Woodrow Wilson. Here he found himself responsible for overseeing the Office of Naval Intelligence. It had been a small and sleepy outfit until the First World War catapulted it into the wider and rougher world of international intrigue.[4]

Roosevelt's enthusiastic embrace of its work marked an important moment in American intelligence. He spent much of 1916 organising the Naval Reserve Force, where he cast aside the pretence that Americans were innocents and recruited like-minded Ivy League friends for secret work. Like him, they regarded it as both glamorous and legitimate. Those destined to run American intelligence in the future would no longer be regarded as social outcasts or political lepers, but could include the best and the brightest.[5] He even recruited an espionage network of undercover agents in Latin America behind the back of an exasperated Director of Naval Intelligence.

In July 1916, in the so-called 'Black Tom' incident, German saboteurs set off an explosion that destroyed the most important loading terminal in New York harbour for munitions to Britain. It convinced Roosevelt that there was an extensive 'Fifth Column' of German–Americans conspiring to sabotage the war effort. After the United States finally entered the war in 1917, he bombarded the new Director of Naval Intelligence, Captain Roger Welles, with requests for information about alleged German–American plots, sent him alarmist reports from his own sources, and even fanta-sised later that he had carried a revolver in a shoulder-holster after becoming a target for assassination by German secret agents.

Welles proved a congenial soulmate and soon the ONI was stuffed with Wall Street lawyers, financiers and stockbrokers.[6] Roosevelt also learned about the significant co-operation that had developed with British naval intelligence in the United States through their naval attaché, Captain Sir Guy Gaunt. A colourful Australian-born *bon vivant*, Gaunt had taken to the murky world of counter-espionage like a duck to water and ran a network of agents penetrating German–American organisations and others considered subversive by the British. When not running his agents from the Biltmore Hotel in New York City, he was carefully cul-tivating Colonel House, President Wilson's confidant and trouble-shooter. '[Gaunt] tells me,' confided House to his diary, 'the British intelligence is marvellously good.'[7] Thanks to Gaunt, ONI files soon bulged with the names of Irish rebels, Hindu plot-ters and Bolshevik terrorists.[8]

Gaunt's superior in London was the legendary Director of British Naval Intelligence, Admiral Sir 'Blinker' Hall, who ran British naval codebreaking (known as Room 40) as well as a mul-titude of secret agents engaged in covert operations around the globe. Admiral Sims, the American naval representative in London who had his own intelligence operations in Europe, told Welles that Hall and the British had broken 'practically every cipher' that they had been put up against.[9] The Zimmerman telegram affair dramatically illustrated the point.

In January 1917 the German Foreign Minister, Arthur Zimmerman, sent a cipher telegram to the German ambassador in Mexico announcing his country's decision to begin unrestricted submarine warfare the following month. If the Americans entered the war, Zimmerman wrote, he would suggest that Germany and Mexico 'make war together, make peace together', with Mexico being rewarded with territory from Texas, New Mexico and Arizona. Audaciously, Zimmerman sent the telegram via Count Bernstorff, his ambassador in Washington, using the American transatlantic cable recently placed at Berlin's disposal by President Wilson to facilitate peace feelers. What neither Wilson nor Zimmerman knew was that British codebreakers were regularly tapping the cable to read American diplomatic ciphers. They quickly intercepted Zimmerman's message, broke its cipher, and by early February its plaintext was lying on 'Blinker' Hall's desk.

How the British naval intelligence chief resolved the dilemma of revealing Zimmerman's plan to the Americans while disguising its source is the stuff of spy fiction and has often been told.[10] Simply put, it involved a British agent in Mexico City stealing a copy of Zimmerman's telegram and claiming it had been intercepted in North America. Thunderstruck at this German duplicity, Wilson abandoned hopes of remaining neutral and publication of the telegram in the press paved the way for Congress to approve his declaration of war in April. German espionage both within the United States and 'at our very doors', as an outraged Wilson declared, proved that Berlin was neither peaceful nor trustworthy.

Roosevelt was entranced by the whole affair, especially as, behind the scenes, one of his oldest Harvard friends had played a part in the coup. This was Edward Bell ('Ned' to Roosevelt) who under cover as Second Secretary of the American Embassy in London was liaison officer with Hall and other British intelligence agencies. It was to Bell that Hall had handed the text of Zimmerman's message once it was sanitised for American eyes.[11]

Roosevelt had done favours for Bell, and soon Bell was able to reciprocate.

In July 1918 Roosevelt arrived in Britain on official navy business. Welcomed at Portsmouth by Admiral Sims, he was whisked off in a Rolls-Royce to the Ritz Hotel in London. Here the British laid out the red carpet. The First Lord of the Admiralty organised an inspection tour of British and American bases, he had a friendly talk with Prime Minister David Lloyd George, he drove out to see Nancy Astor at Cliveden, and he met Arthur Balfour, the Foreign Secretary. He also had a forty-five-minute audience with King George V, proudly writing to his mother that the monarch was shorter than he expected but 'delightfully easy to talk to'.[12]

But the highlight of his visit was a personal call to the Admiralty and Bell's good friend, 'Blinker' Hall. Roosevelt never forgot the encounter. In the midst of their talk Hall suddenly said, 'I am going to ask that youngster at the other end of the room to come over here . . . I want you to ask him where he was exactly twenty-four hours ago.' Roosevelt did as he asked. 'I was in Kiel, sir,' replied the young man. That he was talking to a secret agent supposedly returned from behind enemy lines so impressed Roosevelt that twenty years later he could recount the episode in detail to Hall's successor, Admiral John Godfrey, in the White House. What he probably failed to realise was that it was all a charade designed to divert attention from Room 40's codebreaking work. Roosevelt came away convinced that British intelligence was the best in the world, blissfully unaware that it was also breaking American ciphers and would continue to target them well into the 1920s.[13] It was also on this London visit that he had the encounter with Churchill he later described to Joseph Kennedy.

Back in the United States, Roosevelt's passion for secret agents almost sabotaged his political career. A homosexual scandal had engulfed the Newport naval base. Disregarding advice that the affair was irrelevant to naval intelligence, he set up a special investigative unit. Paid out of a special fund, its work culminated in the arrest and trial of several Newport civilians, including the base's naval chaplain. But the scandal escalated dangerously when it emerged that sexual entrapment had been used and that enlisted men had gone well beyond the bounds of duty in their pursuit of the guilty. The chaplain was acquitted, and a naval court of enquiry severely criticised Roosevelt for his role in the affair. By this time he had resigned as Assistant Secretary of the Navy to run unsuccessfully as Democratic vice-presidential candidate in the 1920 election. The Republican-dominated Senate Naval Sub-Committee strongly condemned his actions, and while Roosevelt claimed he was innocent of the details of the Newport investigations and was the victim of partisan politics, it was clear he had deliberately kept many of his instructions verbal rather than commit them to paper.[14] Already he had learned the skills of plausible deniability.

After he entered the White House in 1933 he quickly resumed his interest in intelligence. Four years before, Henry Stimson, the Secretary of State, had abolished the 'Black Chamber', the nation's first peacetime codebreaking agency, famously declaring that 'gentlemen do not read each other's mail'. Later, in the shadow of Pearl Harbor, critics would claim that this had neutered American codebreaking during the 1930s. In reality, it merely redirected it into more secret channels in order to conceal it from an isolationist nation and Congress.[15] The army set up its Signals Intelligence Service under the codebreaking genius, William Friedman, and by the mid-1930s it was regularly cracking Japanese diplomatic ciphers. By the end of the decade these were being discreetly circulated in Washington under the codename 'Magic'.

Likewise, the navy's cryptanalytic branch, Op-20-G, made significant headway against Tokyo's ciphers, although it was constantly racing against ever more complex machine systems. Then, shortly after the outbreak of the Sino-Japanese war, in December 1937, the gunboat USS *Panay* – the American navy's most successful spy ship of its time, crammed with intelligence material (and the first American warship destroyed by enemy action in the twentieth century) – was sunk in the Yangtse river by Japanese warplanes while observing Japanese operations outside Nanking. Behind the scenes Roosevelt was already contemplating the intelligence alliance he was to forge with Churchill. Four days later the British ambassador in Washington, Sir Robert Lindsay, was a guest of honour at a White House reception. Afterwards, Roosevelt asked him to stay behind for a private conversation.

Here he reminisced warmly about Sir Guy Gaunt and Anglo-American intelligence co-operation during the First World War, hinting strongly that he had been deeply involved. Surely it was time to again inaugurate a systematic exchange of secret information?

Lindsay thought Roosevelt was in one of his worst inspirational moods and that his ideas sounded like 'the utterances of a hare-brained statesman or amateur strategist'.[16] Nonetheless, he said they were worth exploring. Over the next twelve months Roosevelt discreetly supported highly secret talks between the British Admiralty and the US Navy which led to limited intelligence exchanges the following year. After Hitler's occupation of Prague in March 1939 killed off hopes of European peace and intensified demands for naval talks with the British, Roosevelt repeated his praise for Gaunt. Simultaneously an old friend, Admiral William Leahy, the commander of naval operations (and later his wartime White House chief of staff) oversaw an expansion of the Office of Naval Intelligence and its strengthening in the naval hierarchy. Roosevelt also initiated exchanges of military information between the American and British armies.[17]

But Roosevelt was never content with official channels alone. He also developed personal contacts as alternative sources of information. One of the most prolific was the syndicated Washington journalist John Franklin Carter, whose appeal to Roosevelt lay in his easy access to the NBC shortwave radio network and the fact that he could come and go at the White House without attracting suspicion. Roosevelt used him for private investigative work and paid him generously from his Presidential Emergency Fund. Apart from producing over six hundred reports on a huge variety of topics before Roosevelt died, he also investigated the performance and loyalty of unhappy members of the Roosevelt team.

Another personal source was the wealthy and gregarious Philadelphian William C. Bullitt, an influential fundraiser for his 1932 election whom he sent on a private fact-finding mission to Europe and later appointed ambassador in Moscow and Paris. There was also the celebrated aviator Charles Lindbergh, whose isolationist views and admiration for Hitler opened doors that were closed to others. After three inspection tours of Hitler's

Luftwaffe, Lindbergh passed on highly exaggerated estimates of Nazi strength to the White House.

Roosevelt's most prominent informant, however, was Vincent Astor, his wealthy Hudson Valley neighbour and distant cousin in whose heated indoor pool at Rhinebeck, just north of the Roosevelt estate at Hyde Park in upstate New York, Roosevelt had exercised his polio-damaged legs in the 1920s. In 1927 Astor formed a secret society he called 'The Room', a group of about twenty close and influential friends from the world of business that met regularly in New York to discuss financial and international topics. Founded with Astor and Theodore and Kermit Roosevelt, sons of the former President, it included the banker Winthrop Aldrich, the journalist and world traveller Marshall Field III, the publisher Nelson Doubleday, Judge Frank Kernochan, and David Bruce, a foreign service officer and future wartime head of the OSS in London and ambassador to London and Peking. Nearly all had some background in intelligence and one, Sir William Wiseman, a partner in the Wall Street investment bankers Kuhn-Loeb, had headed Britain's intelligence service in New York during the First World War.

Roosevelt highly valued the intelligence they provided, and in 1938 he secretly approved a Pacific cruise by Astor in his luxury yacht, the *Nourmahal*, to spy on Japanese military, naval, air force and radio installations in the Marshall Islands. 'The information-gathering side of our cruise has proved interesting, instructive, and I hope, will be helpful,' cabled Astor enthusiastically to Roosevelt from Honolulu.

But in the long run the most important of FDR's intelligence sources was the wealthy New York lawyer William 'Wild Bill' Donovan. Variously described as America's last hero and its first director of central intelligence, the silver-haired Donovan was a man of indefatigable energy and enthusiasm whose thirst for action and adventure was to leave an indelible mark on America's intelligence community for the next quarter of a century.

Donovan, said movie director John Ford, who worked for him during the war, was 'the sort of guy who thought nothing of parachuting into France, blowing up a bridge, pissing into Luftwaffe gas tanks, then dancing on the roof of the St Regis hotel with a

German spy'.[18] Hollywood hype aside, this neatly captures the swashbuckling spirit of Donovan that Roosevelt admired. He was as adept at waging guerrilla war at home as he was abroad, and left in his wake a trail of wounded bureaucrats and interdepartmental jungle fires.

A former classmate of the President at Columbia Law School, he was a self-made man. Born in Buffalo of a poor Irish immigrant family, he won the name 'Wild Bill' while fighting against Pancho Villa with Pershing's expedition to Mexico in 1916, and he returned from the Western Front in France as the most decorated soldier in the American army; serving with New York's 'Fighting Irish' regiment, he won the Congressional Medal of Honor, the DSC and the Croix de Guerre. Over the next decade he held both state and federal office for the Republicans, then moved to New York to establish a highly successful and lucrative business specialising in international law. Here he made contact with The Room, where his foreign contacts and travel soon recommended him to Roosevelt. In 1935 the President sent him on an unofficial mission to report on Italy's military performance in Abyssinia, and in 1938 he attended German army manoeuvres and investigated the Spanish Civil War from General Franco's side. By the time war broke out in Europe he was an ardent anti-isolationist and knew more than most Americans about European military affairs.[19]

While Donovan, Astor and others gathered foreign intelligence for him, others worked on counter-espionage. Hitler had launched an intelligence war against the United States, and with vivid memories of the 'Black Tom' explosion Roosevelt was soon obsessed again about German spies in America. In 1934 he summoned J. Edgar Hoover, the Director of the FBI, to the White House and told him to investigate fascist and Nazi groups, later extending the order to Communists. In 1938 Hoover's men exposed a massive spy ring operating in Manhattan headed by Gunther Rumrich, a US Army deserter of German background. The trial that followed spawned sensational headlines, deepened Roosevelt's fears of internal conspiracy, and jolted him into seeking increased appropriations for counter-espionage. He also ordered Hoover to co-ordinate his efforts with army and naval intelligence and the State Department. Two years later Hoover reassured him that all potential enemy espionage was under control. Under Roosevelt, the FBI enjoyed an enormous expansion of its powers, including an intensive programme of secret domestic surveillance.[20]

Typically, Roosevelt also liked to be sure himself. Naval intelligence had always dabbled extensively in domestic affairs, and in the 1930s it considerably expanded its domestic surveillance, targeting political and labour radicals and such organisations as the American Civil Liberties Union. To discuss its reports, Roosevelt frequently met as often as three times a week with the Director of Naval Intelligence. To prevent liberal protests he kept such contacts secret. His efforts to centralise and strengthen intelligence even further met with bureaucratic and media resistance. 'No glorified "OGPU" [Soviet secret police] is needed or wanted here,' declared the *New York Times*.[21]

Ironically, Soviet espionage was already at work in America. But Roosevelt, like most others, misunderstood the threat. This was seen in the case of Whitaker Chambers.

A journalist, Chambers was a courier and contact in Washington for Soviet intelligence. In 1938 he recanted his allegiance to Moscow, and after hiding for several months to escape Stalin's assassins re-emerged as a writer for *Time* magazine. Shocked by the brutal cynicism of Stalin's pact with Hitler in August 1939, he told his story to Adolf Berle, Roosevelt's international security adviser in the State Department, and also pointed the finger at more than thirty Communist agents at work in the federal government, including the senior State Department official Alger Hiss. Berle told neither his department nor the FBI, but did, according to one source, pass the intelligence on to Roosevelt. But the President merely 'scoffed at the charge'.[22] He was incredulous that there could be a Soviet espionage ring in his administration; to him Communists were blue-collar trade union militants, not suave representatives of the east coast establishment. Gentlemen like Hiss could simply not be traitors.[23] As a result, no counter-intelligence programme for identifying Communist agents in the federal government was put in place.

Six weeks after the Munich crisis Roosevelt chaired a special conference at the White House to decide on US air power requirements. A full-scale review of national strategy and war plans was already under way, and he was deeply alarmed by intelligence reporting that the Germans were making thousands of military aircraft. Lindbergh estimated annual German production at some 9,000 military aircraft, a figure backed up by the American military attaché in Berlin. Bullitt, now ambassador in Paris, had already passed on similar figures. To Roosevelt, the conclusion was obvious. This huge air capacity had fatally encouraged Hitler and intimidated the allies. To defend the western hemisphere, he announced, America required some 10,000 planes. Thus began the shaping of US rearmament.

The decision throws revealing light on Roosevelt's approach to intelligence. For one thing the figures for German aircraft production were hopelessly exaggerated – the true number was closer to 3,000 per annum. Second, the intelligence came from a mix of unofficial and official sources, with Roosevelt giving as much weight to the former as to the latter. And third, he even came up with numbers of his own – 12,000 – from no identifiable source except his own imagination.

Army Secretary Henry Stimson later complained that Roosevelt rarely followed a consecutive chain of thought, but was full of stories and incidents and hopped around in discussion from suggestion to suggestion. It was all, he despaired, 'like chasing a vagrant beam of sunshine around a vacant room'.[24] This was the Roosevelt method. Unimpressed by professional bureaucracies, he most trusted his own contacts – both inside and outside the government – and combined these with his own instincts and preferences to reach a policy decision. It was a haphazard way of dealing with intelligence. Yet his belief that the European powers had been thoroughly intimidated into appeasement by fears of Hitler's Luftwaffe was correct, and his natural optimism provided a necessary counterweight to the inevitable worst-case scenarios produced by professional naval and military advisers.[25]

Churchill also had a passionate appreciation for intelligence and secret agents, sometimes to the point of being carried away by the romantic character of cloak-and-dagger exploits.[26] He had even been a spy of sorts himself during the war that catapulted Roosevelt's cousin Theodore into the American public eye. In

1895, when the Cubans revolted against Spain's colonial rule, the twenty-year-old Churchill, then a junior officer in the British army, crossed the Atlantic to observe the war from the Spanish side. Before he left London, Britain's Director of Military Intelligence, Colonel Edward Chapman, briefed him on the background and asked him to find out details about Spanish weaponry, thus placing Churchill firmly in the tradition of the 'amateur' gentleman spy typical of the Victorian age. He was fascinated by the ability of the Cuban guerrillas to outwit the Spaniards. 'What their own spies fail to find out,' he noted, 'their friends in every village let them know.'

His exploits during the British army's imperial skirmishes in India, Sudan and South Africa drove home the lesson of how local intelligence could yield valuable dividends and how its lack could sow disaster. On the Indian North-West Frontier he travelled with an army intelligence officer meeting informants. In Sudan, advancing with Kitchener to Omdurman, he was generously briefed and hosted by army intelligence and, in a burst of embarrassing zeal, detained a British agent on suspicion of being an enemy spy. The Boer War, above all, convinced him that good intelligence was a vital weapon of war. What else could explain the success of the Boers – a small, ill-armed bunch of farmers – in humiliating the imperial might of Britain? Its lack, moreover, explained many of Britain's failures. 'The whole intelligence service,' he complained bitterly after he returned home, 'is starved for want of both money and brains.'[27] The Boer War also made him a convert to guerrilla war and covert action. The drama of his own escape from a prisoner-of-war camp, and his dangerous journey home, burnished his fascination with heroic exploits behind enemy lines.

After he entered Parliament in 1900, some of his strongest criticisms of the British army were reserved for its poor intelligence, and he demanded the creation of a powerful Intelligence Department. Events went his way. As the Kaiser constructed a powerful German navy to challenge British maritime supremacy, anxieties over national security sparked a series of spy scares. To keep an eye on German spies in Britain, as well as to improve intelligence about the German navy, in 1909 Britain's Committee of Imperial Defence created the Secret Service Bureau, the fore-runner of the two agencies later to become known as MI5 (the Security Service) and MI6 (the Secret Intelligence Service).

Churchill, who by this time was in the Cabinet, was one of the few ministers to take an interest in the new Bureau's work. Driving his enthusiasm was the firm belief that a powerful German Fifth Column in Britain was poised to carry out sabotage and subversion to assist a German invasion; in truth, no such plan existed, although German spies were certainly at work trying to uncover intelligence about Britain's navy. As Home Secretary (1910–11) Churchill happily gave MI5 extensive powers to carry out secret surveillance on suspected spies, and as First Lord of the Admiralty (1911–15) he kept in close touch with MI5's Director, Captain Vernon Kell. It was Churchill who, on the eve of war in July 1914, gave the order to Kell to round up all suspected German spies in Britain.

Like Roosevelt, he was also 'hands-on' in his approach. He liked to read 'raw' intelligence reports himself, relished what they had to tell him, and even employed an agent to report back to him personally. This was 'Captain' Edward Tupper, a burly firebrand in the seamen's union, who was eager to sniff out German spies at work in British ports. During the First World War Churchill was to find him useful in countering strikes and militancy among British seamen.

But the most important early milestone in Churchill's long con-nection with British intelligence came only weeks after war broke out in 1914. As the airwaves hummed with radio messages between the fleets and ships at sea and their home commands, top-secret coded intercepts began to flood the Admiralty. Quickly alerted to their value for intelligence, Churchill created a special section known as 'Room 40' in the old Admiralty building in Whitehall. With hard work and lucky breaks, it soon broke all significant German codes, and from then until the end of the war Britain could follow the movements of the German High Seas Fleet, trace the departure of U-boats from their home ports, and read most of Germany's diplomatic messages – with the results that Roosevelt and other Americans so vividly learned during the Zimmerman telegram affair. Again, Churchill insisted on seeing Room 40's raw reports with his own eyes. So convinced was he of its significance that he personally wrote out in longhand its early 'charter'.

In May 1915 Churchill became the principal scapegoat for the disaster of the Dardanelles Expedition – a futile bloodletting that attempted to break the stalemate on the Western Front by opening up a southern front in the Balkans. The crisis would have been terminal for most politicians, and it badly damaged Churchill. But he quickly bounced back, and by 1919 was Minister for War and Air. By this time Lenin and the Bolsheviks had replaced the Kaiser's Germany as national bogeyman, and British codebreakers were busily cracking Moscow's codes. Churchill read these with the same enthusiasm he had brought to German codes, using their evidence of Communist subversion in Britain to urge the expulsion of Moscow's representatives from London. He also lent his energies to the efforts of secret agents plotting to overthrow the Bolsheviks. In the chaotic conditions of civil war and famine, a motley collection of passionate anti-Communists and dubious adventurers, including the ex-nihilist assassin Boris Savinkov and the legendary 'ace of spies' Sidney Reilly, courted British intelligence with extravagant plots to topple the Bolsheviks. Churchill gave them all the support he could, and although their plots failed he remained mesmerised by the potential of covert action behind enemy lines to cause mischief and mayhem.

The lessons were reinforced by events in Ireland. In 1922 the British were forced to recognise the Irish Free State after a bloody guerrilla struggle in which Michael Collins' IRA also won a ruthless and protracted intelligence war. Churchill's role is largely remembered because of his support for the 'Black and Tans', a force of British ex-servicemen notorious for its indiscriminate violence. But he also pressed hard for enhanced intelligence. When Sir Henry Wilson, the army's chief of staff, demanded the shooting of hostages in reprisal for Sinn Féin terrorist attacks, Churchill disagreed. 'It is no use . . . saying I should shoot without mercy. The question immediately arises: "Whom would you shoot?" And shortly after that: "Where are they?"' In short, what was needed was an intensified intelligence war.[28]

Out of power after 1929, Churchill created what was almost an alternative private intelligence service at his home in Chartwell in

Kent. With a vast range of contacts and sources inside and outside of government, he battered the governments of Baldwin and Chamberlain with a barrage of facts and figures in his campaign against the appeasement of Hitler. One of his most important sources was Major Desmond Morton, an officer he had befriended on the Western Front. Morton was a senior officer in the Secret Intelligence Service who in the 1930s ran the Industrial Intelligence Centre. He was also a neighbour in Kent, and would frequently stroll over to Chartwell carrying top-secret files to prime Churchill on statistics about German and British rearmament. Churchill also had sources and allies in the armed forces and the Foreign Office who kept him up to date. If Roosevelt was a 'sponge' who soaked up information, Churchill was a vacuum-cleaner who sucked the last particle of intelligence from every corner and crevice he could. When war came in September 1939, he was by far and away the best-informed and experienced minister to mobilise British intelligence for the tasks ahead.

2

━━►●◄━━

EXCHANGING VIEWS

Hitler launched his blitzkrieg attack on Poland on 1 September 1939, and before the month was out Warsaw had capitulated, pulverised by air and artillery attack. More than 20,000 of its population had perished in the ruins. Early in October Hitler flew to the Polish capital to take the salute at a victory parade; almost 700,000 Polish soldiers had been captured and 60,000 killed. 'Take a good look around,' Hitler told journalists. 'That is how I deal with any European city.'

Two days after Hitler launched his attack on the Poles Britain declared war on Germany and Churchill returned to his old office as First Lord of the Admiralty. He was overwhelmed by a sense of *déjà vu*, his old desk in place, many of the same charts still on the wall. The first man he summoned to brief him was his Director of Naval Intelligence, Admiral John Godfrey.

Godfrey presided over Britain's largest intelligence empire after the Secret Intelligence Service. He had patrolled the Yangtse in a gunboat, fought in the Dardanelles, and commanded the battle cruiser *Repulse* in the Mediterranean during the Spanish Civil War. He was also a great admirer of his First World War predecessor, Admiral 'Blinker' Hall, who gave him two pieces of advice about secret intelligence: build links with the City, Britain's financial centre, and forge an alliance with the Americans.

Godfrey did both. From the City he recruited as his personal assistant the son of one of Churchill's old army friends killed in the First World War, Captain Valentine Fleming. Ian Fleming was to learn most of the spy tricks that he turned into his bestselling James Bond fiction while working for Godfrey.[1] Here Godfrey also absorbed the transatlantic spirit. 'The more the Americans have the feeling of being "in" with us . . . the more easily and fluently will the countries [become] allies,' he argued. Captain Alan Goodrich Kirk, the American naval attaché, was only too keen to be wooed. Determined to strengthen relations with the Royal Navy, he had a direct line to Roosevelt and the White House – and eventually returned to Washington as Director of Naval Intelligence.

One of Godfrey's first moves was to give Kirk a personal guided tour around the Admiralty's top-secret operational centre, a bomb-proof concrete bunker squatting next to the old Admiralty building overlooking St James's Park. As he followed Godfrey through the labyrinth of subterranean corridors with their watertight doors bearing such labels as Japanese Room, Italian Room, Code and Signal Room, Kirk was mesmerised by the prospect of intelligence collaboration with the British. But like 'Blinker' Hall's performance in front of Roosevelt two decades before, Godfrey's was a carefully calculated show to cultivate American sympathy without giving too much away. Churchill demanded that sharing be a two-way street. Selected data, such as information about a captured German magnetic mine, kept Kirk happy. But the true information about the submarine war, which was not going as well as Churchill claimed in public, was withheld.[2]

On the very morning that Hitler was crowing to journalists in Warsaw, the British War Cabinet met at 10 Downing Street. When Churchill's turn came to speak, he brought them up to date with the latest naval news. The first two weeks of the war at sea had been grim for Britain, with German U-boats sinking almost thirty ships, more than half the rate of tonnage at the blackest period during the First World War. A welcome lull had followed, but now, Churchill revealed, the picture had darkened again: off the Shetland Islands north of Scotland a whaler had been torpedoed, the first British ship to have been sunk by a

U-boat in fourteen days; and the crew of the 8,000-ton Greek freighter *Diamentes*, sunk two days before off the coast of Kerry *en route* to Britain with a cargo from South Africa, had been landed by the submarine that sank them, the U-35, in Dingle Bay, Ireland.[3]

After this, he turned to a delicate matter of secret service. Preying on his mind was eventual German attack on the Low Countries and the threat it posed to the Channel ports. Belgium's pre-war neutrality had prevented joint military and naval planning. But now a glimmer of hope had been sparked by King Leopold, who was pressing his generals to bypass cautious ministers and begin contingency planning with London. So sensitive was the matter, Churchill told his colleagues, that he was using a secret intermediary named Walter Johannes Stein, an Austrian Jew and economist who had lived in Britain since 1933. The evening before, Churchill's old friend Sir Roger Keyes, the First World War hero of a daring raid on the Belgian port of Zeebrugge who enjoyed excellent contacts in Belgium, had come to see him, bringing Stein along. The Austrian economist, Churchill said, held a position of special influence in the Royal Palace in Brussels and could ensure the entry of any special envoy from Britain. So impressed was Churchill by the possibilities that he proposed to ask Sir Vernon Kell, the Director of MI5, to send an envoy to Brussels to test out Stein's *bona fides*. If they proved satisfactory, then secret talks with the Belgians could begin, perhaps at sea on some British ship far from prying eyes in Belgium.

The War Cabinet approved Churchill's plan and Kell was the first to hear the news. 'Winston sent for me,' he recorded in his diary, 'to discuss a scheme,' and a few hours later an MI5 envoy was on his way to the Belgian capital. Churchill's hopes were soon dashed. King Leopold's ministers got wind of the plan and killed it off by publicly vetoing any idea of Anglo-Belgian staff conversations. From then on they rested comfortably in their illusion of neutral safety until the Wehrmacht's blitzkrieg on the Low Countries prompted their humiliating capitulation in May 1940.[4]

After this intelligence briefing, Churchill turned to his second item of news for the Cabinet. He had just received a personal letter from President Roosevelt in his capacity as commander-in-chief of the US Navy – a warm and friendly note hardly more than a dozen lines long that evoked their shared experiences as naval ministers in the previous war. In particular, what Roosevelt wanted both Churchill and Chamberlain to know was that he would always welcome it if they kept in touch with him personally about anything they wanted him to know, using sealed letters by diplomatic pouch if necessary. He concluded by congratulating Churchill on finishing his four-volume life of his ancestor, the Duke of Marlborough, and thanked him for sending him copies. 'I much enjoyed reading them,' he wrote. He sent a similar letter to Chamberlain.[5]

It was a happy coincidence that just about to be published was a new edition of Churchill's book *Great Contemporaries*, which had originally appeared in 1937. To update it, he had hurriedly included an essay on Roosevelt originally written following the President's first election to the White House. Entitled 'Roosevelt from Afar' it offered a cautious welcome to the New Deal and a warmer embrace of the President. 'It is certain,' declared Churchill, 'that Franklin Roosevelt will rank among the greatest of men who have occupied [the presidency].'[6]

Churchill had already drafted a reply to Roosevelt's offer. That same week a Pan-American conference was meeting in Panama City, where talk of creating a 300-mile maritime 'safety belt' around the Americas was high on the agenda. Churchill thought it a good idea, provided the protected area did not become a shelter for German raiders or U-boats. If that happened he would tell Roosevelt that Britain would feel entirely free to act in its own interests. But if the US Navy were to take care of the problem, it would relieve the Royal Navy of a great deal of responsibility and free up ships to help with Atlantic convoys. After only brief discussion, Churchill's colleagues approved his reply. At four o'clock that afternoon he sent it off to Washington. Carefully, he reciprocated the President's appeal to their shared naval experience and signed it with a personal touch: 'from Naval Person'.[7]

That night he dined with two top Admiralty officials in his Westminster flat, a simply furnished *pied à terre* on whose walls hung many of his own amateur but accomplished paintings. Towards the end of the meal his personal valet, Frank Sawyers, interrupted to say that there was an urgent telephone call. 'Who is it?' demanded Churchill. 'I don't know,' confessed the valet. Annoyed, Churchill at first refused to leave the table and only agreed when Sawyers insisted. To his guests' surprise, they heard Churchill outside in the hall saying, 'Yes, sir,' 'No, sir' into the telephone. Who, they wondered, could provoke such unusual and unexpected deference on the part of Churchill?

It was none other than Roosevelt. He had picked up the telephone to tell Churchill that Admiral Raeder, head of Hitler's navy, had warned on the German radio that the American ship *Iroquois*, sailing from Ireland to the United States, would be struck in similar circumstances to the *Athenia*, a British passenger liner torpedoed on the first day of the war with the loss of over 100 lives, including many Americans. Although in reality sunk by a U-boat, German propaganda had echoed First World War claims about the sinking of the *Lusitania* to allege that Churchill had deliberately ordered a bomb planted on board the *Athenia* in order to blacken Germany's name with the Americans.

As he listened to Roosevelt Churchill furiously scribbled down the gist of his own reply. Ahead of the *Iroquois* lay a thousand miles of ocean before she reached the protective arm of the American navy. Yet the ship was already too far west in the Atlantic for a U-boat to find her, which left only one plausible option to explain a sinking – a time-bomb planted on board the *Iroquois* in Ireland before her departure. The sensible thing, Churchill told Roosevelt, would be to radio the ship and order a thorough search.

Returning to the table, he was in a high state of excitement at being rung up by the President of the United States in the middle of a war. Hurriedly excusing himself he headed for 10 Downing Street to brief the Prime Minister, Neville Chamberlain.[8] The next morning he repeated to the War Cabinet his theory of a bomb, planted either in Liverpool, the port of departure of the *Iroquois*, or in Queenstown outside Cork, where she had briefly put in. Roosevelt ordered a stem-to-stern search, but no bomb was found and the ship safely reached port. The whole affair had been a fruitless German propaganda ploy to discredit Churchill and curry favour with Roosevelt.[9]

Their dramatic radio-telephone conversation about the *Iroquois* was the first of many over the next five years that kept the two men in immediate contact. As a basic protection, security experts installed scrambler devices in Washington and London, but these only countered eavesdropping, not recording and subsequent unscrambling by cryptographic experts. Knowing this, Roosevelt and Churchill used the device sparingly, reserving it for casual chats, emergencies, and elliptical replies to substantive points raised in ciphered telegrams or letters sent by diplomatic pouch. This did not prevent the Germans from intercepting some of the conversations and making transcripts. In 1943 a special intelligence unit of the German Postal and Telegraph Service intercepted a call that Churchill placed to Roosevelt to discuss the armistice they were secretly negotiating with Italy – 'incontrovertible evidence', the Germans reported, 'that secret negotiations between the Anglo-Americans and the Italians are taking place'. Fortunately, it merely confirmed what they already knew.

Such potentially dangerous insecurity was plugged later that year by the Bell Telephone laboratories, which developed new equipment known variously as 'Sigsaly', the 'X-System', or 'Green Hornet', a system unbreakable by cryptanalysis that permitted Roosevelt and Churchill to talk to each other with complete secrecy from telephones installed in the White House and Whitehall War Rooms. At first they were reluctant to use it, partly because the old habits of secrecy and caution died hard, and also because in the end it was a poor or even dangerous substitute for making decisions that required calm reflection – and in Roosevelt's case made it difficult for him to use one of his favoured techniques of decision-taking, procrastination.

For Churchill, however, there was an additional reason. Shortly after Sigsaly was installed he used it to call Roosevelt, only to be deeply disconcerted to hear the President giggle out loud when he heard his voice. He learned later, after he had asked for the reason, that the new equipment had prompted Roosevelt to compare his voice with that of Donald Duck. Churchill often watched cartoons to relieve his mind of the anxieties of war. But even his well-established sense of humour had problems with being compared to a Walt Disney character. 'I'll never use that damn thing again,' he muttered. By D–Day in June 1944 the Bell engineers had ironed out the problem and Churchill was happy to use the link again. Yet both he and Roosevelt remained cautious and discussed little they had not previously dealt with face to face or in written form.[10]

At the heart of this first direct exchange lay Roosevelt and Churchill's shared fear of espionage and subversion. For how else did Churchill believe that a bomb could have been planted on the *Iroquois*? In his mind's eye he saw a German spy at work, or more probably an Irish Republican seeking revenge on the British. He was obsessed by the threat of neutral Ireland as a base for anti-British subversion. 'What does intelligence say about possible succouring of U-boats by Irish malcontents in West of Ireland inlets?' was one of his first queries to Admiral Godfrey. Were German spies at work in Ireland? Was vital intelligence about the Royal Navy leaking out to Germany from Irish sympathisers hostile to Britain and the Crown? Two weeks into the war his worst fears appeared to be confirmed when the Admiralty received intelligence that members of the crew of a German U-boat rescued after it had been sunk claimed to have landed in Ireland and purchased cigarettes.

Churchill instinctively believed it, haunted as he was by ghosts from Ireland's turbulent and violent struggle for independence from Britain, not to mention distant but potent historical memories of French and Spanish armies using it as a base to attack England, and Sir Roger Casement's far more recent landing on the Kerry coast from a German U-boat before the 1916 Easter Uprising. Eamon de Valera, Ireland's Prime Minister, who had launched a bitter civil war against the treaty that left Northern Ireland part of the United Kingdom, had declared Ireland neutral, and the naval bases of Queenstown, Berehaven and Lough Swilly, originally retained by the British under the 1922 Treaty, had been returned to Irish control in 1938. The launch of a major IRA bombing offensive against the British mainland blackened Churchill's view still further. If the IRA could throw bombs in London, he felt, they could surely provide fuel to enemy submarines in Ireland.

As he studied the map of the Western Approaches, Britain's

vital lifeline to North America, he brooded ever more deeply about the U-boat menace. Royal Air Force patrols from Northern Ireland were regularly reporting U-boat sightings, and even as he spoke to Roosevelt rumours were flying that the U-boat captain who had landed the crew of the *Diamantes* in Dingle Bay had local friends from a pre-war visit. 'Give my best wishes to Mickey Long' he was reported as saying before submerging again. True or not, anti-British feeling in the Dingle Bay area was strong enough that eighteen months later a local man rode out across the Dingle Peninsula with a donkey and cart loaded with food and delivered it to a waiting U-boat. And only nine days after Churchill discussed Roosevelt's letter with the Cabinet, the German submarine U-47 penetrated the supposedly impregnable naval base of Scapa Flow, and amidst widespread rumours of a spy at work sank the battleship *Royal Oak* with the loss of several hundred lives. The news was received with joy in parts of Ireland, and one Dingle Bay trawlerman even stuck a picture of the U-boat captain in his wheelhouse. 'It would seem that money should be spent to secure a body of trustworthy Irish agents to keep most vigilant watch,' noted Churchill.[11]

Godfrey could not put agents ashore. But he did the next best thing and launched a top-secret maritime intelligence mission. Within days HMS *Tamara*, an armoured ship masquerading as a civilian trawler and crewed by Royal Navy personnel, was 'fishing' off the Irish coast, carefully scouring its bays and inlets for signs of sheltering German U-boats. Shadowing it off the coast of Cork was a British submarine that was authorised to sink any German U-boat flushed out by the search. Mixing this Churchillian cloak-and-dagger escapade with some genuine fishing, it found not a single U-boat, although it continued its secret probes well into 1940.[12]

Visions of German subversion in Ireland were not the only nightmares troubling Churchill. His close link with Kell had been forged during the spy fever of the First World War and now again he worried about German spies at work in Britain, convincing himself that 20,000 German agents were preparing a sabotage campaign, or worse. As Polish forces fought valiantly against Hitler's Wehrmacht, Churchill summoned back from retirement his faithful bodyguard, Inspector Thompson of Scotland Yard's Special Branch, and armed himself with a pistol against an assassination attempt.

In October 1939, as the nights grew longer, he spoke anxiously of a possible German invasion on England's east coast helped by agents on shore, and warned the Cabinet that German parachutists might descend on Whitehall. Quietly, the First Sea Lord ordered British battleships to shelter from Luftwaffe attacks by taking refuge on the west coast in the River Clyde, off Glasgow. This only brought all Churchill's suspicions about the Irish flooding to the surface. Scotland's biggest city housed a large Catholic and Irish population, and for years Special Branch, Britain's closest equivalent of the FBI, had been reporting that the area was dense with supporters of Sinn Féin. 'There are plenty of traitors in the Glasgow area,' Churchill pronounced, and went on to speculate that a single telephone call to the German ambassador in Dublin could expose the secret that Britain's capital ships had left the North Sea.[13]

His sensitivity to German espionage was fuelled by MI5. Kell had started an undercover investigation into the penetration by German spies of British companies. It soon discovered that one firm, the Concrete Pump Company, run by Karl Heinrich Markmann, a former Hitler Youth activist and naturalised British subject, had supplied British naval bases including Scapa Flow. Another company, also run by a German, had supplied business machines to Admiralty offices. Kell reported this to Admiral Godfrey, who informed Churchill. Immediately he rang up the Home Secretary to demand that both firms be seized and their owners interned. Impatient with legal niceties, he continued to press the case until he got his way.[14]

But weighing far more heavily on Churchill's mind than the state of British counter-intelligence was the future of its foreign intelligence agency, the Secret Intelligence Service (SIS). Its head, Admiral Sir Hugh Sinclair, was dying of cancer. His predecessor and founder of the service, Commander Mansfield Cumming, had also been a navy man, and Churchill was determined to keep it that way. During his battle against appeasement he assumed that SIS was doing a good job but was being thwarted by Chamberlain.

A few weeks as First Lord of the Admiralty quickly dispelled the illusion. With shock he learned that Britain's codebreakers had failed to crack any important German ciphers and that intelligence about U-boats was lamentably meagre. Britain, he concluded, desperately needed a stronger SIS, and he thought he knew the man to run it: Captain Gerald Muirhead-Gould, Britain's naval attaché in Berlin in the mid-1930s and a fan of Churchill's stand against appeasement. Churchill summoned him to the Admiralty and declared he possessed many of the attributes of the original 'C' and was his top candidate. But the prospect of a Churchill protégé in charge of British foreign intelligence seriously alarmed his colleagues, and in a behind-the-scenes Whitehall power play Neville Chamberlain and his Foreign Secretary, Lord Halifax, blocked Churchill's choice. Instead, the post went to Major-General Stewart Menzies, the acting SIS Director during Sinclair's final illness.

While Churchill fought – and lost – this bureaucratic battle, dramatic events were taking place elsewhere. Two senior SIS officers based in the Netherlands, believing that they were in touch with anti-Hitler conspirators anxious to talk peace with Britain, were lured over the Dutch–German border at Venlo in an elaborate 'sting' operation by Gestapo chief Heinrich Himmler's *Sicherheitsdienst*, or security service. Taken to Berlin for interrogation, they revealed devastating details about British intelligence networks in western Europe.

Responsibility for the affair reached right into 10 Downing Street. Both Chamberlain and Halifax had sanctioned the meeting in the hope that it could produce a bloodless victory. Churchill had been hostile from the outset. What if it were a scheme by German intelligence, who would then deliberately leak news of the talks to the French to drive a wedge between the allies? The débâcle only reinforced his determination that whatever else it did, the SIS in future would be forbidden to deal with alleged German peace overtures.

Stewart Menzies quickly learned of Churchill's fascination with cloak and dagger. Early in December 1939 Churchill asked him to devise a sabotage plan to destroy German imports of iron ore from neutral Sweden. This, he was convinced, was an Achilles' heel of the German war economy that could paralyse Hitler. Menzies mobilised his special sabotage section, known as Section D – D for destruction – and early in 1940 the operation was ready to go. Churchill kept a close eye on progress, helped squeeze the £300,000 needed from the Treasury, and pressed its case in the War Cabinet. Impatient at delays, he finally summoned the head of Section D, Major-General Lawrence Grand, to his Admiralty office. What, he demanded, had happened? Grand's complaint of foot-dragging at the top galvanised Churchill into twisting Chamberlain's arm to give it the green light. Then, to his frustration, the plan failed to get off the ground. A crucial agent in Stockholm backed out at the last minute, the Swedish police got wind of the scheme, and the chief SIS man on the spot was arrested.

From this further secret service débâcle Churchill concluded that covert British operations needed a far stronger hand at the tiller. And when intelligence failed to warn effectively of Hitler's offensive against the west in the spring, he decided on a thorough shake-up of the entire intelligence community.[15]

The outbreak of war in Europe brought Roosevelt closer to Churchill. He wrote his first letter to Churchill a week after Britain's declaration of war on the Nazis. Earlier that day Joseph Kennedy told him of a conversation he had had with the King and Queen and Sir Samuel Hoare, the Lord Privy Seal and confidant of Chamberlain. Hoare expected Hitler to call for peace with Britain and France once Poland was defeated, and hoped something would come of this given that continuation of the war would mean Britain's economic, financial and social collapse. Kennedy shared his pessimism and thought the President might play a significant role in any peace talks that took place.

But Roosevelt had little truck for Kennedy's views – 'a pain in the neck' is how he described him to his friend Henry Morgenthau, Secretary of the Treasury[16] – and quickly disabused him. The people of the United States would not support any move for peace by his administration that consolidated or helped prolong a regime of force or aggression. Since Munich Roosevelt had been preparing for the war he knew must come. After Hitler occupied Prague in March 1939 he told Arthur Willert, an old family friend who had been Washington correspondent of *The Times* during the First World War, that he could see no reason at all why the American navy could not patrol parts of the Atlantic and thus free the Royal Navy to concentrate where it was most needed. That same month he also cancelled the Pacific Fleet's scheduled appearance in New York harbour for the World's Fair and ordered it back to its San Diego base. Although he failed to get Congress to repeal the Neutrality Act, he was doing all he could to keep the United States out of the war by helping Britain and France. Only if they were threatened by defeat would he contemplate war. It was in the United States' interest to strengthen the anti-appeasers in Britain. That, above all, meant Churchill.

Up to this point Roosevelt believed that Churchill was a dyed-in-the-wool imperialist whose political future lay behind him. He had, after all, broken with the Conservative Party over its reforming India Act and denounced Mahatma Gandhi as 'a seditious Middle Temple lawyer . . . striding half-naked up the steps of the Vice-regal Palace'. He had also offended Roosevelt and the New Dealers by calling on them to abandon their 'ruthless war on private enterprise'. Nor, as Kennedy learned, had Roosevelt forgotten his rudeness in 1918.

It was foreign affairs, and Churchill's stand on Munich, that redeemed him in Roosevelt's eyes. His blasts against appeasement were broadcast to the world through radio and the press, while behind the scenes influential Americans like the financier Bernard Baruch, a close friend of Churchill since the First World War, brought direct word to the White House of Churchill's private hopes and fears. 'War is coming very soon,' Churchill told Baruch in London during the Munich crisis. 'We will be in it and you will be in it. You will be running the show over there, but I will be on the sidelines over here.' A few days later he broadcast to the American people. 'Britain must arm. America must arm,' he said.

All this struck a potent chord with Roosevelt. His letter of 11 September was a deliberate and conscious attempt to build a personal link with the man he felt in his bones was destined eventually to become Britain's Prime Minister and leader in war.[17] Protocol meant that he should also write to Chamberlain. But Roosevelt had little time for him, fearful of his appeasement instincts, and the letter was formal and restrained. He held similar fears about Kennedy, which is why he suggested that Churchill should communicate directly with the White House by sealed letter.

Roosevelt also strengthened links with his own intelligence networks. The setback over the Neutrality Act was a forceful reminder of how careful he would have to be in his efforts to uncover espionage and subversion by neutral and belligerent powers inside the United States. Private and secret sources were now more important than ever. Vincent Astor's network of agents acquired a new name, 'The Club', and Roosevelt was quick to give it instructions. Among his cornucopia of Wall Street positions, Astor was also managing director of the Western Union Telegraph Company. Secretly he sent Roosevelt excerpts of intercepted cables sent by Axis agents in New York to Latin America – a useful service when federal statute strictly forbade such tampering with communications.[18] The Club also monitored radio messages to detect German spy networks in the vicinity of New York. As ever, Roosevelt carefully absorbed what he read but committed little to paper.

Barely two weeks after he telephoned Churchill to warn him about the *Iroquois*, Vincent Astor told Roosevelt that he now had two men monitoring all frequencies from Mexican, Cuban and Swiss radio stations. A month later he reported that he was opening up a new source of information. One of The Club's leading members was Winthrop Aldrich, Chairman of the Chase National Bank and a future, post-war, ambassador to London. 'Tomorrow I am starting to work on the banks,' Astor told the President. 'Espionage and sabotage need money, and that has to pass through the banks at one stage or another.'

Astor's spycatching quickly revealed that a principal client of the Chase National was the Soviet Amtorg Corporation (American Trading Organisation). Based in New York, this was registered as an American company trading with the Soviet Union. But it also served as Moscow's front for its espionage offensive in the United States and was the conduit for funding such agents as Whitaker Chambers. Astor's bank sources revealed none of this detail, however, merely reporting on the flow of Soviet funds through the bank – some $11 million in January 1940 alone.

Roosevelt was seriously alarmed. 'Can nothing be done to cut this down?' he asked, passing the files along to Henry Morgenthau at the Treasury, who found them of 'great value'. But Roosevelt was mostly focused on Amtorg as an illegal purchaser of strategic war material which might eventually find its way into German hands. All Western intelligence agencies were worried by this. Arthur Purvis, the Canadian-born head of British Purchasing in New York, revealed that month to Morgenthau that 'secret but reliable' sources were reporting that Amtorg was busy buying huge amounts of copper in New York. Morgenthau's Treasury agents were already on to it. Amtorg had used a Connecticut firm, Whipple & Choate, as a front to purchase 100 tons of copper from the Utah Copper Company, ostensibly for domestic consumption. When it attempted to ship the consignment to Russia, it was detained in port. 'We have a man there,' Morgenthau chuckled to Purvis, 'as the boats are being loaded, anything that's going to Russia.' Treasury agents were also wiretapping Jules Bache, a Frenchman expelled from France in 1917 who was reputed to be an Amtorg agent, on whom both Morgenthau and Canadian intelligence had a thick file.[19]

Despite, or more likely because of all this, Roosevelt was distracted from seeing Amtorg as a recruiter for Soviet spies targeted against the United States government; it was only a few months before that he had supposedly waved aside Berle's report on Whitaker Chambers.

More urgent and pressing to Roosevelt was the fear of sabotage by Germany and its supporters of war industry plants. Astor duly prepared a list of security measures and a plan to seal the border with Mexico against infiltration by subversives. For none of these secret operations did Roosevelt issue any official orders or written instructions. Instead, Astor called either at the White House or Hyde Park and Roosevelt told him what he wanted. If anything went wrong, he could deny all knowledge.[20]

More momentous in the long run was the link that Astor's group forged with British intelligence. Soon after Roosevelt made contact with Churchill, he gave the green light for Astor to meet with the head of British intelligence in the United States, Captain Sir James Paget, and his assistant Walter Bell, and ask for unofficial co-operation on counter-sabotage measures. Based in Manhattan, Paget and Bell were professional intelligence operatives working under the standard cover of the day used by SIS, that of the British Passport Control Office. They eagerly collaborated, not just passing on intelligence about German espionage that Astor then filtered to the FBI, but also doing some of the dirty work that Roosevelt could not do as the leader of a supposedly neutral nation. International flights to and from the United States regularly refuelled or touched down in Bermuda or Trinidad, British possessions that were carefully scrutinised by British censorship. With a little help from the British, Roosevelt could keep an eye on suspects. 'In regard to the opening of diplomatic pouches in Bermuda and Trinidad,' Astor told him, 'I have given my word never to tell anyone – with always you excepted.'[21] The risks Roosevelt was running emerged when the State Department found out. Bureaucratic fur began to fly and the information dried up. Anxious not to harm his 1940 re-election campaign, Roosevelt refused to intervene. For the struggle ahead it was far more important that he win the White House that November.

3

KNOWING FRIENDS

Franklin Roosevelt learned of Hitler's attack on Western Europe late on the evening of 9 May 1940 in a telephone call from his ambassador in Belgium. Ensconced in his favourite red leather armchair in the second-floor study of the White House, surrounded by his collection of maritime pictures and models of ships, he listened grimly to the news of simultaneous attacks by more than a hundred German divisions on Belgium, Holland, Luxembourg and France. Ninety minutes later the first reports began to filter in of bombs falling on Brussels, Amsterdam and Rotterdam, and he stayed up until the early hours to digest them. Rising at his usual hour the next day, he convened an emergency meeting in the Oval Office with the chiefs of the army and navy, General George C. Marshall and Admiral Harold Stark; Treasury Secretary Henry Morgenthau; and his Secretary of State, Cordell Hull. After a press conference and lunch, he met with his Cabinet to review the crisis. The pervasive gloom around the table deepened with every bulletin that came in announcing German advances. It was suddenly lifted by a spirited intervention from the Secretary of Commerce, Harry Hopkins.

The fifty-year-old Hopkins was Roosevelt's closest wartime adviser and the indispensable lubricant in his relations with Churchill. Born in Sioux City, Iowa, and fuelled by a powerful conscience gifted by his Methodist mother, he worked for the Red Cross and New York Board of Child Welfare before Roosevelt picked him to head the Works Progress Administration running New Deal programmes for building schools, libraries, public buildings and dams. The previous autumn a major operation for stomach cancer had left him severely weakened, and this was his first Cabinet meeting for months. Gaunt, chain-smoking, his frayed suit hanging off his sagging frame, he resembled, one journalist wrote, 'an ill-fed horse at the end of a long day'.[1]

But to Roosevelt he was an anchor, and to the Cabinet that day he offered a tonic as he outlined an energetic action plan to beef up the United States' strategic supplies of rubber and tin. As he spoke, he was interrupted by yet another news flash. British Prime Minister Neville Chamberlain had resigned and Winston Churchill had replaced him.

To Roosevelt, it was another shaft of light in a dark day. Churchill, he told the Cabinet, was the best man England had – even if, he joked, he *was* drunk half the time.[2] Later that evening, after cocktails, he asked Hopkins to stay on for dinner. 'I'm lonely,' he said. When the meal was over, he noticed his friend looked exhausted and suggested he stay the night. Taking a room on the second floor, he was to stay in the White House for the next three and a half years, the President's closest political ally. Housed in what had once been Abraham Lincoln's study, a suite with high windows looking across the lawn to the Washington Monument and the Virginia hills in the distance, he was available at any hour to advise and console the President. 'Harry tells him everything he needs to know,' confided Eleanor Roosevelt sadly as she lamented her own declining wartime influence on her husband.

After seeing Hopkins installed, Roosevelt left to give a scheduled speech at Constitution Hall and returned to the White House at about nine o'clock. Hardly had he begun to settle down than the telephone rang. It was Churchill, calling to bring him up to date on the momentous affairs that had been taking place in London.[3]

Churchill had been woken up at half-past five in the morning to be told the news of Hitler's attack. Within thirty minutes he was in his office at the Admiralty, and he spent most of the day at emergency meetings of the War Cabinet or Military Co-ordination Committee, which he chaired, fuelling himself first with a hearty breakfast of bacon and fried eggs and then with an expansive lunch with his bosom friend Lord (Max) Beaverbook, the Canadian-born press magnate.

As he threw himself into orchestrating counter-measures against the Germans, the political crisis over Chamberlain's leadership came to a climax. The day before, the opposition Labour Party had decided not to serve under Chamberlain if he formed a national, or coalition, government. It was a fatal blow, and he decided to resign. His first choice as successor was the Foreign Secretary Lord Halifax, but in a tense discussion at 10 Downing Street Halifax declined in favour of Churchill, ostensibly on the grounds that as a member of the House of Lords his position would be hopeless; in reality, because he felt unsuited to the challenge. Afterwards he and Churchill went out into the garden and sat amicably on a bench talking, Churchill recalled later, about 'nothing in particular'. That night over dinner at Admiralty House Churchill discussed his likely Cabinet with Archibald Sinclair, his old comrade-in-arms from the Western Front and now leader of the Liberal Party; his protégé Brendan Bracken; Frederick Lindeman ('the Prof'), his adviser throughout the 1930s on rearmament and science; and Anthony Eden, who had resigned as Foreign Secretary over Chamberlain's appeasement.

The next afternoon, in time for the nine o'clock BBC news, Churchill accepted office from King George VI. By midnight he had formed a coalition War Cabinet that guaranteed him an impregnable parliamentary fortress for the rest of the war. Next he turned to the levers of personal power. He made himself Minister of Defence and forged a direct link with the nerve centre of Britain's war effort, the Chiefs of Staff Committee, which immediately felt the lash of his action-oriented spirit.[4] His private office also experienced the bracing wind of change. He arrived at 10 Downing Street, noted one observer, 'like a wolf on the fold'.[5] Out went Chamberlain's advisers and in swept Churchill's hand-picked team. Principal among them was Desmond Morton, the First World War hero and Secret Intelligence Service officer who throughout the wilderness years had advised him on secret facts and figures about rearmament. Installed in an office directly next to the Cabinet Room, he acted as Churchill's personal adviser and gatekeeper on intelligence and special operations.

Twelve days after he took office Churchill flew to France to discuss strategy with the French High Command in Vincennes. That day codebreakers at their Bletchley Park headquarters sixty miles north-west of London made an historic breakthrough. Thanks to the Poles and French, they had for months been attacking radio messages enciphered on the Enigma machine used by the German armed forces and the Abwehr, SS and railways. Now they had broken the main Luftwaffe operational key. From then on they read it daily until the end of the war. While they wrestled continuously with changing keys and new German techniques, 'Ultra' firmly established itself as the single most important source of secret intelligence about the enemy.

Ultra dazzled Churchill. 'The magic and the mystery,' writes Ronald Lewin, 'had an irresistible appeal for the schoolboy working inside a great man.'[6] Here was the authentic voice of the enemy unaware he was being overheard. Churchill had delighted in signals intelligence (Sigint) since writing Room 40's charter in 1914. Now he described the Ultra transcripts as his 'golden eggs' and demanded daily deliveries of the raw intercepts direct from Bletchley Park. Only thus could he see, touch and feel the enemy and act as his own intelligence officer. Ultra also provided a trump card in his often stormy negotiations on strategy with his chiefs of staff and his allies. He strengthened the Joint Intelligence Committee and ensured its papers went direct to himself, the War Cabinet, and the chiefs of staff. By the end of the war the committee had become the apex of Britain's intelligence system.[7]

But, like Roosevelt, Churchill also wanted his own direct access to intelligence, independent of any bureaucracy. In August, as Ultra was providing the first detailed order of battle of the Luftwaffe and the Battle of Britain was being fought over the fields of southern England, he demanded that all intelligence reports should be sent to him through the faithful Desmond Morton. 'I do not wish such reports . . . to be sifted and digested by the various intelligence authorities,' he instructed. 'Major Morton will inspect them for me and submit what he considers of major importance.

He is to be shown everything, and submit authentic documents to me in their original form.' SIS chief Menzies received a similar instruction from Morton himself. Every day he was to send all Ultra messages to Churchill in a special locked box clearly labelled THIS BOX IS TO BE OPENED BY THE PRIME MINISTER IN PERSON.

Soon the staff at 10 Downing Street were mystified by the arrival of buff-coloured boxes marked with the insignia of Queen Victoria's reign – VRI – that none of them, not even Churchill's Principal Private Secretary, was allowed to handle. Instead, Churchill would take a special key from a keyring he wore at his waist and inspect the contents in private. He allowed only two other people to be present. One was Desmond Morton; the other was Menzies, who frequently brought the boxes himself. He was often Churchill's first visitor of the day, at around nine o'clock, when the Prime Minister was either still in bed or wallowing in his bath. 'Sometimes I had to talk to the PM when he was undressed,' Menzies recalled after the war, 'and once when in the bath he mentioned he had nothing to hide from me.' The meetings gener- ally lasted about half an hour while Menzies discussed the intercepts of the day and other intelligence provided by British secret agents overseas. Churchill called Menzies 'C', although when particularly pleased he lapsed into the more familiar 'Stewart'; but if he was aggrieved over some point or other he adopted the more formal 'General'.[8]

Through his control of Ultra Menzies soon maneouvred Morton aside.[9] 'As the web of Ultra started to extend,' notes Lewin, 'Menzies was at its heart, like a rather elegant and inoffensive spider commanding every point of growth.' He also made himself the indispensable link between Ultra and Churchill, insisted on inter-service co-operation at Bletchley Park, and guarded Ultra's basic security.[10]

Thus began an extraordinary and unprecedented supply of intel- ligence that continued until victory. A secret revealed to the world only thirty years later, popular accounts have focused on its mili- tary and strategic content. But the intercept files passed to Churchill contained significant amounts of diplomatic material from such enemies as Italy, Japan and – after 1943 – Germany itself; from neutrals like Ireland, Turkey, Spain, Portugal, Vichy

France and most Balkan and South American countries. Allies, too, were targeted, such as De Gaulle's Free French, the Dutch, the Czechs and other governments-in-exile. All helped build up a total picture of how friends, enemies and the uncommitted saw the unfolding of the war. In addition, the codebreakers cracked SS and German Order Police ciphers, giving Churchill an early if partial view of German atrocities on the Eastern Front, including the mass shootings of Jews that accompanied Operation Barbarossa. After reading them for several weeks, Churchill stopped, wearied by their sickening predictability.

One source of particular value was intercepts revealing the views of the Japanese ambassador in Berlin, Lieutenant-General Baron Hiroshi Oshima, a crony of Hitler's Foreign Minister Joachim von Ribbentrop, who kept Tokyo fully informed of the state of the German armed forces and the thinking of its war chiefs. Churchill read all his intercepts with scrupulous care.[11] When he travelled abroad special measures were put into place to get the intercepts to him. He could be demanding. 'Why have you not kept me properly supplied with news?' he complained to Menzies from his 1943 Casablanca meeting with Roosevelt. 'Volume should be increased at least five-fold and important messages sent textually.' No doubt he wished to dazzle the President with an impressive clutch of golden eggs.

Churchill was rightfully obsessed with Ultra's security and demanded it be restricted to the tiny inner circle of those who really needed to know. 'The wild scattering of secret information must be curbed,' he ordered. On one occasion he was so concerned about Ultra material appearing in an official document that he ordered its immediate withdrawal. 'The copies circulated,' he instructed, 'are to be destroyed by fire . . .' When Ultra was sent to him at his Atlantic Charter meeting with Roosevelt off the Newfoundland coast, he instructed that it should be delivered in a specially weighted box so that if the aeroplane crashed the documents would immediately sink. Intercepts were withheld from military commanders until Special Liaison Units could ensure top-level security at the regional command level. Some commanders at first discounted Ultra's value precisely because it was disguised as coming from a human source, and hence unreliable.

For that reason the term 'Ultra', initially used only by the Royal Navy, eventually replaced 'Boniface'.[12]

That spring Churchill pushed through another major reform of Britain's intelligence structure by creating the Special Operations Executive (SOE), a top-secret organisation to stimulate and supply sabotage and subversion behind enemy lines and spark a European revolt that would shake off the German yoke. At the Admiralty he had thrown his support behind Section D. Now, his youthful experience of war forged in behind-the-lines action in Cuba and South Africa, he dreamed of a democratic Fifth Column that would pay the Germans back in their own subversive coin.

To run it, he appointed the Labour politician Hugh Dalton, the Minister of Economic Warfare. Dalton held decided views about what was needed. 'Regular soldiers are not men to stir up revolution, to create social chaos or to use all those ungentlemanly means of winning the war which come so easily to the Nazis,' he said. At a late-night meeting on 16 July, after appointing his old friend Sir Roger Keyes as Director of Combined Operations (the Commandos) and discussing with Stewart Menzies the problem of how to get intelligence out of Nazi-occupied Europe, Churchill told Dalton: 'Now, set Europe ablaze!'[13] To do it Dalton imagined that SOE would organise movements in occupied Europe comparable to Sinn Féin in Ireland, the Chinese guerrillas fighting against the Japanese, and the Spanish irregulars who had fought in Wellington's peninsular campaign against Napoleon; even, he admitted, like the Fifth Column organisations operated by the Nazis. 'We must use many different methods,' he declared, 'including industrial and military sabotage, labour agitation and strikes, continuous propaganda, terrorist acts against traitors and German leaders, boycotts and riots.' Churchill shared the vision, but in reality SOE was unable to deliver on its promises for another year or so.

In his heart Churchill knew that for eventual British victory he needed to look west, to the United States. So did Menzies, and soon after Churchill took over he replaced Sir James Paget as head of British secret intelligence in the United States with the deceptively mild-mannered Canadian William Stephenson. A First World War flying ace and amateur boxing champion, he was a millionaire tycoon with business interests in Europe that had made him a valuable source for SIS, and he had been deeply implicated in Churchill's scheme to sabotage Swedish iron ore the year before.

It was an inspired choice, reflected in Stephenson's eventual knighthood and receipt of the American Medal for Merit. 'He radiated warmth and enthusiasm,' noted the head of British intelligence in Buenos Aires, who had much to do with him. 'Being Canadian helped a lot, and a "limey", however talented, would have had a much tougher task.'[14] Although in later life his self-promoted myth as 'Intrepid' did his serious reputation few favours, his personal charm and skill, backed by Churchill's support, opened important doors in Washington and New York. His mission was both to represent 'C' and tighten British security in Canada, the Caribbean and South America. Operating out of New York's Rockefeller Centre, his first moves were to contact J. Edgar Hoover and Vincent Astor. The millionaire New Yorker took Stephenson under his wing, insisted that he stay at the St Regis Hotel, and briefed Roosevelt on the mission of 'The Quiet Canadian'.[15]

Roosevelt's reliance on Astor was unabated, despite the fact that his friend had been summoned to Washington by the irate Director of Naval Intelligence to explain the reasons for his free-lance espionage. 'Maybe I shall need you to protect me from a firing squad,' joked Astor to Roosevelt before departing for the capital. He need not have worried. Only days after the Vichy French leader Marshal Pétain signed the armistice with Hitler, Roosevelt appointed his old shipmate Intelligence Co-ordinator for New York. 'I want you to give him every assistance,' he ordered Admiral Stark, the Chief of Naval Operations, stressing the value he attached to Astor's recommendations on the selection of intelligence officers. Early the next year he elevated Astor even higher by appointing him Intelligence Controller, with authority over all intelligence agencies in the New York area – in effect a local director of central intelligence. But soon his old shipmate began to flounder in the whirlpool of inter-agency intrigue and dirty tricks in New York. Concerned, Roosevelt set John Franklin Carter to investigate and his personal private eye reported that Astor seemed 'confused and suspicious' about his mission. Then

someone leaked Astor's cover, and further damaged his value to
the White House.[16] Before Pearl Harbor his influence was largely
over.

As Astor's position declined, so Bill Donovan's star rose. The
national emergency created by French defeat and the German
invasion threat to Britain stimulated Roosevelt to revitalise his
Cabinet and make it – like Churchill's – a national, cross-party
administration. In June 1940 he appointed as secretaries of the
army and navy two prominent Republicans: Henry Stimson, the
73-year-old scion of the eastern establishment and former Secretary
of State, and Frank Knox, the millionaire publisher of the Chicago
Daily News, whose fondest memory was of charging up San Juan
Hill in Cuba with Teddy Roosevelt and the Rough Riders during
the Spanish–American War.

Knox was also a close friend and supporter of Donovan, and he
was quick to suggest that Roosevelt send him on a fact-finding
mission to Britain. He would have two main tasks: to find out
exactly how willing and able Britain was to carry on fighting
Hitler, and to assess the strength of any British Fifth Column
threatening Churchill. Donovan was already fired up for action.
'Should men of fifty fight our wars?', he asked in the *New York
Herald Tribune*, answering his question with a resounding yes. As
he prepared for the 1940 Independence Day celebrations, the
polio-afflicted Roosevelt summoned him to the Oval Office and
gave him his mission. 'You are my secret legs,' he joked. It was to
mark the inauguration of Donovan's extraordinary career in
American intelligence.[17]

Roosevelt's worries about a Fifth Column had climaxed only weeks
before, over the Tyler Kent affair in Britain.[18] As rumours poured
in of European traitors having opened doors for the Nazis throughout Western Europe Churchill, too, was suffering nightmares.
Quisling's collaboration with the Nazis in Norway opened the
floodgates and lurid accounts poured in from the Low Countries
reporting Nazi agents and sympathisers signalling from clandestine
radios, and female saboteurs disguised as nuns flashing lights for
parachute drops. Most were fantasies to explain unexpected defeat.

Churchill's imagination was also in overdrive. As British forces struggled home from the Dunkirk beaches and Mussolini threw in his lot with Hitler, he sided decisively with MI5 and his chiefs of staff against a foot-dragging Home Office in demanding drastic action against what he assumed would provide the hard core of Britain's Fifth Column – the 70,000 enemy aliens in the country including thousands of recent refugees from Central Europe. In parts of Britain a pogrom-type mood began to take hold. Newspapers demanded general internment, employers fired foreigners, and detainees committed suicide.

Churchill shared his fears with Roosevelt. In his first message to the White House after becoming Prime Minister, he talked of his fear about attacks by parachute and airborne troops. 'We must expect to be attacked on the Dutch model,' he signalled. He found a ready ear. Soon after, on a Sunday, when he knew he would have the largest possible audience, Roosevelt delivered one of his famous radio 'fireside chats'. Sam Rosenman, his friend and personal counsel, who had helped draft the speech with Harry Hopkins, remembered that it was a grim-looking President who took the microphone. Americans, said Roosevelt, should unite to resist the divisive methods of the Fifth Column. 'These dividing forces are undiluted poison,' he warned, using the description with obvious satisfaction. 'They must not be allowed to spread in the New World as they have in the Old . . . today's threat to our national security is not a matter of military weapons alone. We know of new methods of attack, the Trojan horse, the Fifth Column that betrays a nation unprepared for treachery. Spies, saboteurs and traitors are all the actors in the new strategy.'[19]

As the crisis worsened in France Churchill's suspicious gaze extended to British fascists, Communists, and other defeatists. By the time German troops reached the English Channel on 20 May he was in a hawkish mood. Events in London gave him reason to move in for the kill.

That morning, an MI5 officer named Captain Maxwell Knight, a jazz-playing eccentric who ran a network of informers among British fascist groups, knocked at the front door of a house in Gloucester Place, London. The tenant was Tyler Kent, a cipher clerk in the American Embassy. Ambassador Kennedy had already waived his diplomatic immunity, and hidden in a suitcase Knight found keys to the embassy's code and file rooms, as well as some 1,500 documents including copies of telegrams from the Churchill–Roosevelt correspondence. Kent was immediately arrested along with his chief accomplice, a White Russian exile named Anna Wolkoff, secretary of the Right Club, a right-wing and anti-Semitic pressure group. Together they had planned to change the course of history and produce a negotiated peace with Hitler.

In their naïve and conspiratorial minds it would be simple. The Churchill–Roosevelt correspondence revealed – so they believed – a plot to drag a reluctant United States into the war. Exposed to the right people at the right time it would be a bombshell that would destroy its protagonists. Conservatives would revolt against Churchill and replace him with a leader ready to talk with Hitler, while isolationists in the United States would expel Roosevelt from the White House in the 1940 presidential elections. Instead, they found themselves tried *in camera* at the Old Bailey under the Official Secrets Act. The guilty verdicts were withheld until after Roosevelt's re-election.

Kent's treachery was an unprecedented betrayal in the history of American diplomacy, while for Churchill the case conclusively proved the existence of a dangerous Fifth Column. Within forty-eight hours he won War Cabinet approval for a huge round-up of British fascists. The most prominent detainee was Sir Oswald Mosley, long feared by Churchill as the most likely British Quisling. No evidence existed that linked him with the Kent/Wolkoff affair, but Churchill accepted MI5's argument that if an invasion occurred Mosley would either join the enemy or attempt a *coup d'état* to make peace with them.[20]

His ferocity on the home front marched hand in hand with his ruthless determination to fight on against Hitler. In his historic speech promising that Britons would fight on the beaches, on the landing grounds, in the fields and in the streets, he also addressed the internment measures. Many of the internees, he acknowledged, were passionate enemies of Hitler. But things were so critical that distinctions between friends and enemies could not be drawn. No sympathy should be extended to Fifth Columnists, and 'the malignancy in our midst' should be stamped out. He remained in this mood for several weeks until a public backlash, combined with personal misgivings about excesses and mistakes, led him to relent.

The Tyler Kent affair had a profound effect on the White House. To his alarm, Henry Morgenthau discovered that the FBI were not carrying out wiretaps on the German and Italian embassies because this was already being done by the army, and it was forbidden by law to carry out domestic wiretaps to catch Nazi spies. 'I called up General Watson [Roosevelt's personal military aide] and said this should be done,' recalled Morgenthau later. 'I don't think it's legal,' replied Watson. 'So what?', said Morgenthau. Watson called him back five minutes later. He had told Roosevelt, he reported, and he had said, 'Tell Bob Jackson [the Attorney-General] to send for J. Edgar Hoover and tell him to do it.'[21]

Behind this harmony of fears between Roosevelt and Churchill mutual suspicion still lingered. Churchill complained to his War Cabinet three weeks after becoming Prime Minister that, so far, the United States had given Britain no practical help and was holding everything back for its own defence. The USA, he remarked caustically elsewhere, was very good in applauding the valiant deeds done by others. He even decided it would be a waste of time to make a special broadcast to the American people. Still, he had to admit to Mackenzie King, the Canadian Prime Minister, that Roosevelt was Britain's best friend. The President's problem was the need for political caution as he prepared his candidacy for a third term in the White House. And from London Ambassador Kennedy was sending highly tendentious and negative reports about Britain's ability to survive.[22]

This was the background when Bill Donovan arrived on his special White House mission. It was an odd role for an Irish-American with a Fenian streak. Acutely aware of this, Churchill gave him the red-carpet treatment; he had an audience with King George VI and met with Stewart Menzies, Admiral Godfrey and a galaxy of other high British officials, and he returned to Washington confident that Britain could survive. In August he joined Roosevelt at Hyde Park for a couple of days and gave him an enthusiastic briefing on what he had found: Britain would withstand a German invasion, her morale was excellent, and her military needs were urgent. He also helped bolster Roosevelt's decision to release fifty mothballed destroyers to Britain in exchange for leases on British naval and air bases in the Caribbean, Bermuda and New-foundland.[23]

More important, he persuaded Roosevelt to inaugurate full-scale intelligence collaboration with the British. Hardly had he returned to the United States than Brigadier George V. Strong, the American army representative in London, revealed to his British opposite numbers the remarkable headway US Army code-breakers had been making against Japanese cyphers under the brilliant William F. Friedman, their chief cryptanalyst. Indeed, they were on the verge of cracking the secrets of the 'Purple' cipher machine used by the Japanese for diplomatic messages, material that would become known as 'Magic'.

Churchill was immediately informed and agreed in principle to 'a free exchange of intelligence'. In late October Brigadier-General Edwin 'Pa' Watson, the President's military aide, telephoned Henry Stimson at the War Office to tell him that Roosevelt also approved, the only recorded occasion during the Second World War when Roosevelt made known his views on Sigint co-operation with the British. Having agreed in principle, Roosevelt, true to his style of leadership, let his subordinates thrash out the details. A tumultuous bureaucratic battle between the army and navy followed, with the latter being particularly reluctant to share their secrets with the British. But eventually a special joint mission set off for Britain to exchange codebreaking secrets with the boffins of Bletchley Park.[24]

Even Churchill had doubts about sharing secrets. He knew that the British codebreakers' triumphs gave him a powerful card in what was otherwise a feeble strategic hand, and he insisted that the process be a two-way street. 'I am not in a hurry to give our secrets until the United States is much nearer war than she is now,' he told Hastings Ismay, head of his personal military secre-tariat in July 1940. 'Are we going to throw all our secrets into the American lap?' he asked later. 'If so, I am against it. It would be very much better to go slow, as we have far more to give than they. I expect,' he added, 'that anything given to the United States

Services, in which there are necessarily so many Germans, goes pretty quickly to Germany in time of peace.'[25]

This directive, with its curious blend of hard-nosed *realpolitik* and Fifth Column paranoia, sometimes meant applying the brakes, and even after he gave the green light for an agreement on code-breaking he ordered that intelligence being given to the American military attaché in London, including disguised Ultra material, should be cut back. Future reports, he ordered, should become less informative and 'padding should be used to maintain bulk'. This was partly a matter of security; it also reflected his desire not to give away secrets without exacting a price.

Nor did his growing friendship with Roosevelt mean that he exempted the United States as a target for British intelligence. If anything, growing dependence on Roosevelt meant that he needed to know more than ever. 'The greatest thing is to get the true picture,' he declared about Ultra's revelations of Hitler's plans. The same was true for Roosevelt and American policy. William Stephenson's British Security Co-ordination – the name given to the coalition of British intelligence services in New York – spent much of its energy surreptitiously reporting on American affairs as well as exposing German influence on isolationists. And Bletchley Park codebreakers continued to target American diplomatic ciphers even as Roosevelt and Churchill embarked on their early trans-atlantic chats. The task and its results were certainly approved and read by Churchill. While the intercepts revealed little about Roosevelt's personal communications – he distrusted State Department security and relied on naval cryptosystems – the fact that British codebreakers continued this work until Pearl Harbor reveals how anxiously Churchill regarded his new-found friend.[26]

4

MAKING CONTACT

Gathered round the radio at Hyde Park on the evening of 5 November 1940, Roosevelt, his family, and intimate friends such as Hopkins and Morgenthau anxiously awaited the returns on the presidential election. At the mahogany dining table, with tally sheets and a row of sharpened pencils in front of him, Roosevelt charted the results. Worried at first about the Republican Wendell Wilkie's strong showing, by eleven o'clock he was more relaxed, and at midnight, finally sure of victory, he emerged smiling to greet a crowd of local Democrats. 'It looks all right,' he said. Behind him Harry Hopkins performed a little jig.[1] A few hours later Churchill sent him an exuberant message of congratulation.

Roosevelt never acknowledged or replied to Churchill's note.[2] Instead, shortly afterwards, he left Washington for the Caribbean on board the new naval cruiser USS *Tuscaloosa*. This was ostensibly to inspect some of the new naval bases acquired from his destroyers-for-bases deal with Churchill. In reality he planned to relax, fish, and bask in the sun with Harry Hopkins, Edwin Watson and Dr Ross McIntyre, his personal physician, who kept an eye on his hypertension and other ailments. At Guantanamo Bay in Cuba he stocked up on cigars; in the Bahamas he entertained the Governor-General, the Duke of Windsor (the former King Edward VIII); and off the coast of Martinique he got a close-up look through binoculars at the Vichy aircraft-carrier the *Bearn*, lying in the harbour of Fort-de-France. Along the route at pre-arranged points navy seaplanes landed alongside to deliver official mail. One of them brought an urgent letter from Churchill which dramatically highlighted Britain's need for material help.

Chilled by Roosevelt's apparent indifference since his re-election, not to mention his failure to reply to his letter of congratulation, Churchill had carefully worked and re-worked his letter, putting the final touches to it over the last weekend of November at Chequers while he celebrated both his sixty-sixth birthday and the christening of his grandson, Winston Churchill junior, the child of his son Randolph and his wife Pamela Digby (who, after divorcing Randolph, became Pamela Harriman and eventually American ambassador to Paris under President Clinton). Britain had survived the onslaught of 1940, Churchill told Roosevelt, but in the coming year its fate would depend on the supply and protection of shipping, food and munitions that only America could provide. Worse, the moment was now approaching when Britain would no longer be able to pay cash for what it needed. It was a frightening statement of Britain's desperate position.

This plea for help was the longest and most important letter that Churchill ever sent to Roosevelt, and it had a profound effect. Typically, the President concealed his feelings while he digested Churchill's message. 'I didn't know for quite a while what he was thinking about,' confessed Hopkins. But the United States soon found out.

The *Tuscaloosa* headed back to Florida, and in Washington a tanned and jaunty Roosevelt joked with pressmen before telling them he was trying 'to eliminate the dollar sign' in trade with Britain. 'Let me give you an illustration,' he went on. 'Suppose my neighbour's home catches fire, and I have a length of garden hose four or five hundred feet away. If he came to take my garden hose and connect it up with his hydrant, I may help to put out his fire. Now what do I do? I don't say to him before the operation, "Neighbour, my garden hose cost me $15; you have to pay me $15 for it" . . . I don't want $15 – I want my garden hose back after the fire is over.'

In this simple down-to-earth metaphor Roosevelt had floated the idea that was to become Lend-Lease to the American people. Response was positive, but across the Atlantic the speech failed to thaw out Churchill. Angered at the poor condition of most of the American destroyers released by the President – only nine of which proved immediately serviceable – he was also infuriated to learn that Roosevelt had despatched an American warship to Cape Town in South Africa to collect £50 million of British-owned gold to pay for American goods that Britain had already purchased. Overlooking the fact that the deal had originally been proposed by British Treasury officials, he furiously likened Roosevelt's action to that of 'a sheriff collecting the last assets of a helpless debtor'. Only under pressure did he refrain from saying this outright to Roosevelt, waiting instead to hear what the President had to say in his end-of-year 'fireside chat' to the American people.

What Roosevelt delivered was probably his most famous speech ever. There could be no appeasement of Germany, he declared, and if Britain fell all Americans would be living at the point of a gun. The best chance for America to stay out of the conflict was for the United States to become 'the great Arsenal of Democracy'.[3] Churchill now sent a more balanced message, but still remained blunt in his implied criticism of the President's foot-dragging. 'Remember,' he warned, 'we do not know what you have in mind, or exactly what the United States is going to do, and we are fighting with our lives.' The wooing of the President was becoming rough.[4]

As he mulled over this that Christmas Roosevelt suddenly said to Hopkins, 'You know, a lot of this could be settled if Churchill and I could just sit down together for a while.' 'What's stopping you?' replied Hopkins. Roosevelt explained that with neither country having an ambassador in place (Lord Lothian, the British ambassador, had just suddenly died, and Joseph Kennedy was being replaced in London by John G. Winant), it was not a good time.

'How about me going, Mr President?' ventured Hopkins, but Roosevelt turned him down flat. Then, out of the blue, early in the New Year Hopkins heard he was going after all. After two days' frantic preparation he set off in a PanAm Clipper via Lisbon, a gruelling five-day flight that delivered him in his famous battered fedora so exhausted and cadaverous he could barely unbuckle his seat belt. Whisked to London by train in a Pullman car staffed by white-gloved conductors and revived by a glass of wine and a hearty meal, he only narrowly escaped a heavy Luftwaffe raid on the tracks outside Waterloo station. It was his first taste of the relentless German bombing blitz that had been hammering London for most of that autumn and winter.[5]

Housed comfortably in Claridge's, just round the corner from the American Embassy in Grosvenor Square (soon to be dubbed 'Eisenhowerplatz' when the General made his headquarters there), he dined that first night in London with Herschel V. Johnson, the American chargé d'affaires, who quickly warmed to Hopkins' abilities. 'He acted on the British like a galvanic needle,' he noted. CBS's London bureau chief Edward R. Murrow was also impressed by Hopkins' determination to act as a broker between Roosevelt and Churchill. 'I've come here to try to find a way to be a catalytic agent between two prima donnas,' Hopkins told the veteran broadcaster. 'I want to try to get an understanding of Churchill and of the men he sees after midnight.' He was referring to Churchill's well-known habit of brainstorming with close advisers into the early hours of the morning. By contrast Roosevelt liked to be in bed by eleven o'clock for a good night's sleep.

The next day Hopkins arrived at 10 Downing Street for lunch with Churchill. When he had first heard that Hopkins was coming to London the Prime Minister's response was '*Who?*'. Brendan Bracken quickly put him in the picture and ensured that Churchill treated Hopkins as visiting royalty. It was Bracken who now opened the door of Number 10 and showed him around, telling him its distinguished history as the home of British Prime Ministers, before leaving him with a glass of sherry to await Churchill. A few moments later the Prime Minister entered the room. Eager to convey a sense of Churchill's personality to Roosevelt, Hopkins dashed off a vivid sketch in a letter he wrote him later that day: 'A rotund – smiling – red-faced gentleman appeared – extended a fat but nonetheless convincing hand and wished me welcome to England. A short black coat – striped trousers – a clear eye and a mushy voice was the impression of

England's leader as he showed me with obvious pride the photograph of his beautiful daughter-in-law and grandchild.'[6]

The three-hour lunch and five-week visit that followed was a brilliant success, an episode in Anglo-American wartime relations that single-handedly did more to create a personal bond between Roosevelt and Churchill than anything else that happened before their first personal summit eight months later off the coast of Newfoundland.[7]

Yet one obstacle had to be quickly removed. Hardly had Hopkins opened his mouth to pass on Roosevelt's assurance that he was anxious for a summit – an offer that Churchill eagerly accepted – than Hopkins also confessed that there was a feeling in certain quarters that Churchill did not like America, Americans, or Roosevelt. Churchill's fury ignited and he embarked on a bitter attack on Joseph Kennedy, whom he blamed for the misunderstanding. Then, to underline the point, he summoned his private secretary and had him dig from the files the message of congratulation he had sent to Roosevelt after the election.

Conversation then moved into smoother waters. Churchill treated Hopkins to a bravura survey of the war and then took him to the Cabinet Room where they poured over a chart marking the transatlantic convoy routes to Liverpool and Glasgow – and the flight paths of the Luftwaffe bombers sent to intercept them.

'God, what a force that man has,' Hopkins said when he finally left Downing Street late that afternoon. The show continued. That weekend Churchill took Hopkins to Ditchley Park, the stately home north of Oxford where on nights of the full moon, when his official country home Chequers lay vulnerable to German bombers, he regularly stayed at the invitation of its owner, Ronald Tree, a grandson of the original Marshall Field of Chicago. After dinner Churchill told Hopkins that he had just read the text of the Lend-Lease Bill and that it made him feel that a new world had come into being. For his part, Hopkins flattered Churchill. There were two kinds of men, he said, those who talked and those who acted. Both Roosevelt and Churchill belonged to the doers.[8]

In the weeks that followed Churchill took him on gruelling tours to demonstrate the nation's war-winning grit and to meet Britain's top military and political figures. Together they surveyed the gun batteries at Dover and gazed across the Channel at Hitler's 'Fortress Europe'. They visited the blitz-ravaged streets of Southampton and Portsmouth, were mobbed by a friendly crowd in Glasgow, and toured the dockyards of Tyneside. Brendan Bracken drove Hopkins out to Blenheim Palace, Churchill's birthplace, seat of the Dukes of Marlborough, and now the temporary wartime headquarters of MI5. They even travelled in a blizzard to Orkney and the great naval base of Scapa Flow, to see off Lord Halifax, who was on his way to be ambassador in Washington aboard Britain's most recently launched battleship, the *King George V*.

Churchill was so enthused by it all that during the second weekend of the visit he impetuously rang up Roosevelt. 'Mr President – it's me – Winston,' he blurted out.[9] To Hopkins Churchill talked endlessly of the war, of Britain's needs, and of the way ahead. Hopkins was powerfully impressed. 'Churchill is the government in every sense of the word,' he told Roosevelt, the one and only person with whom the President needed to have a full meeting of minds. 'I cannot believe,' he went on, 'that Churchill dislikes you or America – it just doesn't make sense.'[10]

In turn his personal amiability swept away fears that Roosevelt was less than whole-hearted about supporting Britain. One apocryphal and much repeated story summed up the mood. After listening to Churchill talking of creating a post-war British New Deal, Hopkins abruptly cut in. 'Well, Mr Churchill,' he drawled, 'we're only interested in seeing that that goddamn sonofabitch, Hitler, gets licked.' Such sentiments quickly endeared him to Churchill. 'He is an indomitable spirit,' he told Roosevelt. 'I rate him high among the Paladins.' Genuinely moved by his death shortly after the war, Churchill mourned Hopkins as 'a soul that flamed out of a frail and failing body . . . a crumbling lighthouse from which there shone the beams that led great fleets to harbour'. So delighted was Roosevelt at his alter ego's performance that he even bragged to his Cabinet that Hopkins was the first person Churchill sought in the morning and the last one he saw at night.

But not all friends, not even the closest, are necessarily let into intimate secrets, and Churchill carefully rationed and shaped what he told Hopkins. This was especially true of intelligence about

German plans for an invasion. Ultra was one of the few valuable assets now left to Churchill in his bargaining with Roosevelt. Payment for the war had already exhausted British finances and the Lend-Lease Bill faced bitter opposition in Congress. All the more valuable, therefore, were Britain's scientific and cryptanalytical secrets that could be traded for American support.

Churchill was no dupe of Roosevelt, wantonly disposing of British assets for the sake of some sentimental vision of a special Anglo-American relationship. His attraction for the United States certainly had deep personal roots, but these had not stopped him in the past from expressing strong hostility to American policy. Only with the rise of the dictators in Japan and Europe did he begin to sing a different tune.[11] Pragmatism and calculation led the way, followed by hard-nosed bargaining and mutual need, all burnished by personal diplomacy. Ultra represented special potency and influence, and Churchill used it carefully. Throughout the autumn and winter of 1940–41 this had governed his use of intelligence about Hitler's invasion plans. Not least in his mind was Roosevelt.

Hitler had signed his infamous Führer Directive No. 16, ordering planning to begin for Operation Sealion, the invasion of Britain, in July 1940. Yet despite the increasing flow of Ultra intelligence about his plans, information remained partial and opaque. That he was assembling an invasion fleet was apparent, but where and when the attack would come was a matter of intense debate. Fears had peaked early in September, when church bells had rung out in alarm across England's southern counties and Churchill warned on the BBC that invasion could come at any time. 'We must regard the next week or so,' he stirringly told the nation, 'as a very important period in our history. It ranks with the days when the Spanish Armada was approaching the Channel, and Drake was finishing his game of bowls; or when Nelson stood between us and Napoleon's Grand Army at Boulogne.'

But his public rhetoric contrasted with his inner conviction. The operational demands of a successful invasion made him sceptical, and the Royal Navy still enjoyed command of the seas and the Royal Air Force had won air supremacy. So he privately discounted the gloomiest intelligence predictions, but found it useful not to say so in public. Anti-invasion preparations stimulated morale and bolstered his political health. Many Tories were still wary of him, and it was not until after Chamberlain's death that November that he actually took over leadership of the Conservative Party. Who, at a time of supreme national danger, would dare rock the boat?

Even more important, his strategic gaze was directed firmly across the Atlantic. As he warned the War Cabinet, 'If the picture was painted too darkly, elements in the United States would say that it was useless to help us, for such help would be wasted and thrown away. If too bright a picture was painted, then there might be a tendency to withhold assistance.' When intelligence analysts finally conceded that the invasion risk was reduced and Churchill informed the Defence Committee that it was relatively remote, he deliberately withheld the news from Roosevelt. 'I cannot feel that the invasion danger is past,' he told the President in late October. 'We are maintaining the utmost vigilance.' Two days after Ultra finally revealed that Hitler was abandoning his invasion plans that year, he reminded Roosevelt yet again of the difficulty of defending Britain against sixty German divisions and a powerful air force. To Mackenzie King, his principal Dominion ally, he confessed that he did not intend to let the Americans view too complacently the prospect of a British collapse.[12] 'I got a report from Switzerland, from a usually reliable source,' Roosevelt cabled Churchill early in 1941, 'that invasion will be attempted in near future – somewhat prior February 15.'[13] Churchill's ploy had obviously worked.

The day after hosting Hopkins at Ditchley Park, Churchill received an Ultra report that further confirmed the unlikelihood of invasion by revealing that German wireless stations linked with the headquarters responsible for Luftwaffe equipment in Belgium and northern France would no longer be manned after 10 January. Churchill kept this carefully to himself, and with Hopkins continued to stimulate invasion talk. At Chequers one evening he even enthralled him with an account of 'Victor', an anti-invasion exercise taking place on the south coast of England. If the Germans landed and he had to deliver a speech, he joked, he would begin by saying, 'The hour has come: kill the Hun.' But later that night he privately confessed to his Assistant Private Secretary, John Colville, that he did not think the Germans would invade.[14]

Hopkins, however, took it at face value. In his extensive account to Roosevelt of his stay in Britain, a cable some thirty pages long, he declared that the most important single observation he had to make was that almost everyone thought invasion imminent. No matter how fierce the attack, Hopkins promised, the British, led by the defiant Churchill, would resist and defeat it. 'I cannot urge too strongly,' he cabled the President, 'that any action you may take to meet the immediate needs here must be based on the assumption that invasion will come before May 1. If Germany fails to win this invasion then I believe her sun is set.'[15] Churchill had generously gifted Hopkins with his hospitality and rhetoric. On their last night together at Chequers they had listened together until well after midnight to records of American music brought by Hopkins, and waxed sentimental about Anglo-American friendship. But Churchill had only too obviously not shared Ultra with the President's confidant.

Neither did Roosevelt share all *his* secrets with Hopkins, either. As usual, he was keeping a clandestine eye on his intimates, and that included his personal envoy. Back in London from his round-Britain trip, Hopkins had found himself as guest of honour at a dinner at Claridge's hosted by Max Beaverbrook and attended by editors and owners of the major British newspapers. Speaking in emotional terms, off the record, about his reactions on seeing Britain's blitzed and devastated cities, Hopkins cast a spell on his audience that convinced them, in the words of one witness, that 'should we stumble America would see we did not fall . . . we were happy men all; our confidence and our courage had been stimulated by a contact for which Shakespeare, in *Henry V*, had a phrase: "A little touch of Harry in the night."'

Soon after, in Washington, FBI Director J. Edgar Hoover sent a letter to 'Pa' Watson for Roosevelt's private and personal information with his own account of the dinner. Many of those present, he reported with pleasure, had praised Hopkins' charming manner, his keen insight into current problems, and his vigorous and dynamic approach to issues. It delighted Roosevelt to know that

G-Men in London were checking up on the performance of his personal emissary.[16]

They were even checking up on his host. Released to the author in 1998 under a Freedom of Information request, the FBI file on Churchill shows that Hoover himself took the first step in April 1941 when he ordered his New York office to purchase copies of Churchill's collections of speeches, 'While Britain Slept' and 'Step by Step'. The file attracts a bizarre miscellany of curious items, including death threats against the Prime Minister, allegations by self-proclaimed 'inside sources' about his personality and drinking, and even items about his son, Randolph.[17]

If Churchill held back on Hopkins, he was likewise discreet with Roosevelt's other envoy, 'Wild Bill' Donovan. As Roosevelt was embarking from Miami in early December 1940 on his Caribbean cruise aboard the *Tuscaloosa*, Donovan left Baltimore on yet another fact-finding tour to Europe. Blessed by Roosevelt, his mission was to carry out a strategic survey of the Balkans, Mediterranean and North Africa. The fate of the Balkan states still hung in the balance and in the Mediterranean and North Africa the British were fighting on land and sea against Mussolini's forces, who were soon to be stiffened by the German Wehrmacht.

Donovan also had a secret agenda: to brief himself on British intelligence methods and organisations with a view to pushing through an intelligence revolution in Washington with himself as director of central intelligence. A powerful ally was William Stephenson in New York, who regarded Donovan almost as his own creation. He extravagantly told his boss in London, Stewart Menzies, that the Republican Donovan had Knox 'in his pocket', and that he enjoyed more influence with Roosevelt than Colonel House had enjoyed with Woodrow Wilson. The two men flew together to London via Bermuda, where Stephenson initiated Donovan into the secrets of British censorship and other intelligence operations carried out on the island.

Within two days of arriving in London Churchill invited him to lunch and they spent the best part of an afternoon discussing the war. What intrigued Donovan especially was Churchill's desire to avoid a repeat of the bloodletting of the First World War. Donovan, with his own bitter experience of the Western Front, felt the same. It made him especially receptive when Churchill expounded on his hopes of setting Europe ablaze – the idea of stimulating Europe to rebel as a prelude to invasion – the task he had given to SOE.[18] Donovan already knew of its work, and he was to learn more over the next few weeks.

The day after Christmas 1940 Donovan left the comfort of Claridge's for a gruelling three-month tour that took him to British military headquarters in Cairo, the battlefront in Libya, every major Balkan capital, Baghdad, Ankara, Cyprus, Palestine, Malta, Gibraltar, Spain, Portugal and Ireland. He spoke to kings and prime ministers, generals and diplomats, and everywhere visited SIS stations and SOE training schools to learn as much as he could about British secret intelligence, special operations, psychological warfare and guerrilla units.

Churchill had arranged for His Majesty's Government to pick up the bills, and carefully provided him with a hand-picked escort from the War Office to guide him around – Lieutenant-Colonel Vivian Dykes, a brilliant ex-military intelligence officer who was later to become the first British secretary of the Combined Chiefs of Staff Committee in Washington, in tandem with Brigadier-General Walter Bedell-Smith, the future Director of Central Intelligence under President Harry S. Truman.

On his return to London Donovan briefed the War Cabinet and had another long meeting with a delighted Churchill. 'I must thank you for the magnificent work done by Donovan,' he told Roosevelt. 'He has carried with him throughout an animating, heart-warming flame.'[19] Yet Churchill had again been selective, and did not tell Donovan about the cancellation of German invasion plans, nor indeed of the existence of Ultra.[20]

Things were about to change, however. Shortly before both Donovan and Hopkins had arrived in London, the fruits of the initiative inaugurated in October 1940 by Roosevelt and Churchill began to ripen when the text was signed of a still secret and unacknowledged Anglo-American pact on sharing cryptographic secrets. It opened the door for the arrival in Britain of a top-secret American army and navy cryptographic mission.

Three days before Hopkins returned to Washington, the Royal Navy battleship *King George V* – on board which he and Churchill had wished godspeed to Lord Halifax on his way to Washington – arrived back at the Scottish naval base of Scapa Flow in a snowstorm.[21] On board were four American officers accompanied by four wooden crates. They were transferred to a British cruiser which made its way down the east coast to London. A heartstopping strafing attack by a German bomber put a dent in the crates, which had been stored on deck, but none of the contents were harmed. At Sheerness, on the Thames estuary, they were met by car and driven north through the blacked-out capital. Eventually they reached a red-brick Victorian mansion where they were warmly welcomed before being whisked off to a nearby country estate for a good night's sleep.

The first American cryptanalysts had arrived at Bletchley Park. Head of the American mission was Abraham Sinkov, an army reserve officer and mathematical cryptanalyst. Greeting them at Sheerness was Commander Edward ('Jumbo') Travis, its second-in-command, and their welcoming host at Bletchley was its Director and Room 40 veteran, Alastair Denniston. Carefully packed in the crates was a reconstruction of the Japanese diplomatic cipher machine known as 'Purple'. In exchange for handing it over to the British, the Americans were to be given the secrets of Ultra.

Some historians have argued that the British held back on their cousins. But this was not the recollection of Prescott Currier, a naval captain in the group. 'We went everywhere,' he remembered, 'including Hut 6 [where German army and air force Enigma codes were broken]. We watched the operation of the bombe [the deciphering machine]. We were told in great detail about the solution of the Enigma.' The Bletchley Park boffins also briefed them on other ciphers used by the Germans and Italians, as well as the Russians (still then allied to Hitler). In addition, they were given a great deal of information about the codes and ciphers of a host of Latin American countries. They also travelled extensively through Britain visiting intercept stations – invariably staffed, Currier warmly remembered, by elegant young females. On one memorable day they even watched a dogfight between German and

RAF fighters over Dover Castle. 'We were told a good many things that we didn't know we wanted until after we were told the information existed,' confessed Currier.[22]

Now Churchill could be more generous. In Washington top-secret staff talks had begun to discuss joint military planning in the eventuality of the Americans joining the war. Roosevelt had also been massaging him. Late in January Wendell Wilkie arrived in London, and over lunch at Downing Street he handed Churchill a letter that contained a verse by Longfellow: 'Sail on, O ship of State! / Sail on, O Union, strong and great! / Humanity with all its fears, / With all the hope of future years / Is hanging breathless on thy fate.' Sentimentally touched, Churchill replied that he would have it framed as a souvenir and mark of their friendly personal relations. The next day, he also sent Roosevelt happy returns on his fifty-ninth birthday, and a few days after that, in a BBC broadcast from Chequers carefully crafted for American ears, read out the Longfellow verse. What was the answer he would give to this great man, the thrice-chosen head of a nation of 130 million? 'Put your confidence in us. Give us your faith, and your blessing, and under Providence, all will be well. We shall not fail or falter; we shall not weaken or tire. Neither the sudden shock of battle, nor the long-drawn trials of vigilance and exertion will wear us down. Give us the tools, and we will finish the job.'[23]

But still, for all this sentiment and rhetoric, it was only when the Bletchley Park experts and the chiefs of staff had fully satisfied themselves of Purple's value – some three weeks into Sinkov's visit – did he finally agree to tell the Americans about their success in deciphering German military cryptography. 'The chiefs of staff informed me,' Menzies told him in a 'Most Secret' letter dated 26 February 1941 and signed 'C', the legendary initial traditionally used by heads of the Secret Intelligence Service, 'that, on balance, they favour revealing to our American colleagues the progress which we have made in probing German Armed Forces cryptography. Before I give permission to open discussions, which will be confined to the mechanised devices which we utilise *and not to showing the results*, the chiefs of staff desire me to obtain your assent.'

As Churchill pondered Menzies' proposal, news of two depressing military setbacks highlighted Britain's plight and plunged him into gloom. A Commando raid to seize one of the Italian-held Dodecanese islands off the south-west coast of Turkey was spectacularly repulsed by the Italians. Far worse was news that arrived after midnight detailing another serious disaster to a British Atlantic convoy. John Colville, Churchill's private secretary, decided not to pass on the news so that Churchill could get a good night's sleep. But at 3 A.M. Churchill woke up and asked him point-blank if there was any news from the Admiralty. Colville told him, adding feebly that it was all very distressing. 'Distressing!' responded Churchill. 'It is terrifying. If it goes on it will be the end of us.'[24] That morning, in red ink, he scribbled underneath 'C's initial, 'As proposed.'[25]

Astonishingly, the official history of British wartime intelligence passes over in silence the Sinkov mission. Yet with these two laconic words, Churchill inaugurated the most important intelligence alliance in history. The American cryptographers departed Britain having gained priceless insights into the successful marriage of cryptanalysis and intelligence assessment, as well as inter-service co-operation, that characterised Bletchley Park's work and contrasted so vividly with the grim army/navy gridlock in Washington. They also witnessed the work of the Admiralty's Operational Intelligence Centre in London and agreed on the security procedures to be used for exchanging intelligence across the Atlantic. 'It all could save years of labour,' reported Sinkov when he got home.

But, as Churchill agreed with Menzies, the Americans were told only about the process, and no agreement was reached about sharing Ultra itself, the finished intelligence product. At least not yet. But this embargo was to change dramatically that spring as the Battle of the Atlantic went from bad to worse.

Churchill's alarm over the Atlantic convoys was deepening by the day, and a week after giving Menzies the go-ahead he issued his famous Battle of the Atlantic Directive, ordering a full-scale offensive against Doenitz's U-boats. Within weeks British codebreakers also made a vital crack in Doenitz's hitherto impenetrable ciphers. In a sensational intelligence coup, early in

May 1941 a British destroyer, the *Bulldog*, captured a German submarine, U-110, off the coast of Iceland. Inside it, hurriedly abandoned by the crew, was an intact Enigma machine with its current settings and key tables. This, along with other material, enabled Bletchley Park to break the U-boat cipher. On 1 June, a message intercepted eighteen minutes after midnight was ready for action at the Admiralty's Operational Centre in under five hours. This set the pattern for the rest of the year, enabling U-boats to be located and convoys re-routed. The graph of convoy losses levelled off dramatically, and over three hundred ships, or one and a half million tons of shipping, was saved during the next six months.[26]

But how much of this material did Churchill dare pass on to Roosevelt, who for his part was stretching American non-belligerency to breaking-point by authorising the US Navy to extend its escorting of convoys to and from Britain further and further eastwards into the Atlantic? Churchill did not tell Roosevelt about the *Bulldog*'s coup. But not long after, he told Menzies to do something about sending Ultra to Roosevelt. But his security-conscious intelligence chief dug in his heels. 'After considering, from all angles, the possibility of divulging to the President the information regarding US Naval Units being chased by U-boats,' he told Churchill, 'I find myself unable to devise any safe means of wrapping up the information in a manner which would not imperil this source, which should, without fail, play a vital part in the Battle of the Atlantic.' To back up his caution, he also told Churchill that the chiefs of staff had recently agreed that Ultra should be passed to the American naval and military authorities only when they were completely satisfied that the source would not be endangered. 'I believe,' Menzies emphasised, 'that any other decision as regards weakening the veil of secrecy would cause the greatest regret at a later date.'[27] Reluctantly, Churchill took his intelligence chief's advice. But the exchange merely marked the opening volley in a campaign by Churchill that within weeks was to open the intelligence door for Roosevelt.

Menzies' worry about passing Ultra secrets to Washington was that the Americans were notoriously less security-minded than he and Churchill demanded. To underline the point, he drew

Churchill's attention to an article in Beaverbrook's *Daily Express* based on a report from New York. Headlined 'COLONEL BILL, NOW GENERAL, GETS HUSH-HUSH JOB', and accompanied by a photograph of a beaming 'Wild Bill' Donovan, it announced that Roosevelt had just appointed him to supervise 'the United States Secret Service and ally it with the British Secret Service'. For Churchill's intelligence chief, used to the British culture of official secrecy, it was all too much. If the American and British secret services were really to work together the news should never have been made public.[28]

Roosevelt's appointment of Donovan as Co-ordinator of Information – for that was what the garbled report was about – was the result of high-powered lobbying by the Irish–American as well as Roosevelt's own urgent need for better intelligence. Within twenty-four hours of his return from Europe a buoyant Donovan spent an hour locked in conversation with Roosevelt, Harry Hopkins and Frank Knox, during which he almost certainly floated the idea of a central intelligence agency launching operations along the lines of SIS and SOE. Sabotage, subversion and undercover war were obviously much on his mind. Speaking on the radio soon after, he highlighted the help it had given the Nazis. 'Just as in the schoolbooks,' he said, 'where we read that the soldiers of ancient days prepared for the taking of a city by first undermining its walls.' That he had made a hit with Roosevelt was obvious from the reaction of Henry Morgenthau, a man as close to the President as anyone. 'Donovan is the first man I have ever talked to I would be willing to really back,' he confided. 'I think he knows more about the situation [in Europe] than anybody I have talked to by about a thousand per cent.'[29]

Events in Europe since Donovan's return from the Balkans had taken a serious turn for the worse. In April, after months of relative calm, Hitler's Wehrmacht struck with devastating force against Greece and Yugoslavia. They quickly capitulated and British forces in Greece were forced to evacuate. The next month, Crete also fell victim to Hitler's onslaught. In North Africa General Erwin Rommel's arrival with battle-hardened German troops helped turn the tide of the desert war in the Axis' favour. Hitler's rule now stretched from the Arctic to the doors of Egypt. In the Atlantic, his U-boats continued to sink British convoys with appalling results.

Roosevelt watched events with growing alarm. Two days before Hitler launched his Balkan offensive he met in the Oval Room with his Cabinet. Spring had arrived and the cherry blossoms were in bloom, but he was weary and irritated, torn by his desire to do more to help Britain and his need to tread carefully at home. Lend-Lease had finally passed through Congress, but the gruelling struggle had sharpened divisions within the country between interventionists and isolationists. He had set the FBI on to the leading isolationist group, America First, where Hoover's men were eagerly assisted by Stephenson's British Security Co-ordination. Fifth Column fever was running high, and Donovan was warning everyone about the dangers of further aggression by Hitler and of a Nazi threat to Spain and North Africa, not to mention subversion in Latin America and the United States itself.

Roosevelt felt more than ever that he needed better intelligence. Already he had approved the creation of an American intelligence network in Vichy-controlled North Africa. Now, he told his Cabinet, what he wanted was a thorough re-organisation of American intelligence, and an intelligence 'supremo' analagous to Churchill's 'C' in Britain, a man who would draw all the strings together and report directly to him.[30]

Churchill and his intelligence chiefs, all too aware of the bewildering intelligence maze in Washington, applied what pressure they could. Late in May Admiral Godfrey arrived in the United States with his personal assistant, Lieutenant-Commander Ian Fleming, of later James Bond fame. After fruitlessly trying to penetrate the Washington bureaucratic maze for a few days, Godfrey decided that only Roosevelt could cut through the red tape. With help from Sir William Wiseman, Britain's First World War intelligence chief in New York, he got an invitation to the White House. Dressed in his dinner jacket, he encountered the usual Roosevelt welcome for his British guests:

> . . . there was the inevitable, 'Hallo, Admiral, how did you come out?', and when I mentioned the Clipper via Bermuda he said, 'Oh, yes, those West Indian Islands; we're going to

show you how to look after them . . . every nigger will have his two acres and a sugar patch.' Rough stuff, and rather brash . . .

But later, after dinner and a movie ('a rather creepy-crawly film of snake worship', noted Godfrey), the two men had a long tête-à-tête about intelligence. Roosevelt reminisced enthusiastically about his visit to London in 1917 as Assistant Secretary of the Navy, and about the First World War triumphs of 'Blinker' Hall and British intelligence, recalling the episode when he had supposedly met a British spy in Hall's office. Godfrey did not disabuse him, but encouraged him instead in his idea of establishing a central intelligence agency.[31]

Behind the scenes, encouraged and helped by William Stephenson, he pushed hard for Donovan, in whose gung-ho enthusiasm and vitality he detected an American version of Hall. Two weeks later Roosevelt summoned Donovan to the White House and offered him the job of Co-ordinator of Information, with a mandate to report directly to him on all information relating to national security. He did it in his usual casual manner. 'Jack,' he scribbled to his acting director of the budget, Jack Blandford, 'get together with Bill Donovan and fix this up.' Fighting off heavy opposition from his army and navy chiefs, Roosevelt made the appointment official by executive order on 11 July 1941. Spending millions of dollars in unvouchered money, Donovan was accountable to Roosevelt alone. Within months he was to transform COI into the Office of Strategic Services (OSS), the forerunner of the CIA, with added responsibility for subversion, sabotage and guerrilla warfare.[32]

Stephenson was jubilant at Roosevelt's decision. 'You can imagine,' he cabled London, 'how relieved I am . . . that our man is in a position of such importance for our efforts.' It all created a euphoric mood in Downing Street and Desmond Morton was especially pleased. Churchill knew, he recorded, that 'to all intents and purposes US security is being run for them at the President's request by the British'.[33]

Yet the notion, heavily peddled by contemporary and post-war British sources, that Donovan was 'their' man, and that Roosevelt's decision to appoint him was the result of British pressure, was a profound illusion. It was also dangerous and could backfire, as even Ian Fleming recognised at the time. Roosevelt was enthusiastic about Donovan, cabled Fleming to London, but rumour that he was a British nominee and 'a hireling of British SIS' was spreading and should be watched.

Donovan shared the worry and was blunt about being first and foremost an American when he went on his Balkan tour. After being briefed in the combined operations room at Plymouth on how the Atlantic convoys were guided between Ireland and Scotland, he pleaded that false sentiment should be cut out and that both British and Americans should look at matters from the standpoint of mutual interest only. The violently pro-English American, he insisted, was liable to be one of Britain's worst friends in America.[34] Churchill was soon to learn that in the President's intelligence supremo he had a prickly and obstinate ally.

5

—⊳•⊲—

UNDECLARED WAR

Hitler launched Operation Barbarossa, his onslaught against the Soviet Union, on 22 June 1941. It sent the Red Army reeling, and within twenty-four hours Churchill was urging Stewart Menzies to send Ultra intercepts of Wehrmacht messages on the Eastern Front to the Russians. Since the spring Roosevelt and Churchill had passed intelligence warnings about the impending attack to Stalin, only for the paranoid dictator in the Kremlin to dismiss them as deliberate tricks to embroil him with Hitler. The bizarre flight to Britain of Hitler's deputy, Rudolf Hess, on his one-man mission of peace the month before, only deepened Stalin's suspicion that Churchill, the veteran anti-Bolshevik, was a wily and duplicitous trickster. Even Roosevelt suspected there was more to the episode than Churchill was letting on. But now all had changed, and they were at one in seeing Stalin as an ally.

Yet Menzies refused Churchill's request about the intercepts. 'It would be fatal,' he said bluntly. To be of any use the intercepts would have to be sent immediately from Moscow to Russian field commanders. But, as the Bletchley Park codebreakers well knew – because they had broken them – Russian military ciphers were insecure. Menzies pointed this out to Churchill: 'It would be only a matter of days before the Germans would know of our success, and operations in the future would . . . be hidden in an unbreakable way.' Churchill took the point. 'Certainly,' he scribbled, 'run no such risks.'[1] Eventually, after he persisted and Menzies was sat-isfied about security arrangements, Ultra intelligence from the Russian front *was* passed on to Moscow.

The Soviet Union's forcible entry into the war dramatically changed the strategic picture. It also gave the final push to plans for Roosevelt and Churchill to have their first face-to-face meeting of the war. It came in August 1941 and was marked by low skul-duggery and high emotion. To keep it secret, both men resorted to the tricks of deception they so loved. Roosevelt left a sweltering Washington by train from Union Station, telling journalists he was taking his yacht, the *Potomac*, on a fishing cruise off the New England coast. Twenty-four hours later, under cover of darkness off Martha's Vineyard, he boarded the USS *Augusta*, flagship of the Atlantic fleet, and headed north with his military advisers towards Newfoundland, a British Dominion still separate from Canada. The next day the *Potomac* passed in broad daylight through the Cape Cod Canal with four men sitting on the after-deck impersonating the President and his personal aides,while fake messages were transmitted such as 'Pa Watson got the big fish today'. Neither Stimson nor Knox – not even his wife or mother – knew of Roosevelt's plans.[2]

Churchill's departure from London followed a similar pattern, its preparations having all the hallmarks of the opening of a good John Buchan spy thriller.[3] Before departing, Churchill had a pho-tograph taken of himself outside 10 Downing Street buying a flag from a beaming woman – a picture published on Flag Day in Britain when he was already across the Atlantic. Some members of the party only learned of their destination when they boarded the battleship *Prince of Wales*.

Churchill was thrilled by feeling he was personally challenging Hitler's U-boats to find him – although in reality the battleship could outrun any of them. The first night aboard, he also chuckled over a tongue-in-cheek spy film, *Pimpernel Smith*, starring the British cinema idol Leslie Howard as a modern English prototype of the 'Scarlet Pimpernel' rescuing victims from Nazi Germany.[4] Virtually none of those watching with him knew about his 'golden eggs' or the steps he had taken to receive them. 'C' himself selected the military intercepts, while Desmond Morton chose the diplomatic.[5]

Throughout the journey he constantly visited the ship's Map Room, a miniature replica of the famous Map Room at the Admiralty fitted for the journey on his personal orders. On one wall hung a map of the Russian Front, on the opposite one a chart of the Atlantic. As intelligence reports came in, every ship and submarine was plotted, hour by hour, with the U-boats represented by sinister little black coffin-shaped pins. From time to time the officer in charge, Captain Pim, would receive a message and remove a pin. 'Has that U-Boat been sunk?' queried a visitor one day. Behind him Churchill had quietly entered the room. 'Only British submarines are sunk,' he smiled, 'German U-boats are – *destroyed*.'[6]

Both leaders worried how they would react to each other. What sort of man was Roosevelt? Churchill endlessly grilled Harry Hopkins, who had joined the British party after a gruelling mission to see Stalin in Moscow. What did he think of this and that? And always: 'Tell me more about Roosevelt.' Hopkins later told his friends: 'You'd have thought Winston was being carried up into the heavens to meet God!'[7] Roosevelt had been posing similar questions in Washington, anxiously asking the only woman in his Cabinet, Frances Perkins, his Labor Secretary, who had known Churchill before the First World War: what kind of fellow is he? Will he keep his word? Is he angry at anybody? Does his anger cloud his judgement?[8]

Yet it was Roosevelt's pique that almost spoiled the show. The *Prince of Wales* steamed into Placentia Bay off Argentia in Newfoundland on the morning of 8 August, where the *Augusta* already lay at anchor. The bosun's pipes shrilled, the band of the Royal Marines played the 'The Star-Spangled Banner', and from the *Augusta* came the sounds of 'God Save The King'. On shore, the building of an American seaplane base under the terms of the destroyers-for-bases deal was already in full swing, the Stars and Stripes flying proudly within the perimeter fence and trucks and automobiles driving on the left; Roosevelt had insisted on this symbolism of place as a reminder that Churchill, not he, was the supplicant.

Dressed proudly in his blue uniform of the Warden of the Cinque Ports, Churchill crossed by barge to the American flagship,

mounted the gangway, and handed the waiting Roosevelt, dressed
in a tan Palm Beach suit and leaning on the arm of his son Elliott,
a letter from King George VI formally introducing his Prime
Minister. They shook hands, exchanged greetings (lost to posterity when the British sound recording machine broke down), then
moved into the captain's cabin for lunch.

How delighted he was to meet the President for the first time,
Churchill began. But they had met before, interjected Roosevelt.
When? asked Churchill. Why, at a dinner at Gray's Inn in 1918,
replied the President, bringing up the encounter that still irked.
Churchill covered his error quickly, pretending to remember, and
later polished the false memory by describing the vivid impression
Roosevelt had made on him.[9] Roosevelt, equally keen to get the
summit off to a good start, went along with the deception. But he
was irked. Churchill the bumptious and arrogant British imperialist
would never quite go away, it seemed. 'We've got to make it clear,'
Roosevelt told his son, 'that from the very outset we don't intend to
be simply a good-time Charlie who can be used to help the British
Empire out of a tight spot and then be forgotten for ever.'[10]

Yet, over the next four days, the two prima donnas laid the
foundations of personal trust and understanding that endured until
Roosevelt's death. Each man gained a mental picture of the other
vital in handling problems that threatened to derail them, and they
shared an instinctive feel for the potency of symbolism as a lubricant of diplomacy. This reached its emotional climax in the
Sunday morning service they choreographed on the deck of the
Prince of Wales, an event that Churchill vested with such importance that he personally conducted a full rehearsal two days before
as the battleship ploughed through heavy seas.

Supported by his son, the President boarded the British battleship, and with obvious difficulty and determination walked the
length of the ship to join Churchill on the quarterdeck. Seated side
by side in the centre of a hollow square, with their military advisers behind, ranks of British and American sailors on each side, and
the Union Jack and Stars and Stripes draped together on the
pulpit, Roosevelt and Churchill sang together the hymns they had
selected: 'For Those In Peril On The Sea', 'Onward Christian
Soldiers' and 'God, Our Help In Ages Past'.

'You would have been pretty hard-boiled not to be moved by it all – hundreds of men from both fleets all mingled together, one rough British sailor sharing his hymn sheet with one American,' recorded John Martin, Churchill's Principal Private Secretary. 'I have established warm and deep personal relations with our great friend,' cabled Churchill to Clement Attlee in London. Roosevelt felt the same. 'If nothing else had happened while we were here,' he said, the joint service 'would have cemented us.'[11]

But plenty did happen: the two men agreed on the Atlantic Charter, a bold statement of principles about a post-war world of freedom, self-determination and economic liberation that adeptly skirted around the awkward existence of the British Empire and its colonies; they explored hypothetical strategic planning; they discussed supplies and aid to the Soviet Union; and they talked about the vexed issue of Japan and its Pacific ambitions. Here, Roosevelt exuded caution, as he had been doing for most of the year. So much so, indeed, that he had already vetoed a British cloak-and-dagger operation put to him by Churchill. It involved Operation Marchioness, a sabotage plan for destroying the Japanese cargo ship *Asaka Maru* in the early months of 1941. Highly sensitive, only the recent opening of SOE archives has revealed Churchill's personal hand in the affair.[12]

The *Asaka Maru*, a single-funnelled 7,200-ton passenger-cargo ship armed with 2.5-inch guns, sailed with a Japanese naval crew from Yokohama in January 1941 bound for Lisbon and Bilbao, carrying over thirty members of a high-ranking naval mission headed for technical discussions in Berlin. Even as Sinkov and his American team were learning about Ultra and delivering 'Purple' to his opposite numbers at Bletchley Park, British codebreakers discovered that for its return voyage the ship would load up in neutral Lisbon or Spain with supplies for the growing menace of the Japanese war machine, such as electrical transformers, Oerlikon guns, optical goods and strontium and cyolite (used in aluminium production).

This was a blatant challenge to Britain's attempts to strangle trade in war matériel from Europe – as well as political dynamite. Foreign Secretary Anthony Eden referred it straight to the War Cabinet. The affair came at an acutely sensitive time in the Pacific.

Japan was seen as an increasing menace to Britain's position in the Far East, its formal neutrality an increasingly empty charade as it fell under the sway of army nationalists with imperialist goals. Tokyo had joined the Tripartite Pact with Germany and Italy and was planning its moves into southern China and south-east Asia to create its 'Greater East Asia Co-Prosperity Sphere' – a thinly disguised version of Hitler's European 'New Order'. Already, the French had been browbeaten into granting Japan bases and transit rights in Indo-China from where they could strike against China and threaten British and Dutch imperial possessions in Malaya and Indonesia.

As the *Asaka Maru* prepared to sail, rumours of war reached a crescendo. Hugh Dalton, in charge of SOE, noted in his diary that Japanese entry into the war seemed 'very imminent', and Churchill himself cabled Roosevelt about 'reliable drifting straws' indicating the same.[13] Lord Halifax, who was still finding his feet in Washington, was instructed to raise the affair with Roosevelt, and a total censorship blanket was imposed on the British press. British High Commissioners in Canada, Australia, New Zealand and South Africa were secretly instructed to tell the Prime Ministers of their countries, on a 'most secret and personal' basis only, that if London decided to seize the *Asaka Maru* it could provoke war.

The War Cabinet was cautious. It accepted the argument for seizing the ship, but also noted Dalton's suspicion that Tokyo might deliberately be 'trailing their coats', hoping to lure Britain into a trap without American support. This could be disastrous for relations with Washington if war appeared to have been needlessly provoked by Britain. Churchill decided to wait for Roosevelt's response. In the meantime, he ordered, British intelligence should find out exactly what the *Asaka Maru* proposed to take aboard in Lisbon.

Such, at least, was all that was *officially* recorded in the War Cabinet minutes. But a vital point was deliberately left out. Churchill, who chaired the meeting, had a bolder idea. As Dalton cryptically noted in his diary that night: 'A hint [was] dropped to me from the chair.' He hurried back to his office and immediately issued orders. Less than forty-eight hours later he sent a plan marked 'Immediate and Most Secret' direct to Churchill for the clandestine destruction of the *Asaka Maru*.

Codenamed Operation Marchioness, it presented two options. One was to purchase a ship in Gibraltar in the name of a fictional Yugoslav, man it with a hand-picked crew including a sabotage expert, and in radio liaison with SOE agents in Lisbon, fake a breakdown and enter the Tagus river for repair. Here, they would 'accidentally' ram the *Asaka Maru*. 'Possibly,' Dalton helpfully footnoted for Churchill, 'some inflammatory material might be placed in the bows of our ship which would ignite at the moment of impact . . . [and] . . . ensure the destruction of the cargo.'

An alternative was to send to Lisbon, disguised as a diplomatic courier, a specially trained agent supplied with sabotage material and plenty of money to arrange for incendiary devices to be smuggled on board and limpet time-bombs placed on her hull. Both options could be pursued simultaneously. The first scheme was more likely to succeed, but it ran the higher risk of being exposed as a British plot which could be both embarrassing and damaging to Britain's relations with neutral Portugal. If Churchill approved, added Dalton, the project would need absolute top priority to be ready for the ship's arrival. And, he added hopefully, knowing Churchill's delight in scrutinising the operational details of skulduggery, 'If you desire to see the plan itself, which has been elaborately worked out, I should, of course, be delighted to submit it to you.' Should he now proceed?[14]

Churchill was clearly tempted. This was exactly the sort of covert action that appealed to him, especially after Ministry of Economic Warfare intelligence experts pieced together a far more detailed picture of the cargo due to be loaded on to the *Asaka Maru*: electrical transformers and rectifiers for the Fuji Electrical Company, strontium and possibly cryolite for Mitsui, Swiss-made Oerlikon guns, and range-finders and binoculars manufactured by the Società Galileo of Florence, Italy.

But by this time signs had arrived from Halifax that Roosevelt feared a showdown with Japan and was opposed to drastic action, and even as Dalton's sabotage experts in Baker Street were plotting the details Churchill began to back off, telling the War Cabinet that it would be best to let the *Asaka Maru* load up at Lisbon and detain her if necessary on her return journey. In the meantime, he would think further about what to do.

So no sooner did he read Dalton's plan than he decreed that any action against the *Asaka Maru* should be put on hold, to be reactivated if Roosevelt changed his mind. A week later, he intervened again to postpone any action at least until the return journey had begun. Roosevelt was now signalling firmly that he was opposed to any action at all, and the State Department believed the case for interception was legally extremely weak. Throughout March, as the *Asaka Maru* loaded up with its sensitive cargo in Bilbao and Lisbon, Churchill prevaricated. The ship finally headed home via the Cape of Good Hope and the Indian Ocean. British intelligence closely monitored its return in case of a last-minute change of mind. But none was forthcoming, and the cargo safely reached Japan at the end of April. Roosevelt's caution had won out.[15]

But by the time of the Argentia talks he was balancing caution in the Pacific with boldness elsewhere. Three topics on the agenda carried important intelligence implications: American patrols in the Atlantic, policy towards Vichy France, and the threat from Franco's Spain, which Churchill feared would soon fall victim to Hitler. Here the two men were fighting an undeclared intelligence war whose tempo was rapidly speeding up.

In mid-June 1941 one of Doenitz's submarines, the U-203, had encountered the American battleship *Texas* in the Atlantic. From the decrypts of its signals to Berlin Churchill learned that Hitler was desperate to avoid any incident that might bring the United States into the war. At Argentia he passed the news to Roosevelt, who became confident enough to permit his navy to escort North Atlantic convoys as far as Iceland. Soon after he authorised the US Navy to shoot at U-boats on sight.[16] From then on, the Americans were to benefit from an increasing volume of naval Ultra and other British intelligence including daily reports from the Submarine Tracking Room at the Admiralty. Even then, however, raw U-boat messages were held back and Bletchley Park refused to ask for American technical help in the continuing battle to keep on top of Enigma. The need-to-know principle still excluded the Americans from the greater part of Britain's intelligence harvest. Peacetime Washington was still desperately insecure, and Churchill had no desire to trade secrets needlessly. He believed that Britain should keep its monopoly of work against Enigma for as long as possible.[17]

Sharing of air force or army Ultra took even longer. Need and trust had to be built first. Here, again, Churchill and Roosevelt set the direction and applied the accelerator or brake as they thought fit. Even as they met at Argentia, the Director of Bletchley Park, Alastair Denniston, made his own personal journey across the Atlantic to visit New York, Washington and Ottawa and establish personal relations with his opposite numbers. With the American William Friedman he struck a lifelong friendship. 'I like to think,' he wrote at the end of the war, 'that I, the first to visit you, had a hand in founding an efficient and successful co-operation which had fine results in every field of operation.' He also sorted out teething problems that troubled Canada's fledgling codebreaking operation after Ottawa appointed the legendary but now ageing American codebreaker Herbert Yardley to set up its Examination Unit. The delicate task of replacing Yardley with a British expert required the personal touch.[18]

Vichy France and its North African possessions was also high on the Argentia agenda. Britain had broken its links with Pétain but Roosevelt kept America's doors and windows open. Because he feared both that Hitler might seize the Vichy Fleet, and that North and West Africa were a potential staging-post for attacks on the Americas – as well as a launching pad for allied assaults on Europe – he kept a heavy personal hand on America's Vichy policy. To carry it out, he even sent his old navy friend William Leahy as ambassador to Pétain.

Churchill was sceptical about Leahy's chances of keeping Vichy sweet, but Roosevelt's policy enabled the Americans to establish an intelligence network in North Africa. In March 1941 the American chargé d'affaires in Algiers, Robert Murphy – another of his friends – had struck a deal with General Maxime Weygand for twelve American observers to be posted there. Ostensibly overseeing the delivery of American imports, they doubled as intelligence officers and were quickly nicknamed 'the twelve disciples'. Simultaneously Lieutenant-Colonel Robert Solborg, of the US Army's G-2 Division (intelligence), travelled through the region and concluded that it held high intelligence potential. When Roosevelt made Donovan Co-ordinator of Information, North Africa was to become one of the earliest happy hunting grounds of American intelligence. Much of it was to benefit the British as well.[19]

Roosevelt regarded Donovan's expansive ambitions for his intelligence empire with benevolence and brainstormed with him frequently about the burgeoning secret war. He found the free-wheeling Republican a man after his own heart. Donovan's links with Stephenson and British Security Co-ordination in New York also proved useful, giving the White House instant access to British intelligence material and reports from sources around the world. This link was to prove particularly valuable as Roosevelt pondered how to deal with a nation reluctant to commit itself to Britain.[20]

Barely had he set sail from Argentia than news arrived that the House of Representatives had passed his Selective Service Bill by a single vote, a sobering reminder of the strength of isolationist sentiment and the climax of a summer of bitter political recrimination and invective. Isolationists denounced the President for deceiving the nation about his intentions, and he retaliated by letting loose the FBI and Justice Department against America First, their principal mouthpiece. He also hinted strongly that its money was tainted by Nazi origins. 'Will you please speak to me about the possibility of a Grand Jury investigation of the sources behind the America First Committee?' he asked his Attorney-General, Francis Biddle.[21] Meanwhile, the undeclared war against Hitler in the Atlantic was intensifying. The USS *Greer* was attacked by a U-boat early in September and then, in October, American lives were lost with an attack on the USS *Kearney* and the sinking of the *Reuben James*.

Casting around for an issue that would dramatise the danger to the American people, he seized on the Nazi threat to South America, America's back door. On Navy Day, 27 October 1941, he went on air again to justify his use of force to keep the Atlantic shipping lanes open. 'America has been attacked,' he began, 'the shooting has started.' Then, to emphasise the peril they all faced, he dropped a bombshell.

'I have in my possession,' he announced, 'a secret map, made in Germany by Hitler's government – by planners of the new world order. It is a map of South America and part of Central America as Hitler proposes to organise it.' The Nazis, he claimed, planned to divide South America into five vassal states, one of which would include the Panama Canal, the 'great lifeline' of the United States. It was a clear signal, he warned, that Nazi designs were directed against the United States itself. He also claimed to have uncovered evidence of a Nazi plot to do away with all religion and replace it with an international Nazi church. Only the month before he had also revealed details of a recently foiled Nazi-backed plot to overthrow the Bolivian government, masterminded by Major Elias Belmonte, its military attaché in Berlin.

The revelation stunned the nation, and at a press conference the following day he elaborated on the threat. But he refused to produce the map itself. It contained clues, he suggested, that would endanger the source.[22]

It also worked politically, and Congress finally agreed to amend the Neutrality Act so that American ships could carry arms directly into British ports. But his isolationist critics were quick to smell a rat, and claimed the map was a fake. Equally vehemently, he denied the charge. The truth is that both the Belmonte letter and the Nazi map were the products of a major dirty-tricks campaign to manipulate American public opinion in favour of war. At the centre of it all sat British intelligence and William Stephenson's New York-based British Security Co-ordination.

A great deal of myth has attached itself to Stephenson, from the claim that he carried the personal codename 'Intrepid' to the notion that he served as a personal intermediary between Roosevelt and Churchill masterminding secret operations around the world. These are a fantasy, fuelled by a sustained campaign of post-war mythmaking by Stephenson himself about his wartime deeds.[23] Yet even stripped bare of the myths, Stephenson accomplished a lot. Sent to New York to represent the Secret Intelligence Service, he also acted as an agent of influence using clandestine means such as wiretapping and disinformation to discredit Roosevelt's opponents and counter Nazi propaganda. The Belmonte plot and the Nazi map provide vivid examples of British dirty tricks at work. Like most effective operations of their kind, they exploited real events to gain their maximum effect.[24]

In Bolivia, as throughout South America, genuine Nazi sympathisers were at work, and plenty of evidence existed implicating Major Belmonte in a plot to overthrow the democratic government in La Paz, a major supplier of wolfram to the Allies. Alerted by the FBI, Stephenson sent Harford Montgomery Hyde, one of his officers – and his first biographer – to investigate the Bolivian scene and plan a counter-offensive. Hyde, as he confessed in a post-war memoir, decided to forge a letter and give it maximum publicity.[25] A copy of Belmonte's signature was obtained, a suitable typewriter found, and a bogus letter concocted from Belmonte to the German minister in La Paz promising a coup in mid-July that would put an end to the Allied wolfram supply.

Telling the FBI that sensitive documents had been filched from a German agent in Buenos Aires, Stephenson's men then forwarded the letter to J. Edgar Hoover, who alerted the White House. 'We cannot vouch for [its] authenticity,' Hoover cautioned 'Pa' Watson, 'although it was received from a reliable source.'[26] After a copy was flown to La Paz, the Bolivian government declared martial law, the German minister was declared *persona non grata*, and a number of army officers suspected of disloyalty arrested. Belmonte prudently stayed put in Germany.

The sensational 'Nazi map' took a similar course, being handed over personally to Roosevelt by Donovan after coming his way from Stephenson with the claim that it had been secretly purloined from a courier of the German Embassy in Rio de Janeiro. Ivar Bryce, another of Stephenson's agents (and a great friend of Ian Fleming) claimed later that he had personally sketched it out and had it produced by expert British forgers. On the other hand, Stephenson, to the end of his life, insisted it was genuine. Recent research suggests that it may well have been produced, not in Berlin, but by the local Abwehr representative in Argentina before being touched up for dramatic purposes by BSC's forgery factory in Canada, 'Station M'.[27] Whatever its origins, its impact and use by Roosevelt is not in doubt.

So does all this prove that Roosevelt was manipulated by Stephenson and British intelligence? The *Washington Post* claimed as much when rumours surfaced that the recently deceased Sir William Stephenson had left behind a secret history of British Security Co-ordination.[28] Such suspicions continue to surface, embraced in the United States by those anxious to denounce Roosevelt as a British dupe or even worse, and in Britain by claimants eager to proclaim the superiority of British intelligence over a gullible President.[29]

Yet the truth is far more sensational, revealing a Roosevelt fully conscious of the power of intelligence and highly adept at manipulating it for his greater political goals. For him the First World War, with German sabotage plots and the Zimmerman telegram affair, was a vivid living memory, and he allowed Stephenson to operate on American soil because he understood that British intelligence would help fight Nazi espionage and his own policy of discrediting the isolationists. For most of 1940 and 1941 he resisted attempts by State Department watchdogs to put a curb on BSC, and instead turned a benevolent blind eye to its 'convenient white lies'.[30]

But he also did more than that. Evidence just released in Britain demonstrates conclusively that he was fully informed and actively complicit in Stephenson's dirty tricks. Nor was Donovan his only source on British special operations. Averell Harriman, his even closer and trusted personal emissary to both Churchill and Stalin, was another. Visiting London in the spring of 1941, after Donovan's return to Washington from his Balkan trip, Harriman met with SOE minister Hugh Dalton on 11 May to discuss the whole question of Anglo-American subversive co-operation. It was an encounter crucial to bringing Roosevelt personally even further into the picture, and yet was significantly whitewashed from Harriman's published memoirs. His promise that he would approach Roosevelt through Harry Hopkins quickly bore fruit because two weeks later a happy Dalton noted in his diary that Harriman had delivered 'a verbal message to the President about my show'.[31]

What Roosevelt's green light for British dirty tricks might mean in practice became clear that August. For several months Stephenson's men had been compiling a report about Vichy French activities in the United States. The French ambassador,

Gaston Henry-Haye, had declared on his arrival in Washington that his prime objective was to establish that Britain had betrayed France and was therefore the real enemy. 'Every means at our disposal,' he urged, 'must be used to convince America that this is true.' Vichy secret agents in the United States also opened files on the supporters of the Free French, threatened reprisals against them and their families in France, shanghaied French sailors contemplating joining up with De Gaulle, and lent a hand to known German secret agents.

Soon after Roosevelt returned from his historic first meeting with Churchill Stephenson ensured a copy of the report reached him. 'He is "fascinated" by it,' reported the British intelligence chief personally to London, 'and has given his approval to necessary action which involves a newspaper campaign now being organised.' This press offensive involved careful editing of the report, which was then passed to a safe contact at the *New York Herald Tribune*. The article appeared as a front-page story, a dramatic exposure that accused the French Embassy in Washington of working hand-in-glove with the Nazis to make France a vassal state of Hitler, and striving actively against the United States. More articles followed, accompanied by facsimile letters and photographs of incriminating evidence. Reproduced in over a hundred papers throughout the United States and Canada, it was a scoop. Henry Morgenthau was so impressed that he said he wanted to meet the *Herald Tribune* reporter who'd uncovered the story and congratulate him personally.[32]

Roosevelt thus knowingly supported and approved of British special operations because it suited his purpose. Both the State Department and the FBI told him they had reservations about the authenticity of both the Belmonte letter and the Nazi map, but this did not bother him. Even if the letter was a forgery, it expressed a deeper truth. And if the Nazi map sprang from the cunning intrigues of British intelligence, it also laid bare Hitler's goals of world hegemony that would awaken the American people to the Nazi threat. Far from being a dupe, Roosevelt gladly played along with British 'dirty tricks' for his own ends.

6

➤━◆━◆━

THE LAST PIRATE OF
THE MEDITERRANEAN

Henry Morgenthau's enthusiasm for British dirty tricks was no accident. He was both staunchly anti-Nazi and Roosevelt's keenest Cabinet ally for waging secret war. As Secretary of the Treasury responsible for the Secret Service he already had a taste for it. Created by Lincoln's last Cabinet meeting before his assassination, the service's main task had rapidly expanded from the detection of counterfeiters and the physical protection of the President to criminal investigation and the pursuit of spies. Since the First World War the FBI had steadily taken charge of federal crime and espionage, but the Secret Service, and hence the Treasury, still enjoyed extensive powers of investigation and surveillance.[1]

Of all the President's men Morgenthau was one of the closest. A wealthy landowner and neighbour in Dutchess County, New York, he was a Roosevelt protégé and came from a family of impeccable Democratic Party pedigree. His father, Henry Morgenthau Sr, an immigrant from Mannheim, had prospered as a lawyer and real-estate magnate in New York and chaired the finance committee for Woodrow Wilson's successful 1912 presidential campaign. Rewarded with the post of US ambassador in Turkey, he later investigated anti-Jewish pogroms in Poland, oversaw the resettlement of Greeks from Anatolia after the

Greco-Turkish war, and was a technical expert at the World Monetary and Economic Conference in London at the nadir of the Depression in 1933.

His son's public career reflected Roosevelt's rising public fortunes. Fifty years old in 1941, Henry Morgenthau Jr had been neighbours with Roosevelt since he acquired his fruit and dairy farm before the First World War. They became lifelong friends, sharing similar patrician instincts, a love of the Hudson Valley, and enjoying an elevated social status. As Assistant Secretary of the Navy Roosevelt found Morgenthau a job during the First World War, appointed him Chairman of the New York Agricultural Advisory Commission when he was Governor of New York, and as President made him Chairman of the Federal Farm Board and Governor of the Farm Credit Administration – for the previous ten years Morgenthau had been publisher of the *American Agriculturist*. Then, in 1934, Roosevelt appointed his old friend Secretary of the Treasury. It was his job to finance the New Deal, and, eventually, America's war effort.

But Morgenthau was always more than that. In personality they were quite different. Roosevelt's broad smile and *bonhomie* charmed total strangers, whereas Morgenthau could be brusque, thin-skinned and morose. On a good day he resembled a buoyant Wall Street banker. On a bad one he looked like a mournful small-town undertaker. Yet Roosevelt liked Morgenthau's hard-headed practicality, his sense of humour, and his discretion.

Above all, he valued Morgenthau's loyalty. Roosevelt revealed his inner thoughts to very few people, but he did to Morgenthau because he understood Roosevelt's moods, shared his jokes, and was neither a rival nor a sycophant. Eleanor Roosevelt once said that only two men dared to tell her husband when he was wrong. Louis Howe, the trusted political adviser who had helped him to the White House in 1932, was one, and Henry Morgenthau was the other. 'To Henry,' Roosevelt once scribbled across a photograph of the two of them riding side by side in an automobile, 'from one of two of a kind.'[2]

The fourth of November 1941 was another long day in Washington for Morgenthau: a multi-agenda Treasury group in the morning, a telephone tussle with the State Department over Lend-Lease funds for Russia followed by a hurried meeting on Foreign Funds Control after lunch, and then an interminable wrangle over Social Security for most of the afternoon. By late evening he was back at home.

As the lights went out in the forest of temporary government buildings downtown, Morgenthau was about to play banker to a top-secret multi-million-dollar subversive operation that would have caused uproar in Congress had it seen the light of day. Remarkably, it has remained largely secret until now.

At 9 P.M. Morgenthau opened the door of his home to two men. One was John Pehle, the Treasury official he had met with after lunch to discuss Foreign Funds. An able young lawyer, he was eventually to head the War Refugee Board which belatedly energised America's efforts to rescue Jews from Europe. Pehle had demonstrated energy and imagination in recruiting staff he urgently needed. That summer, the funds of most European countries – including the neutral, or quasi-neutral, states of Switzerland, Sweden, Spain, Portugal and Russia – had been frozen, but it had been done so hastily that background checks had not always been completed, or even started, before they began work.

This muddle had angered Morgenthau. 'The point I make is, hell, put a spy in there for a month, and that is all he needs,' he reprimanded Pehle. 'It isn't whether a fellow pays his bills and whether the butcher and the baker and the doctor says he is all right, it is what does he think, and what has he got inside him. Does he want to lick this fellow Hitler, or does he want to sit down and do business with him . . . does this fellow hate Hitler's guts or does he like him?' Pehle was left in no doubt where Morgenthau stood on Hitler or on the need for tight security.[3]

The other visitor that evening was Robert Jemmett Stopford. He had arrived in Washington the year before as Second Financial Adviser to the British ambassador, Lord Halifax. Four years younger than Morgenthau, the Cambridge-educated bachelor had been a banker in the City of London and arrived with an impeccable reference from Lord Simon, the British Lord Chancellor and former Foreign Secretary and Chancellor of the Exchequer. 'He is a close friend of mine and a man of high capacity and accomplishment,' Simon told Morgenthau, adding that in particular Stopford had a wide experience of financial problems in Europe.[4] These were now, as Morgenthau was about to learn, fully in play.

The reason for the visit was a letter Pehle had received the day before. Morgenthau decided the content was far too sensitive to discuss in his office and asked Pehle to bring Stopford along that night for a private briefing. The letter carried a personal appeal from Churchill to help with a top-secret intelligence operation. So complex and potentially explosive was it in its ramifications, Churchill laundered it completely from the record when he wrote his multi-volume history of the Second World War. Even his official biographer, Sir Martin Gilbert, writing in the 1980s, fifty years later, merely hints at an affair of 'considerable importance and delicacy', without giving any idea of what was at stake.[5]

The story began after the fall of France. The two main characters were a trusted personal agent of Churchill and a mysterious Majorcan millionaire who had bankrolled Franco's rebellion in Spain in 1936.

The agent was Alan Hillgarth, a bushy-eyebrowed and fiercely patriotic Englishman cut from the swashbuckling cloth of a Boy's Own adventure story. The son of a Harley Street surgeon, Hillgarth had entered Osborne Naval College at the age of eight, been wounded as a midshipman at the Dardanelles, got caught up in the 1920s Rif rebellion in Morocco, prospected for gold in Bolivia, and had a successful stab at writing adventure novels, one of which even won plaudits from the critical eye of Graham Greene.

Churchill, then out of office, had met him in Majorca *en route* to a holiday to Marrakesh with his wife Clementine on the eve of the Spanish Civil War. The 36-year-old Hillgarth, British vice-consul on the island, invited them to his villa for lunch, where Churchill signed a treasured copy of *The River War*, his vivid eye-witness account of Kitchener's campaign in the Sudan and the great battle of Omdurman in 1898. When Clementine also complained about the drains in their local hotel, Hillgarth put them up for a couple of days. It marked the beginning of a bond that stretched into the Cold War.

'Adventure,' Hillgarth lamented in one of his books, *The War Maker*, 'was once a noble appellation borne proudly by men such as Raleigh and Drake . . . [but is now] reserved for the better-dressed members of the criminal classes.'[6]

The Spanish Civil War offered the chance for him to reclaim adventure for nobility. He rode to the aid of stranded British expatriates, helped negotiate the handover of Minorca to the victorious Nationalists without loss of life, and won a guarantee of safety from Nationalist air attack that allowed the Royal Navy battle-cruiser HMS *Repulse* to enter Republican-held Barcelona to evacuate British subjects. Throughout, he was a valuable source for the Foreign Office and Admiralty as they anxiously tracked the impact of the Spanish Civil War on the Mediterranean balance of naval power. For all this he was awarded the OBE. More soon followed. John Godfrey, captain of the *Repulse*, had been struck by Hillgarth's dash and bravado. When he became Director of Naval Intelligence two years later, he made Hillgarth assistant naval attaché in Madrid.

War in Europe instantly transformed the capital of neutral Spain into a super-sensitive post. Franco was indebted to the Axis powers for arms, and one of Hillgarth's major tasks was to deter the Spaniards from refuelling and resupplying German U-boats. To help him he enlisted the local police, stevedores and dock watchmen, and rapidly acquired a thorough knowledge of German espionage networks and their numerous Spanish sympathisers. He revelled in these Iberian cat-and-mouse games, while at the same time doing nothing to provoke Franco's government to take action against the British. So impressed was London that Hillgarth quickly found himself handling and co-ordinating a broad portfolio of clandestine SIS, SOE and naval intelligence operations.

Normally, attachés kept well clear of clandestine intelligence, but because of his link with Churchill the rule was broken and Hillgarth was ordered to report directly to Stewart Menzies. Kim Philby, the notorious British intelligence officer later exposed as a KGB mole, was then running SIS Iberian affairs in London. He thought the whole arrangement fuelled delusions of grandeur on Hillgarth's part, including his grandiose use of the codename 'Armada' for his correspondence with the SIS chief. Once, Philby remembered, the SIS chief revealed that Hillgarth was authorised to spend a large amount of money to buy details about leading Abwehr officers in Spain. When Menzies handed Philby the list he thought it 'distressingly short', and in any case told him nothing he did not know already from his own network. Philby concluded that Hillgarth's source, whom he identified as a high official in the Spanish Security Service, was levying too high a price for his services.[7]

Yet Philby, writing in Moscow after his defection, liked to pour malicious scorn on his former colleagues, and is hardly a reliable source. Naval intelligence in London found Hillgarth excellent value for money, as did Sir Samuel Hoare, the British ambassador in Madrid, who placed considerable trust in his judgement and discretion. Even Sir Alexander Cadogan, the permanent under-secretary at the Foreign Office, who once described Hillgarth as a 'charlatan', agreed he was an effective one.[8]

So did Jack Beevor, a canny lawyer from the blue-chip City firm of Slaughter & May sent by SOE to run its Lisbon office. One of Slaughter & May's many leading talents to enter SOE, he was, remembered British wartime intelligence officer Sir Alexander Glen, 'one of its most able members, quietly competent with exquisite manners and great kindness'. His main mission, to plan sabotage and resistance in case the Germans invaded Portugal – his top targets were oil installations along the Tagus river – meant he kept in close touch with fellow operatives in Gibraltar. He was strictly forbidden to have any links with Spain, but – another measure of Hillgarth's standing in London – was instructed to maintain close contact with Hillgarth. They worked smoothly together, sharing pragmatic views about the harsh *realpolitik* of intelligence.[9]

Hillgarth's success rested on his extensive network of Spanish contacts acquired during his long years at Palma, the capital of Majorca. The most important of these was the man at the centre of the operation that Stopford outlined to Morgenthau in November 1941: Juan March.

For decades Juan Ordinas March remained a shadowy financial power behind the throne of General Franco's Spain. Glimpses would be caught in hotel lobbies in Palma, Madrid, Lisbon,

London or Geneva of a pale and birdfaced man wearing thick spectacles and smoking a cigar, his path cleared by a burly body-guard handing out tips to porters and doormen. Rumours abounded of his wealth, of his power, and of his menacing ability to inspire fear in those who crossed him.

But not until after his death in 1962, and, more important, that of General Franco in 1975, ending thirty-five years of dictatorship in Spain, did even the basic facts of his life become known. Two biographies appeared in Spanish, then the *New Yorker*, under the title 'Annals of Finance', published a revealing portrait of the man widely canonised in Spain as 'the last pirate of the Mediterranean'.[10]

Born into poverty in Santa Margarita, Majorca, in 1880, March rapidly scrambled his way to riches through real-estate speculation and smuggling. By the age of thirty he owned the monopoly to sell tobacco throughout Spanish North Africa. His fleet of launches, faster than any of those deployed by the Spanish authorities, made him master of a sea later described as 'an invisible and mysterious city that sprawls from Tangier to Cape Creus' at the eastern end of the Pyrenees.

During the First World War, using his Transmediterranean Shipping Company, he dealt with both the British and Germans, often double-crossing both. By the 1920s he was the millionaire owner of oil companies, banks and newspapers, and the undisputed political baron of his native island. Under the dictator General Miguel Primo de Rivera, after an unhappy interlude when the dictator vainly tried to dispense with his services, his tobacco monopoly in North Africa was extended to take in the enclaves of Ceuta and Melilla.

By this time his *modus operandi* had become legendary in his homeland. 'In some ways,' observed the *New Yorker* piece, 'he outdid all our Carnegies, Rockefellers, and Vanderbilts: he was bolder, more guileful, and less inhibited by restraints of either prudence or conscience . . . [his] outstanding characteristics as a financier were patience, nerve, subtlety at negotiation, crude skill at bribery, and prodigious political adaptability . . . He took corruption for granted, and used it casually and openly.'

The overthrow of the monarchy and creation of the Second

Spanish Republic in 1931 were to test March's political and financial skills to the utmost. First he lost his tobacco monopoly, then was condemned in the Cortes (Spain's legislative assembly), arrested, and imprisoned for bribery in connection with its operations. 'This is a man,' declared the Minister of Finance, Jaime Carner, in the Cortes, 'of the Middle Ages, with modern means and instruments . . . [who] centuries ago cruised the Mediterranean in search of their destiny, seeking to realise their will, who considered as their enemies only those who crimped or attempted to alter the course of that will. This is a man possessed . . .'

Even while in jail (where he enjoyed the privileges of a private suite and the use of his personal staff) March acquired a virtual monopoly of the Madrid press, masterminded a change in Prime Minister, and capped it all by carrying out one of the more sensational prison escapes of modern history. After a quiet word with the warder, his door was left unlocked and he was escorted by his personal prison guard to a waiting chauffeur-driven limousine, which whisked him on a twelve-hour trip to the Gibraltar border crossing point. Here neither the Spanish nor British border guards even asked him to step out of the car, and only after he had safely left Spanish territory was his absence from prison finally 'discovered'.

On his arrival in Marseille, the prison guard who had accompanied him cheerfully told reporters that he had decided to retire from the prison service and go and live in Greece. Even his enemies admired March's cheek. 'All Spain was chuckling,' reported Claude G. Bowers, the American ambassador in Madrid. 'In the cynical, ribald laughter of the cafés, men told this story and roared with the joy of it.'[11]

Not surprisingly March was a heavy backer of the right wing during the Spanish Civil War. He personally paid for the Dragon Rapide aircraft, chartered from a British company, that flew General Franco from the Canary Islands to Spanish Morocco to launch his rebellion. He found £1 million to buy twelve Italian Savoia-81 bombers from Mussolini for the rebels and guaranteed a $4.5 million line of credit from Kleinwort's Bank in London for Franco's forces. One recent historian of Spain has described him as 'the millionaire enemy of the republic'.[12]

March's prime motivation, however, was neither ideology nor politics, but making money. Above all, he was a capitalist, careful to keep his money in accounts throughout the world from where he could move it quickly into other currencies or commodities whenever his antennae sensed political trouble. His loyalty to Franco was as provisional as to anyone else. When he returned to Spain after the Civil War and found the dictator's brand of fascist-regulated capitalism burdensome, he moved to Lisbon. March, it was said, was neither friend nor foe of Monarchy, Dictatorship or Republic: March, quite simply, was for March.[13] Yet this *éminence grise* of manipulation and deception was also deeply enmeshed in international intrigue and espionage. Here, while the complex webs he wove are even harder to disentangle, recent releases of intelligence material reveal that in this field, too, March was a master player.

During the First World War March enjoyed shadowy links with British intelligence, trading with the Germans in food and fuel while providing information to his British contacts on shipping movements in the Mediterranean. Spain, as it was again to be twenty-five years later, was a fertile centre of espionage and intrigue, with a neutral government, a divided public opinion, strong German commercial influence, and a powerful British navy sitting astride its lines of communication in the Atlantic and Mediterranean.

The cloak-and-dagger-minded 'Blinker' Hall, Britain's legendary Director of Naval Intelligence, sent two of his men to Spain. One was the popular novelist A. E. W. Mason, whose private income and love of yachting provided perfect cover for missions along the Mediterranean coast picking up information about German submarines. Later he drew on this experience for his bestselling historical romance, *Fire Over England*, the tale of a young Englishman sent on a mission to Spain by Sir Francis Walsingham, the legendary founder of England's first secret service, which was immediately made into a major movie starring Laurence Olivier and Vivien Leigh.[14]

Hall's other agent was Major, later Colonel, Charles Thoroton, known to colleagues as 'Charles the Bold'. Based in Gibraltar, he built an extensive network of agents throughout Spain, the Balearic

Islands and North Africa. One of them was Juan March. Little is known of Thoroton's links with the Majorcan, because in a fit of security-mindedness after the war he made a bonfire of most of his papers. But Sir Basil Thomson, the flamboyant head of Britain's wartime Special Branch, captured a rare and revealing glimpse of March in a diary entry from 1916:

> He [March] keeps the government quiet by bribing officials and occasionally permitting captures of cargo, but he turned over the services of his staff to watch the coast for German submarines. The Germans offered him money, and he replied that they might as well offer him an elephant, and then they tried a decoration, and he said he could buy things to hang on his coat whenever he wanted them. Then they tried a lady from Hamburg, who first would and then would not, though he offered her 30,000 pesetas. This infuriated him. Thoroton had told him she was a spy. He said he did not care what she was. He meant to have her. Thoroton became nervous, but early this month he [March] returned triumphant from Madrid with a scratch across his nose inflicted by the lady, who resented having received only 1,000 pesetas. Now the smuggler [March] is in harness again.[15]

It seems doubtful, however, that March was ever truly and exclusively in British harness, and he appears to have traded information to both sides. However, enough was believed in London for Roosevelt's buddy 'Ned' Bell, the American Embassy's liaison officer with British intelligence, to describe Britain's Spanish network as 'immensely powerful'. Bell was a major source for Roosevelt's great admiration of British intelligence, and probably told him about March.

The Second World War offered even more glittering prizes, and March was quick to seize them. Hardly had Hitler's forces attacked Poland than he approached Hillgarth with a proposal to buy up over fifty German ships now forcibly lying idle in Spanish ports because of the British blockade. Not only would this deprive Germany of their use, he pointed out, but the British could then buy them from him for their own use. If they could strike a deal, he told Hillgarth, he would again put his vast intelligence network at British disposal. March also added that through his stranglehold of oil supplies in Spain he could ensure that no German U-boats would refuel at Spanish ports. He hinted strongly that Franco approved of his plan.

Hillgarth immediately suggested a trip to London to sell the idea there. Prudently, March had recently established his own 'import–export' firm there, J. March & Company, and he travelled under the cover of a business trip. His arrival in Whitehall in September 1939 sparked consternation. Many officials were horrified by his murky Francoist past, and a widely circulated intelligence profile described him as 'a scoundrel of the deepest dye'. But John Godfrey, the inheritor of 'Blinker' Hall's robust approach to naval intelligence and espionage, suffered no qualms. After meeting March, he decided he was quite genuine in his desire to help Britain, adding cynically (and accurately) that by doing so he was obviously going to benefit mostly himself. March, he thought, was 'an honest rogue'.

From behind his desk as First Lord of the Admiralty Churchill was even more enthusiastic. He brushed aside doubts about March's personal background, endorsed the intelligence appreciation of the Majorcan, and seized on his naked commercial motivations as a frankly positive asset. Besides, Churchill felt some sympathy for March's attitude towards the Spanish Republic because of his own inclination to see the Spanish Civil War as a battle against Bolshevism.

'This man is most important,' he declared, 'and may be able to render the greatest services in bringing about friendly relations with Spain . . . The fact that during the last war . . . he made money by devious means in no way affects his value to us at the present time or his reputation as a Spanish patriot . . .' He had no doubt, he concluded, that March's interests, and probably his sympathies, were with Britain.[16]

To Churchill's chagrin, March slipped out of London before he could see him personally. Back in Spain he reported to Hillgarth. Churchill's agent shared his master's cynical view. 'It would be a mistake to trust him an inch,' concluded the naval attaché, who thought him the most unscrupulous man in Spain, 'but, as long as that is kept in mind and every possibility of trickery provided against, it need not in itself prevent the scheme going through.' Its advantage was that March's organisation was entirely Spanish, totally under his personal control, and Hillgarth would have to deal with no one but March himself. Besides, it would cost the British nothing, and March could be perfectly ruthless when necessary, thus saving Hillgarth from getting his own hands dirty. 'He has already had two German agents shot in Iviza [Ibiza], though I did not ask him to do so and knew nothing about it till afterwards,' Hillgarth noted after yet another meeting with March shortly before Christmas.[17]

Churchill was delighted with Hillgarth, who by now was sending him personal handwritten reports. But foot-dragging in Whitehall and hard-nosed bargaining by the wily Majorcan meant that by early 1940 the scheme was not yet under way. Finally, reports that German U-boats were refuelling in the Spanish port of Vigo galvanised Churchill and Godfrey into action. Through his City of London merchant banking contacts, Godfrey's dynamic personal assistant, Ian Fleming, who was rapidly losing patience over a plan half-throttled with paper, discovered that March possessed an Achilles' heel. A £1 million loan from Kleinwort's Bank had been called in as soon as the war began, forcing the financier to replace it with a similar loan from Barings. 'A vague hint that it might be called again,' noted Fleming, 'would certainly bring M to his senses and get him to come back to brass tacks . . . we must bind him body and (if any) soul to the Allied Cause before we can go ahead with any of our main plans.' This idea, along with Fleming's suggestion that Barings – along with 'a sharp financier from "C"' (Menzies' Secret Intelligence Service) – should be recruited to help, had the desired effect. After SIS City contacts did their work, and to everyone's relief, the scheme was soon in place. 'Blinker' Hall's legacy of marrying intelligence with City finance had once again borne fruit.[18]

Hillgarth's standing as a fixer in Spain thus stood high when Churchill became Prime Minister and faced the strategic fall-out from the collapse of France. Neutral Spain, with Nazi troops now poised on her border in the Pyrenees, held the key to the Mediterranean and Gibraltar, guardian and pivot of the Royal

Navy. Which way, if any, would Franco jump? The Spanish dictator was militarily indebted to both Mussolini and Hitler, but he
had inherited a ravaged country whose rebuilding demanded peace.
Would he abandon neutrality and throw in his lot with Mussolini
and Hitler? If he refused, would Hitler simply invade Spain
instead? How could Churchill help ensure the best outcome for
Britain?

Basically he counted on Franco's unheroic attitude of self-inter-
ested caution. The 'narrow minded-tyrant', he wrote later, 'only
thought about keeping his blood-drained people out of another
war'.[19] As ambassador to Spain he sent Sir Samuel Hoare. It was
an astute move. His reputation tarnished by the notorious 1935
'Hoare–Laval' pact and rumours that he favoured a negotiated
peace, Hoare was nonetheless a shrewd operator, and keeping
Franco happy was exactly what Churchill wanted. It also got a
potential threat out of London, for Hoare was rumoured to be
angling for Churchill's job.

Hoare had other skills, too. In 1916, after a crash course in basic
spycraft, he had been sent to Russia by Britain's first SIS chief, Sir
Mansfield Cumming, and became head of station. A year later, dis-
mayed by Czarist and British intelligence red tape in Petrograd, he
transferred to Rome, where he spent SIS gold freely on subsidis-
ing the anti-pacifist faction in the Italian socialist movement. This
included its newspaper *Il Popolo d'Italia*, whose editor, Benito
Mussolini, used it as a springboard for his seizure of power five
years later.

In Madrid, therefore, Hoare found himself well-equipped to
deal with the intelligence jungle. On the one hand he strenuously
vetoed SOE links with ex-Republican guerrilla and resistance networks for fear of provoking Franco. But he warmly embraced
quieter forms of intelligence and was fully briefed on Bletchley
Park's breaking of Abwehr hand ciphers which enabled SIS to
track German espionage efforts. Kenneth Benton, the intelligence
officer handling them at the embassy, recalled that Hoare showed
'much interest' in the material.[20]

Hoare knew the pay-off that intelligence and subversion could
deliver. Such experience was useful. For Churchill could not be
sure that diplomacy alone would work, and he soon had a second

string to his bow. Four weeks after Churchill became Prime Minister, Hillgarth arrived in London carrying another typically audacious plan.

If the Treasury could unloose the purse strings the right people in Spain might be persuaded to pressure Franco to stay neutral. The 'right people', in Hillgarth's view, were certain high-ranking officers of the Spanish army opposed to becoming expendable parts of Hitler's war machine. Negotiations would be conducted by March, who would carefully cover up the British tracks and make it appear an entirely Spanish move financed by Spanish banks and businesses in order to spare the country the horrors of another war. Patriotism and money would do the rest.

Churchill hardly blinked before saying yes, and Hillgarth returned to Spain to mobilise March knowing that Hoare, the Chancellor of the Exchequer and the Foreign Secretary were fully on board as well. David (later Viscount) Eccles, Hoare's economic adviser and later Minister of Education in Churchill's post-war government, admitted bluntly that bribery was a major British weapon. 'We couldn't fight for Gibraltar. Nothing to fight for. So we bribed,' he said in 1983.

In its first phase, which took several months for March to organise, $10 million was released by the British Treasury and deposited via byzantine SIS manoeuvres – which still remain secret – into an account at the Swiss Bank Corporation in New York. From here, the Spanish officers could draw down instalments in Spanish pesetas as a credit against the final pay-off sum. Of the $10 million, it has been estimated that at least $2 million went into the pockets of General Antonio Aranda Mata, a nationalist hero of the Civil War and commander of the Spanish War College, who was expected to head the Spanish armed forces if Franco were toppled. Another ready recipient was the fervently monarchist General Luis Orgaz y Yaldi, high commissioner and commander-in-chief of Spanish Morocco. The relatively liberal-minded Aranda had been horrified by the post-Civil War brutality and massacres of Republicans and, like Orgaz and other generals, resented the power the pro-fascist political movement, the Falange, was acquiring in Madrid.

By the spring of 1941 this clandestine and highly sensitive

scheme, oiled by Hillgarth's energy and Juan March's facility in lining pockets, was running smoothly. Concrete evidence came in May, when Franco clipped the wings of his ambitious Falangist son-in-law, Ramon Serrano Suner, by appointing an army officer, Colonel Valentin Galarz a Morante, as his Minister of the Interior, in what has been described as a decisive battle in the ongoing war between the fascist ideologists of the Falange and the military high command.[21]

Hugh Dalton, who was head of SOE and Minister of Economic Warfare, and thus fully briefed on details of the scheme, noted cryptically in his diary that month that in Spain, 'the Cavalry of St George have been charging, which explains recent changes . . . hence Attaché H.'s concern for J.M.'s tinplate'. The 'Cavalry of St George' was a coded reference to British gold sovereigns, which carry on one side a depiction of St George slaying the dragon; Attaché H. was Hillgarth; and 'J.M.'s tinplate' referred to Juan March and the money being deployed to bribe the generals.[22]

That month, too, the British Treasury also released £2 million, channelled through Kleinwort's, to help March purchase a Spanish shipping company that would secretly work for Britain. Plotted by Hillgarth, Ian Fleming and the Admiralty, and sold to General Franco and the Spanish government as an initiative of South American financiers, the deal was consummated with March in the very week that Churchill and Roosevelt met off Newfoundland. The shrewd financier received a 5 per cent commission.[23]

At first, the Americans had been kept in the dark about all this. But early in 1941 Bill Donovan arrived in Spain during his Balkan and Mediterranean reconnaissance trip, which was enough to convince him that Spain needed urgent attention. Franco refused to see him. Instead, Foreign Minister Ramon Serrano Suner delivered a tirade against Britain and France, made no secret of the regime's pro-German sentiments, and declared his hope for a German victory that would deliver Gibraltar to Spain. If by some miracle Britain won, he said contemptuously, Europe would become 'a congeries of peoples too weak to resist the Red attack'. He also denied rumours of German infiltration and intervention in Spain.

Donovan vigorously disagreed, proclaimed his and Roosevelt's faith in Britain, and pointed out that America could supply Spain's desperate economy if it adopted a less hostile stance. Reporting on the confrontation to Washington, Alexander Weddell, the American ambassador, grimly underlined the need for a policy of 'bald realism' towards Spain, along with a careful calculation of the value of Spanish neutrality and how it should be secured.[24] Chill winds were obviously blowing. Two weeks later the Spaniards returned to the Third Reich its consulate building in Tangier, which the Germans quickly transformed into a major espionage base.[25]

By this time Hillgarth was up to his neck in more skulduggery. Churchill was increasingly desperate about Hitler's designs on Spain, and early in 1941 approved a scheme to be activated if Hitler's forces invaded. Codenamed 'Goldeneye', and master-minded by British naval intelligence with the help of SOE and SIS, it was a massive covert operation which was designed to pre-pare the way for a campaign of sabotage and guerrilla war against the Germans and the building of a post-occupation network of communications with London.

This prompted Admiral Godfrey to decide that Donovan should be told about the British plan. 'We can achieve infinitely more through Donovan,' he pronounced, 'than through any other indi-vidual.' With the Battle of the Atlantic entering a crucial period, bringing the President on-side was uppermost in Godfrey's mind, so he sent out his dashing assistant, Ian Fleming, to brief Roosevelt's man.

Donovan flew down to Gibraltar to meet him. Here, on the rock off Spain's southern coast that had been a colony since 1704, British intelligence had established its major base in the region. Eisenhower was also to make it his operational HQ for Operation Torch. J. C. Masterman, the MI5 officer who ran Britain's wartime double agents, described it as 'one of the most difficult and complicated places on the map'. On the one hand it was ideal for operations into neutral Spain; on the other, its very proximity to what also provided a hunting ground for German spies made it highly vulnerable to the attentions of Admiral Wilhelm Canaris's Abwehr.[26]

Here Fleming and Hillgarth spent an evening briefing Donovan, stressing the mutual interest of Britain and the United States in keeping Spain neutral. By the summer of 1941 a Joint Anglo-American Committee had made its base there to co-ordinate intelligence from North Africa and the Iberian peninsula.[27] In the end, of course, 'Goldeneye' never had to be implemented, but it was immortalised nevertheless when Fleming used the codename for his post-war Jamaican hideaway, where he wrote his James Bond novels. Like the future 007, however, Fleming knew when to be discreet, for it appears that the two young British officers kept their lips sealed about both the bribery scheme and Juan March.[28] Nonetheless, Donovan had been left in no doubt at all that Spain was a major playground for British agents.

Churchill himself soon told Roosevelt about the secret plans for guerrilla war in Spain if Hitler invaded. 'It is of the utmost importance,' Roosevelt agreed, 'to make every practical effort to keep Spain out of the war or for aiding the Axis powers.'

The Nazi victories in the Balkans that spring, followed by Britain's ignominious expulsion from Greece and the fall of Crete, made the situation worse. Then, in June 1941, Franco's response to Hitler's attack on the Soviet Union further deepened their fears. Addressing the National Council of the Falange, the Spanish dictator sneered at the destroyers-for-bases deal as 'the exchange of fifty old destroyers for the shreds of an empire', and announced that Roosevelt and Churchill had already lost the war. By contrast, he claimed, in Russia Hitler and the Wehrmacht were leading the battle against communism for which 'Europe and Christianity have for so many years longed'. To prove his point, he despatched the infamous 'Blue Legion' to fight alongside Hitler's troops on the Eastern Front.[29]

Not surprisingly, when they met off Newfoundland two months later, Churchill told Roosevelt that the situation in Spain was going from bad to worse. For that reason, he confided, the British had developed a highly secret plan, codenamed 'Pilgrim', to occupy the Spanish-owned Canary Islands as a way of protecting the southern Atlantic convoy route to Britain. Roosevelt had similar plans for the Americans to occupy the Portuguese-owned Azores.[30]

The Argentia meeting deepened the harmony of views on Spain of the President and Prime Minister. This was fortunate, because hardly had he returned to London than Churchill was alerted to a major crisis in the bribery campaign.

Early in September Hillgarth once again hastened to Chequers from Madrid with alarming news. The scheme had been extended for a second phase, with a further $3 million thrown into the pot. But then the Swiss Bank account in New York had been suddenly blocked by the US Treasury following the general freezing of European neutral assets over the summer. It was urgent, Hillgarth pleaded with Churchill, that at least $10 million be released immediately to keep the Spanish generals on-side. Only a personal appeal to Roosevelt would get the decision quickly reversed.

Churchill's faith in Hillgarth had continued unbounded. 'I am finding Hillgarth a great prop,' he once told Hoare. So he responded rapidly to Hillgarth's heartfelt plea. His first step was an attempt to mobilise his Chancellor of the Exchequer, Kingsley Wood, but the Chancellor's pusillanimous response – that the Spanish generals should be promised they would get their money after the war – exasperated the impatient Churchill. 'Can't you give them something on account?' he protested. 'We must not lose them now, after all we have spent – and gained. Vital strategic decisions depend on Spain keeping out or resisting. Hillgarth is pretty good.'[31]

Giving up on Wood, Churchill turned to Anthony Eden, his Foreign Secretary, and told him to order Lord Halifax in Washington to make a personal approach to the President through Henry Morgenthau. He was to make it plain that the appeal to lift the freeze came personally from the British Prime Minister. Eden obliged. Halifax was alerted, and he handed over the task to one of his two embassy financial advisers. Thus, on that November evening, Robert Stopford found himself telling the details to Henry Morgenthau.

7

THE CAVALRY OF
ST GEORGE

Morgenthau was no novice to the shadow war, and was probably not greatly shocked at the British plan for financial
subversion of Spain. Quite apart from the Secret Service, the US
Treasury enjoyed extensive and highly sensitive investigative
powers of its own, and had brushed up frequently against international espionage, for example during the Amtorg affair of 1940 (see
pp. 29–30). His outburst to Treasury official John Pehle about the
need for vigilance within the department showed that he was convinced of the dangers from Hitler's agents at work in the United
States. Indeed, he had recently let loose Treasury agents into
Swiss banks in New York to investigate possible Nazi connections,
where they had uncovered plentiful and damning evidence of the
banks' complicity in transferring ownership of companies from
German or Italian hands into American or Swiss names. They had
also discovered that some senior bank officials were directly implicated in the running of firms that were camouflaging German
interests. His agents were also on the trail of 'Nazi gold'.[1] The
Treasury had its own Cryptanalytic Unit, and within days of his
surreptitious meeting with Stopford, Morgenthau told Roosevelt
alarming news of what his codebreakers had unearthed about the
undercover operations of Nazi agents in South America.

He also had extensive dealings with the FBI, where there was a

considerable overlap of tasks. One of the items of his Treasury
agenda on the morning of his meeting with Stopford had been a
dispute with J. Edgar Hoover over who was to carry out security
checks for defence industry employees. Traditionally this had been
done by the Treasury, but Morgenthau was eager to palm it off on
to the FBI and Hoover was digging in his heels. 'His position is,'
Morgenthau grumbled, '[that] he would like us to do it, and whenever we run into a subversive matter, just turn it over to him.'
After a personal meeting with Hoover, Morgenthau agreed that the
FBI could have use of a room in the Treasury building to carry
out interrogations of suspects.[2]

Stopford thus found a sympathetic listener in Roosevelt's
Treasury Secretary when he explained the Spanish bribery scheme,
Churchill's interest, and the problem that had arisen from the
freezing of the funds. It was not just the practical fact that payments could not be made, he emphasised. It could jeopardise the
entire scheme if the Spaniards felt the British were conniving
with the Americans to withhold the funds.

Morgenthau listened intently, and when Stopford finished,
asked one question. What if Spain *did* enter the war and Britain
then asked him to re-freeze the funds? The three men decided to
cross that bridge when they came to it. Morgenthau then confirmed that the Treasury would release the money by issuing the
requisite licence.[3]

Stopford immediately passed on his response to Halifax. In
London, Churchill was waiting anxiously. 'Good,' he noted when
Halifax confirmed the deal, and asked him to convey his personal
thanks to Morgenthau.[4]

In Washington Pehle and Stopford now set the bureaucratic
wheels in motion. Three weeks later Pehle received through regular channels an official application from the Swiss Bank
Corporation to unfreeze the account. At 2.06 on the afternoon of
28 November he telephoned Morgenthau. Throughout the war
Morgenthau kept detailed transcripts of every official telephone
discussion he held. This is how the transcript of the relevant section of his talk with Pehle reads:

JOHN PEHLE: . . . this old matter we discussed with Stopford.

HENRY MORGENTHAU: With who?

PEHLE: Stopford.

MORGENTHAU: Stopford?

PEHLE: Yeah. For over ten million dollars.

MORGENTHAU: Oh, yes.

PEHLE: And the application has now come through.

MORGENTHAU: Yes.

PEHLE: It indicates nothing except that they want the account put in a free account.

MORGENTHAU: I see.

PEHLE: Now, the only further information we have is that a man by the name of Myorga came over here on the clipper to see about the matter and he talked to Stopford.

MORGENTHAU: I see.

PEHLE: And that's all.

MORGENTHAU: Okay.

PEHLE: Right. I'll put it through. Goodbye.[5]

José Myorga, the man who flew to Washington to talk to Stopford, was a top official of Kleinwort's Bank and handled Juan March's account. He had also sat in on March's meeting with Britain's naval intelligence chief, probably to assist with interpretation: March, somewhat surprisingly, spoke only fractured English. *En route* to Washington, he had stayed over in Lisbon to consult the financier. The British authorities could have stopped him by refusing him a visa, but they obviously thought his presence vital to the negotiations. 'Make people be pleasant to Myorga' urged Hillgarth. Nonetheless, there were worries about his discretion. Stopford should be told to take him in hand and 'shut him up', urged officials in SOE's Baker Street headquarters.[6] But neither Pehle nor Morgenthau enquired more deeply about him, and within hours of this telephone conversation, Pehle unblocked the Spanish account.

What did Roosevelt know of all this? Did Morgenthau win his approval in advance, or at any point even tell him about the operation? Strictly speaking, the President did not *have* to approve the deal, because Morgenthau was already empowered to grant exemptions in the case of foreign funds. Yet it seems implausible that he kept the President in the dark about an operation of such sensitivity and potential political backlash, especially when Churchill was involved. Neither Morgenthau's nor Roosevelt's papers reveal any evidence one way or another. Two days after Stopford's visit Morgenthau had one of his regular tête-à-tête sessions with the President at the White House, which would have been the natural time to brief him. Often he recorded in writing what they discussed, but in this case nothing appears in the notes he kept.

This, of course, proves nothing except to confirm Roosevelt's faith in Morgenthau's discretion: the President discouraged any records being kept of sensitive matters. It seems certain that Morgenthau told him all about it and agreed not to commit anything to paper. There were no secrets between him and the President, and as well as the political and international importance of the operation, Roosevelt's fascination for the secret war was well known to Morgenthau. His approval can safely be assumed. Here, too, he was waging undeclared war against Hitler.

Indeed, an episode that occurred soon after would have been inconceivable without White House approval. In December, with America still reeling from Pearl Harbor, the *Isla de Tenerife*, a freighter owned by March's Transmediterranean Shipping Line and bound for Lisbon, was seized while docked at Staten Island. The captain, the chief radio operator and three others found on board – including a Spanish-born shipping broker carrying a British passport – were charged with attempting to export prohibited commodities and violating the Trading With the Enemy Act. Aboard, federal agents had found large quantities of radio parts, parachute silk, and, on the dockside waiting to be loaded, 155 gallon-drums of oil, which had been innocuously listed on the ship's manifest as 'ship's stores'. All of it was suspected of being destined for Germany.

Mysteriously, despite a huge outcry in the press, the affair was quickly settled. Some of the charges were dismissed, the captain and broker were allowed to plead guilty to the charge of shipping prohibited material, Transmediterranean paid a small fine, and in January 1942 the *Isla de Tenerife* was permitted to sail away, having forfeited only part of its cargo. The broker's lawyer praised the Department of Justice for its 'fairness', and later reports from the Treasury attributed the handling of the case to 'British inter-cession'.[7]

Roosevelt's connivance at such undercover operations – comparable to his nods and winks for BSC's campaigns in the United States – went hand in hand with Donovan's ambitious plans to transform his new office as Co-ordinator of Information into a centralised intelligence agency. The month before Morgenthau met Stopford, Donovan told the President that he was taking over responsibility from the army and navy for all US covert operations. At the same time he appointed two chief subordinates to head up separate secret intelligence and special operations divisions. In charge of the latter was Lieutenant-Colonel Robert Solborg, who almost immediately went to Britain to find out more about SOE and visit the various sabotage and guerrilla warfare training camps around the country.

Solborg was a key figure in Donovan's early subversive efforts, and was to play a role in the Spanish bribery plot. The émigré son of a Czarist cavalry officer, at the outbreak of war in Europe he was a senior executive of Armco Steel. Soon after, he joined G-2, US Army intelligence, which sent him on a mission to North Africa, Spain and Portugal using his Armco business cover. It was after he returned, profoundly pessimistic about the lack of pro-Allied sentiment, that Donovan recruited him. After his visit to Britain he urged that both sabotage and revolution should be high on the American intelligence agenda.[8]

Early in 1942 Solborg arrived in Lisbon under cover as the American military attaché, to implement Donovan's intelligence plans for the Iberian peninsula. These were being co-ordinated with the British, and Solborg had been fully briefed on SOE plans for action.

'You know that I shall never fail you,' Solborg wrote privately to his boss. 'I have pledged my life to my country . . . We must unite behind our commander-in-chief (God bless him) and we must be *angry* if we are to win and win we shall.'[9]

As soon as he landed in the Portuguese capital – a notorious hotbed of intrigue, awash with spies – he met with British agents from London, Madrid and Tangier to discuss their mutual plans. 'There is lots to be done,' he reported back to Washington, 'and I can see that I shall be kept very busy.' He also set about arranging meeting places and cut-outs in and around Lisbon for his agents, and establishing communications with Madrid, Bilbao, Barcelona, Marseille, Tangier and Casablanca.[10] Driving it all was fear of German invasion, and keeping in step with the British kept him frantic – so much so, indeed, that they even offered to find him an expert secretary fluent in French, Spanish and Portuguese. They also provided him with rich material for intelligence reports back to Washington. So trusted did he become that they made him privy to plans not yet shared officially with the OSS in Washington. The most sensitive of these secrets was that in August 1941, while Churchill and Roosevelt met for the first time, staff talks began in Lisbon between representatives of Portugal and Britain to blow up oil refineries, docks, arsenals and shipbuilding yards along the Tagus river if the Germans invaded. Known as DAPI (Demolitions Anglo-Portuguese No. 1), the plan acknowledged that Britain's SOE could not do the job alone. Hillgarth's friend, Jack Beevor, was behind the scheme, and although his London chiefs kept it secret from Washington there was one American he trusted. 'Months ago,' he finally confessed in late 1942, '[I] told G50,200 [Solborg's code number] of [its] existence.' He would almost certainly have been unhappy to know that Solborg immediately sent details to army intelligence in Washington.[11]

In April 1942 Solborg travelled to Madrid, where he spent a week as Hillgarth's guest. Here the British naval attaché filled him in on the bribery scheme. After sending a long account of it all to Brigadier-General Raymond E. Lee in Washington, Solborg left with Hillgarth by plane for London. The Englishman, he reported, was taking back with him a proposal to Churchill from the Spanish generals for a 'definite, written pact' in which London would agree to support them when they decided to overthrow the present government and join the allies. The arrangement for Solborg himself to fly to London was not, he assured Lee, 'of sheer coincidence'.[12]

No sooner had the two men landed in London than Hillgarth hotfooted it again to Chequers to bring Churchill up to date on the Spanish scene. He arrived just as some other guests, including

Lord Vansittart, the former anti-appeasement head of the Foreign Office, were coming out of the dining room. Churchill, a cigar clenched between his teeth, was slapping Vansittart on the back. 'Extraordinary fellow,' he chuckled to Hillgarth as they watched him leave. 'He actually likes Dr Dalton.'[13]

What transpired next is indicated by one tantalisingly brief clue that exists in an undated and handwritten note from the Lord Privy Seal, the Labour politician Sir Stafford Cripps, to Churchill. 'My dear Prime Minister,' scrawled Cripps, 'I have seen Captain Hillgarth and Colonel Solborg today, and entirely approve their plans which they put before me at your suggestion.'[14]

Was this, as Solborg hinted before leaving Lisbon, for a written pact with the Spanish generals? Why else would Churchill send two intelligence operatives, one British and one American, to see such a high-ranking colleague as Stafford Cripps? And to what extent were the Americans now actively involved in the scheme?

Certainly, top officials in the British government took Solborg very seriously. He knew a great deal about Anglo-American subversive planning for Operation Torch, and that summer the British chiefs of staff, keen to be briefed on the American angle, asked if Solborg could come to London. 'We should like Solborg and Murphy [Roosevelt's man in North Africa] sent over here secretly,' they cabled to Washington, 'under assumed names, as soon as possible.' Churchill, according to the Cabinet Secretary, had already been briefed verbally by Solborg.[15]

Morgenthau, Solborg and US Army intelligence now knew about the bribery scheme. But who else? There were surely others, for just the month before General Aranda himself had approached the American Embassy in Madrid with a plea for American arms if a military junta seized power. This would happen, he said, if the war ended and Franco could not keep law and order, or if Germany invaded Spain and Franco failed to mount effective resistance, or if he refused to do so or gave transit rights for German forces through Spain to North Africa.[16] But nothing came of this, because the Americans had already agreed that Spain should be left to the British.

In the United States, however, Donovan had just unleashed against the Spaniards one of his most celebrated agents, Donald

Downes. 'No agent for the Office of Strategic Services,' writes Robin Winks in *Cloak and Gown*, his study of American scholars in the secret war, 'appears to have been so nearly "the complete spy" as Donald Downes.'[17] The Yale-educated Anglophile, whose career can almost stand as a metaphor of the Anglo–American special intelligence relationship, had first volunteered his services to British intelligence, which put him to work in Istanbul. Later he transferred to William Stephenson's British Security Co-ordination, where he spied on fellow citizens to sniff out Nazi money destined for isolationists.

In March 1942 Roosevelt sent a new ambassador to Madrid, Carleton J. Hayes, a Columbia University professor of history. At two separate briefings in the Oval Office he told him that his urgent task was to resist to the utmost any attempt by the Axis powers to invade the Iberian peninsula.[18]

Roosevelt's raising of the diplomatic pressure went hand in hand with other, clandestine, moves. By now Downes had left BSC and joined Donovan. That same month David Bruce, Donovan's intelligence chief, approved a plan to burgle the Spanish Embassy in Washington for documentary proof that the Spaniards were sending information to the Germans, spying on American aircraft factories and refuelling German submarines at sea.

Donovan warned him of the dangers. 'If you get caught we're in terrible trouble,' he said. At first his fears were unfounded. In July 1942 Downes's break-in team spent several hours one night in the embassy, and emerged with more than 3,000 photographs as well as details of the Spanish diplomatic cipher to help Allied code-breakers continue their reading of Madrid's traffic in the run-up to the North African landings. Similar operations succeeded in August and September.

J. Edgar Hoover, enraged by Donovan's trespassing on his domestic turf, then had Downes and his men arrested as they arrived for the October break-in. A furious Downes appealed to Donovan. 'Won't the President do anything about such war treason?' he asked. 'No' came the reply. 'No President dare touch John Edgar Hoover.' To get Downes out of the clutches of the FBI boss, Donovan sent him on an overseas mission.[19]

By this time, back in Spain, Juan March had made himself even more indispensable to British intelligence, this time over the so-called 'Wolfram War'. Spain was a major source of wolfram, vital for the production of tungsten used in the hardening of steel for such items as machine tools, armour plate and armour-piercing projectiles. Germany had none of its own and relied heavily on Spanish imports. To prevent the Germans getting their hands on it, the British and Americans had been busy with pre-emptive buying. As they did so, the price inexorably went up. Soon the British ran short of pesetas, most of which were provided through the Anglo-South America Bank, the only English-language bank in Spain.

What brought matters to a head was a sudden demand for the immediate withdrawal of some 35 million pesetas from the Bank's Barcelona branch by its largest client, the Riegos y Fuerzas del Ebro, the main subsidiary of the Barcelona Traction Company, a request that made it impossible for the bank to continue helping the British. Sir Samuel Hoare, the British ambassador, turned to Hillgarth, who immediately approached March. Could he help? Of course he could, replied the eager financier. Hillgarth later described what happened in a post-war affidavit for the International Court of Justice. 'He [March] put on his hat and asked me to introduce him to Mr Glaisher [Anglo–South America's manager in Madrid]. When we got to the bank he opened an account and lodged in it the necessary millions to enable the bank with its other resources to meet the withdrawal of the Ebro funds.'[20] Implicit in this deal was that March would be repaid by the British at some later date. As will be seen below, this British obligation led to persistent rumours after the war that in his campaign over the Barcelona Traction Company March found ready and willing allies in the byzantine corridors of British intelligence.[21]

Meanwhile the 'Cavalry of St George' – British gold – continued its work with the Spanish generals until 1943 and the final victories of the Allies in North Africa. The 'Torch' landings of November 1942 produced some particularly anxious moments. Hoare was so concerned that Franco would retaliate by granting transit rights to the Germans that he asked London for permission to make yet another payment to the Spanish generals. 'Agreed,' noted Eden's private secretary.[22]

Whether or not this British secret cavalry rode to war accomplishing anything more than enriching a handful of Spanish generals who would have argued the neutrality case anyway remains a controversial point. It may even be that as their pockets filled with British gold, General Aranda Mata and his friends lost any enthusiasm they had ever possessed for provoking Franco's anger; they simply had too much to lose. There were even doubts in London, and at one point Anthony Eden himself wondered whether Hillgarth and Hoare had become little more than dupes of the Spaniards, who, despite their smiling promises, were showing little bite.

But Churchill and Roosevelt clearly thought the operation worth the vast expense, and the hopes Churchill pinned on the scheme certainly checked more aggressive and belligerent moves against Spain – such as the occupation of the Canary Islands – that could easily have backfired. As a result, Hillgarth's credit with Churchill as a brilliant intelligence officer rose to new heights, Stewart Menzies and the Secret Intelligence Service added another successful subversion operation to their files, and Juan March became even wealthier.

As for Henry Morgenthau, in 1942 he found himself at dinner with Churchill and Eleanor Roosevelt during the First Lady's successful official visit to Britain. Churchill and Eleanor rarely saw eye to eye, and provocatively Churchill brought up the subject of Spain. Why couldn't we have done more to help the anti-fascists during the Civil War? asked Eleanor. 'Because both of us would have lost our heads if they had won,' replied Churchill, thinking of the Communists. Eleanor briskly answered back that she didn't care, whereupon Churchill riposted that he didn't want either of them to lose their heads. An attempt by Clementine to cool the rising temperature round the table only made things worse. 'I have held certain beliefs for sixty years,' growled Churchill, 'and I'm not going to change that now.' With that, he abruptly rose from the table. Dinner was over. Morgenthau can only have smiled wryly to himself at how shocked the First Lady would have been to know exactly what her husband and Churchill were up to in Spain.[23]

*

An intriguing post-war chapter to this story suggests that Juan March's links with British intelligence, and perhaps even Churchill, long outlived the war.

Hillgarth stayed in Spain until the Mediterranean was finally secured for the Allies, and in one of his last messages to Churchill reported that 'Sicily has impressed everyone and delighted most. Mussolini's resignation and what it presages has stunned opponents.'[24] By late 1943 he had moved to Ceylon to be chief of intelligence to Admiral Sir James Somerville, commander-in-chief of Britain's Eastern Fleet, and then became naval intelligence chief for the entire Eastern region. Again he reported directly to Churchill, once being brought by the Prime Minister to address the War Cabinet on the Far East naval scene.

After the end of the Pacific war and retirement from the navy, he moved to Ireland but kept alive his links both with Churchill and Juan March. Churchill, by now in opposition, was as hungry as ever for intelligence to throw light on Soviet aims in a Europe divided by the Iron Curtain. Hillgarth frequently visited London, kept in touch with old intelligence contacts, and regularly sent Churchill reports on defence and intelligence affairs based on the snippets he picked up in Whitehall or at the service clubs he frequented. He also visited him privately at Chartwell or at Churchill's London apartment; once he even saw him in Switzerland.[25]

The main reason for Hillgarth's frequent trips across the Irish Sea was his continued interest in Spain, and, more particularly, his links with Juan March. The Majorcan's field for personal enrichment had grown vastly larger with General Franco's post-war emphasis on the 'Hispanicisation' of Spanish business and his personal indebtedness to March. This reached its climax in the affair of the Barcelona Traction, Light and Power Company.

Through a series of dubious but skilful financial manoeuvres, March acquired and stripped the assets of the company after having it declared bankrupt with the complicity of the Spanish government. The stratagem he deployed was breathtakingly simple and densely camouflaged by typical March-ian subterfuge.

Early in its corporate life Barcelona Traction had issued a series of fifty-year bonds whose interest was payable in sterling. These payments were stopped by the Spanish government during the Civil War and Franco continued the ban after 1945. Quietly, March began buying them up. Then, when he owned a majority share, he successfully petitioned a mysteriously compliant and obscure Spanish court to have the company declared bankrupt on the grounds of non-payment of the sterling interest – despite the fact that in reality it was a large and prosperous concern that controlled almost 20 per cent of Spain's power output. This startling coup accomplished, March then set about acquiring the devalued assets of the company. By 1952, after interminable legal wrangles, he had succeeded. *The Times* guessed that by investing a total of between £2 or £3 million in the bonds he had acquired a company with nearly £20 million in book value alone. By his own estimation, March was now the seventh wealthiest man in the world.

The Barcelona Traction Company's owners furiously fought back. The majority of shareholders were Belgian, and after several attempts at settlement had failed, in 1958 the government in Brussels brought a case against the Spanish government in the International Court of Justice at The Hague.

The case dragged on until 1970, when the Court finally declared that Belgium lacked standing in the case as the company was technically Canadian; it had been incorporated in Toronto before the First World War. By this time March was long dead, having been fatally wounded in a car crash outside Madrid in 1962. His laudatory obituary in *The Times*, an accurate gauge of British Establishment views, praised him as '*par excellence* the self-made man, tough, shrewd, gifted with the power and will to survive'.

The case generated mountains of documents which exposed intriguing glimpses of March's intelligence contacts. One of the counsel for the Belgian government was a British QC, Mr Francis Mann, of the distinguished City law firm Herbert Smith & Company. In his pleading before the Court he repeatedly suggested that March's success in smuggling the proceeds of his Barcelona Traction, Light and Power Company manoeuvres out of Spain could only be due to the help of his contacts in British intelligence. How did March, a resident of Spain and thus subject to the very Spanish exchange control that had vetoed sterling payments on the ill-fated Barcelona Traction bonds, manage to purchase the vast amounts of sterling bonds he had accumulated in the first place? 'Did he illegally extract money from Spain into the United Kingdom,' asked Mann rhetorically, 'by assisting the British Secret Service?'[26]

The hint of an SIS pay-off was all the more apt because March had established a nominee business in London, called the Helvetia Finance Company, to hold the bonds. By happy coincidence Alan Hillgarth was one of Helvetia's directors. The records reveal that even as he supplied Churchill with intelligence he was working actively for March. Curiously, he soon forgot his 1940 conviction that March was 'the most unscrupulous man in Spain', swearing on oath before the Court that he was 'not only a very clever man but a scrupulously honourable one'.[27]

He and March were in close touch with the British Treasury. Four weeks after Churchill returned to Downing Street for his second premiership in October 1951, Hillgarth arrived in London for a meeting with the aggrieved shareholders. He immediately reported the details to Sir Herbert Brittain, a senior Treasury official. 'I spoke to Mr March by telephone after the meeting,' he told him, 'and he expressed himself as in complete agreement and very pleased.'[28]

Why, it might be asked, was the British Treasury so interested in March's reaction? The answer could be quite innocent, of course: the Treasury, after all, was already deeply involved for purely financial reasons. But it adds fuel to speculation about complicity with March. And, in a case replete with odd coincidences and intriguing connections, there was yet another to catch the eye.

Only the month before, Hillgarth had attended yet another meeting in the City of London, this time to discuss a legal suit over Barcelona Traction brought against March and his companies by Belgian shareholders. Defending March were Slaughter & May, where the senior partner handling the case was none other than Jack Beevor, ex-head of SOE Lisbon, senior executive in SOE's Baker Street headquarters – and Spanish contact of Alan Hillgarth at the height of the bribery scheme. He and Hillgarth had remained close friends, and Beevor would sometimes invite him to dinner at his home, where they would chuckle over 'the old crook'

Juan March; and on at least a couple of occasions he also hosted Juan March himself at the family dinner table.

Beevor was also an unabashed apologist for the use of bribery as a weapon of secret war. 'The word has of course unpleasant connotations,' he wrote in his memoirs, 'implying corruption and criminal liability. But in secret work in wartime it may include the giving of a secret and well-deserved reward for important services.' Above all, he went on, it was vital for the intelligence officer in charge of such operations to be imaginative in removing any criminal aspects, 'or at least put the transactions into a different form, and so reduce the risk of exposure and punishment'.[29]

Again, this is no more than circumstantial, the considered and dispassionate remarks of a former intelligence officer reflecting on a career now firmly, perhaps, interred in the past.

Yet, when all is said and done, the coincidences are just too glaring to ignore. When Hillgarth died in 1978, a letter appeared in *The Times* in response to its rather perfunctory obituary of Churchill's former protégé and favourite intelligence officer. Quoting Sir Samuel Hoare's encomium to Hillgarth as 'the embodiment of drive' who gave Britain vital contacts in wartime Spain, the letter's author, identified only by the initials 'J.G.B.' and described as a 'businessman and former government adviser', added that prominent among the contacts was Juan March. 'Wrongly believed to be anti-British,' wrote J.G.B., '[he] was in fact a sincere admirer of this country and rendered services to this country unsurpassed in any neutral country.'[30] J. G. Beevor's praise of Juan March – for who else could J.G.B. be? – and his own and Hillgarth's involvement in the Spanish bribery scheme, offers powerful evidence that the Cavalry of St George had ridden to the help of Juan March in grateful pay-off for his work for Winston Churchill and Franklin Roosevelt in fighting the shadow war against Hitler.

8

——◆——

INTERCEPT MAGIC

The Newfoundland summit boosted other aspects of the growing intelligence alliance. Early in September Tommy Davies, a top SOE official, flew to the United States to strengthen links with Donovan. A former executive with the textile firm Courtaulds, Davies had already made his mark by stripping his company's Paris factory of its platinum stocks only a step ahead of the advancing Nazis.

By this time Stephenson's British Security Co-ordination empire in New York had added special operations to its security and intelligence work. On the evening of Saturday 6 September, Davies met with Stephenson and some of the Canadian's friends in his private suite on the fourteenth floor of the St Regis Hotel in midtown Manhattan. Among the group was Alfred James Towle Taylor, a wealthy Vancouver businessman whose contacts in Canada proved useful. Most of his New York secretarial staff had been recruited thanks to his help.

High on Davies' agenda was strengthening links with the Americans. Specifically, he flew over to set up a secret-agent training camp in Canada for Americans as well as Canadians. Taylor, with his finger in real-estate affairs, knew of a site close to Toronto with quick and easy access to the United States. 'We think the Americans are going to come into the war and they have to learn about all this stuff,' SOE's training supremo Major Colin Gubbins told the camp's first chief instructor. 'Your job is to help train them and tell them everything we know.' Secretly, 'Camp X' – Special Training School 131 – was built on an isolated stretch of Lake Ontario. Its first commandant and training staff arrived from Britain on Saturday 6 December. Within twenty-four hours the world, and Anglo–American relations, were to be transformed by Japan's surprise and devastating attack on Pearl Harbor.[1]

For all the personal chemistry established with Roosevelt off Argentia, Churchill had conspicuously failed to unlock what he described as the 'inscrutable mystery of American politics': would Roosevelt take the plunge and formally enter the war? Returning home on HMS *Prince of Wales* he was no clearer in his mind than before. His encounter with Roosevelt, he wrote to his son Randolph, had undoubtedly marked the beginning of a great and lasting friendship. But there was something about the President that troubled him deeply. This was his obsession with public opinion and the instinct to follow rather than lead it. 'Our greatest single preoccupation today,' he confessed, 'is with how the United States is to be brought boldly and honourably into the war.'[2]

The Japanese Air Force gave the answer on 7 December 1941. To this brutal commencement of war in the Pacific was added the enlargement of the European struggle when Hitler, throwing caution to the wind, declared war on the United States. The conflict was now truly global. But had American entry come honourably, to use Churchill's words, or as the result of some machiavellian manoeuvre by Roosevelt – or even by Churchill himself? In particular, had either the President or the Prime Minister received prior intelligence of the Pearl Harbor attack and deliberately concealed or ignored it in order to bring Americans into the war? Conspiracy theories have been endlessly recycled since the day of infamy itself. Yet no convincing evidence exists to support them.

On the evening of Saturday 6 December 1941 Roosevelt was sitting quietly with Harry Hopkins in the oval study on the second floor of the White House, having excused himself earlier from a dinner party. Shortly after 9.15 a knock on the door announced the arrival of a junior naval officer, Lieutenant Lester R. Schulz, a communications specialist. In his hand Schulz clutched a pouch, which he solemnly unlocked. Inside was a sheaf of intercepts of Japanese 'Magic' forming a thirteen-part message from Tokyo to Ambassador Nomura in Washington, rejecting Cordell Hull's latest proposals for a peaceful settlement; the final, fourteenth, part had not yet been transmitted.

Roosevelt studied it carefully for ten minutes or so, then handed it over to Hopkins, who had been pacing backwards and forwards across the study. When he had finished, Roosevelt said softly, 'This means war.' Hopkins agreed. 'Too bad,' he said, 'that we can't strike the first blow and avoid a surprise.' The President demurred. 'No,' he replied firmly, 'we can't do that. We are a democracy and a peaceful people.' Then, raising his voice, he said, 'But we have a good record.' After that he returned the papers to Schulz, who locked them back in the pouch and left.[3]

Early next morning, Sunday, Roosevelt's senior naval aide, Captain John R. Beardell, brought to the President in his bedroom the final part of the message that had been deciphered overnight. 'It looks like the Japanese are going to break off negotiations,' Roosevelt observed before handing back the pouch. At lunch he sat again with Hopkins in the oval study, talking about things far removed from the war. At about 1.40 P.M. he was interrupted by a phone call from the Secretary of the Navy, Frank Knox, break-ing the news that the navy had picked up a radio report from the Commander-in-Chief Honolulu, advising his forces that an air-raid was on and that it was 'no drill'. Hopkins was flabbergasted. 'There must be some mistake,' he sputtered. 'They'd never attack Honolulu.' Roosevelt shook his head. 'It is just the kind of unex-pected thing they'd do,' he replied grimly. Yet he was also relieved. 'If the report is true,' he told Hopkins, 'it has taken the decision out of our hands.'

An hour later Admiral 'Betty' Stark telephoned with preliminary details of the heavy damage and loss of life inflicted on the Pacific Fleet. When the President met with Stimson, Hull, Knox, Stark and Marshall half an hour later, he was still visibly in shock.[4] As they talked, the phone calls kept coming in, mostly from the navy, and Roosevelt would excuse himself to take down the details.

In the midst of it all, Eleanor Roosevelt came in to share the news and be at her husband's side. 'He was completely calm,' she remembered. 'His reaction to any event was always to be calm. If it was something that was bad, he just became like an iceberg . . .' Roosevelt than rang his son James and asked him to come over. 'He was sitting at his desk,' his son remembered. 'He didn't even look up. I knew right away we were in deep trouble. Then he told me. He showed no sign of excitement, he simply and calmly discussed who had to be notified and what the media campaign should be for the next forty-eight hours.'[5]

Then came the call Roosevelt must have expected. It was Churchill on the transatlantic line.

It was evening in Britain when Admiral Isoroku Yamamoto's carrier force struck, and Churchill was dining at Chequers with two of his closest American contacts: John G. Winant, the American ambassador in London, and Averell Harriman, Roosevelt's special envoy. Winant had arrived earlier that day to find the Prime Minister pacing up and down at the entrance steps. Churchill already knew from intelligence reports that Japanese forces were preparing for an attack southwards. 'Will there be war with Japan?' he asked abruptly. 'Yes,' replied Winant. 'If they declare war on you, we shall declare war on them within the hour,' said Churchill. Then he asked, 'If they declare war on us, will you declare war on them?' Winant gave the only answer he could. 'I can't answer that, Prime Minister. Only the Congress has the right to declare war under the United States Constitution.'

It was a brutal truth that haunted Churchill, and Congress was still in the grip of isolationism. If Japan struck only at the British Empire, there was every chance that Britain would still have to fight on alone. For a minute, he stood in silence. Then he turned to Winant. 'We're late, you know,' he said quietly. 'You get washed and we will go in to lunch together.'[6]

By nine o'clock that evening his resilience and courtesy had wilted as he brooded on events. He was tired and dispirited, and said little during the meal. Over the previous few days he had been more than usually alert to the products of Bletchley Park. Only the day before he had read the text of a message from the Foreign Ministry in Tokyo to the Japanese ambassador in London, instructing him to destroy codes and secret documents. 'As these are precautions envisaging an emergency,' instructed Tokyo, 'you should communicate this to no one but your own staff and you should redouble your attention to your duties and maintain your calm and respect.'[7]

Not content to wait for such intercepts, Churchill took active steps to find out if his codebreakers had spotted signs of a move by Japan. Captain Malcolm Kennedy, a Japanese-language specialist at Bletchley Park, secretly kept a diary of his work. On the day that Churchill read the emergency telegram from Tokyo, Kennedy recorded that 'the All Highest [Churchill] is all over himself at the moment for latest information and indications re: Japan's intentions and rings up at all hours of the day and night, except for the four hours in each 24 [2 to 6 P.M.] when he sleeps . . .'.[8] But not even from the codebreakers did Churchill receive a whisper of Pearl Harbor.

Shortly after finishing his dinner with Winant and Harriman, Churchill switched on the BBC nine o'clock news and barely caught an announcement of a Japanese attack on American shipping at Hawaii as well as on British ships in the Dutch East Indies. Not sure he had heard correctly, he asked his butler to confirm the news. 'It's quite true, we heard it ourselves,' replied Sawyers. 'The Japanese have attacked the Americans.' The three men at the table stared at each other incredulously, and then Churchill leaped to his feet. 'We shall declare war on Japan!' he shouted, heading for the door. He was halted by Winant. 'You can't declare war on a radio announcement,' said the American. 'What shall I do?' asked Churchill. 'I will call up the President by telephone and ask him what the facts are,' declared Winant. Churchill said he would to talk to Roosevelt as well.

They were through to the White House within minutes, and Roosevelt briefed Winant on the news. Then Winant said, 'I have a friend on the line who wants to speak to you. You will know who it is when you hear his voice.' Churchill took the phone. 'Mr President, what's this about an attack?' he asked. 'It's quite true,' said Roosevelt. 'They have attacked Pearl Harbor. We are all in the same boat now.' The next day, he told Churchill, he would ask Congress to declare war.

For Churchill the news was bliss. Like his military advisers he had feared a Japanese attack in South-East Asia would hit British possessions and leave the Americans on the sidelines. Now the United States was fully in the struggle. 'I went to bed,' he recalled, 'and slept the sleep of the saved and thankful.'[9]

The fact that Roosevelt was genuinely surprised by Pearl Harbor clears him of conspiracy charges but hardly of responsibility for one of the greatest intelligence failures of history. Why did he himself not anticipate the attack, and why did American intelligence, despite its mastery of Japanese diplomatic ciphers, fail to alert him to Pearl Harbor as the likely target?

Too often forgotten in discussions of Pearl Harbor is that the Japanese exercised the very tightest security. Not a single reference to Pearl Harbor as a target appeared in the Magic intercepts, and the task force that left Japan in late November sailed under total radio silence – it could not even be detected by radio traffic analysis.

Apart from Magic, however, the Japanese navy had its own separate cipher. This was known as JN-25, and it, too, was cracked by American codebreakers. Conspiracy theorists claim that they therefore must have identified the target. Again, however, the awkward facts intrude. JN-25 was continuously upgraded by the Japanese, and the version in use by December 1941 was causing codebreakers so much trouble that while most were being *intercepted*, only about 10 per cent were being successfully *decrypted*. Of those that were read, none referred to Pearl Harbor or gave clues that could point to it.

Nonetheless, JN-25 is significant because post-war National Security Agency inquests discovered that clues existed in the non-deciphered messages which could have pointed to the actual target. Some 26,000 Japanese naval messages for the month before Pearl Harbor lay undeciphered at the time of the attack. Hidden among them were details of training in torpedo and dive-bombing raids against battleships, references to a six-carrier strike force, fuelling at sea, and weather surveys of the north Pacific: all clues that could have pointed to Pearl Harbor, although whether analysts would have drawn the right conclusions can never be known. It is only with hindsight that the clues acquire the significance they now possess.[10]

Why were so many JN-25 messages not decrypted? Because the codebreakers were undermanned and short of resources, and their energies were heavily focused on Magic and the Battle of the Atlantic. And why was that? Because ultimately, critics have argued, the President and commander-in-chief failed to appreciate how important signals intelligence (Sigint) could be.

Is it true that Roosevelt, by contrast with Churchill, neglected intercepts in favour of human intelligence (Humint)? 'No existing account of Roosevelt's policy before Pearl Harbor quite does justice to the staggering ineptitude with which the best foreign intelligence in American history was handled before the Japanese attack,' writes the historian Christopher Andrew. 'Among the most inept was the President himself.' Roosevelt, he argues, was uninterested in codebreaking, slow to grasp its potential, and failed to ensure it received the resources and priority it required. On all these counts Roosevelt's behaviour contrasted unfavourably with Churchill's, who avidly consumed his intercepts, nurtured the producers of his 'golden eggs', and created a centralised inter-service codebreaking centre at Bletchley Park which gave him immediate access to the very best the codebreakers could produce.[11]

Such a conclusion is easy to reach. Graphic examples abound of absurdities spawned by Washington's bureaucratic jungle, none so fantastic as the arrangements over Sigint. The triumph of Magic was won by the army's Signals Intelligence Service. But inter-service rivalry meant that it had to share its success with the navy, so both would analyse the material, the army attacking messages carrying an even date, the navy an odd one. This was bizarre enough, but was made worse when it came to deciding which service would have the responsibility – and hence the credit – for delivering the material to the White House.

Japanese diplomatic intercepts first began to be delivered to the White House in 1937, when they averaged one a day. By early 1941 this had risen to about fifty. At this point the army and navy cut a deal to share deliveries to the President: the army would deliver the intelligence during odd months, the navy during even months. This routine lasted only a few months, until the army abruptly halted it. The reason was a gross breach of security within the White House itself, the guilty party being none other than the President's own military aide, Brigadier-General Edwin 'Pa' Watson. Some time after receiving an army delivery of Magic, he thoughtlessly threw one of the summaries into a wastepaper basket instead of returning it to its source. This cancellation meant that in September, an 'army month', no intercepts at all were shown to Roosevelt, although he *was* briefed on their contents. November – the next army month – began the same way.

But by this time Roosevelt had lost patience, and told his naval aide, Captain John Beardell, that he insisted on seeing the raw material. Within two days a new procedure was put in place. From now on, the navy took entire responsibility for deliveries to the White House throughout the year, with the army concentrating on deliveries of Magic to the State Department. This division of labour lasted until the end of the war, the navy delivering Magic to the President through Beardell and his successors – despite the fact that six weeks after the Pacific war began it was agreed that the actual interception and decryption of diplomatic messages would be an exclusively army responsibility.

Beardell's office was in the Navy Building. Here, late each afternoon, he would ask a Japanese-language expert working on the Magic traffic if there was anything for the President. If there was, he would carry it over to the White House in a special pouch at about 5.30 or 6.00 in the evening. Usually he would open the pouch himself; other times Roosevelt would do it himself and then, after reading the material, hand it back. Beardell never discussed the intercepts with the President, but he did draw his attention to items of importance. From January 1942 his successor, Captain John McCrea, followed much the same procedure.

McCrea either saw or telephoned the President every day from his office in the Navy Building. Here the army would deliver its Magic intercepts daily by courier, while the navy provided a selection of significant naval messages. Important items in Magic had already been flagged, but McCrea would carefully highlight other items that he knew would interest Roosevelt. If the President was at home in Hyde Park or at his Maryland retreat he would give him the gist by telephone. Otherwise, stuffing the messages into his briefcase – and even into his pocket – he would head for the White House. In the mornings he would usually find Roosevelt in bed, or in the bathroom shaving. If the former, he would hand the documents over and wait quietly while the President spread them out on the bedcovers and shuffled through them. If the latter, he would go into the bathroom, close the toilet seat cover, sit down, and read out loud while Roosevelt stood at the mirror. Thus did the President of the United States receive some of the greatest secrets of the Second World War.

McCrea would visit the White House again in the afternoons. Here he would usually find Roosevelt in the Map Room or closeted with his personal physician Admiral Ross T. McIntyre, who had fulfilled the identical task the year before as the President's official naval aide. Most often with McIntyre Roosevelt would be having his polio-deformed legs massaged, in which case McCrea would again read the documents out loud to him. McCrea, and those who succeeded him as couriers of Sigint, all agreed that Roosevelt struck them by his responses and questions to the intelligence carried by Magic as extremely well-informed. Like Churchill, Roosevelt also took care to see that it travelled with him. At Casablanca in January 1943 he received several so-called 'Colonel Boone' messages, named after the Marine Corps Colonel, Ronald Boone, an intelligence specialist in the Navy Department, who provided summaries of the daily Magic material. Later that year, in Quebec with Churchill, he again received messages from Boone. There can be little doubt that Roosevelt's appetite for Sigint matched that of Churchill. Alfred McCormack, architect of the army's Special Branch, declared that Roosevelt read Magic 'avidly'.[12]

The byzantine sharing arrangement between army and navy in America contrasted sharply with the smoother mechanism that delivered the products of Bletchley Park to Churchill. There was another significant difference. Whereas Churchill read intercepts that ranged from the diplomatic traffic of enemies, neutrals and allies through to enemy naval, air, army and police intercepts, Roosevelt's intercept files contained exclusively diplomatic material. In May 1942 the army, navy and FBI decided not to burden the President with military material or enemy spy messages.[13] The significance and amount of Sigint reaching Roosevelt was thus considerably less than the golden eggs delivered to Churchill.

But was Roosevelt alert to the material he *did* see? Or was he slow to realise its significance, preferring to focus on human espionage? Encounters such as that experienced by Henry Stimson early in 1941 might suggest a casual approach by the President. Stimson arrived at the White House at 10.30 one morning to find Roosevelt still in bed. 'I told him that he should read certain of the [Magic] reports which had come in from Berlin giving the summary which the Japanese ambassador there had made of their situation and others like it . . . They were extremely interesting [and] reported a very serious situation . . . Germany had her troops in good condition and . . . she probably was going to make an attack upon Great Britain and attempt to end the war this year.' But to his dismay Stimson discovered that Roosevelt hadn't yet read the material.[14] Early in 1944 George C. Marshall, the chief of staff, chided his commander-in-chief in similar vein. 'I have learned,' he deplored gently, 'that you seldom see the army summaries of "Magic" material.'[15]

Yet these examples are far from conclusive. Roosevelt's leadership style contrasted with Churchill's, and he was far more willing to delegate, trusted his military commanders to get on with the job, and gave no great urgency to matters he could not control. It was far from meaning he was uninterested. In reality, Roosevelt took a lively and active part in Sigint which, if it did not fully match Churchill's obsession, certainly justified the codebreakers' efforts.

Only the month after Stimson's rebuke, Roosevelt received a visit from the new Japanese ambassador in Washington, Admiral Nomura, a friend whom he had known since the First World War. Nomura assured him of his determination to secure peace, but after carefully reading the Magic intercept revealing the instructions Nomura had received from Tokyo, Roosevelt had doubts about the feasibility of this: they appeared, he said, to be 'the product of a mind which is deeply disturbed and unable to think quietly and logically'.[16] He scrutinised the intercepts of Nomura's account of his audience with him, as reported back to

Tokyo. 'Yes, I said that,' he commented as he read the translation.[17] Brigadier-General Watson's indiscretion and the interruption of army deliveries in September left him far from indifferent. Indeed, he complained so strongly that the army grudgingly agreed to let the navy provide him with a selection. It was also his own forcible insistence that guaranteed the resumption of raw Magic in November.[18]

During the last days of peace for the Americans, Roosevelt was as avid a consumer as Churchill of his intercepts. On 5 November the Japanese government opted for its surprise attack on Pearl Harbor and told its embassy in Washington to settle its dispute with the United States before the end of the month. 'After that,' remarked the new Foreign Minister, Togo Shigenori, 'things are automatically going to happen.' By the end of the month Japanese troops were on the move, a huge expeditionary force heading south from Shanghai in the direction of Indo-China. American intelligence alerted Washington, and by 25 November Roosevelt was warning his Cabinet that 'we [are] likely to be attacked next Monday [1 December] for the Japs are notorious for making an attack without warning'. But his eyes were focused on the Philippines, Burma, the Dutch East Indies and Thailand – not Hawaii.

On 1 December, the day of the anticipated attack, Roosevelt received the intercept of a message from Tokyo to Hiroshi Oshima, the Japanese ambassador in Berlin, instructing him to see Hitler. 'Say very secretly,' it read, 'that war may suddenly break out . . . and that . . . this may come quicker than anyone dreams . . .' So struck was Roosevelt that after handing this message back to Beardall he changed his mind and asked for it back. Two or three days later Beardell drew his attention to a further message revealing that the Japanese were burning their code books. 'Mr President,' he ventured, 'this is a very significant dispatch.' Roosevelt read it. 'When will war happen?' he asked. 'Most any time,' replied Beardell.[19] Within hours Roosevelt had also heard alarming intelligence from Frank Knox. 'The Japanese fleet is out. They're out of harbor. They're out at sea.' But Knox was talking of the fleet movements off Japan, not the carrier force that, unseen, was on its way to Hawaii. Roosevelt was thus fully prepared for a Japanese

strike by all the intelligence that reached him. But he was also determined that Japan should take responsibility for the conflict.

Should Roosevelt have anticipated Pearl Harbor and taken
measures to protect the Pacific fleet? With hindsight, obviously so.
But does the failure to provide more resources to the Far East
codebreakers also support the idea that Roosevelt was far less
interested than Churchill in intelligence interception, mishandled
it, and starved it of resources? An episode that occurred soon
after Churchill returned from Argentia reveals that two years into
the war, and eighteen months after Churchill entered Downing
Street, the codebreaking scene in Britain itself was far from perfect
and that it, too, suffered from a lack of resources.

On the very day that SOE's Tommy Davies was meeting
Stephenson in New York, Churchill paid his first – and only
recorded – visit to Bletchley Park. Accompanied by Desmond
Morton and Stewart Menzies, he talked and joked with a group of
forty or so cryptographers, toured the huts where they worked, and
gave them one or two graphic examples of how their work had
helped him. He left in high good humour and with the codebreakers' morale greatly enhanced.

Yet in reality all was far from well. Staffing and resources had
failed to keep up with demand, the intelligence war in the Atlantic
was balanced on a knife edge, delays in breaking Luftwaffe ciphers
in North Africa were frequent, and the bombes – the primitive
computers coming into use – were understaffed. Frustration was
mounting, and, emboldened by Churchill's visit, a few weeks later
senior staff appealed directly to him over the head of their
Director, Alastair Denniston. On 21 October 1941 – Trafalgar
Day, a date whose significance they knew would not be lost on
Churchill – they told him that lack of resources meant their work
was being held up or not being done at all. So desperate were they
that, to ensure the letter encountered no bureaucratic block, one of
them travelled to London and handed it in personally at Downing
Street. Churchill reacted immediately. In one of his famous 'Action
This Day' orders he instructed that the codebreakers' demands be
given 'extreme priority'. Early the next year a new Director took
command of Bletchley Park.[20]

*

At 8.30 P.M. that fateful Pearl Harbor Sunday, members of Roosevelt's Cabinet began to gather in his White House study. Normally he greeted them warmly, deploying his legendary charm and friendliness. Tonight he was withdrawn and silent, hardly noticing them at all. Frances Perkins described his face and lips as being 'pulled down'. 'His complexion didn't have that pink and white look that it had when he was himself,' she noted. 'It had a queer, gray, drawn look.' Finally he pulled himself together and thanked them for coming for what he said was probably the most serious crisis that any Cabinet had confronted since the Civil War. Congressional leaders then joined them for a briefing and throughout the evening a succession of visitors entered the Oval Office.

The last two to arrive, at midnight, were Bill Donovan and Ed Murrow, the CBS reporter. They found Roosevelt sitting in the pool of light cast by his desk lamp, the rest of the room in darkness. 'They caught our ships like lame ducks! Lame ducks, Bill!' he exclaimed. Yet he was also relieved that the position had been clarified and that America was unified. There was a good chance that the country would now accept total war against the Axis. 'It's a good thing,' he added to Donovan, 'that you got me started in this intelligence business.'[21] Ironically, however, Donovan was not even on the Magic distribution list.

At noon the next day, after driving to the capital in tight security, he denounced the events of the day that would, in his famous phrase, 'live in infamy', and called on Congress to declare war on Japan. Approval was unanimous, except for a single voice in the House of Representatives. Overnight, isolationism had collapsed.[22] Afterwards, Roosevelt telephoned Churchill: 'Today, all of us are in the same boat, and it is a ship which will not and cannot be sunk.'

But were they sailing on the same course? Churchill immediately worried that American priority would be diverted from the Atlantic to the Pacific. On 8 December, even as Roosevelt addressed Congress, he decided to go to Washington. Roosevelt hesitated, but Churchill was unstoppable. Four days later he left London by night train for the River Clyde, where he boarded the *Duke of York*, sister battleship to the *Prince of Wales*, which had already fallen victim to Japan off the coast of Malaya. Battling rough seas and gales, the ship arrived off the Hampton Roads at the mouth of Chesapeake Bay ten days later. Twenty-seven cipher staff on board had helped him keep abreast of the catastrophe in south-east Asia as the Japanese swept all before them. But above all he was anxious, as he wrote to his wife from on board, to find out 'what is the American outlook and what they propose to do'. His impatience unbounded, he completed his journey on a US naval plane. As it approached Washington, he could see the city below with its myriad dancing neon signs. It looked, remembered his naval aid, 'like a fairy city'.[23] Roosevelt was at the airport to greet him. For the next three weeks he was to live in the White House as the President's personal guest.

9

———◦◦———

THE TIES THAT BIND

The American press greeted Churchill like a long-lost member of the family. 'A son returning to his mother's land,' glowed the *New York Times*, in tune with the nation's seasonal celebrations. Gifts and mail for Churchill deluged the White House, including a six-foot-tall V-sign of lilies, carnations and irises, as well as hundreds of boxes of cigars. Eventually the Secret Service decided that only those sent by specially cleared people should be accepted: there was no way to X-ray for poison injected by syringe. One eager columnist even compared the apple-cheeked and twinkle-eyed Prime Minister to Santa Claus.

On Christmas Eve, the President and Churchill stood on the south portico of the White House for Washington's annual tree-lighting ceremony and the singing of carols. With a crescent moon above and a Marine band playing 'Joy To The World', Churchill beamed seraphically as Roosevelt pressed the button that set the tree ablaze with light. He did not feel distant from home, he told the eager crowd gathered on the lawn. Ties of blood, friendship, language, religion and ideals meant that far from feeling a stranger he felt he had a right to sit at their fireside and share their Christmas joys.

This proved literally true. Roosevelt installed his British guest in the White House Rose Suite, on the second floor of the family quarters that also housed Harry Hopkins and his nine-year-old daughter, Diana. On the wall hung prints of scenes of Victorian England. Next door slept Sawyers, Churchill's valet, and across the hall his two private secretaries. Every afternoon Churchill disappeared for his afternoon nap, and into the early hours of every morning, while the capital slept, he and the President stayed up talking, drinking brandy, and smoking cigars.

Two days after his arrival Churchill struck the family chord again when he addressed a packed joint session of Congress. In a speech he prepared with agonising care, he reminded his audience of his American forebears, regretted that his mother had not lived to witness the day, and joked that if only his father had been American and his mother English then he might have made it to Congress on his own, without an invitation. But then, he added mischievously, it might not have been unanimous. The effect was electric. Laughter and cheers engulfed him, and Senators and Congressmen stood and cheered and waved their papers until he had left the chamber. 'I hit the target all the time,' he chuckled to his personal physician Charles Wilson. Highly publicised church attendances and the laying of a wreath at George Washington's tomb at Mount Vernon completed the Anglo-American bonding. Roosevelt carefully added his own personal touch. 'Our very warm Christmas greetings,' he cabled Mrs Churchill on 25 December. 'It is a joy to have Winston with us. He seems very well and I want you to know how grateful I am to you for letting him come.' Churchill was just as happy. 'We live here as a big family,' he told his deputy, Clement Attlee, in a cable to London.[1]

But like many a family Christmas, the outward show of merriment masked at least one unhappy figure. Eleanor Roosevelt confided to her daughter that for her this was 'a very sad time'. It was not just that the festive rhetoric brought home painfully the emotional void at the heart of the Roosevelt marriage. At least until then she had been able to take solace in their joint commitment to the New Deal programme of social reform. Now, to her dismay, her husband's priorities and passions were being transformed into those of a President at war. No longer could she count on him as a companion in arms on the home front. One day in the White House she spotted her husband and Churchill through a doorway, eagerly discussing some military topic. 'They looked like two little boys playing soldier,' she observed. 'They seemed to be having a wonderful time – too wonderful, in fact. It made me a little sad somehow.' Increasingly, as the war progressed, Eleanor Roosevelt was sidelined in the interests and affections of her husband.

By contrast, Clementine Churchill felt no such loss. She was already deeply immersed in war work as head of the Red Cross Aid to Russia Fund, and had long granted her husband his own separate interests. Theirs was a marriage built on the rock of complementary roles. Apart from his youthful fling as a rebellious Liberal, Churchill's passions had always lain in war and foreign affairs.[2]

That the Washington visit was superbly orchestrated by two skilled professionals in no way diminishes the genuine bonds that were forged or the real achievements accomplished during these hectic three weeks, the longest of their wartime meetings. The two men, so different in style and temperament, learned significantly more about how the other worked.

For Roosevelt, it also provided a challenging initiation into becoming a war leader, and, above all, the eventual head of an alliance in which national strategy would sometimes yield to the greater interests of victory. 'I am responsible,' Roosevelt once told George C. Marshall during an argument over strategy, 'for keeping the grand alliance together. You cannot, in the interest of a more vigorous prosecution of the war, break up the alliance.'[3] Nor, as was to become vividly clear, would he permit differences between the secret warriors of both sides to disrupt his links with Churchill.

Churchill's enthusiasm was infectious, and their competitive sparring stimulated Roosevelt into transforming the White House into a battle headquarters. To match Churchill's mobile Map Room – now set up temporarily in the Monroe Room (an irony that would not have escaped the author of the Monroe Doctrine) – Roosevelt created one of his own in an easily accessible ground-floor room that had previously served as a women's cloakroom. Staffed by three shifts operating around the clock, its walls were covered in fireboard on which his aides pinned large-scale charts of the Atlantic and Pacific theatres of war, updated two or three times a day to display the changing locations of enemy and Allied forces culled from information flowing into the Departments of the Army and Navy. The whereabouts of the 'Big Three' Allied leaders were also highlighted by special pins: a cigar for Churchill; a cigarette-holder for Roosevelt; and a briar pipe for Stalin. Access to this inner sanctum was highly restricted. Apart from the Map Room staff, only the President, Harry Hopkins, General Marshall, Admiral King and (after July 1942, when he became Roosevelt's personal chief of staff) Admiral William Leahy.[4]

Roosevelt and Churchill hammered out agreements with their military experts on some basic principles. Already, early in 1941, Anglo-American military planners had agreed on giving precedence to joint action in Europe in the event of American entry into the war (the 'ABC-1' agreement). Now, the 'Europe First' strategy, which defined Germany as the prime enemy whose defeat was the key to victory, was given formal approval. So was the need to tighten the ring around Germany by sustaining Russia, strengthening the Middle East and gaining control of the North African coast. The leaders also embraced the hope that 1943 might see the 'clear return' of Allied forces to the European continent.

Above all, in the Combined Chiefs of Staff Committee based in Washington, they built a joint machinery for war unprecedented in history. Here again, personal trust at the highest level came into play in the person of Field Marshal Sir John Dill as Churchill's informal representative with the American Joint Chiefs of Staff. He and Churchill had not seen eye to eye in London, but in Washington he crucially won Roosevelt's trust as another personal link with the Prime Minister. Roosevelt felt his premature death early in 1944 as a personal loss, and accorded him a burial in Arlington cemetery – the only foreigner to be so honoured.[5]

By 1945 almost ten thousand British officials had crowded into the steamy capital to staff a plethora of Anglo-American sub-committees and their clones. Churchill exuberantly told King George VI that Britain and America were now 'married' after many months of walking out. The President felt much the same: 'Trust me to the bitter end,' he told Churchill as they bade each other farewell. Two weeks later, mindful of the personal touch, Churchill sent him birthday greetings. 'It is fun,' Roosevelt replied in the same spirit, 'to be in the same decade with you.'[6]

Burnished by post-war memory and transatlantic myth, this 1941 White House Christmas, so rich in family and festive symbolism, has become a metaphor for the Churchill–Roosevelt wartime relationship. One much re-told story, still potent on the after-dinner Churchill circuit, is that of Roosevelt suddenly entering Churchill's bedroom to find the Prime Minister, fresh from his bath, dictating in the nude to his secretary. Never lost for words, the Prime Minister cheekily quipped: 'You see, Mr President, I have nothing to conceal even from you . . .' Told many times by Hopkins, it also appears in the official Churchill biography. Yet when Robert Sherwood, the chronicler of Hopkins' years in the White House, asked Churchill if it was true, he replied firmly that it was nonsense. Not only had he never received the President without at least a bath towel wrapped around him, he could never conceivably have made such a statement. 'The President himself,' he told Sherwood, 'would have been well aware that it was not strictly true.'[7]

Of course it wasn't. Indeed, what might have been the most momentous event of all during that White House Christmas was carefully concealed from Roosevelt. Lying in bed on the night of his triumphant speech to Congress, Churchill felt the need for fresh air, and forcefully tried to open his bedroom window. Suddenly he felt short of breath and a pain over his heart travelled quickly down his left arm. 'Is my heart all right?' he anxiously asked Charles Wilson the next day. His physician did some quick thinking and came to a political rather than medical conclusion. To announce that Churchill had suffered a minor heart attack at such a critical moment would be disastrous, and even to tell Churchill himself would induce paralysing self-worry. 'You have been overdoing things,' he replied. At that point there was a knock at the door. It was Harry Hopkins, coming in for one of his regular chats. Wilson quietly slipped out and kept the secret until after Churchill's death.[8]

Not concealed, however – although often laundered from postwar memory, especially on the British side – were reminders that the carefully nurtured family *bonhomie* masked a dynamic tension between two prima donnas who represented differing political ideologies and conflicting national objectives. Churchill congratulated himself on the respect he showed the President on their first White House dinner by pushing him in his wheelchair to the elevator, and even skilfully appropriated him into the tapestry of British history by comparing his action to that of Sir Walter Raleigh spreading his cloak before Queen Elizabeth. Yet Roosevelt was quick to remind Churchill of his own anti-British stance during the Boer War, and for much of the dinner, as in those that followed, the two men competed for attention. Churchill, when denied centre stage, would lapse into moody silence. He was all too aware that he was mortgaging the future of Britain as a world power by seeking American help.

To Roosevelt, moreover, imperialism was more than the Boer War of his youth or – as he constantly reminded Churchill – the real if distant British rule in India. There were less awkward reminders far closer to home, such as Canada – its very existence a testimony to the staying power of British influence at America's own back door. Churchill travelled there after Christmas, stayed with the Governor-General, met the Canadian War Cabinet, and addressed Parliament in Ottawa. Roosevelt and the Canadian Prime Minister, Mackenzie King, got on, but even as Churchill and Roosevelt sang carols under the White House tree an event occurred north of the border that threatened Allied harmony.

On Christmas Eve three corvettes and a submarine under the command of Admiral de Muselier, head of the diminutive Free French navy, seized control of the islands of Saint-Pierre-et-Miquelon, in the Gulf of St Lawrence, old French colonial possessions which since 1940 had remained under Vichy control. The affair had its roots in intelligence, for the islands were an ideal base for spying on transatlantic convoys using the important base at Halifax, Nova Scotia, and a powerful transmitter on Saint-Pierre was sending a constant stream of messages to Europe. Codebreakers at Canada's Examination Unit could decipher some, but not all, of their content, and pressure mounted for action to put the transmitter out of action. Mackenzie King, true to his reputation for caution, rejected the idea, so it was floated to the Free

French. De Gaulle, sensing a great propaganda coup for his Free French forces, seized on the idea, and Churchill, who was reading Free French ciphers, gave it a complicit nod.

But Cordell Hull, the Secretary of State, who was wedded to the policy of keeping in with Vichy France, reacted violently to De Muselier's action, and in a rage denounced the 'so-called Free French movement'. The row raged on while Churchill was in Ottawa, but Roosevelt knew immediately what he should do. This was not an issue on which he wanted a break with Churchill, and the needs of the coalition came first. On New Year's Day, he firmly told Hull to let the issue drop.[9]

Churchill was equally inclined to take a lead. While Cordell Hull sulked over De Gaulle, in London Churchill's intelligence chiefs decided that despite Pearl Harbor they were not yet ready to let the Americans know about Britain's sources of intelligence and 'most secret methods of acquiring it'. Yet, soon after, closeted with Roosevelt in one of their late-night sessions in the White House, Churchill initiated a wide-ranging discussion of ciphers and cipher security by revealing that until Pearl Harbor British codebreakers had been breaking State Department ciphers. But now, he added, he'd told them to stop, although it meant as allies they should work jointly to make all their cipher systems more secure. He almost certainly then gave Roosevelt the big-picture view of Britain's most closely guarded secret: Ultra. Exactly how far he went, and how much he omitted, remains a secret. However, after he got back to London, he sent Roosevelt a letter, delivered personally by Halifax, reminding him of their conversation. 'I shall be grateful,' he wrote, 'if you will handle this matter entirely yourself and if possible burn the letter when you have read it. The whole subject is secret in a degree which affects the safety of both our countries. The fewest possible people should know.'[10]

Churchill's admission demonstrated an extraordinary degree of trust. Nations are ready to acknowledge that they spy on their enemies. But to admit that they also eavesdrop on their friends is something they rarely admit. Roosevelt, however, took it all in his stride. He instructed Harry Hopkins to draft a reply, and over the next few months kept on demanding to know what was happening about signals intelligence co-operation with his ally. Most of this paper trail – as is the case with much of Roosevelt's intercept archive, in stark contrast to Churchill's – is missing from the records, including Hopkins' draft reply, if he ever produced one. But on 11 July 1942, General Marshall finally confirmed in writing that he had taken up the matter with Dill and that all was 'satisfactory'. Such were the beginnings of the greatest intelligence alliance in history.

Churchill was pushing his intelligence advisers to the limit, and his revelations had a significant impact on Roosevelt. With the national inquest already raging about the intelligence failure at Pearl Harbor, the President acted. While Churchill took a well-earned rest in Florida from his Washington exertions, Roosevelt pressed Cordell Hull about the communications systems of various foreign embassies in Washington. He was particularly interested in the Vichy French, the Spanish and the Portuguese. Did they have the right to send messages in code, and if so, were American codebreakers doing anything about it?

Then, ten days later, Secretary of State for War Henry Stimson appointed a high-flying New York lawyer named Alfred McCormack to bring sense to the US Army's handling and analysis of Sigint through the creation of its Special Branch, which shortly afterwards moved into the newly built Pentagon building. By the end of the month the diplomatic traffic of Spain, France, Portugal and other countries being targeted by American codebreakers was given exclusively to the army's Signals Intelligence Service. The bizarre compromise between the army and navy over the production of Magic was also ended at this time.[11]

During the early months of 1942 the eyes of both the President and the 'Former Naval Person' were fixed firmly on the high seas, whose mastery was vital to victory both in the Atlantic and the Pacific. Since the summer of 1941 Churchill had brushed aside the protestations of his intelligence chief Stewart Menzies to ensure that Washington should be given the fruits of Ultra to help in the struggle against Doenitz's U-boat packs in the Atlantic. Then, less than a month after he initiated Roosevelt more fully into the secret, disaster struck. On 1 February 1942 the Germans changed their U-boat cipher. Suddenly British codebreakers were plunged into the dark. Simultaneously, German codebreakers mastered a critical British naval cipher that opened a window on to the movements of Allied convoy traffic across the Atlantic.

The German coup opened a year that saw some 8 million tons of Allied shipping sunk – by far the worst twelve-month period of the war. The loss of U-boat Ultra plunged Churchill into a profound depression. This was compounded by disaster in the Far East. Here, in short order, the Japanese captured Hong Kong, Malaya, Singapore, Burma, the Philippines, Borneo and Java, taking prisoner over 100,000 British soldiers and inflicting unprecedented humiliation on the British Empire. In the Philippines, at Roosevelt's personal order, General Douglas MacArthur finally left the island fortress of Corregidor in Manila Bay – the Gibraltar of the Far East – vowing famously: 'I shall return.' The euphoria of the White House Christmas had quickly evaporated. 'When I reflect how I have longed and prayed for the entry of the United States into the war,' confessed Churchill to Roosevelt in early March, 'I find it difficult to realise how greatly our British affairs have deteriorated since 7 December.'[12]

Those close to Churchill noticed with alarm a sharp deterioration in his buoyancy and spirit. Charles Wilson found him one day in the Map Room staring fixedly at the chart of the Atlantic with its dense collection of little black pins representing the U-boat packs. 'Terrrible,' he was muttering to himself, so absorbed in his inner thoughts that he failed even to notice his doctor as he stumped out of the room. 'He is desperately taxed,' noted his worried daughter, Mary. Sir Alexander Cadogan, head of the Foreign Office, confided to his diary that Churchill was in a sour mood and bad way. Desperately casting around for new offensive strategems, Churchill brought Lord Louis Mountbatten, the head of Combined Operations, on to the Chiefs of Staff Committee and quietly replaced its ailing chairman, Admiral Dudley Pound, with the industrious and forceful General Alan Brooke, Chief of the Imperial General Staff (CIGS). Averell Harriman, reporting to Roosevelt from London, guessed that Churchill would quickly bounce back.[13]

Roosevelt worked hard to bolster Churchill's morale. 'A cheery word from you and Harry always lightens the load,' reported Winant. Roosevelt obliged. 'Dear Winston,' he wrote in March, 'I am sure you know that I have been thinking a lot about your troubles during the past month. I know you will keep up your optimism and your grand driving force.' Then he went on to urge Churchill to take a leaf out of his own book. 'Once a month I go to Hyde Park for four days, crawl into a hole and pull the hole in after me . . . I wish you would try it, and I wish you would lay a few bricks or paint another picture.'[14]

'Crawling into a hole' was not Churchill's style, and he painted only one picture during the entire war. What he did enjoy, however, and what also gave him heart in these dark days of the war, was sharing tidbits of intelligence with Roosevelt. Increasingly, these *were* tidbits. By mid-1942 the sheer volume of daily Ultra intercepts – several thousand – made it simply impossible for Churchill to master them. The best he could do was monitor a selection and let everyone around him know that he was doing so in order to keep them on their toes. The same was true for Roosevelt. Occasionally there was some substantive issue at play, but often it was a way for them to reinforce the mutual trust they had built.

'President Roosevelt has asked that this message should be brought to the attention of the Prime Minister,' noted a Bletchley Park codebreaker on a Magic decrypt that March from the Japanese ambassador in Berlin, Hiroshi Oshima, to Tokyo. On this occasion Roosevelt's move was explained by the significance of the decrypt. The 'most secret' message, sent to Churchill via Bletchley Park's new Director, Commander (later Sir) Edward Travis and SIS chief Stewart Menzies, revealed the contents of a long discussion that Oshima had held with Hitler's Foreign Minister Joachim von Ribbentrop about a separate peace with Stalin.

Oshima provided no material of any immediate operational significance. But to Churchill and Roosevelt this decrypt provided comforting reassurance. Rumours of a separate peace between Hitler and Stalin were continually surfacing, never more so than when Stalin was pressing hard for Churchill and Roosevelt to announce the opening of a second front in Europe. It was a form of blackmail, hinting that if they did not deliver he might strike a deal with Berlin. Heavy pressure from Moscow for just such a second front was already under way and Churchill was trying desperately to reassure Stalin of Allied support. Intelligence pointed to a renewed German onslaught on the Russian front once the winter snows began to melt, and Hitler himself predicted in a bombastic broadcast to the German people that Russia would be 'annihilatingly defeated'. Churchill responded by ordering that everything should be done to take the weight off the Russians. The strategic bombing attacks on Germany would be sustained, and he promised Stalin that if the Germans used poison gas against the Russians British aircraft would drop deadly loads of gas bombs over western Germany. And he himself would personally fly to Moscow to talk things over.

Insights into Hitler's thinking about a deal with Stalin at such a black moment of the war, and from a source so close to the Nazi dictator, were like gold dust. Churchill received the Magic intercept only hours after holding a top-level meeting of his military advisers at Chequers to discuss ways of helping the Russians. Reading it, he learned that Oshima had visited Ribbentrop at the latter's request in his Wilhelmstrasse office, where they spent two hours surveying the global strategic picture in the aftermath of Pearl Harbor. After a few opening remarks about the future military and naval plans of the two Axis allies, Von Ribbentrop welcomed Japan's incursion into the Indian Ocean and confirmed that a new German offensive was soon to be expected on the Eastern Front. Then he turned to the issue of a separate peace. 'Germany,' he told Oshima, 'has no intention of making a separate peace with Stalin.' It followed from this that the only way of settling the Soviet question was 'by force'. He then further elaborated his views. 'Even supposing Stalin entertained such an idea,' he added, 'peace terms would be such as he could not accept – the closing of Murmansk and Archangelsk and the cession of territory.'

Churchill was forcibly struck by this piece of intelligence. Reaching for his red pen, he carefully sidelined the words. Then, after he had finished the entire document, he initialled it and returned it to Menzies.[15] A week later he kept Brooke up until after one o'clock in the morning exploring the chances of launching an offensive in northern France to take pressure off the

Russians. Demands for a second front were coming to a climax. 'All now depends,' Churchill told Roosevelt, 'upon the vast Russo-German struggle.'[16]

For the rest of the war against Germany Oshima's reports provided Roosevelt and Churchill with a unique intelligence source. The son of a former Minister of War, Oshima had arrived in Berlin as Japanese military attaché and quickly struck a close relationship with Von Ribbentrop. Then, from 1938 until the Red Army entered a shattered Berlin, with only one brief interruption, Oshima was Tokyo's ambassador to the Nazi state.

An ardent friend of the Third Reich, he enjoyed unique access to its leaders, including Hitler. Joseph Goebbels, the Nazi propaganda minister, described him as one of the most successful champions of Axis policies – 'A monument ought later to be erected in his honour in Germany,' he scribbled in his diary. Oshima reported back to Tokyo continuously and at length on his conversations with Hitler, Von Ribbentrop, Albert Speer and other top Nazis who spoke to him frankly about their strategic plans and views on the war. Just as continuously, unknown and unsuspected by Oshima, American codebreakers deciphered, translated and sent his messages to the Army and Navy Departments and the White House within a matter of hours. So immediate and momentous was the intelligence it conveyed that one American cryptanalyst and translator who worked on it later confessed that he felt 'it was coming from the very heart of the evil enemy and that he was standing at the center of the universe'.[17]

Through Oshima's Magic intelligence Roosevelt learned in advance about Barbarossa, followed the Wehrmacht's devastating advances on the Eastern Front and then, when the tide of battle turned against the Germans in late 1942, was able fully to appreciate, through Oshima's trained military eye, the full scale of the disaster that had befallen the Third Reich. Magic also carried detailed tactical material and insights into Nazi strategic thinking as well as shedding light on the plans of Japan. Tokyo kept back a great deal from its ally and there was no co-ordination of strategy with Berlin. Nor did Minister for War Tojo share all his thoughts or knowledge with Oshima. Yet even a little light on Japanese plans was useful. Hitler's attack on the Soviet Union stirred up a heated debate in the Japanese Cabinet. Should they join in the attack, or should they head towards south-east Asia?

Roosevelt followed the debate as it found echoes in Oshima's messages. The Japanese, he noted, were 'having a real drag-down and knock-out fight amongst themselves'. Later, after Pearl Harbor, when hints of a Japanese attack on Russia briefly resurfaced, he sent a warning to Stalin. Then, when Oshima was told in unequivocal terms by Tojo that no such attack was planned, Roosevelt passed the intelligence on to Stalin. The source was completely 'authentic', he assured the Soviet dictator in August 1942.[18] Oshima's final major contribution to the Allies was detailed information about German defences along the French coast he picked up during an official tour he made of the Atlantic Wall, not long after Roosevelt and Churchill agreed on Normandy as the site of Allied landings. It was an intelligence windfall that proved invaluable to the D-Day planners.[19] Germany's and Japan's defeat guaranteed that Oshima did not get the memorial that Goebbels planned. Instead, his true contribution to the war is memorialised in the thousands of his messages that now lie in the Washington archives.

By 1942 Roosevelt was beginning to receive a rich harvest of signals intelligence in addition to Magic. Among this was JN-25, the Japanese naval code. The complex variants that had resisted the codebreakers' efforts before Pearl Harbor were finally yielding rewards. Ironically, the first results came from the Sigint outpost at Pearl Harbor, codenamed Hypo, whose output was beginning to turn the tide of battle in the Pacific. Its greatest victory in these critical months of 1942 was to reveal the plans of Admiral Yamamoto to attack Port Moresby in New Guinea, intelligence that helped Chester Nimitz, Commander-in-Chief of the American Pacific fleet, to halt the Japanese advance towards Australia at the Battle of the Coral Sea. Shortly afterwards Station Hypo helped guarantee the decisive victory of the Pacific fleet over Yamamoto's aircraft-carriers at the Battle of Midway. Errors by the Japanese admiral were compounded by skilful American radio deception. More crucial, however, was the success of American codebreakers in uncovering Yamamoto's battle plan and Nimitz's confidence in using the intelligence to launch a surprise and devastating attack on the Japanese fleet that destroyed four of their carriers. The defeat forced Yamamoto on the defensive for the first time since Pearl Harbor and shifted the Pacific balance in favour of the Allies. Within weeks American forces had begun their long island-hopping advance towards the Philippines and Japan by landing at Guadalcanal in the Solomon Islands.

10

---⟫•⟪---

FIFTH COLUMNS

By mid-1942 Roosevelt and Churchill were overseeing the creation of the greatest intelligence alliance in history, a vital underpinning for the joint military plans they were forging for their offensive in Europe. Roosevelt sent Harry Hopkins and George Marshall to London in April to discuss the second front and then, in June, Churchill again crossed the Atlantic. This time he met Roosevelt at the presidential retreat of Hyde Park before travelling on to Washington and the White House.

Churchill's second Atlantic crossing in six months – this time by Boeing Clipper, a huge flying boat fitted with sleeping bunks, a dining salon and a steward's office – was prompted by his urgent sense that he had to intervene personally to prevent Roosevelt's pressing demand for action in 1942 from becoming a cross-Channel bloodbath. The President, he feared, 'was getting a little off the rails'.[1]

He began his journey in apprehensive mood. As he left the quayside at Stranraer in Scotland, dressed in his black Homburg hat and with a gold-topped malacca cane in his hand, he suddenly, like an anxious Winnie the Pooh, began humming, 'We're here because we're here because we're here.' It could hardly, felt Field Marshal Sir Alan Brooke, have been more appropriate. Flying the Atlantic was still a rare adventure and 'we were both doubtful . . .

whether we should get there, what we should achieve while we were there, and whether we should ever get back. We were facing a journey of twenty-seven hours in the air . . .'[2]

In the event, all went well. Roosevelt, along with his son James, was there to greet him at Hackensack airfield, the closest landing strip to Hyde Park, for what Churchill described as the roughest bump landing he had ever experienced. From then on, however, things got smoother, although not until after an interlude that smacked of the Keystone Cops.

Roosevelt was in a cordial and jovial mood. Taking the controls of his specially modified Ford V8 automobile himself, he drove Churchill to the bluffs overlooking the Hudson river. The ride provided Churchill with – as he tactfully put it later – some 'thoughtful moments'. As they approached the cliffs, he anxiously voiced the hope that Roosevelt could handle the controls. 'Feel my biceps' joked the President.

After they had admired the view Roosevelt amused his guest with a hair-raisingly boyish game by trying to outwit the Secret Service men following him in another car. They were under standing orders never to let him out of their sight, and the President used his intimate knowledge of the woodland tracks to throw them off. The Secret Service countered by stationing cars equipped with radio, waiting for him at strategic points. This time, however, Roosevelt won the game. Suddenly he swerved off the road, crashed through some dense foliage, and emerged on to a track barely wide enough for the Ford. The Secret Service men followed, but this was part of the President's plan. Ahead was a hairpin bend which, as he gleefully told Churchill, the following car could never negotiate. The ruse worked beautifully, and when the two leaders glanced back they could see the escort charging backwards and forwards on the hairpin making no headway at all. Then the President kept to the woods and they saw no other Secret Service car until they broke cover close to the house.[3]

After this, Churchill was grateful for some sleep. Up early next morning, he padded around barefoot on the lawn and then, still shoeless, went in to see Harry Hopkins in his bedroom. 'He sure is an informal house guest,' noted one of the President's assistants.[4] After lunch, with Harry Hopkins sitting in the corner of

Roosevelt's ground-floor study, a room at the front of the house shaded from the intense heat outside, Churchill and Roosevelt discussed 'Tube Alloys' – the codename for the atomic bomb project. They had agreed on a joint project after their first face-to-face meeting, American and British scientists had already begun the preliminary work, and what was required now was a firm decision to proceed. No one could guarantee success, and the project would consume huge resources.

But both leaders knew that the Germans were also working in this field. 'I received a report about the latest developments in German science,' Goebbels had noted in his diary only a few weeks before. 'Research in the realm of atomic destruction has now proceeded to a point where its results may possibly be used in the present war. It is essential that we should keep ahead of everybody.'[5]

Fully determined to stay first in the race, Roosevelt and Churchill quickly agreed to give the project the green light, with production based in the United States: two months later, the Manhattan Project was launched. After this portentous decision, the two men adjourned for tea. Later that evening, they left together by overnight train for Washington.

Again, Roosevelt put Churchill in the Rose Suite he had occupied at Christmas. 'There was something so intimate about their friendship,' noted General Ismay, Churchill's personal chief of staff. 'They used to stroll in and out of each other's rooms . . . as two subalterns occupying adjacent quarters might have done. Both of them had the spirit of eternal youth.'[6] The stamina of youth was sorely needed, for barely had he finished his breakfast than Churchill was told of the fall of Tobruk and the surrender of 25,000 British troops. This, the heaviest blow he received during the war, was made all the more humiliating by suffering it while in the White House. 'I am ashamed,' Churchill confessed to Charles Wilson. Yet Roosevelt's response was immediate. In a gesture that caught their relationship at its best, he asked quietly: 'What can we do to help?' By lunchtime, when Eleanor joined them, Churchill had recovered and spirits were high. 'To neither of these two men,' she noted, 'was there such a thing as not being able to meet a new situation . . . This attitude was contagious.'[7]

It underpinned, too, their decisions over strategy: plans for a 1943 cross-Channel operation and, for 1942, landings in North Africa – Operation Torch. George Marshall disagreed, dismissing Roosevelt's strategic thinking as 'cigarette-holder' strategy. General Dwight D. Eisenhower, the newly created commander of American forces in Europe, felt likewise. But Roosevelt held firm. Action, and action soon, was vital for domestic morale, as well as to keep Stalin happy. For Churchill, it also guaranteed that Roosevelt would stick to the 'Europe First' agreement reached at Christmas, and not be lured off-course by temptations in the Pacific.

After a final dinner with Roosevelt and Hopkins at the White House, Churchill left for Baltimore and the Boeing Clipper. When he got there, it was to find a mood of high excitement. Roosevelt's chief Secret Service agent, Mike Reilly, revealed that only a few moments before his men had arrested an Irish–American employee of the British Overseas Airways Corporation (BOAC) who had been standing close to the aircraft muttering Churchill's name over and over again. When the Secret Service men pounced, they found a loaded revolver in his pocket. Assassination, as both Churchill and Roosevelt well knew, was always on the agenda.

These Washington talks gave a further powerful boost to intelligence collaboration, and Marshall's guarantee to Roosevelt that all was satisfactory followed soon after. Even as the President and Churchill were huddled in Washington, the first permanent American cryptographers arrived at Bletchley Park to learn the secrets of British techniques in cracking Enigma.

Then, in September, Bletchley Park's Director, Edward Travis, travelled to Washington to sign a deal on a joint Anglo-American codebreaking effort in the Atlantic, the first of two remarkable wartime agreements that broke the taboo on keeping one's closest secrets hidden even from one's allies. The second accord, this time between the Allied armies, followed in March 1943 (see Chapter 16). No such intimate an intelligence alliance between two sovereign powers had been seen in history before.[8]

So drastically did Allied warfare sweep aside traditional inhibitions that when General Eisenhower arrived in Britain as commander of Operation Torch, Churchill personally told him about Ultra. He also took the shrewd and unprecedented step of giving him a British intelligence chief. Overruling Sir Alan Brooke, he approved the appointment of Major-General Kenneth Strong, an army officer who had first cut his teeth in intelligence during Britain's struggles against Michael Collins' guerrillas in Ireland during the independence war of the early 1920s. Then, to complete the transatlantic intelligence axis, almost a year to the day after Churchill's arrival for his White House Christmas, a joint U-boat tracking room began work in the main Navy Building in Washington. From now on US Naval Intelligence and Bletchley Park agreed to exchange all U-boat signals, and from early in the New Year all naval Enigma work was carried on the basis of a single programme. The Canadians, too, formed an integral part of this combined intelligence offensive.[9]

Not surprisingly, neither Roosevelt nor Churchill felt much inhibition about sharing the fruits of Ultra with their pipe-smoking ally in the Kremlin. Churchill's reaction to Barbarossa, Hitler's June 1941 attack on the Soviet Union, was straightforward. He immediately told the British people over the BBC that he would help Russia in whatever way he could. This even included Ultra, and within twenty-four hours he asked for an item to be sent to Stalin.[10]

This deeply alarmed Stewart Menzies. Ultra, he told Churchill, had revealed that the Germans were breaking Soviet ciphers and thus might learn indirectly about Britain's Ultra successes. Churchill overruled him, but kept an eagle eye on the ground rules that insisted information should be passed on only in paraphrased form, with the source concealed. When the Director of Military Intelligence demanded that information passed to subordinate Russian commanders should never be identified as coming from British sources, Churchill scrawled a note to Menzies in red crayon: 'Does this satisfy you?' Back came the reply in the famous green ink used only by 'C'. 'I am satisfied, as all drafts of wires to Moscow based on Most Secret material will be submitted to me.' Even then Churchill fiercely scrutinised the Moscow traffic. In September General Mason Macfarlane, head of the military mission in Moscow, passed Ultra information about German troop concentrations in the Smolensk sector to his Moscow contacts. 'I stressed secrecy and value of source,' he told London. Churchill sent an urgent note to Menzies: 'Has he told them the source?' Only when Menzies assured him that he had not did Churchill relax.

This extraordinary intelligence-sharing operation between London, Washington and Moscow lasted until the end of the war. Once the pattern of transmissions was securely established Churchill regularly demanded that a particular decrypt be sent, or queried why an item had been withheld. 'Has Joe [Stalin] seen this?' became a regular refrain. Occasionally, he pushed Menzies beyond the limits of professional comfort. By 1942 the lack of Soviet reciprocity, as well as continuing evidence of Soviet cipher insecurity, was leading British air and army intelligence to cut back on what they sent to Moscow. But the battle for Stalingrad refuelled Churchill's demands. Menzies was again unhappy. The Germans were tightening their signals security, he pointed out, and to provide the Russians with information only gleaned from Enigma could be dangerous to Ultra. 'I am always embarrassed,' he told Churchill, 'at sending the Russians information only obtainable from this source, owing to the legibility of many Russian ciphers.'[11] Nor was it an entirely one-way street. As late as December 1944 the Soviets handed the head of the American military mission in Moscow, General John Deane, a copy of the Luftwaffe's complete order of battle on the Eastern Front.[12]

Domestically, the Pearl Harbor shock sparked a reaction by Roosevelt similar to Churchill's after the collapse of France. Convinced of the dangers of an enemy Fifth Column, Churchill had ordered the internment of thousands of enemy 'aliens' in makeshift camps scattered throughout Britain, and a massive programme to ship them overseas was only halted by public outrage after several hundred drowned with the torpedoing of the *Arandora Star*, bound for Canada, in the north Atlantic. Many British subjects, some of them prominent social or political figures, were imprisoned under emergency regulations for pro-Nazi or fascist sympathies. Only after the invasion threat had passed did Churchill begin to press for their release.

Increasingly, as the war progressed, he deplored the arbitrary judgements and wartime powers of MI5, the domestic security service, and in 1943 firmly stamped on a proposal to unify all Britain's intelligence services under a single head. Behind it, he suspected, lurked the predatory ambitions of MI5. Soon after, the Cabinet Secretary commissioned a report which condemned the security service for a lack of proper ministerial control, abuse of its powers, and 'injustices to the public' – especially in the treatment of aliens. 'Look what has happened to the liberties of this country during the war,' Churchill complained bitterly in a newspaper article that year. 'Men of position are seized and kept in prison for years without trial and no "have your carcase" [*habeas corpus*] rights . . . a frightful thing to anyone concerned about British liberties.'

Uppermost in his mind was the case of the British fascist leader Sir Oswald Mosley, detained without trial since 1940. Churchill was keen to see him freed, and his release that year on medical grounds detonated a huge political row. Was Churchill showing favouritism for a man of his own class, as so many alleged and as is hinted at in his complaint about the fate of 'men of position'? Perhaps. But Churchill also evoked a matter of principle. By now he was personally eager to see the repeal of Regulation 18b, the order permitting such detentions, but his hands were tied by the political realities of his coalition with Labour. Nonetheless, he stated his conviction in typically forthright manner: 'The power of the Executive to cast a man into prison without formulating any charge known to the law,' he declared, 'is in the highest degree odious and is the foundation of all totalitarian government whether Nazi or Communist.' Ironically, his own Home Office vetoed the circulation of his comments as being far too subversive of wartime orthodoxies.[13]

Roosevelt was far less bothered by such violations of civil liberties. He, too, genuinely believed in a subversive Fifth Column threatening national security, but he also blatantly manipulated it for political purposes. Memories of German sabotage in America during the First World War had convinced him, like Churchill, that a Nazi Fifth Column had opened the doors to Hitler's stunning conquest of western Europe in the spring of 1940. Speaking to the nation in a 'fireside' radio chat as France collapsed and British forces streamed back in disarray towards Dunkirk, he told the American people: 'We *know* of new methods of attack. The Trojan Horse. The Fifth Column that betrays a nation unprepared for treachery. Spies, saboteurs and traitors are the actors in this new tragedy.'

Now, with Pearl Harbor, another act of treachery had taken place, and Roosevelt was swift to respond with draconian measures foreshadowed in a revealing scene in the White House. Francis Biddle, the Attorney-General, was due to arrive after lunch with a report. As Roosevelt finished off his meal with Harry Hopkins, Robert Sherwood and Sam Rosenman, he told them that Biddle was worried about civil liberties. 'He has been on my neck asking me to say that the war will not curtail them too much. Now don't laugh and give me away,' he asked, 'but I'm going to hand him a little line.'

After Biddle had arrived Roosevelt turned to him and said seriously, 'Francis, I'm glad you've come. All of us have just been discussing here the question of civil liberties in the war, and I have finally come to a decision to issue a proclamation – which I am going to ask you to draft – abrogating as far as possible all freedom of discussion and information during the war. It's a tough thing to do, but I'm convinced it's absolutely necessary . . .' Thunderstruck, Biddle looked at the others, who all kept a straight face. Assuming it was all in earnest, Biddle launched into a vehement defence of civil liberties, becoming so passionate that he began to walk up and down the room declaiming against the idea. He went on for fully five minutes before the others burst out laughing and he realised the joke.[14]

Biddle took it in good spirit, but such a scene with Churchill would have been inconceivable. It was not that he lacked humour – far from it – but he would have thought civil or constitutional liberties far too serious and important to joke about. That Roosevelt could make such light of them, even in jest – and, even more revealing, that his own Attorney-General could believe he could contemplate such a thing – suggests a disturbingly casual attitude. Proof followed very quickly.

Roosevelt's fears of a Fifth Column came together with a popular outcry on the west coast of North America against the Japanese population there. Rumours of treachery, of mysterious men with maps, and of shore-to-ship signalling, ran rampant. Bill Donovan seized the chance to enhance himself as a special intelligence channel to Roosevelt by showering him with all kinds of material on what the Japanese were up to and what to do about it. They ranged from wild press reports that hordes of Japanese soldiers in disguise were about to pounce on San Diego from across the Mexican border, to a polemic from the film director John Ford, then filming in Hawaii, about how most Japanese–Americans were tainted and that the hundreds of Japanese spies were hiding out on Oahu.

Yet Donovan carefully balanced such rumours by also sending the President a passionate defence of the Japanese–American community from the unlikely hand of General Ralph van Deman, the head of American military intelligence during the First World War. A prominent anti-Communist crusader, his nose for 'subversives' was otherwise among the most finely tuned in the nation.[15]

It did no good. In February 1942 Lieutenant General John de Witt, the officer in charge of Western Defense Command, admitted that nothing had been proved against Japanese–Americans. But in a mad twist of logic, and operating on the principle that 'a Jap is a Jap', he argued that this only provided 'a disturbing and confirming indication that such action *will* be taken', and recommended the evacuation of all Japanese from the coastal areas of California, Oregon and Washington state. Racial animosity, always latent, became virulent, with the Japanese being labelled 'mad dogs, yellow vermin, nips'. Walter Lippman, otherwise a darling of the liberal intelligentsia, also came out in favour of evacuation. Saboteurs could be native-born Nisei (US citizens) as well as aliens, he declared. Besides, he added, 'nobody's constitutional rights include the right to reside and do business on a battlefield' – a remarkable description by any standard of the Californian coast.[16] Similar hysteria infected British Columbia, on Canada's Pacific coast.

The President caved in to the panic. Despite strong opposition from both Attorney-General Biddle and FBI Director J. Edgar Hoover – who argued that racial feeling and not factual evidence was driving the panic – in February 1942 he signed Executive

Order 9066. It had a drastic impact on some 120,000 Japanese –
approximately half of them American citizens living along the
West Coast. Forcibly relocated in camps in the interior, they lost
their homes, farms and livelihoods. The expulsions, in the words
of the American Civil Liberties Union, were 'the worst single
wholesale violation of civil rights of American citizens in our
history'.

Churchill at least expressed sympathy for the innocent aliens he
had interned in 1940, justifying his action on the grounds of
regrettable and urgent necessity, and later pushing hard to get the
policy reversed. Roosevelt demonstrated no such feelings and the
policy remained in force, supported by two Supreme Court decisions, until December 1944.[17] His own racial animosity for 'the
Japs' was palpable, and dissident members of his Cabinet kept their
mouths prudently closed. They were used to Roosevelt's out-
bursts. 'Have you pretty well cleaned out the alien waiters in the
principal Washington hotels?' he asked J. Edgar Hoover in April
1942. As late as D-Day in Europe, June 1944, he still resisted
releasing the West Coast internees. Whatever else it was, the
wartime White House represented an uncertain bastion of civil
liberties.

Roosevelt's national security fears were grimly demonstrated a
few weeks after Churchill had returned to Britain. At two o'clock
on the afternoon of Saturday, 8 August 1942, in a downpour of
rain, Roosevelt left the White House for his recently acquired
weekend retreat in the Catoctin Hills of Maryland. Joining him
were chosen guests with whom he felt comfortable: his secretary
Grace Tully, Margaret ('Daisy') Suckley, a close friend; the
Librarian of Congress, Archie MacLeish, and his wife Ada; and
his long-time legal counsel and speechwriter, Sam Rosenman,
with his wife. There was no motorcycle escort, but a handful of
Secret Service men rode in the small convoy of cars, and the regular White House licence plates, with their quickly identifiable
low numbers, had been changed to avoid attracting attention. A
couple of hours later they reached their destination, a group of
rudely constructed small pine cabins furnished sparsely with used
furniture and rugs that had once been a summer vacation camp
for boys and girls. It contrasted sharply with Roosevelt's beloved

presidential yacht, the *Potomac*, which was now laid up for the war, and with Springwood, his Hyde Park home, an overnight train ride away. Roosevelt found it a rejuvenating haven from the pressures of the White House and the steamy summer heat of the capital. He'd christened it 'Shangri-La', after the fictional paradise of that name in James Hilton's 1933 novel *Lost Horizon*. Today, transformed, it's known as Camp David.

Roosevelt's cabin was the largest, with a combination living/dining room, a kitchen, four bedrooms and two baths, all looked after by the Filipino crew from his yacht. It also had a stone-floored screened-in porch where, casually dressed in sports shirt and old slacks, he would sit for hours playing solitaire, arranging his stamp collection, chatting with his friends or gazing out over the valley below. It was secluded, and its secret was well kept. A direct line linked it to the White House switchboard. If necessary, the President could quickly summon anyone from the capital he needed to see.

The small group gathered for cocktails just after six-thirty, for dinner at seven. As they sat down to eat, the White House telephone link rang and Roosevelt listened intently before hanging up. Then, over dinner, he told story after story of cases where as Governor of New York he had exercised executive clemency over the death sentence. But the tale – no doubt apocryphal – that he enjoyed telling the most was that of the butcher during the siege of Paris in 1870 who sold delicious 'veal' supplied by the local barber, several of whose customers had gone missing. His relish in telling the story made Ada MacLeish shiver. She was plump enough herself, she laughed nervously, to make excellent veal. Afterwards, Roosevelt worked on his stamps, then began reading a detective novel. His guests peacefully played cards, and at ten o'clock they all went to bed.

Everyone around the table understood the grim reality behind Roosevelt's gruesome choice of dinner-table talk. At exactly eleven minutes past noon that day, in the Washington District Jail, the first of six Nazi saboteurs captured by the FBI had been executed in the electric chair, followed at regular ten-minute intervals by the other five. The last electrocution had occurred at 1.04 P.M., less than an hour before Roosevelt and his party had left the White

House. As they were settling in at Shangri-La, two Army Medical
Center ambulances removed the bodies to the army's Walter Reed
General Hospital, where they were identified by two army wit-
nesses to the execution, signed for, had name tags attached, and
were stored in refrigerated compartments at the hospital morgue
prior to being embalmed. That night, as the President joked with
his guests, a German group of Nazi sympathisers at the Ellis
Island detainee centre in New York held two minutes' silence for
the dead men and then sang the 'Horst Wessel' song, the Nazis'
unofficial anthem.

The saboteurs had done no damage and been quickly picked up
by the FBI. Along with two others, who escaped the electric chair
in exchange for long terms of imprisonment in the US Penitentiary
in Atlanta, Georgia, for co-operating with their interrogators, they
had landed by submarine in two separate groups along the eastern
coast of the United States on the night of 13 June: one group of
four on Long Island, the other near Jacksonville in Florida.
Trained by the Abwehr in a Nazi sabotage school close to Berlin,
they learned about explosives, detonators and timing devices, and
were given false identities along with fake birth certificates, Social
Security cards and driving licences. They were also handed over
$100,000 between them. All had spent several years in the United
States before the war, and two of them were American citizens.
Their mission, codenamed Pastorius, included destroying bridges,
power plants, and railroad and water facilities. But their principal
target was America's aircraft industry: aluminium manufacturing
plants in Tennessee, New York and Missouri were all on their list.

Their grandiose ambitions ran aground straight away.
Demonstrating remarkable ineptitude, the northern group landed
only a stone's throw away from the coastguard station at
Amagansett, and as they were unloading their supplies shortly
after midnight were surprised by one of its officers. John Dasch,
the saboteurs' leader, tried to bluff it out by pretending they were
local fishermen. When that failed, he offered a bribe to the officer,
who was unarmed, and made clear the alternative by waving a gun
at him. Prudently taking the cash, the officer returned to the
station and immediately reported the affair. At daylight, a search of
the beach revealed the saboteurs' supplies, and the hunt was on.

But Dasch and another member of the group saved Hoover's men a lot of time. Unnerved by the fiasco on the beach, they turned themselves in to the FBI's New York office. Spilling the beans at Hoover's headquarters in Washington a few days later, they revealed the full details of the operation along with the identities of their fellow saboteurs. All were rounded up within a matter of days.

Roosevelt heard the news about the Amagansett escapade from Attorney-General Biddle as soon as FBI interrogators began grilling Dasch in Washington. After being warned by Hoover that it was the first of a wave of such attacks heralding an intensive German drive against the nation's vital resources and factories, he took an extraordinarily detailed interest in the case.[18] From the outset he believed that nothing less than the death penalty would do. The American Revolution and the fate of captured British and American spies offered him a clear-cut analogy. '[The saboteurs] were apprehended in civilian clothes,' he told Biddle. 'This is an absolute parallel of the case of Major André . . . and Nathan Hale. Both were hanged.'[19]

He got his way. A civil trial for espionage or treason, which raised difficult problems of proof and risked delays and appeals, was dismissed in favour of a military commission applying the laws of war. Across America, the media whipped up public opinion. U-boats had been roaming almost at will down the eastern seaboard since January. One aroused citizen from Lakewood, Ohio, sent the President a $4 money order to buy the saboteurs neckties – 'not the Japanese silk we used to buy,' he explained, 'but good old manila hemp about twelve feet long'. Another urged that the Nazis be shot and the event broadcast live across the nation. A man from Evanston, Illinois, offered to pay his own air fare to join the firing squad.[20]

Roosevelt signed the military commission's order early in July. The day before he left for Shangri-La, his naval aide, Captain John McCrea, carried his personal order, sealed in a large envelope, for the executions to proceed. News of their fate prompted another flood of mail to the White House, nicely summed up by a woman from Baltimore. 'Just read the headlines,' she telegrammed. 'That is the greatest thrill I have read lately.'[21]

The morning after the executions it was still raining heavily at Shangri-La and Roosevelt stayed in his room talking on the phone until noon. When he emerged, he joined his guests in giving birthday greetings to Grace Tully, then sat down to work on some papers. Shortly before one o'clock, Captain John McCrea turned up from Washington and sat whispering in a corner with Roosevelt out of hearing of the guests. He declined an invitation to stay and eat and returned to Washington as quickly as he'd appeared. 'Where will the Nazis be buried?' asked Sam Rosenman, taking a guess at what they'd been discussing. He didn't know, responded Roosevelt, he'd been talking it over with McCrea and hadn't yet decided.

He quickly did. The day after he returned to Washington, when the evening rush hour was over, the bodies were placed in individual plain pine boxes and driven in a light army truck with three armed guards to Potters Field, Blue Plains, within the District of Columbia. An army detail from Fort Myer had already dug the graves. Protestant and Catholic burial rites were read out by two army chaplains and numbered stakes, without names, were placed above the graves. The whole affair was conducted in complete secrecy with no photographs taken, and those taking part were warned to keep quiet. Roosevelt received details several days later, and over the following weeks and months J. Edgar Hoover fed him intelligence gleaned from the case, such as Hitler's expectations of a second front and German transportation facilities and fuel supplies. Publicly, Roosevelt had played the affair for all it was worth. At a time when American forces had still not joined combat in Europe, the smashing of the Nazi plot sent the message that America still meant business.

Spies were not the only thing on Roosevelt's mind that weekend. McCrea had arrived with a large map, and he and the President had spent a lot of time poring over it. Sam Rosenman could see it was of the Pacific. The Marines had landed just two days before at Guadalcanal in the Solomon Islands, and the US Navy had lost four heavy cruisers to the Japanese. 'Things are not going well in the Pacific,' Roosevelt soberly told his guests. The one bright spot on the war front was his relations with Churchill, and he'd spent much of the morning working on a draft message to the Prime Minister celebrating the first anniversary of the Atlantic Charter.

Roosevelt and his friends had not been the only occupants of the pine cabin complex up in the hills that weekend. Bill Donovan, scouting around for a training camp for his agents close to Washington, had already claimed possession of part of the site and men about to be sent overseas were living in some of the cabins. Soon, British instructors from Camp X in Canada were coming down to help him train his own staff for the independent American spy training school that eventually took root there. Donovan's agency was rapidly finding its feet, and his own relations with Roosevelt were changing as the secret war moved into top gear.

11

━━⊷◈⊶━━

ACTION STATIONS

As soon as Churchill had become Prime Minister he had created the Special Operations Executive 'to set Europe ablaze' with covert action behind enemy lines. A bold vision in 1940, two years later it was becoming a reality, with serious operations run by skilled secret agents across Nazi-occupied Europe.

After Pearl Harbor Roosevelt was likewise impatient. Once his British guest left Washington he urged Donovan to come up with unorthodox plans for taking the war to the enemy. Hungry to expand his empire, Donovan responded with a succession of outlandish schemes, including sending the Hollywood actor Errol Flynn to Dublin as a spy, undermining the loyalty of Vichy sailors with subversive musical lyrics, flooding Italy with counterfeit currency, and using Prince Otto of Habsburg, the claimant to the Austro-Hungarian Imperial throne, as a recruiter for pro-Allied groups in Hungary.

His most bizarre scheme even caught the eye of the President himself. Soon after Pearl Harbor, a private citizen from Irwin, Pennsylvania, wrote to the White House alleging that the Japanese had a mortal fear of bats and suggesting they could be used in a return 'surprise attack' on Japan. Roosevelt turned it over to Donovan, who enthusiastically investigated how vast quantities of the animals could be bred to bombard the Japanese. The project was abandoned only when huge numbers of bats persisted in freezing to death during high-altitude experiments. No one bothered to check whether the Japanese were, as alleged, frightened of bats.[1]

Alongside the bizarre and crazy, Roosevelt initiated more serious projects. He and Churchill had agreed during the White House Christmas that North Africa provided the gateway to the Mediterranean as well as a stepping-stone back to Europe. Most of it was controlled by Vichy France, but General Franco's Spanish army also occupied part of Morocco, from where it could pose a serious threat to Allied operations. Roosevelt had already initiated American intelligence-gathering in the region. Early the previous year Robert Murphy, the chargé d'affaires in Vichy, had established 'the twelve apostles', a network of vice-consuls throughout North Africa. Under the cover of control officers supervising the distribution of American goods, they provided intelligence on pro-Allied elements among the general population and within the armed forces.

Roosevelt now brought Donovan in on the plan. In a brief informal meeting at the White House only twenty-six days after Pearl Harbor, he instructed him to prepare for an American invasion through a major campaign of intelligence and propaganda that would identify and soften up pro-American elements, particularly in the French armed forces, to help ensure a friendly or at least neutral reception for the Americans when they landed. He was also to penetrate Spain and Spanish Morocco and ensure that Spain remained neutral. In case of German or Italian moves to occupy the Iberian peninsula or Spanish North Africa, he was also to prepare a campaign of sabotage to disrupt their plans. In all this, Roosevelt stressed, he was to keep in step with British intelligence. Soon after, he told Churchill how important he considered this American penetration of Vichy and North Africa. 'Should France go over it would mean, of course, that the Iberian peninsula as well is lost to us. We are obtaining for our common cause vital military and strategic information by the presence of our observers in North Africa . . .'[2]

To oil wheels and grease palms, Roosevelt authorised an initial expenditure of $5 million in gold coins. Donovan was so excited by this that it almost – literally – killed him. The bullion was to be shipped out of New York with the help of Stephenson's BSC. On April Fool's Day, rushing from his Washington office to Union Station to catch the New York overnight sleeper, his car collided roughly with a taxi and he was hurled across the back seat. In considerable pain he boarded the train and later that night suffered an embolism – the collision had loosened a blood clot in his knee that travelled up to his right lung. On arrival in New York, he was immediately confined to bed for six weeks in his suite at the St Regis Hotel. 'I hope you will do what the doctors tell you,' a concerned Roosevelt told his intelligence chief, 'and take the proper rest at this time.'[3]

To implement Roosevelt's post-Pearl Harbor plans in North Africa, Donovan turned to Lieutenant-Colonel William Eddy, the Syrian-born son of missionary parents who had worked for military intelligence in the First World War and taught at the American University in Cairo. (Eventually he was destined to become Harry Truman's ambassador in Saudi Arabia and head of State Department Intelligence.) Under Eddy 'the twelve apostles' suddenly found themselves smuggling explosives and weapons and building underground communications networks and new code and cipher systems. Eddy himself made important contacts among the French military, who pledged to help the Americans, and asked Donovan for massive amounts of financial and material support for a North African resistance high command. He also linked up with SOE in Gibraltar, and by the time Roosevelt and Churchill opted for Operation Torch Donovan's network was the logical lead player in preparations for the landings.

Roosevelt briefed Churchill from the beginning about Donovan's plans, and the Prime Minister lent his strong support. 'It seems to me vital,' he told the President, 'that Donovan's activities . . . should have full play . . . otherwise what becomes of [Torch]?'[4] The American lead role in North Africa was the result of yet another of Donovan's visits to London. In June 1942 he hammered out a co-ordination pact on subversion and sabotage with Sir Charles Hambro, the operational head of SOE, a global version of Monopoly with two teams dividing up the world and agreeing on joint tenancies and the pooling of technical resources, training and finance. To be shared 'fifty-fifty' geographically were Burma, Malaya, Sumatra, Germany, Italy, Sweden, Switzerland, Portugal and Spain. The British were to have primacy in India, East and West Africa, and – at least until the American strategic role was better defined – in western Europe. The Americans were to lead in the rest of Asia and the Pacific, Finland, and North Africa. Here, predictably, Eddy was appointed Chief of Special Operations.

The American secret warriors had arrived in Europe. Their British counterparts began by regarding them as upstarts, but by the end of the war detractors had come to respect their skills in the great game of intelligence. 'I personally thought,' recalled one of SOE's leading lights, the international banker Bickham Sweet-Escott, 'that they were doing it better.'[5]

Few had pushed so eagerly for the European mobilisation of Donovan's agents as Churchill's intelligence chief in the United States, William Stephenson. The Canadian's British Security Co-ordination office in New York's Rockefeller Center ran a sprawling intelligence empire that embraced security, counter-sabotage and counter-intelligence, propaganda and special operations. Most of this took place in the United States, but Stephenson's mandate also covered Canada, Mexico, the Caribbean and Central and South America. For over fifty years after the war little that is accurate was known about it. Two popular biographies of Stephenson only muddied the waters. One, *The Quiet Canadian* (published in the United States as *Room 3603*), written by a former BSC and Secret Intelligence Service officer, Harford Montgomery Hyde, was specifically commissioned by Stephenson to paint a glamorous portrait of him as a man of drive and initiative running an essentially one-man show in New York. Indeed, the *New York Times* obligingly compared its revelations to D. H. Lawrence's *Lady Chatterley's Lover* in their ability to shock.[6] The other, penned by a Canadian journalist, was unreliable at best.[7]

The BSC files were deliberately burned at the end of the war after being trucked in convoy from New York to Camp X, the SOE training school in Canada. Before being consigned to the flames, they provided the raw material for a hand-picked team of

authors to write the official history of BSC. To prepare the project, Stephenson first chose Gilbert Highet, a professor at Columbia
University married to the well-known American thriller writer
Helen MacInnes. Later, two other writers took over. One was Tom
Hill, a Canadian journalist who had spent the war in the
Rockefeller Center writing BSC's weekly intelligence bulletin. The
other was Roald Dahl, the children's author and short-story writer
whose book *The Gremlins* became a favourite of the Roosevelts'
grandchildren. The final gloss was added by the British journalist
and broadcaster Giles Playfair, the eyewitness author of a vivid
account of the fall of Singapore and counter-espionage expert for
Stephenson.[8]

This secret history, of which only twenty bound copies were
made, is still kept under lock and key by the British government.
The reason is simple. Revelations about British intelligence activities in the United States would be profoundly embarrassing to
relations between what since the Second World War have been two
close intelligence allies. Not least of the awkward facts in the
United States would be Roosevelt's passive complicity and active
connivance in British intelligence operations on American soil.

For many years significant clues about its contents existed in the
papers of Montgomery Hyde deposited in the Churchill Archive,
which houses the Prime Minister's own vast collections in the
Cambridge college to which he gave his name, including a partial
history of BSC written by Hyde himself in New York in 1943.
Then, in the 1980s, learning of its existence, security-obsessed civil
servants from Whitehall declared it closed.

But it was too late. Copies had long been circulating in private,
and in 1998 the full in-house version was finally published in
Britain.[9] All these sources reveal clearly how strenuously British
intelligence chiefs worked to get Donovan's men involved in special operations. Early in 1942, as Roosevelt pressed Donovan hard
for action, the British decided that the COI chief needed help in
Washington. Stephenson had already vigorously encouraged
Solborg's schemes in North Africa and Spain and provided special
training for American recruits at Camp X. Now he was told by
London to prepare for a greatly expanded special operations division. So important was it considered that, instead of being based in

New York, it worked hand in glove with Donovan's outfit in Washington.

But it is also clear that its mission was as much to contain as to encourage Donovan. Its members were senior SOE veterans hand-picked to 'advise' Donovan on the Balkans and Middle East, the Far East, West Africa, South America and western Europe. Here, on Donovan's home ground, they could spot and neutralise any American moves to harm British interests. One of the earliest damage-limitation challenges was to lobby hard against Donovan's attempts to insert his men into Yugoslavia, which London regarded as British territory. And a straw in the wind for future discord was the choice of man to advise Roosevelt's intelligence chief on Far Eastern matters: John Keswick, a partner and domi-nating figure in the firm of Jardine Matheson, the British trading company forming one of the principal pillars of the British Empire in the Far East.[10]

Donovan and Stephenson had been the closest of allies until then, each using the other to enhance his position: Donovan to demonstrate to the White House his valuable links with British intelligence, Stephenson to show Stewart Menzies – and through him, Churchill – how he could harness the Americans to the British secret war. So long as the United States was neutral Roosevelt was prepared to turn a blind eye to this subversive counterpart to his own undeclared war against Hitler. Pearl Harbor changed all this. Now Roosevelt could take the gloves off America's own efforts while rationalising and harnessing them properly to the war. In addition, America's own security needs now justified giving greater powers to the FBI, whose Director, Hoover, had little time for Donovan. The subsequent bureau-cratic turf wars bruised both Stephenson and Donovan.

Only days before Roosevelt launched Donovan on his North African scheme, Congress passed the McKellar Bill, a move to place all foreign agencies in the United States under the tight supervision of the Justice Department. Stephenson immediately protested that this would make his BSC work impossible. This in turn provoked the far from Anglophile State Department intelli-gence point man, Adolf Berle, to lobby Roosevelt not to exempt the British. A British espionage service functioning in the United

States, he told the President, while ostensibly or actually fighting the enemy, might at any time be turned against them. 'I do not see,' he said, 'that any of us can safely take the position that we should grant blanket immunity from any spy system, no matter whose it is.'[11]

So threatened did Stephenson feel that he desperately resorted to dirty tricks. Seeing in Berle a deadly enemy, he instructed one of his agents to uncover any 'dirt' he could on him for a press leak. But the vigilant FBI quickly spotted the campaign and reported it to the White House. In the row that followed Halifax found himself carpeted by Berle, Attorney-General Francis Biddle and FBI Director Hoover. The President was so unhappy about Stephenson and his BSC operations, they told him, that Stephenson would have to go and BSC be reduced to a mere liaison role. Only strong protests from Stewart Menzies that Stephenson's links with Donovan were crucial for Eddy's North African exploits saved him.

But it was a sign of things to come, and Roosevelt's intervention inaugurated a steadily diminishing role for Stephenson's operations. By the end of the year his chiefs in London were beginning to query their worth and Menzies ordered cut-backs in his staff. Early in 1943 he took back operational control of SIS's Latin American stations, while SOE simply shut down its special operations activities there altogether. 'It was inevitable,' toll the doleful words of Hyde's BSC history in speaking of the Berle affair's aftermath, 'that independent investigations by the 4800 station [the code number for the New York SIS station] within the United States would have to cease altogether.'

Roosevelt's anger produced another casualty. His patience with Donovan's empire-building and the Washington turf wars they provoked was also running thin, and to Berle one lunchtime over trout and eggs Benedict he confessed that he was thinking of putting Donovan on 'some nice, quiet, isolated island, where he could have a scrap with some Japs every morning before breakfast.' It was at this time, too, that J. Edgar Hoover hit the roof over Donald Downes' exploits. But Donovan was too deeply entwined with the British by now to be exiled like some Robinson Crusoe, and far too indispensable to Roosevelt in North Africa and the President's politically driven desire for a major American offensive in 1942. The Americans would be welcomed in North Africa, Donovan's agents were reporting with misleading optimism.[12]

Instead, in June 1942, Roosevelt clipped his wings. While Donovan was in London briefing the War Cabinet on his tasks, he abolished the position of Co-ordinator of Information, placed the Foreign Intelligence Service under the Office of War Information, and made Donovan Director of the newly formed Office of Strategic Services, reporting directly to the Joint Chiefs of Staff. In theory, if not always in practice, Donovan's intelligence empire was now an integral part of America's rapidly expanding machinery of war.

The decision also represented Roosevelt's recognition that his personal intelligence system was inadequate for waging global war. It had been well enough tuned for his domestic and peacetime needs – 'It was a beaut,' recalled Ernest Cuneo, one-time Democratic Party counsel and Roosevelt troubleshooter; 'The Court of Franklin the First [was] the greatest since Louis XIV'[13] – but as absolute monarchy had yielded to republican rationality, so Franklin Roosevelt gave way to the bureaucratic demands of modern war.

Churchill also made changes in the top command of his shadow warriors. During the political and personal crisis that faced him after his return from Washington he replaced the Labour minister Hugh Dalton, who had all too obviously failed to win his affections, with Lord Selborne, a die-hard Conservative and long-standing Churchill loyalist. Churchill was a crucial SOE ally in bureaucratic struggles that came to a head that spring. Quarrels with the Foreign Office, complaints from governments-in-exile, demands for greater co-ordination of subversive plans with strategy, and often bitter rivalry from the Secret Intelligence Service, coalesced to threaten SOE's very survival as a separate agency. Only with deep reluctance had Stewart Menzies agreed even to let it have its own independent ciphers and radio organisation.

For all that he valued Menzies, Churchill stoutly defended Selborne's secret agents and vetoed a plan to place them under SIS control. Prudently, Selborne sent him quarterly reports designed to press the right Churchill buttons. 'As my department works more in the twilight than in the limelight,' he told him, 'I should like to keep you informed regularly of the progress of the brave men who serve in it.' The reports, finally released in 1992, reveal that Sir John Peck, one of Churchill's private secretaries (and later British ambassador in Dublin), who handled most of the files, judged Baker Street's achievements 'impressive'. Churchill read them closely and demonstrated unfailing concern for the fate of individual agents. Had they been rewarded for their efforts, he would scribble in the margin, or did SOE know their fate when captured?[14]

After the initial shock of occupation, Europe was beginning to stir. The previous autumn, the first SOE officer had penetrated Yugoslavia and made contact with both Communist and royalist partisans. Churchill ordered all-out help, and the 'Cavalry of St George', the British gold sovereigns already generously deployed in Spain, went to work in the Balkans to help pry loose valuable weaponry for the guerrillas from the arms of Italian soldiers.[15] Then, in the spring of 1942, as Roosevelt began to unleash Donovan's agents on Europe, Churchill's imagination was re-ignited by a powerful and bestselling novel by the American writer John Steinbeck.

The previous October, the bestselling author of *The Grapes of Wrath* had met Robert E. Sherwood, the Pulitzer Prize-winning playwright and newly appointed head of the United States Foreign Information Service, which was still part of Donovan's empire. The subject was anti-Nazi propaganda. After meeting European refugees who electrified him with stories of double agents, collaborators and resistance heroes, Steinbeck sat down to write. Barely two weeks after Pearl Harbor he delivered a completed manuscript to Viking, his New York publisher. In March 1942, under the title *The Moon is Down*, it appeared in bookstores across the United States as well as in Britain. A powerful fable of resistance to foreign occupation in an unspecified northern country, clandestine editions quickly circulated throughout occupied Europe. Its story was simple. Assisted by a local collaborator, a battalion of invaders overrun a small town where they hope to keep open the local coal mine. At first, all is peaceful. Then one of the miners impetuously kills an enemy soldier and is executed in the square. The towns-people become sullen, and small acts of defiance and sabotage begin. The occupying troops become isolated and demoralised, and the mayor is taken hostage. Resistance escalates, young men flee across the sea to Britain, and the mayor is taken away to be shot. 'Free men cannot start a war, but once it is started, they can fight on in defeat,' are his defiant last words.[16]

Churchill read it enthusiastically, his imagination set alight by a scene in which British planes drop thousands of small explosive devices to the population of the town, where they are collected and hidden by adults and children like so many Easter eggs. Churchill immediately asked Selborne whether similar small arms and sabo-tage devices could be dropped to civilian populations all over Europe. Yet this typically bold and visionary idea ran counter to the reality of SOE policy, which was to discourage isolated civil-ian direct action until Allied landings in Europe could protect civilians from German reprisals. Selborne, firmly, had to restrain him from what Jack Beevor, Alan Hillgarth's companion at arms in Spain and now one of Baker Street's inner circle, described as 'his attractive heresy'. Reluctantly, Churchill backed down. But his hopes for European resistance remained high.[17]

Concern about reprisals did not block SOE's major coup that spring, the assassination of SS leader Reinhard Heydrich, head of the German secret police, deputy to Heinrich Himmler, and con-venor of the fateful Wannsee Conference that approved details of the 'Final Solution'. He was also 'Protector' of Bohemia and Moravia, where he initiated a dangerously effective campaign against Czech resistance. In May 1942 he was fatally wounded in a grenade attack on his car in Prague. Hitler gave him a state funeral and the attack made headlines around the world. Nazi reprisals were brutal and widespread. The village of Lidice was razed to the ground, its menfolk murdered, the women sent to Ravensbruck concentration camp, and the children farmed out to German families for 'Aryanisation'. Nationwide arrests effectively liquidated Czech resistance for the rest of the war.

The assassins were two Czech agents who had parachuted into the country just as Churchill was arriving in Ottawa following his

Christmas 1941 meeting with Roosevelt. They carefully reconnoitred Heydrich's movements, striking as he journeyed from his
country home to his HQ in Hradacny Castle. Betrayed by a fellow
agent turned Gestapo informer, and surrounded by German troops
in the crypt of a Prague church, they committed suicide.

For decades after the war the British hand in the killing
remained a guarded secret. But SOE files released in 1994 reveal
conclusively that its top officials were fully implicated in the mission, codenamed 'Anthropoid'.[18] The dramatic elimination of such
a hated symbol of Nazi terror would put heart into European
resistance and a spanner into Hitler's machinery of repression.
Hand-picked by Czech intelligence chief General Moravec for a
mission agreed with Eduard Beneš, the Czech leader-in-exile, the
agents were placed in the care of Major Peter Wilkinson, the head
of SOE's Czech section, and his deputy, Captain Alfgar Hesketh-
Prichard. Carefully isolated from other agents they received special
training and were provided with two .38 revolvers, six percussion
bombs, a sten gun, and a lethal hypodermic syringe before being
dropped into Czechoslovakia from a Special Duties Squadron
Halifax. 'The two agents,' reported Hesketh-Prichard, 'have been
trained in all methods of assassination known to us.'[19]

Churchill applauded the news of Heydrich's death. In the
United States a few weeks later Roosevelt asked him if the British
had been involved. Churchill simply gave him a knowing wink.[20]
The affair of the Irish–American with the loaded revolver at
Baltimore a few days later must have vividly reminded him of
Heydrich's fate.

Anglo-American bridge-building on the secret intelligence front
was far more difficult than that between the 'Baker Street
Irregulars' (SOE) and Donovan's special operations experts. In
charge of American secret intelligence was Colonel David Bruce, a
forty-year-old blue-blooded Virginian and son-in-law to one of
America's wealthiest men, Andrew Mellon. As Churchill was
hastily improvising his visit to Washington, Bruce was in London
wining and dining with British intelligence chiefs and exploring the
ground for American operations into Europe.[21]

For most of 1942 Stewart Menzies imposed strict limits on SIS co-operation with the Americans. In Donovan his suspicious eye readily detected an arm of Roosevelt's anti-imperialism – in its own way, as dangerous to British interests as the Communist aims of the Kremlin – and with whom he felt he should sup with as long a spoon as possible.

Churchill backed his caution. He was happy to see Donovan's intelligence men at work in French North Africa, which was difficult territory for the British. But closer to home he became nervous, and conspicuously failed even to acknowledge a personal message from Roosevelt reporting that he had authorised Donovan to send a small staff to London. When Donovan's first secret intelligence chief in London, William Dwight Whitney, took up his post, Churchill ordered Ismay to watch him 'vigilantly'.[22] Only in 1943, with the Americans fully engaged in joint military operations, did Menzies finally agree to work together on counter-intelligence, and only then did Donovan gain limited access to codebreaking intelligence from Bletchley Park and decrypts of hand-ciphered German Abwehr material. Even then, Menzies jealously resisted American efforts to launch intelligence operations into Europe from British soil. One result was to make the OSS station in Switzerland Donovan's most important European base – and to launch its head, Allen Dulles, on the trajectory that within a decade made him Eisenhower's Director of Central Intelligence.[23]

Roosevelt and Churchill were still slowly assembling the building-blocks of the special intelligence relationship. On the eve of Montgomery's Eighth Army offensive in North Africa, another was put into place when Churchill read an Ultra report revealing that the Germans were worried about Allied intentions towards Crete. He immediately sent a message to General Harold Alexander: 'Anything that can make them more nervous would act as good cover.' Two weeks later he met with three British deception officers expert at making the enemy nervous: Colonel John Bevan, Colonel Dudley Clarke, and Major Peter Fleming, the explorer brother of Ian. Churchill was instinctively drawn to deception as a stratagem of war. 'All kinds of Munchausen tales can be spread about to confuse and baffle the truth,' he declared in 1940, inimitably throwing himself into the building of dummy ships and phony targets. Such ploys were tactical and defensive, appealing as much to his schoolboy delight in gadgets and wizardry as any considered military theory of deception as a force mutiplier.

By 1942 he had awoken to the vastly greater potential of strategic deception. By creating imaginary threats the Allies could confuse the enemy about their offensive plans. Critical to deception was Ultra, which, by exposing Abwehr intelligence operations, also opened the door to the Double Cross system used to plant misleading information on the Germans.

By the time Roosevelt and Churchill met at Hyde Park in the spring of 1942 to plan the return to Europe, the system was fully tested and running and watertight security guaranteed that no suspicion of duplicity troubled the Nazis.[24] The London Controlling Section (LCS) was created in the deepest secrecy to prepare strategic deception plans. Its head was a former City stockbroker and First World War holder of the Military Cross, Lieutenant-Colonel John Bevan. His deputy was Lieutenant-Colonel Sir Ronald Wingate, eldest son of 'Wingate Pasha', Kitchener's intelligence officer who had personally briefed Churchill on the River War over forty years before.

Located in the Cabinet Office complex, the LCS became integral to Allied planning and Churchill quickly came to trust Bevan, the two often cooking up deception plots in late night sessions over brandy. 'Bevan and Churchill sparked each other off,' noted one LCS member, 'and pulled out what were all the old tricks of Eton and Harrow and polished them up for the task at hand.'[25] Its first main test was to come with Operation Torch, when two aborted invasion plans were re-adapted for deception use: 'Jupiter' for an invasion of Norway, and 'Sledgehammer' for France. Churchill was quick to get Roosevelt on board. 'All depends upon secrecy and speed,' he told him. 'Secrecy can only be maintained by deception.' Briefed on the details, he insisted that to make doubly sure the Germans would not guess the target, Casablanca should be called 'Dunkirk', Oran 'Calais' and Algiers 'Boulogne'. 'No one,' he ordered, 'should use the guilty names in conversation.'

The Americans joined in, with a permanent American member in London and an equivalent staff in Washington known as the Joint Security Control. Even before this, Admiral Chester Nimitz had brilliantly used deception against the Japanese to squeeze the maximum he could from his meagre resources. It provided a crucial 'bodyguard of lies' for his victory over the superior force of the Japanese at Midway, and went on to significantly shorten the war and save lives in the Pacific.[26]

12

<hr>

OUR MAN IN MANILA

'Bataan has fallen' came the announcer's voice over the coast-to-coast NBC broadcast on 19 April 1942, 'but stout Corregidor fights on. The Japanese bombers smash away at the dogged defenders of the Rock on Manila Bay, and still the gun-crews rally, still the shells go screaming up with their messages of death for the invaders.'

Japan had invaded the Philippines the day after Pearl Harbor. On Christmas Eve 1941, after days of heavy bombing, the American General Douglas MacArthur had declared Manila an open city and moved his headquarters to the heavily fortified island stronghold of Corregidor across Manila Bay – the 'Gibraltar of the Far East' – riddled with underground tunnels and stocked with a hospital and supplies enough for 10,000 men to survive a six-month siege. American and Filipino forces retreated to the Bataan peninsula. After a hard-fought battle they had surrendered just ten days before – and already embarked on the notorious march that saw thousands of them clubbed and bayoneted to death by Japanese troops.

But Corregidor still held out and NBC had relayed its broadcast to its defenders as well as to the BBC in London. And it was for them that the second voice now came on air, a man who had lived on the Rock for several weeks as British Liaison Officer with

Hymns at sea: Roosevelt and Churchill at the Atlantic Charter meeting off Newfoundland, August 1941.

'Wild Bill' Donovan, appointed head of the OSS by Roosevelt.

Henry J. Morgenthau, US Secretary of the Treasury, who approved Churchill's Spanish bribery scheme.

FBI Director J. Edgar Hoover, who kept a file on Churchill.

Captain John McCrea, Roosevelt's naval aide, who delivered his secret intercepts.

Churchill and Roosevelt at Shangri-La, Maryland, fishing.

Roosevelt consults Harry
Hopkins in his White
House study.

'A romantic Limey':
Gerald Wilkinson,
Churchill's 'spy' on
General Douglas
MacArthur.

Roosevelt at the Quebec Conference in 1943, framed by the
Stars and Stripes and the Union Jack.

Churchill celebrates his honorary degree at Harvard, 1943.

Roosevelt and Churchill at the 1943 Cairo Conference, with
Generalissimo and Madame Chiang Kai-shek at either side.

Yalta: an ill and exhausted Roosevelt confers with Churchill.

MacArthur and who was now speaking from Washington. 'I can see the guns now and the men who man them,' he reported, 'stripped to the waist, burnt by the sun, with their pet signs painted on their gun barrels – blue devils, green dragons, and their favourite emblems. The ground around them will be mostly scars and craters now, and they'll all be taking a cruel, incessant pasting . . .'

Then, highlighting the vital importance of air power, he concluded: 'The bombardment may even be too heavy to permit *any* of them to hear this broadcast. But if any of them are listening today, I would like, as a British officer, [to say] that the hearts of men and women throughout America are inspired by Corregidor today. So, too, are the hearts of free men everywhere.'

The voice was that of Major Gerald Hugh Wilkinson, a thirty-year-old Englishman caught in the Pacific maelstrom who was to play an intriguing clandestine role in Churchill's efforts to know his American allies better – and yet another example, like Alan Hillgarth, of the Prime Minister's desire for personal sources of his own. Thanks to official secrecy, his story until now has remained obscure.[1]

A few weeks after Bataan's fall, on a Saturday in June 1942, a khaki-camouflaged Humber Pullman car driven by an army sergeant pulled up outside Chequers. Out stepped Wilkinson, promptly on time for lunch with Winston Churchill.

As he gazed on the weathered brick mock-Tudor frontage, he must have been all too aware of the burdens troubling the Prime Minister. In North Africa Rommel's forces had reached the gates of Tobruk, Stalin was pressing hard for the second front, and in the Atlantic Doenitz's U-boats were reaping their grim harvest of Allied merchantmen. Even the one bright light in the general gloom, the stunning American victory at Midway, had its downside, raising acute concerns for Churchill: would Roosevelt now stick to their agreed 'Europe First' strategy? Or would popular enthusiasm force him to give priority to the Pacific? Only the night before at Chequers, he'd brainstormed into the early hours with Lord Louis 'Dickie' Mountbatten, freshly back from Washington with news of the swirling tides of American opinion. The dashing chief of Combined Operations had hit it off with the President and the two of them had had a long meeting over dinner at the White House about Allied strategy. Roosevelt had made it abundantly clear that politically he needed to get GIs into the fighting as soon as possible, with a foothole somewhere in Europe before the end of the year. Above all, Mountbatten told the Prime Minister, Roosevelt was showing a vivid interest in North Africa. All this had convinced Churchill he urgently needed to pay another visit to his friend in the White House, and before the end of the day he'd sent Roosevelt a message inviting himself back.[2] By the time he left Chequers Wilkinson had a far clearer idea of what was troubling the Prime Minister.

Standing in front of the fire in the large lounge room to welcome him was the Prime Minister's daughter-in-law, Pamela. An attractive and vivacious redhead, she was already estranged from Churchill's son Randolph and engaged in a passionate affair with Roosevelt's personal emissary in London, the multi-millionaire Averell Harriman. Soon after, Clementine Churchill joined them, followed by Commander Thompson, her husband's naval aide, and Major-General Sir Hastings Ismay, his personal chief of staff.

As they engaged in small-talk over sherry Churchill entered the room dressed in his famous 'zipper' suit – an air-force-blue boiler suit with a zip fastener running from crotch to collar – and was in a buoyant mood. As he led his guest to a couple of high-backed wooden chairs slightly to one side of the room, where they could have a private chat, Wilkinson found himself surprised at the nordic lightness of his colouring. The hair was sandier and the eyes a paler grey-blue than appeared in the photographs he had seen.

'Well,' began Churchill truculently, 'I understand your man is a bit of a prima donna and that he hasn't much use for the President or even me.' This no-nonsense opener gave Wilkinson the chance he'd been waiting for since linking up with MacArthur after Pearl Harbor. Taking a deep breath, he spoke equally frankly back to give the Prime Minister the full benefit of his eyewitness experience of the Pacific scene.

MacArthur had been through a six-month hammering, he told Churchill, during which he'd vented his frustrations in words distorting his true opinions. Above all, he had never been fully briefed on the hard-headed reasons for the 'Europe First' strategy, concluding instead that it was driven by selfish and insular British interests. He'd finally been corrected on that, and seen the reason for it. But now, Wilkinson told Churchill, it was essential to capture his *heart* as well as his head.

'So you'd like me to write him a letter,' Churchill grunted as soon as Wilkinson had finished. 'It's very important to have him with us.' Then, draining his glass, he jumped to his feet, shouting, 'Lunch – lunch,' and marched off into the dining room with the others following behind.

The meal was a simple affair, with plenty of drink at hand, although most of the guests successfully resisted their host's constant promptings to refill their glasses. He was in top form, cracking an endless series of jokes. 'I really believe,' he grinned while gesturing at the bottles on the table in front of him, 'that we shall be out of all this sort of thing – *all* of it, except whisky – before we are through this war. That will be the time I'll have to send a note to Goering . . . "Can't go on – down to liquor parity."' Wilkinson glowed in the *bonhomie*, fascinated by Churchill's performance. 'There was something young about the constant spark of humour,' he noted. 'Everything was middle-aged about his shape . . . and much of both youth and age in the terse and wholesome grasp [of] his simplest remarks . . .'

Throughout, Churchill shouted questions at him down the table about the Pacific campaign, and when the lunch was over marched him off to the study so that Wilkinson could explain it all to him on a globe. 'Pug – come on, Pug,' shouted Churchill to Ismay as he and Wilkinson headed off enthusiastically together.[3]

Who was this man who could hold Churchill spellbound with tales of Pacific strategy and have the Prime Minister's personal chief of staff trail behind him like some junior subordinate? If the British Cabinet Office had its way, his career would still remain a secret. It's no accident that Churchill made no mention at all of Wilkinson in his multi-volume history of the Second World War, or that he also fails to appear in the official Churchill biography by Sir Martin Gilbert. Wilkinson's papers, including a detailed diary he kept during the war, were deposited after his death by his family in the archives at Churchill College, Cambridge, alongside those of Churchill himself. For several years researchers were free to consult them. Then, in 1993, after the government had launched its so-called 'Open Government' liberalisation plan for official records, the Cabinet Office abruptly ordered the bulk of them closed.

The reason was that there existed another dimension to Wilkinson's life than that of the army major (and later lieutenant-colonel) whose uniform he wore. For years he had worked for the Secret Intelligence Service, and throughout the Second World War was on its payroll collecting intelligence on the Pacific and United States. His role remains particularly sensitive today because of his work as a protégé of Churchill, one of the most eager consumers of his reports. In Wilkinson the Prime Minister saw a gallant young man of the world who could deliver pungent and independent views on significant personalities and issues of priority to him.

Fortunately for posterity, before the heavy hand of officialdom fell, miscellaneous material from Wilkinson's diary and papers had appeared in academic writings scattered around the world, while a copy of his diary has recently surfaced outside Britain. From this, as well as from items in his papers overlooked or thought harmless by the official weeders, the jigsaw that was Gerald Wilkinson's secret life can finally be pieced together.[4]

A dark and handsome man, he was born in Rajputana, India, the son of an Indian civil servant who had himself served as an intelligence officer during the First World War. He was educated at Winchester, joined the insurance business, and by his mid-twenties was running the Philippines branch of the British Hawaii-based firm of Theo Davies & Co., dealers in sugar and other commodities with offices in Manila, Honolulu, San Francisco and New York. His rapid rise owed much to his native talents, but was substantially assisted by marrying Lorna, the daughter of Clive Davies, eldest son of the firm's founder, and its driving force. His brother, and Lorna's uncle, Sir George Davies, was a Conservative Member of Parliament, a Lord High Commissioner of the Treasury, and a friend of Churchill.

By the late 1930s the Wilkinsons had two young children and

were leading the privileged life of Britain's Asian merchant class, with a large house in one of Manila's exclusive neighbourhoods, a nanny, a driver, and a bevy of houseboys and kitchen staff, as well as a busy round of social life among the Americans and Europeans who luxuriated in the city's wealth. But Gerald Wilkinson's social ebullience concealed a forceful and deeply serious religious man who wrote poetry, loved Bach and Telemann, and held strong patriotic convictions.[5]

There were other hidden aspects, too, for by this time he had been recruited by the Secret Intelligence Service to report on Japanese activities in the Philippines. Business links were the lifeblood of SIS, as the Juan March case in Spain has shown, but nowhere was British intelligence more dependent on the help of the private sector than in Asia and the Pacific. Here it had only two full-time intelligence officers, and what they produced from their agent networks was widely regarded by its consumers, especially the military, as at best unreliable and at worst useless. Far better were the private intelligence networks of big Western trading companies in the region and well-placed individuals such as Wilkinson, a man who, in the words of the *Philippines Herald*, 'knew how to make friends and get along with people'.[6] Reg Spear, an OSS officer who got to know him later in the war, described him as 'a hell of a salesman, smart as hell, and nobody's fool'.

After being driven out of Singapore by the Japanese, SIS re-established itself in India under the cover title of the 'Inter-Services Liaison Department' (ISLD). With its agent networks destroyed, it took until 1944 before it even partially recovered, and by then it had lost considerable ground to its wartime rival, the Special Operations Executive, which in Asia took the cover name 'Force 136'. Besides organising sabotage, subversion and guerrilla warfare, it filled in much of the secret intelligence gap left by its crippled rival.

At first Wilkinson concentrated on tracking Japanese, German and Italian commercial and subversive activities in the Philippines, material valuable to the Ministry of Economic Warfare in London. But as time passed he increasingly focused on Japan's wider military ambitions in east Asia. So worried was he by early 1941 that

he even booked steamship tickets for his family to move to
Honolulu, only to have second thoughts and cancel them at the
last moment. When Japanese forces moved into French Indo-
China that summer, he made his first contacts with American
intelligence. In Manila the American army and navy were
exchanging items from Magic and Wilkinson began to swap
British intelligence with them. He also flew out to Hawaii to tell
the FBI agent in charge of Honolulu, Robert Chivers, that from
now on he would pass on SIS material to American army and
naval intelligence in Honolulu through his intelligence colleague
there, Harry Dawson, who was operating under cover as the
British vice-consul.

And it was to Dawson that, just four days before Pearl Harbor,
he sent an urgent cipher cable based on a mix of Magic and
human intelligence revealing a dramatically heightened level of
military activity, warning him of an impending Japanese attack on
Britain and the United States, and authorising him to pass this on
to the Americans. The next day, after receiving a similar message
from Wilkinson, John Russell, the president of Theo Davies in
Pearl Harbor, telephoned his San Francisco office to cancel all outstanding orders for goods as well as all sugar contracts in the
pipeline. The official American investigation into Pearl Harbor
later revealed that Dawson had passed his message on to the
Americans. It also emerged that between July and December 1942
Wilkinson had sent some 200 SIS messages from Manila to
Hawaii.[7]

Prepared for war as he was, Wilkinson was nonetheless stunned
by the attack on Pearl Harbor. 'The news was staggering,' he
recalled, 'and I sat down on the verandah looking over our peaceful lawn, at its best in the slanting shades of early morning, to try
and grasp the full implications of the assault.' They quickly made
themselves felt. Ironically, late in November he'd again booked his
family on an American ship bound for Honolulu, but this time the
sailing was delayed because of the war scare. Now it was too late.
Even as he sat absorbing the news, Japanese planes were leaving
their airfields on Formosa to launch a devastating assault on the
huge American air base at Clark Field just outside Manila. Here,
too, as at Pearl Harbor, the Americans were caught napping. Most

of their heavy bombers were destroyed, caught in the open on the unprotected runways.

As Manila braced itself for invasion, Wilkinson realised he was vulnerable as a civilian with known intelligence contacts. His American friends came to the rescue. Telegrams flew between Manila, Singapore and London, and within days he found himself appointed as British Liaison Officer to American forces in the Far East, with the rank of major. Every morning he reported to its HQ inside the old walled city to pass on intelligence that was still coming in from Singapore and elsewhere in the region. In return he reported back on developments in the Philippines. A few days after his arrival he was summoned to meet the officer commanding – General Douglas A. MacArthur.

MacArthur remains the most flamboyant and controversial American general of the twentieth century, the Pacific war hero and Republican icon dismissed by Harry S. Truman for defying presidential orders during the Korean War in 1951. 'A great thundering paradox of a man,' writes William Manchester, 'noble and ignoble, inspiring and outrageous, arrogant and shy, the best of men and the worst of men, the most protean, most ridiculous, and most sublime.' He was also imperious, apocalyptic, devious, paranoid and charming.[8] Even as he prepared to defend the Philippines, his reputation had marked him out as a larger-than-life figure meant for some remarkable destiny. No one was more aware of this than Franklin Roosevelt.

Soon after launching his bid for the presidency in 1932, Roosevelt, then Governor of New York, was having lunch with family and friends in his mansion in Albany when he was interrupted by a phone call from the notorious Senator Huey Long of Louisiana. 'He's one of the two most dangerous men in the country,' said Roosevelt after he'd finally hung up on a lengthy harangue. 'Who's the other?', someone asked, suggesting the name of Father Coughlin, the leading voice of isolationism. 'No,' replied Roosevelt, 'it's Douglas MacArthur,' and he went on to voice his fear that the Depression could easily pave the way for the proverbial man on a horseback, a charismatic soldier who would step forward to save the nation in its hour of distress. And who was a more likely candidate than MacArthur, at that time the army's chief of staff?

Prompting Roosevelt's warning was not MacArthur's West Point graduation with the highest points ever scored, nor even his brilliant service as the army's youngest brigadier with the Rainbow Division during the First World War, in which he won a gallery of medals. It was an incident just two years before, known as 'The Battle of Anacostia Flats', when troops under his command had dispersed unemployed veterans marching on Washington. Using tear gas and with weapons at the ready, MacArthur had pursued them down Pennsylvania Avenue, past Capitol Hill, and then – against the specific orders of President Herbert Hoover – across the Anacostia river, where he burned down their shantytown in a fire whose glow could be seen around the city.

'The mob down there was a bad-looking mob,' declared a defiant MacArthur to the press, 'animated by the essence of revolution.' Then, with a typical rhetorical flourish, he added that in his day he had rescued 'more than one community which had been held in the grip of a foreign enemy'. The remark was to dog him for years to come, hinting at a belief that he was above the civil authority. As a dyed-in-the-wool Republican hostile to the New Deal, MacArthur's was an ego that clashed with Roosevelt's more than once after 1932, until the President put him firmly in his place. The tension between them was now to surface again.[9]

As he entered MacArthur's inner sanctum, Wilkinson was all too aware of his reputation in Manila, where since 1935 he'd commanded the army of the Philippines with a bombast and theatricality that grated harshly with traditionalists. He was also familiar with MacArthur's physical presence, the long, aquiline features and the thinning black hair parted low at one side and brushed flatly across the head. But his own misgivings were quickly swept aside. MacArthur greeted him warmly, gestured him to a comfortable sofa, and sat beside him quietly while he explained his mission. Over the next few battle-hardened weeks Wilkinson's admiration for this 'American Caesar' was to grow by leaps and bounds.

News of the Pearl Harbor attack reached Wilkinson early on the morning of 8 December. Soon after, Japanese troops landed on Luzon and MacArthur began pulling his forces back to the Bataan peninsula at the north entrance of Manila Bay. On Christmas Eve, after three weeks of daily bombing attacks on Manila's port facilities, Wilkinson – now officially appointed British Liaison Officer with US Forces Far East – was summoned to MacArthur's headquarters. Here the general told him that he had decided to declare Manila an open city, abandon Luzon, withdraw his headquarters to Corregidor, and take Wilkinson with him that night. The rest of the day saw Wilkinson frantically packing a suitcase, making last-minute arrangements for the handling of his company's business, and the welfare of his family and servants. Then his chauffeur drove Wilkinson and his wife to the docks, where they bade farewell to each other, neither knowing when, where, or if they would ever see each other again. Soon after, MacArthur arrived, and they embarked with the rest of his staff for the short journey to Corregidor. They arrived at the fortress shortly after midnight, and Wilkinson turned in for an uneasy night's sleep on one of the steel bunks lining the side tunnels bored into its hillside. Thus, in the flickering light of a few bare electric bulbs, with trucks grinding ceaselessly along the main tunnels, and metal desks and filing cabinets being scraped into place, Gerald Wilkinson began the adventure that would eventually lead him to Chequers and Downing Street. Back in Manila, his wife and children waited for the Japanese to arrive. They were to spend the rest of their war, alongside other expatriate families, in an internment camp. Their fate and release was to be a constant pre-occupation for Wilkinson until they were safely reunited after MacArthur's liberation of his beloved islands in 1945.

Two weeks after the retreat to Corregidor, MacArthur asked Wilkinson to fly out to General Wavell, head of the ill-fated inter-Allied ABDA Command in Java, to make a verbal report. The flight almost ended in disaster. Seventy miles into its 2,000-mile flight the small two-seater plane, piloted by Major Reggie Vance, MacArthur's personal air officer, developed an oil leak and was forced to return. It was nighttime, and the anti-aircraft batteries on Corregidor mistook it for an enemy plane and began to blaze away at them. They made a rapid descent, crashed on landing, and the plane broke into three. Miraculously, Wilkinson and Vance emerged only scratched and bruised. 'What happened to you, boys?' asked MacArthur cheerfully as they limped back into the fort.

Several weeks later Wilkinson made another try, this time by submarine. After several cramped and claustrophobic days he eventually arrived in Java. After reporting to Wavell he flew on to Washington, his NBC broadcast, and his meeting at Chequers.

13

---◆◆◆---

'JUST A ROMANTIC
LIMEY'

L ater that summer, after his meeting at Chequers, Wilkinson
 re-joined MacArthur at his headquarters in Australia. 'I shall
return,' MacArthur had famously promised the people of the
Philippines. Over the next few months Wilkinson was to be
Churchill's inside source on his steps to redeem the promise.

'I am to be absolutely freelance,' Wilkinson noted happily. Soon
he was commuting regularly between Melbourne, home of the
Central Bureau; MacArthur's signals intelligence agency, staffed by
an inter-Allied group of codebreakers whose American contingent
was headed by Abraham Sinkov, the man who had delivered the
Purple machine to Bletchley Park the previous year; and Brisbane,
MacArthur's command headquarters.[1] Here he also met regularly
with Roy Kendall, the Secret Intelligence Service's station chief in
Australia, whose secret cipher he used for contact with Stewart
Menzies in London. He also carried a watching brief over the
affairs of SOE, which had retreated from Singapore to Melbourne
with the cover name of 'Force 137'. John Chapman-Walker, its
deputy head, became one of his closest companions during his
months in Australia. On top of this came a constant round of
meetings with top British officials and Australian politicians, picking up news, gossip and opinion about the volatile political
temperature in the unhappy British Dominion.

Most significant of all, however, was his deepening relationship with MacArthur. This ranged from the trivial and familial to the most portentous: one day taking Mrs MacArthur out for a drive, the next listening to campaign plans still unknown to MacArthur's superiors in Washington. Throughout, he provided a sounding-board for MacArthur's often explosive views.[2]

Through the alchemy of tireless self-promotion and brilliant publicity MacArthur had transformed defeat into victory. In reality, his defence of the Philippines had been badly flawed. But with the help of Washington's spin-doctors and Hollywood films like *Bataan* and *Wake Island*, the surrenders of Corregidor and Bataan were transformed into heroic dramas, with MacArthur centre stage. Babies were named after him, the Blackfeet Indians gave him the title 'Chief Wise Eagle', and Roosevelt awarded him the Congressional Medal of Honor.[3] Edwin 'Pa' Watson even claimed after Bataan that MacArthur was alone worth five army corps.

His fame spread far beyond America, and in Australia he was greeted as a saviour, the warrior who would thwart a Japanese invasion and protect their interests far better than far-distant Britain under Churchill, the general scapegoat for the First World War campaign at Gallipoli that killed and wounded thousands of Australian troops. The fires of colonial resentment burned bright, fuelled by fear and panic that followed the sinking of the British battleships *Prince of Wales* and *Repulse* and the fall of Singapore. Darwin was bombed and Japanese midget submarines attacked Sydney harbour. John Curtin, the Prime Minister, exchanged bitter words with Churchill and publicly declared that Australia now looked to America, not Britain. The Australian press magnate Sir Keith Murdoch – father of the global media mogul Rupert Murdoch – founded the Australian–American Co-operation Movement, which worked for an alliance with the United States. So delighted was Curtin with MacArthur that, in MacArthur's own words, he 'more or less offered him the country on a platter'. American observers like Walter Lippman rejoiced at the possible break-up of the British Empire.

Talk like this prompted Churchill to fear the political and strategic damage that MacArthur could wreak, especially as it found powerful echoes in American public opinion. Bataan and Corregidor intensified the American public's demand for action in Asia. The notoriously isolationist and anti-Roosevelt *Chicago Tribune* pronounced that Japan was both 'the principal and proximate enemy'. Pearl Buck, the bestselling novelist, claimed that the American stake in the Far East was far greater than that in Europe, and that if the American way of life was to prevail in the world it first had to be safeguarded in the East. The month MacArthur arrived in Australia the Office of War Information told Roosevelt that Americans wanted action against Japan first, while Harry Hopkins warned that if American public opinion had its way the weight of the American war effort would be turned against Japan.[4] 'Asia First' became a battle-cry for opponents of Roosevelt and, with his well-known hatred of the New Deal, MacArthur became their irresistible magnet and a potential rival as President. A Gallup poll taken on a hypothetical Roosevelt-versus-MacArthur presidential race gave the latter 42 per cent of the vote.

Churchill was determined to keep a close eye on MacArthur. Soon after his arrival Wilkinson heard that an official British army and liaison team under Major-General Dick Dewing was on its way to MacArthur's headquarters. Far from replacing him, however, Churchill insisted that Wilkinson remain his personal link with MacArthur using his SIS channels. 'He'd go through the sky' if the contact were broken, promised Dewing when he met Wilkinson: Churchill had obviously remembered Wilkinson and his views even more than he had hoped. So, regularly and faithfully, he continued to send the Prime Minister his observations on the volatile moods and opinions of MacArthur. This way he also provided a back-channel for MacArthur to communicate with Churchill over the heads of Roosevelt and the American chiefs of staff.

American biographers of MacArthur have ignored the extraordinary revelations to emerge from Wilkinson's meticulously kept diaries during his months at MacArthur's side. Even more remarkable is the depth and frankness of his indiscretions to a British intelligence officer he knew was in direct touch with Churchill. At times, this could be breathtaking. Once MacArthur confessed that because of jealousies in Washington and the American navy he felt that Churchill was his only real ally, and that he would be glad to give him his views, provided it was to *Churchill alone*. Churchill, prompted by Wilkinson's report, referred flatteringly to MacArthur's brilliant generalship in the House of Commons. In turn, Wilkinson drew this to the delighted general's attention.[5]

MacArthur made no effort to hide his dislike for his President and commander-in-chief. 'Roosevelt has his spies right down to the kitchen sink,' he exploded when Wilkinson floated the idea of going to Washington. 'Your outstanding loyalty to me is too well known, Gerry, they'd seek you out and destroy you.' So paranoid was he about Washington conspiracies that he even denounced the appointment of Dewing, who had served under Eisenhower, as 'sinister'. He talked endlessly of plots by Roosevelt to get rid of him, and flew into a rage when Roosevelt nominated a Democratic Party crony, the scandal-prone Bronx political boss Ed Flynn, as Minister to Australia. Flynn would be a spy on him for Roosevelt, he protested, and his feelings were only soothed when Senate opposition killed the nomination.

Nor did he mask his contempt for Eisenhower and the entire North African and European strategy. He dismissed Eisenhower, who had once served as his chief of staff in the Philippines, as a man of no original ideas or fighting experience. Worse, he told Wilkinson, he suspected that Eisenhower was enhancing his own position and ambitions in Europe by stirring up anti-MacArthur feeling in the White House. As for North Africa, the whole campaign was a vast blunder that would soon deteriorate into a mess from which the Allies would be unable to escape. Eisenhower's elevation as Allied commander in North Africa was an even more terrible mistake, explicable only by Churchill's willingness to help Roosevelt along with American public opinion. On the subject of Churchill himself, MacArthur was understandably restrained, balancing his views on Allied strategy with fulsome praise for the Prime Minister's generosity and magnanimity. If criticism there was, it was for being too amenable to Roosevelt.

To another visitor with British intelligence links, however, MacArthur was even more indiscreet. Early in 1943, soon after Roosevelt and Churchill met at Casablanca, Sir Campbell Stuart flew into Australia. A Canadian-born businessman long enmeshed in the affairs of the global British telecommunications empire Cable & Wireless, ex-managing director of *The Times* and chairman of the Imperial Communications Committee, Stuart was also a former head of Britain's secret Foreign Office propaganda department and enjoyed close links with BSC chief and fellow Canadian, William Stephenson.

Wilkinson quickly arranged a tête-à-tête for him with MacArthur, who took the opportunity to let fly with a litany of all his pet grievances: Roosevelt and Churchill were dominating the whole direction of the war and the Combined Chiefs of Staff were mere pawns in the game; Eisenhower's campaign would end up as 'the greatest disgrace ever suffered by American arms'; Japan, not Germany, was America's main enemy and forces had to be diverted to the Pacific before Japan got too strong; if it all went wrong Churchill and Roosevelt 'may yet have to answer to the American people' and the voice of the fighting services would have to be expressed (he left it to Stuart to guess who he had in mind); and finally, he pronounced, it was Roosevelt's strategy and ambition to let Churchill wage the war while he, Roosevelt, could have his way over the peace and win a fourth term in the White House to become head both of the United States *and* the British Empire. In one explosive outburst MacArthur had vented all his prejudices and fears.

As he dined with Wilkinson that night, retelling the details of this extraordinary encounter, Stuart was convinced that MacArthur was the only man capable of displacing Roosevelt. He would, he predicted, be the next Republican candidate for the presidency. The threat was so great, he believed, that it was even more imperative for Wilkinson to stick by MacArthur's side.[6] Wilkinson quickly travelled to Brisbane to report all this to London using Kendall's cipher. Stewart Menzies decided that Wilkinson should return to London for an immediate in-depth debriefing.

Before he left, he had one final meeting with the mercurial MacArthur, who was in a more benevolent mood. Churchill should fly out and see him, he said. 'The effect would be electric,' he told Wilkinson. 'Militarily I would rather have him come here than to be supplied with another army corps.'

Late in February 1943 Wilkinson took the long flight back across the Pacific via Washington, where he gave Field Marshal Sir John Dill and Lord Halifax a detailed report. Despite the friendly farewell with MacArthur, he took the opportunity to deliver a powerful warning about the likely consequences of American victories in the Pacific to post-war British interests. Halifax was both fascinated and disturbed, and sent a message to Churchill urging him to listen to Wilkinson's views. 'I think you will find it useful to see him,' he told him.[7]

Wilkinson arrived in London something of a minor celebrity, having been awarded the Legion of Merit and the focus of American press attention for his adventures with MacArthur at Corregidor. With typical stiff upper lip he downplayed any talk of heroism. He was just, he told one American reporter in New York, a 'Limey on a romantic errand'.[8]

After reporting to SIS headquarters, he went to stay with his mother at Lottisham Manor, the family's eleventh-century home in Somerset, for a much-needed rest. At midnight on 14 March the phone rang. It was 10 Downing Street. Could Mr Wilkinson please come for lunch with the Prime Minister the next day? Churchill obviously considered it urgent. He had spent most of the time since his return from Casablanca recuperating at Chequers from a serious bout of pneumonia. The meeting with Wilkinson would be his first working lunch in London for weeks.

Wilkinson rose early the next morning, took the train to Paddington Station and ordered a taxi to take him to Downing Street. On the way, he asked it to stop in Trafalgar Square, where he vanished for a few moments' prayer into the peaceful precincts of the church of St Martin-in-the-Fields. Downing Street was barricaded with barbed wire, and a policeman escorted him to the front door. A manservant ushered him through the entrance hall and downstairs to a pleasant informal living room with a low white-raftered ceiling that overlooked a lawn. A few moments later he was joined by Sir Charles Portal, Chief of the Air Staff, and over a glass of sherry they discussed the progress of the war in MacArthur's South-West Pacific Command.

Then Churchill entered, wearing his famous siren suit. Wilkinson noted that he looked paler and thinner than when they had met at Chequers the year before. But he greeted his guests cheerfully and with a friendly glint in his eye. As they moved to the small table that had been prepared for their lunch, the Prime Minister invited Wilkinson to start talking.

In his history of the Second World War Churchill is exceptionally discreet about MacArthur, acknowledging the brilliance of his generalship while refraining from any character assessment or speculation about his political ambitions – an omission explicable by Churchill's desire not to rock the boat of American post-war politics, where MacArthur was not just Pacific war hero but a Republican candidate. Yet it was precisely MacArthur's personality and ambition that entranced him as he listened to Wilkinson. Early fears about his stirring up trouble in Australia and widening imperial cracks had now largely vanished. After initial problems MacArthur had gone out of his way to minimise friction and the honeymoon with Curtin and the Australians had long since cooled.

Churchill's darkest anxiety now was the threat MacArthur might pose to Franklin Roosevelt. It was not just Wilkinson's reports that had him worried. Events in Washington could be read as ominous. MacArthur himself denied any interest, but many of his allies were lobbying hard in the capital, and that year saw the formation of an informal MacArthur-for-President Committee.[9] Some inkling of his fear was provided by Brendan Bracken, a friend who often echoed his master's thoughts. MacArthur, Bracken confided to Wilkinson, was one of the most important figures on the international scene, because as a successful general and great public figure he was a potential threat to the conduct of the war as a whole if he should ever exert his full influence to rock the boat of Allied strategy – that is, to join up with the Chinese lobby in Washington, the Pacific-minded elements of the US Navy and any Republican and isolationist groups who preferred the 'Asia First' strategy.

The idea of MacArthur finding an ally in the US Navy, where his rivalry and loathing for Admiral King was an open secret, was ludicrous. Yet rumours of his presidential ambitions were rife, and not surprisingly Wilkinson turned first to the question of MacArthur's relations with Roosevelt. Here, to Churchill's relief, he was able to reassure him that Roosevelt was not at risk.

Vain, ruthless, unscrupulous and self-promoting MacArthur certainly was, Wilkinson admitted. Yet he was also a strong leader with a vivid imagination, a quick capacity to learn, and a powerful sense of loyalty to the men under his command. Yes, he acknowledged, MacArthur was a political general, a sort of 'American [Jan] Smuts'. But this was not in the sense of desiring to enter politics. Rather, it signalled MacArthur's powerful appreciation of personalities and politics. Only if some great national disaster traumatised the United States would MacArthur need to be taken seriously, and it would only be as a national saviour – a general on a white horse – that the Republicans could hope to sell him to the American people or that MacArthur himself would be prepared to run. His contempt for the 'stewpot' of political intrigue in Washington was a complaint all too familiar with Wilkinson.

The SIS officer had one further observation to make. MacArthur, if he ever did run for and win the White House, would make a terrible President, as he was completely ignorant of politics. In his heart he knew it. Far better and more congenial was the glamour of being a pan-American hero without any of the burden of office.

Churchill listened intently, interrupting only once to observe that there was no reason in a democracy why *any* man should not honourably hold political office. Then, after grilling Wilkinson on the touchy subject of Australia, he steered the talk back to Anglo-American relations. The massive mobilisation of American power was all too obviously tilting the balance in American favour, and Churchill knew of MacArthur's reaction to Eisenhower's appointment through Wilkinson's earlier reports. Now he confirmed that his decision was essentially political. The relatively green American forces had recently suffered a battering in Tunisia. What would have happened to public opinion in the United States, he asked Wilkinson, if the losses had taken place under a British general? American troops were still underperforming, but Eisenhower was doing an excellent job in building relations with his British counterparts. Then, with some final remarks about the bombing campaign in western Europe, Churchill terminated the lunch. He was obviously well satisfied with Wilkinson and hardly had he left than the Prime Minister sent a personal message to MacArthur. 'I have had a long talk with Colonel Wilkinson,' he began, before saying that although weight of business made a personal visit to Australia impossible, he hoped Wilkinson could return in order to keep in touch.[10]

But the SIS man was now *persona non grata*. Although MacArthur liked him personally he was profoundly suspicious of his intelligence links, arguing that they would cause trouble if uncovered by the Australians. But this was an alibi for his own objections, because he stirred up the Australians himself. 'The activities of Colonel Wilkinson [require] careful watching as he [expresses] views . . . critical of Australia,' he warned Australian Prime Minister Curtin.[11] To bolster his opposition was his own intelligence czar, General Charles Willoughby.

'A stout, obdurate German–American officer like a bull,' according to a candid Japanese officer who worked with him after the Second World War at MacArthur's Tokyo headquarters, Willoughby was a fervent Anglophobe who jealously guarded his turf and had taken an active dislike to Wilkinson. So deep had this penetrated that in 1945, during the Pearl Harbor Hearings, he roundly (and inconsistently) denounced the Englishman both as a sinister spy serving British imperial interests and as an untrained civilian extending the long tradition of the British amateur agent peddling largely useless information. 'The whole story,' he swore, 'is one of duplicity, evasion, bargaining, horse-trading of information and a sort of E. Phillips Oppenheim international intrigue.'[12] He even accused Wilkinson of callously deserting his family and leaving them to the Japanese – an unfounded allegation that Wilkinson publicly forced him to withdraw.

Thwarted by MacArthur's veto on Wilkinson, Churchill tried a second tack by proposing that Wilkinson join the personal staff of Lord Gowrie, the Governor-General of Australia, from where he could make frequent visits to MacArthur. 'A relief to know that the message has been sent,' noted Wilkinson after Menzies gave him the news. 'I anxiously await Gowrie's reply.' But despite his own praise for Wilkinson, Gowrie also refused on the grounds that his presence would only make already shaky Anglo-Australian relations more difficult.

'This is all very tiresome,' Churchill spluttered testily to Stewart Menzies. 'Why cannot Wilkinson go back in the same capacity which he had before? Let me know what you propose.' Wilkinson suggested a brief two- or three-month visit to the south-west Pacific as the Prime Minister's personal observer – a trip that would be agreed in advance through a private note from Churchill to Roosevelt that he himself would carry to the White House. Menzies agreed, only to have Hastings Ismay squash the idea. It was both 'impossible and undesirable', he said, for Churchill to try to get Washington's permission on an issue so touchy for MacArthur. Unknown to Wilkinson, the general had already turned down a third request from the Prime Minister. There was to be no return to the Pacific for Wilkinson.

'I feel,' he noted forlornly, 'like a politician who has lost an election after a rather busy spell in office . . . untidy, uncomfortable and not knowing quite what to do.' Menzies tried to reassure him by pointing out that there were very few people whom Churchill had tried not once, but three times, to appoint to any area.[13]

It still left them in a quandary. What was Wilkinson to do and where could his intelligence skills be best applied? His Whitehall visitors' round that summer included Ian Fleming, Brendan Bracken, Clement Attlee, Desmond Morton, Sir Stafford Cripps, Sir Alan Brooke, Sir Charles Hambro, Ernest Bevin and Admiral Sir James Somerville, Commander-in-Chief of the Eastern Fleet; he also gave a personal briefing to the Joint Intelligence Committee, spent hours discussing his future with colleagues at the SIS Broadway headquarters, and had several inconclusive meetings with Stewart Menzies. He rejected a posting to Turkey and another to India to head up Far East intelligence, a backwater where SIS intelligence, he noted dismissively, 'has now dwindled to a trickle from a few Chinese coolies'. Finally William Stephenson settled the matter for him.

During one of the BSC chief's many transatlantic trips Wilkinson had two satisfactory meetings with him at Claridge's Hotel. He instantly endeared himself to the intrepid Canadian by saying that useful intelligence was not obtained in the Travellers' Club and that the SIS professionals in Broadway had little comprehension of the United States and how its power would increase after the war. Stephenson promptly invited him to join him in America.

Thus, in the summer of 1943, Wilkinson left for the United States, ostensibly to liaise with the OSS, but in reality as head of BSC's Far Eastern Division (Section VI), charged with procuring from North and South American sources, and from American areas of command in the Pacific and Far East, all secret intelligence 'of imperial interest relating to Far Eastern matters' not available through official channels (i.e., overtly from the Americans), or from other SIS sources. He was also to supply London with any secret intelligence concerning military, air and naval matters of interest to Mountbatten's South-East Asia Command (SEAC). American Far Eastern intelligence as well as Japanese military information was now Wilkinson's target, and for the next two years he reported regularly on American challenges to British interests in the region. 'America's ability to manufacture and ship capital goods and heavy machinery with rapidity after hostilities cease should enable her to steal a march on British manufacturers,' read one of his reports on post-war trade with China, while many others covered Sino-American relations that threatened to squeeze Britain out. All were circulated under the security codeword 'Guard', meaning not to be read by the Americans. These reports are still considered too sensitive to be seen and have been closed in Wilkinson's papers.[14]

And what of Churchill and MacArthur? Who could now help him decipher the enigma of this American Caesar? MacArthur strenuously excluded Donovan's men from his command, so not even this indirect route could help, and Churchill felt Wilkinson's absence acutely. 'I have felt greatly the gap between us which has prevented all continuous exchange of thought,' he cabled MacArthur in a Most Secret and Personal message early in October 1943. At the Quebec Conference the month before he'd already persuaded Roosevelt of the merits of a direct link with MacArthur, and chosen Lieutenant-General Sir Herbert Lumsden, formerly commander of the 30th Armoured Corps in the western desert, as his man to fill the gap. 'I will be delighted,' replied MacArthur on hearing the news.[15]

He would have been far less pleased had he known of the

advance briefing provided to Lumsden by none other than his old friend 'Gerry'. Reflecting his own growing apprehensions about post-war American rivalry in the Pacific, and doubtless influenced by Washington opinion, Wilkinson produced a damning assessment. MacArthur, he wrote, was undoubtedly a potential danger: 'shrewd, selfish, proud, remote, highly strung and vastly vain', he noted. 'He has imagination, self-confidence, physical courage and charm, but no humour about himself, no regard for truth, and is unaware of these defects. He mistakes his emotions and ambitions for principles. With moral depth he would be a great man; as it is he is a near-miss, which may be worse than a mile . . . His main ambition would be to end the war as a pan-American hero in the form of generalissimo of all Pacific theatres . . . He hates Roosevelt and dislikes Winston's control of Roosevelt's strategy . . . [He] is not basically anti-British, just pro-MacArthur . . .' So dangerous to Anglo-American relations was this considered that after being read by Lumsden and other top British officials it was destroyed. The copy that remained in Wilkinson's papers is among those that have since been closed.[16]

When Lumsden was killed by enemy air action on the bridge of the USS *New Mexico* early in 1945 and replaced by General Charles Gairdner, MacArthur promptly denounced the new arrival as 'Churchill's spy'. Yet neither had been an adequate substitute for Wilkinson, and Churchill had turned to a stalwart in his stable of personal agents: Alan Hillgarth.

After leaving Juan March and his Spanish exploits in October 1943 Hillgarth had joined Admiral Somerville's staff as naval intelligence chief. Early in 1944 he visited Australia to discover MacArthur's plans for his attack on the Philippines and the use of Australian troops – an issue of burning interest to the Australian High Command as well as Mountbatten. But MacArthur was deliberately evasive and Hillgarth concluded he did not intend to use Australians – but was unwilling to say so in case they were taken from him. Hillgarth's report, as with those from Spain, went straight to Churchill, this one under a covering note that it should not be read by American eyes.[17]

Wilkinson, too, spent the rest of the war penning reports often too sensitive for Americans to read. Nothing, he once said, could ever reduce 'the love for America that a man feels when he owes to American arms and American arms alone the liberation of his wife and children from a Japanese internment camp'.[18] But, as Churchill also made clear, knowing one's friend was a patriotic duty.

14

'I LOVE THESE AMERICANS'

'Rarely,' one of Roosevelt's biographers has written, 'has an American President commanded a major military enterprise as bizarre, doubt-ridden, and unpredictable as the invasion of Northwest Africa in early November 1942.' Mounted not against Germany, but against America's oldest ally, France, it began with American politics and ended mired in those of the divided French. On the periphery roamed agents and double agents, adventurers and mercenaries, opportunists and innocents. All in all, Operation Torch tested and gratified to the full Roosevelt's skill at deception and surprise, and his flair for the complex and indirect.[1]

The Torch landings began four days after General Bernard Montgomery's victory over Rommel at El Alamein and two weeks before the Red Army's fatal encirclement of General Paulus's Sixth Army at Stalingrad – the turning point of the German-Soviet war. With General Dwight D. Eisenhower as commander-in-chief of the Allied forces, 65,000 American ground troops, transported and protected by over 600 British and American warships, came ashore on the Moroccan and Algerian coasts. By way of preparation Eisenhower's deputy, General Mark Clark, landed secretly from a British submarine near Algiers and heard from a senior French officer, Major-General Charles Mast, that French forces would offer no serious resistance.

Two days after the landings, Admiral François Darlan, the commander-in-chief of Vichy French forces, and one-time defence and foreign minister under Pierre Laval, signed a general ceasefire in exchange for which he became High Commissioner in North Africa. Against all the odds the landings represented a triumph for Allied intelligence, deception and security. Despite watching eyes on both sides of the Straits of Gibraltar, the Germans were taken by complete surprise. Ultra provided a valuable and reassuring window on German behaviour, the deception planners hinted successfully at forthcoming landings elsewhere, and the convoys evaded detection until they were inside the Mediterranean.

If the landings were a success, however, the political fallout was disastrous. In London and Washington an outburst of anger greeted the deal with Darlan, a living symbol of Vichy's collaboration with Hitler. De Gaulle and the Free French had been kept entirely in the dark about it all. Was this what the democracies were fighting for? 'Prostitutes are used,' thundered Freda Kirchwey in *The Nation*, 'they are seldom loved. Even less frequently are they honoured.' With Darlan denounced as 'America's first Quisling', the White House was flooded with hostile mail. In London, cries of 'Munich' resounded in Parliament.

Neither Roosevelt nor Churchill was prepared for the onslaught. Robert Murphy, Roosevelt's personal emissary in North Africa, had worked hard and secretly for the deal, and Darlan's arrival in Algiers on the eve of Torch was not, as Churchill later claimed, 'an odd and formidable coincidence'. While he agreed that Darlan had an 'odious record', he had a huge row with Eden and several harangues with De Gaulle. Henry Morgenthau, normally one of Roosevelt's most loyal friends, almost resigned over the deal. The President was stung by the chorus of liberal protest. 'I do not remember his ever being more deeply affected by a political attack,' noted Sam Rosenman. Eventually, in the face of a mounting tide of protest, he and Churchill climbed down and announced that the deal was only a temporary expedient.

It lasted until Christmas Eve. At three o'clock that afternoon in Algiers, the capital of French North Africa, a twenty-year-old Frenchman climbed out of a black Peugeot and entered the Palais d'Été, Darlan's official residence. Here he waited patiently for

Darlan to return from a lengthy lunch with Admiral Andrew Cunningham, Allied naval commander of the Torch expedition, and when he arrived coolly shot him twice in the stomach with a 7.65mm calibre pistol. Two hours later Darlan died at the Maillot Hospital. Over lunch he had confessed that he knew of at least four plots against his life.

Darlan's murder, wrote Churchill in his war memoirs, 'however criminal, relieved the Allies of their embarrassment at working with him'.[2] This was putting it mildly. The deal had presented him with a major dilemma. Despite the storms in his relationship with De Gaulle, he had forged a powerful emotional bond with the leader of the Free French that went back to the desperate days of 1940. Yet the alliance with Roosevelt was crucial to victory, as were the landings themselves. At stake was the political future of France. By the end of 1942 the choice was becoming clear. He could either support Roosevelt and Darlan, or opt for a France that included De Gaulle. It was a crisis that cried out for special action. The assassination solved his problem.

Berlin and Rome were quick to point fingers at the British secret service, while Churchill was equally prompt to deny it and Admiral Cunningham was instructed formally to rebut the charges. Whatever might be claimed, he was told by London, nothing could incriminate any branch of the British secret service, 'who do not indulge in such activities'.[3]

Yet extensive evidence exists of an active behind-the-scenes effort to rid the Allies of Darlan. 'If France one day discovers that because of the British and Americans the liberation consists of Darlan,' De Gaulle bitterly told Churchill, 'you can perhaps win the war from a military point of view but you will lose it morally, and ultimately there will only be one victor: Stalin.' Churchill feared he was right, and within a week of the deal told the Free French leader that Darlan should be shot.

In December De Gaulle despatched General Francois d'Astier de la Vigerie as his personal emissary to Algiers, ostensibly to seek a *modus vivendi* with Darlan. His journey was arranged by SOE, where opinion was unanimous that Darlan had to go, and he was given several thousand dollars on the understanding that any action should not be traceable to either the British or the Free French. By this time even Churchill's personal intelligence adviser, Desmond Morton, who actively disliked De Gaulle, felt that Darlan 'will not do', and flew out to Gibraltar to confer with British agents on the spot. Just hours before the assassination, Lord Selborne told Anthony Eden that any expediency in using Darlan had finally vanished.

Curiously enough, SIS chief Stewart Menzies also flew to Algiers, one of the very rare occasions he ever left London during the war, ostensibly to discuss the start-up of a new French intelligence service. It was perhaps no more than a 'formidable coincidence', therefore, that he was enjoying Christmas Eve lunch on a sunny Algiers rooftop when Darlan was shot only a few hundred yards away. Whatever the truth of his mission, one thing is certain. He could never have left London without Churchill's personal consent.[4]

How far was Roosevelt implicated? Two days before d'Astier's arrival in Algiers, Eisenhower issued a warning that if SOE gave any help to anti-Darlan or pro-Gaullist elements he would immediately close its North African operations down. Yet Darlan himself said he was 'a lemon which the Americans will drop after they have squeezed it dry', and the Americans were closely involved with SOE. 'We have before us,' Bill Donovan said early in December, 'the very practical problem of eliminating the political leadership of Darlan.'

But what about physical elimination? The assassin, Fernand Bonnier de la Chapelle, belonged to a small paramilitary group known as the Corps Franc d'Afrique, based at Ain Taya, a camp about thirty miles outside Algiers run by SOE close to its North African headquarters. Among the instructors was an early graduate of the Camp X training camp in Canada, the OSS officer and eccentric Harvard professor Carleton S. Coon, who spent much of his time training French recruits in weapons and explosives. 'They were all young, enthusiastic, and eager to learn,' he recalled.[5] Later Bonnier transferred to another camp close to Algiers, where he met Henri d'Astier, a brother of De Gaulle's emissary, who just happened also to be the Algiers police chief, as well as his son Jean-Bernard, and, through him, an army padre called Father Cordier. Both OSS and SOE had given Bonnier pistols, but it was

Cordier who provided him with the actual weapon that killed Darlan. Henri d'Astier's son, Jean-Bernard, drove him to the scene. Naïvely, Bonnier believed he would be hailed as a hero. Instead, hauled before an *in camera* court-martial, he was silenced by a firing squad less than forty-eight hours later and buried in a coffin thoughtfully ordered before his trial.[6]

'Good morning,' announced the BBC in its first news bulletin of Christmas Day, 1942, 'a very Happy Christmas to you all. Last night, in Algiers, Admiral Darlan was assassinated.' At Baker Street champagne corks popped at what everyone considered was the best thing that had happened since Heydrich's assassination.[7] Churchill was in a conspicuously cheerful mood, sitting up in bed reading, one of his secretaries reported, and looking 'like a benevolent old cherub'. As for Roosevelt, while apparently innocent of any foreknowledge of Darlan's death, even he was feeling better by New Year's Eve. Celebrations at the White House were far more cheerful than the year before. Champagne was served at midnight and even Henry Morgenthau and his wife were there, along with the Hopkinses, the Sherwoods and the Rosenmans, to toast the United States and the President. To this, Roosevelt added a new salute: 'To the United Nations.' Then they all sat down and watched a movie. Its title was *Casablanca*. The choice was apt. Ten days later Roosevelt left for Morocco and his fourth face-to-face meeting with Churchill.[8]

'I pray that this great American enterprise,' Churchill had told Roosevelt on the eve of Torch, 'in which I am your lieutenant and in which we have the honour to play an important part, may be crowned by the success it deserves.'[9] Clearsighted about the changing balance of power between himself and Roosevelt, Churchill also went out of his way, in his famous Mansion House speech ten days later, to reassure Britain that he had 'not become the King's First Minister in order to preside over the liquidation of the British Empire'.

The wooing of Roosevelt had ended, and from now on the build-up of American troops in Britain for D-Day was to be a visible reminder that the big battalions now belonged to the United States. Churchill called Operation Torch and El Alamein 'the end of the beginning'. The description more accurately fits the Casablanca Conference. For here the Churchill–Roosevelt romance began to lose some of its sheen. 'We make a perfectly matched team in harness and out – and incidentally we had lots of fun together as we always do,' Roosevelt told King George VI when it was all over. The behind-the-scenes reality was more nuanced. Had the King been a devotee of the cinema, he would have known that in *Casablanca* the British are conspicuous by their absence.[10]

Yet so far as the outward performance was concerned, Roosevelt was right. President and Prime Minister, basking in their first joint triumph of arms, apparently revelled in each other's company and dreamed of a *Pax Anglo-Americana*. Roosevelt's journey, a gruelling forty-eight-hour endurance test by rail and air, was the first time a President had ever left the United States in war, and not since Lincoln had the commander-in-chief visited American troops in a war zone. The presidential train took him from Washington to Miami, where he boarded a Pan-American Clipper for a flight across the Caribbean and then down the South American coast to Belem, in Brazil, for the long overnight flight across the Atlantic to Bathurst, in British Gambia, and the waiting cruiser *Memphis*, where he caught up on sleep. The next day, aboard a Douglas C-54, he flew into Casablanca. Here, after greetings from his son Elliott and Secret Service chief Mike Reilly, an armoured car rapidly whisked him to his bungalow. Security was even tighter than normal because of fears of retaliation for the assassinations of Darlan and Heydrich. To muddle the scent, as well as to indulge Roosevelt's taste for deception, he travelled under the *nom de guerre* of 'Admiral Q'. Churchill gave him the codename 'Don Quixote'; Hopkins, inevitably, was 'Sancho Panza'.

The Prime Minister travelled as 'Air Commodore Frankland', and his RAF plane (a converted B-24 bomber) was booked in Averell Harriman's name. Roosevelt's envoy told senior members of his staff he was flying to Algiers and arrived at the airfield near Oxford with two of his assistants and their luggage clearly marked 'Algiers'. When Churchill arrived to board the plane after dark, the two assistants quietly disappeared.[11] Such precautions were understandable but not, in fact, necessary. The Germans had got whiff of Casablanca, but correctly translating it as 'White House' wrongly concluded the meeting was being held in Washington. Codenamed Symbol, the conference was an Anglo-American extravaganza of luxury and opulence fuelled by excellent food, drink, and an inexhaustible supply of freshly pressed orange juice from the groves that surrounded Casablanca. Vivian Dykes, Bill Donovan's British 'minder' during his Balkan mission the year before, and now British Secretary of the Combined Chiefs of Staff Committee in Washington, described it as an *Arabian Nights* affair that made him feel like he was in some *Esquire* cartoon.[12]

The venue, at Anfa, a couple of miles outside the city, was a compound of gleaming snow-white villas centred round a luxury modern hotel on a hill overlooking the rolling breakers of the Atlantic. Until just a few weeks before it had housed the German Armistice Commission. Churchill, taking a walk along the beach in the enormous clouds of foam, marvelled that anyone could have got ashore during the landings. His villa, the Mirardor, was only fifty yards from Roosevelt's, the Dar es Saada, and here he greeted the President with what he described as 'intense pleasure'.[13] Over the next ten days, in a frenzied atmosphere of *bonhomie*, they and their military staffs were to carve out a path to victory. Roosevelt also seized the chance to review American troops in company with General George S. Patton. Security was again intense, with Secret Service men training tommy guns in the direction of the troops from the President's car. For Roosevelt it was all a tonic. He and the men lunched in the open air on boiled ham and sweet potatoes while an army band played such favourites as 'Chattanooga Choo-Choo' and 'Deep In The Heart Of Texas'.

Hard work and often heated military debate behind the scenes resulted in important strategic decisions: to defeat the U-boats in the Atlantic and secure lines of communication across the Atlantic; to attack Sicily with a view to knocking Italy out of the war and diverting German pressure from the Eastern Front (Operation Husky); to build up forces and create a planning command (Cossac) in Britain for the invasion of France in 1944; to intensify the strategic bombing attack against Germany, with General Ira Eaker's Eighth Air Force complementing the RAF night attacks with daylight raids; to open the Burma Road supply line to China; and to continue supply convoys to Russia. These decisions largely confirmed what Roosevelt and Churchill had already decided. George Marshall was again unhappy, but the American chiefs were divided among themselves, and Roosevelt got his way.

He and Churchill also glowed with pleasure at the final press conference, when General de Gaulle reluctantly agreed to shake hands for the cameras with General Henri Giraud, his American-backed rival for the political leadership of France. 'I take it that your bride and my bridegroom have not yet started throwing the crockery. I trust the marriage will be consummated,' joked Roosevelt.

Finally, the two leaders agreed on the policy of unconditional surrender – making clear, among other things, that they would remain partners to the bitter end in the war against Hitler and Tojo, and that there would be no more damaging and demoralising Darlan deals. While Roosevelt's public announcement of this to the fifty eager reporters startled Churchill, he had fully consented to the substance of the policy.

The climax came after the final press conference. 'I must be with you,' Churchill insisted to Roosevelt, 'when you see the sunset on the snows of the Atlas Mountains.' His chosen venue was the bustling city of Marrakesh, and their overnight resting spot 'La Saadia', a luxurious Moorish villa hidden behind a high, rose-coloured wall, with an inner courtyard and a tower giving spectacular views over the Atlas Mountains. It was, Churchill enthusiastically wrote to Clementine, 'a fairyland villa'.

No more appropriate venue could have been selected to celebrate the North African triumph, with all its clandestine pre-landing manoeuvrings and political intrigues, for its occupant, and their host for the night, was Kenneth Pendar, nominally the American vice-consul in the city, but in reality one of 'the twelve apostles' who had served as Roosevelt's eyes and ears under Robert Murphy in the run-up to Operation Torch. In this witch's brew of international intrigue and internal French bickering, Pendar had operated in what he described as an 'E. Phillips Oppenheim atmosphere of mystery and intrigue' that pitched him from a peaceful job at the Harvard University Library into 'two years of adventure, spying, political manoeuvring and international intrigue almost incredible to Yankee minds'.[14]

The journey from Casablanca to the villa took five hours by car, broken by a picnic lunch, during which the two leaders caught up privately on what they had agreed. At regular intervals along the route American soldiers stood at guard, fighter aircraft patrolled overhead, and Secret Service men whispered into their radios keeping track of the convoy. It was early evening before Pendar showed them to their rooms. They then took tea on the terrace overlooking an emerald-green pool and the garden with its shade-giving cypress trees. Robert Hopkins, Harry Hopkins' son, took some home-movie footage of the scene. After a while Churchill climbed the tower with Pendar to inspect the view. 'Don't you believe that it can be arranged for the President to be brought up here?' he asked. As the stairs were too narrow for the President's wheelchair, two of his Secret Service detail made a cradle of their arms and carried him to the top. Behind followed Churchill, humming and singing a little tune with the words: 'Oh there ain't no war, there ain't no war.'

For half an hour they sat drinking in the spectacular view of the purple mountains with their snow-capped peaks, the setting sun over the palm oasis to the west shedding a gentle pink light on their flank. Below, they could see the whole of Marrakesh spread before them, the mosque towers glowing pink, innumerable Arabs on camels and mules coming in and out of the city gate of Bab Khemis, and the entire scene dominated by the famous Koutoubia tower, built by Arab invaders in the twelfth century. Silence fell over the group as the sun set and the electric light at the top of every mosque tower flashed on to indicate the hour of prayer. 'There was a feeling of suppressed drama,' said Pendar. 'Both Mr Roosevelt and Mr Churchill were spellbound . . .'[15]

Soon it grew chilly and Churchill sent for a coat which he placed over the President's shoulders. 'It's the most lovely spot in the world,' he murmured. After they descended and Roosevelt had been carried back to his room, he took a stroll in a nearby orange grove. 'I love these Americans,' he told Charles Wilson. 'They have behaved so generously.'[16] Descending for cocktails at eight, Pendar found the President stretched out on one of the couches near the dining-room door. He held out his hand, smiled, and said, 'I am the Pasha, you may kiss my hand.' Then Churchill arrived, wearing his famous siren suit and embroidered black velvet slippers. Roosevelt was wheeled into place, with Pendar sitting between him and the Prime Minister and Averell Harriman and Harry Hopkins beyond.

Dinner was, indeed, fit for a Pasha: lobster, *filet mignon*, pâté, and a magnificent profiterole dessert, three feet high, a reproduction in nougat of the Koutoubia tower with a candle inside to make the whole affair more dazzling, and a substructure of spun sugar.

'I see the pastry cooks have been busy for days and days, preparing for our secret visit,' observed Churchill. 'How on earth does one attack a thing like that?'

'Why, that's easy, Winston,' said Roosevelt. 'This is the way,' and he took off the top of the tower and laid it on his plate.

Churchill remembered dinner as 'a jolly affair with speeches, songs, and toasts', and a solo rendition by himself that Roosevelt, he claimed, was about to repeat until someone interrupted him.[17] At about midnight, when they had demolished the food, they sat down to work on messages to Stalin and Chiang Kai-shek about their meeting. It was 3.30 A.M. before they were finished. 'Now Winston,' said Roosevelt, 'don't you get up in the morning to see me off. I'll be wheeled into your room to kiss you goodbye.' 'Not at all, Mr President,' replied Churchill, 'I can get into my rompers in two twos, and I'll be on hand to see you off.'

Early next morning, as promised, he insisted on seeing his friend to the airport. Throwing on a flamboyant dressing-gown covered with red dragons, and wearing only slippers on his feet and an Air Marshal's blue cap on his head, he drove with Roosevelt to the airfield, the inevitable cigar stuck in his mouth. Above the early morning mist rose the sunlit peaks of the High Atlas and before them the plane with its wooden ramp for Roosevelt's wheelchair already in place. Churchill jumped out of the car, ran up the ramp, and inspected the plane. Then he bade farewell to the President and turned to Pendar saying, 'Come, Pendar, let's go home. I don't like to see them take off.' As they climbed into the limousine taking them back to La Saadia, he again shared his dread: 'Don't tell me when they take off. It makes me far too nervous.' As the President's plane shrank to a small dot and disappeared over the horizon, he put his hand on Pendar's arm: 'If anything happened to that man,' he said, 'I couldn't stand it. He is the truest friend: he has the farthest vision; he is the greatest man I have ever known.'[18] As if profoundly at peace with himself and the world, the next day he painted the only canvas he produced during the war, a colourful panorama of the distant Atlas.

Yet Churchill's memory of the dinner was as impressionistic and sketchy as his art, and he omitted some discordant but significant details. Pendar remembered no jolly singing at all, but instead a lengthy disquisition by Roosevelt about Morocco, the Arab world, and the future of France that left Churchill sitting mostly silent. Post-war Morocco, the President declared, should be independent and have money poured into it for education, health and birth control. Nor did Churchill record an earlier dinner for the Sultan of Morocco, where Harry Hopkins described a glum-looking Prime Minister absorbing a lecture from Roosevelt on how the post-war world would see a radical revision of the colonial scene. Indeed the entire trip had reinforced Roosevelt's anti-colonial zeal. On both the outward and inward stages of his journey he was forcibly struck by the poverty and squalor of Bathurst, the capital of British Gambia. He found it, he told Churchill, an 'awful, pestiferous hole'. On building global peace and the future of colonial empires their visions remained far apart. 'Winnie is a great man for the status quo,' quipped Roosevelt to his son. 'He even *looks* like the status quo.'[19]

Yet the cords of war binding them were becoming stronger by the day. Each man was by now umbilically attached to Ultra and Magic. Throughout the conference Roosevelt regularly received intelligence sent by the White House Map Room prefaced by the codeword 'Colonel Boone', indicating material gleaned from intercepts. Those designated 'Utah' were for the eyes of Captain John McCrea, his accompanying naval aide, who received over a hundred during the entire journey. Churchill similarly received daily summaries of Ultra in the form of the so-called 'Sunset' series prepared by naval intelligence, or in a morning telegram from Stewart Menzies. True to form, Churchill never found his supply enough. 'Why have you not kept me properly supplied with news?' he impatiently tasked his SIS chief halfway through the conference. 'Volume should be increased at least five-fold, with important messages sent textually.' This last demand, with its request for the actual texts of intercepts, posed a security nightmare, and not until Special Liaison Units equipped to handle this material were in place was Menzies ready to relax his guard over the 'golden eggs'.

In addition, each man knew broadly what the other was receiving, and in a haphazard way this enabled them to keep an eye on each other as well as the enemy. On the eve of his departure for Casablanca, Churchill sent Roosevelt, by the hand of Lord Halifax, a top-secret Magic intercept recounting a conversation the Japanese ambassador in London had recently had with Spain's ambassador in London, the Duke of Alba, in which the Spaniard gave details of two meetings he had recently had with Churchill. The Prime Minister had exuded confidence, but talked rather incautiously of future Allied plans, mentioned Italy as the next target, and gave Alba grounds to talk of a rift between London and Washington on strategy.

'There is hardly anything in this which represents what I said,' Churchill assured Roosevelt. 'Most of it is the ambassador's own impressions but a lot of it looks as if it were fathered on me. I am sure that I need not tell you that I have no claim to paternity.'[20] True or not, and knowing that the Americans would see the same message, Churchill was obviously trying to discredit Alba's account. He was also signalling that if Roosevelt's discussions with foreign statesmen were to be similarly captured, he, Churchill, would quickly know what he'd said.

By now, Anglo-American codebreaking was reaping a rich and nourishing harvest. Within weeks of Casablanca the Bletchley Park codebreakers finally cracked the new U-boat cipher that had eluded them for most of 1942. They never looked back, and with the help of improved air patrolling and other techniques, by the end of the year the first Casablanca priority, control of the Atlantic, had been achieved.

In the Pacific, too, triumph over enemy ciphers delivered a dramatic reward. After the American navy's victory at Midway, the assault on Guadalcanal in August 1942 had turned into a six-month slogging match, and even as the two leaders met in Morocco Australian and American ground troops were battling to expel the Japanese from their beach-head in Papua, north of Port Moresby. While Churchill strenuously resisted the diversion of too many resources from Europe, he agreed with Roosevelt that the New Guinea campaign should continue and that efforts be made to capture the important stronghold of Rabaul to the east. Meanwhile, the codebreakers had continued with their steady and relentless advance against Japanese codes, and radio intelligence remained the cornerstone of the American effort. Early in April 1943 it delivered gold.

That month Admiral Isoroku Yamamoto, Commander-in-Chief of the Japanese Combined Fleet and genius behind the Pearl Harbor attack, moved his headquarters to Rabaul in order to direct an all-out offensive against Allied forces in the Solomon Islands and New Guinea. Shortly after waving off a 200-bomber attack on Guadalcanal – the largest raid since Pearl Harbor – he decided to make a personal tour of Japanese bases in the northern Solomons. At Station 'Hypo' on Oahu, several thousand miles away, American codebreakers picked up the message detailing his itinerary. It revealed the vital information that his flight would take him within reach of long-range P-38 American fighters. Admiral Nimitz sent an urgent message to the Secretary of the Navy, Frank Knox. Should they go for Yamamoto? Or would a strike only reveal to the Japanese how far their codes were broken?

Knox asked Roosevelt, who promptly said yes to a strike. Provided the pilots were told – in case of capture – that the intelligence had come from Allied coastwatchers near Rabaul, the operation would remove an inspirational and dangerous enemy. 'Best of luck and good hunting,' scribbled Nimitz on the order giving the go-ahead. Soon after, on the morning of 18 April 1943, a squadron of P-38s shot down Yamamoto's plane as it approached Bougainville. Tokyo kept the news secret for a month before finally admitting that Yamamoto's ashes had been returned for burial after his 'gallant death' in a war plane. In the space of twelve months General Reinhard Heydrich, the butcher of Prague; Admiral François Darlan, Vichyite and embarrassment; and now Admiral Yamamoto, the brain behind Pearl Harbor, had been conveniently eliminated from the equation of war. In each case nods and winks had come from the top.[21]

15

~~=⇒·◦·⇐=~~

MISSION IMPOSSIBLE

General Bernard Montgomery's Eighth Army had launched its offensive against Rommel at El Alamein on 23 October 1942. Ten days later, with the North African coastal road littered with wrecked and fleeing German vehicles, it was clear that Hitler's forces had suffered a major defeat. Fifteen hundred miles to the west, American forces under General Eisenhower had landed at several points along the coast of French North Africa. Two days later fighting ended with a general ceasefire.

As these Allied triumphs reverberated in the world's press, Churchill was the guest of honour at a luncheon held at the Mansion House by the Lord Mayor of London. Seizing the moment, he delivered a speech powerful in imagery and promise. Up till then, he began, he had promised nothing but blood, toil, tears, and sweat. But now in Egypt, victory's bright gleam 'had caught the helmets of our soldiers'. The battle in Egypt, he went on, was designed and timed as prelude and counterpart to the American operations under Eisenhower. Yet their author, as commander-in-chief of the armed forces of the United States, was the President himself to whom, in all of the undertakings, he – Churchill – had been his 'active and ardent lieutenant'.

Then, as if instantly to negate the image of himself as Roosevelt's subordinate, he added that Britain meant to hold its own. He was proud to be a member of the Commonwealth and society of nations gathered around the British monarchy, 'a veritable rock of salvation in this drifting world'. No thought of territorial gain or commercial profit was in Britain's mind, only liberation from Nazi and fascist tyranny. The African campaign was a combined effort. The whole event, he hoped, would be a new bond between the English-speaking peoples.

Churchill's defiant claim that Britain would hold its own was prompted by Eisenhower's appointment as allied commander of Operation Torch and the overwhelmingly American nature of his campaign, developments that heralded a shift in the balance of power between the two allies that was to tilt massively in American favour over the next two years. Only eighteen months before, Britain had 'stood alone'. Now she risked being swamped by her American ally.

Yet this did not by itself explain Churchill's anxiety. Even more potent was the rising tide of American criticism of European colonialism and especially of the British Empire in Asia, now an active theatre of war involving the Americans. Were American boys fighting to save these colonial empires? The self-righteous tone of American anti-colonialism quickly grated on British opinion, especially viewed against the open segregation enforced against blacks among the increasing number of American troops in Britain and news of race riots in the United States. Discord over the future of the British Empire became a challenge to both Roosevelt and Churchill if they were to preserve the alliance. The crisis was to get worse before it got better.[1]

Photographs from Casablanca showed Roosevelt and Churchill beaming happily side by side to the cameras – the image of harmony echoed in the Holofcener bronze in Bond Street. Yet barely had they left Morocco than friction erupted over an issue on which both men held strong but bitterly opposed views: the future of India.

To Churchill, India was the lynchpin of Empire and guarantor of the greatness of Britain. During his fight against appeasement in the 1930s he resisted even the most modest concessions to Indian self-government with apocalyptic warnings of chaos and blood. His passionate stand came from the heart. He would 'sooner give up political life at once, or rather go out into the wilderness and fight', he swore after he became Prime Minister, 'than to admit a revolution which meant the end of the Imperial Crown in India'. When the *Bombay Chronicle* deliriously greeted the Atlantic Charter as the 'Magna Carta of the world', he made it clear that it did not apply to India. Even close colleagues threw up their hands. 'He knows as much of the Indian problem as George III did of the American colonies,' groaned his Secretary of State for India, Leo Amery.[2]

But in the Viceroy of India, the Scottish laird and Presbyterian elder Lord Linlithgow, Churchill found a soulmate. This 'Churchill of the East' had one basic strategy in dealing with the rising tide of nationalism: ruthlessly crush any disturbance that could disrupt the war effort. Eagerly assisted by Britain's huge intelligence networks directed from London and New Delhi, he kept Indian dissidents under close and constant surveillance, their letters opened, their meetings infiltrated, their movements followed. Mahatma Gandhi, the eccentric but charismatic nationalist leader, was their principal worry. He had first called for Indians to be neutral in the war, and then, in August 1942, with the Japanese knocking at India's gates, launched an immediate campaign of non-violent struggle to force Britain to quit India. 'I am engaged,' Linlithgow told Churchill, 'in meeting by far the most serious rebellion since that of 1857 [the Indian Mutiny].' Already alerted by spies and informers, he had Gandhi and other Congress Party leaders arrested and locked up. Maulana Abdul Kalam Azad, the Muslim President of Congress, was even detained while drafting an appeal to Roosevelt. Over the next few months more than 100,000 nationalists were put behind bars. Yet, for reasons of military security, heavy press censorship concealed the full gravity and extent of the crisis.[3]

Churchill and Roosevelt had barely left Casablanca when the imprisoned Gandhi went on hunger strike. The prospect that his death might spark a national uprising electrified the world's press and put British intelligence on high alert. One of its most vigilant and excited arms was in the United States itself.

Even as Gandhi fasted in Poona, William Stephenson was fighting for his job with Stewart Menzies and other British intelligence

chiefs in London, now doubtful of his value with the Americans in
the war and their own intelligence services in place. One of
Stephenson's weapons was a detailed account of his agency that
highlighted the tasks accomplished and the challenges ahead.
Protecting the future of the British Empire, and not least India,
was one of these, he argued. His men had long targeted nationalist Indian movements in the United States such as the Indian
League, as well as on pro-Gandhi material reaching the White
House. But more damaging now, insisted Stephenson, were
Americans bent on giving the United States a major role in the
post-war development of India, and already embarked on 'preliminary reconnaissance'. New targets for British intelligence, he
concluded, had to be 'the aims and ambitions of influential
American circles and political parties . . .' Prominent among these,
although he tactfully omitted his name, was none other than
Franklin D. Roosevelt himself.[4]

He was right. The British Raj was a red rag to the anti-colonialist Roosevelt, whose views on this emotional issue were as
instinctive and even less informed than those of Churchill. India's
patent lack of democracy was an offence to basic American values,
and independence should come as soon as possible. If nothing else,
Roosevelt believed, freedom would encourage the Indians to fight
harder against the Japanese. Soon after Pearl Harbor he had sent
an old friend, Louis Johnson, to the sub-continent to prod the
British into making concessions to the nationalists. A visit by the
Chinese leader Chiang Kai-shek early in 1942 calling for 'Asia for
the Asians' had added steam to the campaign.

But Roosevelt quickly learned the dangers of raising the matter
directly with Churchill. The Prime Minister had bitten his head
off when he raised the idea of Indian independence during their
1941 White House Christmas get-together. 'I reacted so strongly
and at such length,' recorded Churchill with satisfaction, 'that he
never raised it verbally again.' Instead the President got advisers
such as Harry Hopkins, Averell Harriman or John Winant to do it
for him. The results were little different, as Harry Hopkins quickly
found out.

In April 1942, again back in Britain, he had set off in high spirits for a social weekend at Chequers. Spring was in the air, and as

Hopkins travelled by car through the English countryside he felt he'd finally grasped why the English had produced 'the best god-damn poetry in the world'. But a far from lyrical encounter awaited him. Under pressure, Churchill had recently sent Sir Stafford Cripps to negotiate a deal with the Indian Congress Party. As both he and Linlithgow hoped, Cripps reported failure. Roosevelt took the news badly and blamed Britain. His comments arrived at three o'clock in the morning while Hopkins and Churchill were still up talking over brandy and cigars. 'I feel,' recorded Roosevelt, 'I must place the issue before you very frankly. If India was to be invaded by the Japanese and heavy defeats followed there would be a powerful hostile reaction by the American people.'

Churchill erupted in a violent outburst of anger, and for a full two hours Hopkins listened to a 'string of cuss-words' that heatedly included a threat to resign if Roosevelt did not stop interfering. 'I cannot feel,' dictated a furious Churchill to his White House friend, 'that the common cause would benefit by emphasising the serious difference which would emerge if it were known that against our own convictions we were conforming to United States public opinion in a matter which concerns the British Empire and is vital to our successful conduct of the war in the East. I should personally make no objection at all to retiring into private life . . .'

By the next morning he had cooled off, dropping the threat to resign. Nonetheless, he remained adamant that this was not the moment to risk turmoil in India through political change and pleaded with Roosevelt to drop the subject. 'Anything like a serious difference between you and me would break my heart, and would surely deeply injure both our countries at the height of this terrible struggle.' Churchill made this a purely private message, all too aware of what damage it might do if it reached the War Cabinet. He also refused to tell the Viceroy, Lord Linlithgow, what had happened.[5]

There was no mistaking the depth and passion of Churchill's plea, one that he reiterated less than a month later to Harry Hopkins when rumour reached him of a possible invitation to the White House for Jawaharlal Nehru, another prominent leader of the Congress Party (and India's first Prime Minister). As one of Churchill's closest associates later told Robert Sherwood, the chronicler of Harry Hopkins' White House days, 'The President might have known that India was one subject on which Winston would never move a yard.' Indeed, it was the one subject on which the normal, broad-minded, good-humoured, give-and-take attitude which prevailed between the two statesmen was stopped cold.[6]

Roosevelt certainly got the message, for never again did he raise Indian independence directly with Churchill. Yet conditions in India still bothered him. Bill Donovan's intelligence agency had established a British Empire section in Washington to gather information about its ally. Only days after Churchill's explosion, Donovan gave the White House a lengthy report its experts had prepared on the collapse of the British Empire in Asia at the hands of the Japanese, which blamed fifth column subversion and native defections to the enemy as playing an important role. In Burma entire units had gone over to the enemy and even now were forming a 'Free Burmese Army' to assist the Japanese against the British colonialist oppressors. Colonialism was bankrupt, Donovan told Roosevelt: 'You can't win a war with slaves,' he added, concluding grimly that the British were 'beaten and groggy' and that the only hope for Burma and India was American power, especially air power.[7]

Not surprisingly, British authorities in the Raj regarded American interference as almost as subversive as the efforts of the Japanese, suspicions that rose acutely after Gandhi's 'Quit India' call. Indian intelligence secretly began opening the mail of American journalists and letters addressed to American consulates, while the American mission in New Delhi was banned from passing any messages from Roosevelt to Gandhi. The head of the film division of the Office of War Information even earned her own security file when writing home to object to American boys dying for the British Empire.

But despite all this Roosevelt kept his deal with Churchill, vetoing any American action that could further destabilise the situation. Yet the very turmoil sweeping the British Raj made him as eager as ever to receive intelligence about it. Much of it was bloodcurdling, anticipating the worst for American troops stationed there if violence broke out.

The American press was also in uproar, both deploring Gandhi's move as a blow to the fight against Japan and demanding American action to hasten independence. *Time* magazine stated baldly that if the United Nations' aim was to build a better world then India was the best place to start. Labour unions joined in, and the *New York Times* published a full-page petition signed by fifty-seven public figures demanding the re-opening of negotiations. Prominent among them were Pearl Buck, Clare Booth Luce, William Shirer and Upton Sinclair. Then the 1940 Republican presidential candidate Wendell Wilkie struck a blow of his own. He had just finished a world tour to demonstrate his bipartisan support for the war. Speaking to a national radio audience of almost 36 million Americans, he denounced the President's policy on India as 'wishy-washy'. America's silence on the issue, he thundered, had drawn heavily on the reservoir of goodwill in the east. 'They cannot tell,' he warned, 'whether we really do stand for freedom, or what we mean by freedom.'[8]

Roosevelt now decided to send yet another personal agent to scout out the Indian scene. This was a habit of his, a way of bypassing the 'stripey pants' bureaucrats of the State Department – a prejudice against professional diplomats he shared with Churchill. Ironically, the man he chose was a seasoned diplomat. Yet he was also a long-standing personal friend and skilled in the politics of inter-Allied intelligence.

William Phillips was a wealthy Harvard-educated Bostonian. A grand-nephew of Wendell Phillips, he had been a member of President Theodore Roosevelt's 'Tennis Cabinet', the group of athletic young men who played tennis, hunted, rode, boxed or rock-climbed with the muscular President, and his first diplomatic posting had been in London before the First World War. He got to know Franklin Roosevelt during Woodrow Wilson's presidency, when Roosevelt had an office on the same corridor in the then combined State, War and Navy building in Washington. Phillips' wife had known Eleanor and Franklin for years, and soon Phillips was part of a regular dinner group with the future President. 'Brilliant, lovable, and somewhat happy-go-lucky' is how Phillips remembered him.[9] A decade and a half later his friend, now the polio-stricken Governor of New York, mobilised his support for the 1932 presidential election, and his reward was appointment as Under-Secretary of State to Cordell Hull. Three years later Roosevelt sent him as ambassador to Rome to report on the growing menace of Mussolini's Italy. He stayed there until Italy and the United States went to war after Pearl Harbor.

Phillips was clear-eyed about Roosevelt. A frequent attender at Cabinet meetings in Cordell Hull's absence, he knew the President's foibles: his weakness as an executive; his ability to wound with a casual remark; the provisional nature of his promises. Yet he admired his vision, his intelligence, his courage, and his superb ability to sell himself to the American people. A Republican by blood, Phillips, like thousands of his countrymen during the grim Depression years, embraced the optimism and courage radiated by the Democrat Roosevelt. Donovan, another instinctive Republican, had done much the same. Not surprisingly, Phillips and Donovan soon found themselves drawn together.

With the prospect of serious American intelligence operations in Europe becoming a reality, by mid-1942 Donovan urgently wanted to establish a base in London and cast around for a candidate to head it. His eye lit on Phillips as a senior Roosevelt protégé experienced in Europe. Invited to breakfast in Donovan's Georgetown home, Phillips was quickly seduced by the Colonel's immense vitality and conviction. Here, he told himself, was a man after his own heart. But he was careful to secure Roosevelt's approval. 'Delighted with the idea,' responded the President. 'I know you could do it extremely well. If you accept, come in and see me before leaving.'[10] By mid-summer Phillips was hard at work in London.

Up till then Donovan's men had operated out of two cramped rooms in the American Embassy. Phillips' job was to oversee its shift into a separate building close by in Upper Grosvenor Street, smooth OSS relations with the various and often suspicious American military and civilian authorities in the British capital, and build up contacts with the intelligence services of the European governments-in-exile. Above all, his mission was to establish good relations with British intelligence chiefs. 'In all these circles,' he recorded, 'I found only the most agreeable response.'

This was certainly true for relations with SOE, where the treaty earlier that summer was yielding early fruit. The 'Baker Street Irregulars' showered him with their expertise on training techniques and communications and in return accepted the badly needed supplies and personnel the Americans could provide. In September 1942 Donovan flew to London, and seated in Phillips' office hammered out further deals with Sir Charles Hambro, the SOE boss. One was for the opening of an OSS office in Cairo. Another was over financial transactions between their two agencies. And another saw the Americans given the direction of all special operations in Portugal, where the British were having problems and a high priority was to undermine German influence over the Portuguese dictator Dr Antonio Salazar. In return, the OSS agreed to keep out of Spain.[11]

Such close Anglo-American co-operation was a different matter when it came to secret intelligence. Here, Stewart Menzies was determined to maintain the SIS monopoly on operations into Europe and, if the Americans did enter the field, control what they got up to. Phillips strongly resisted this approach. One of Donovan's principal goals, with his eye already firmly fixed on the post-war world, was to establish an independent global American intelligence service. His intelligence men in London knew they had a battle on their hands. It was not a question of being anti-British but of being independently American while co-operating with their allies. 'We are to a considerable degree conducting our affairs here in London on sufferance,' complained Whitney Shephardson, the head of American intelligence in London, 'and from time to time events and comments have reminded us of our position.'[12] Phillips needed no convincing and knew he had Roosevelt's backing. 'My duty,' he stressed, 'was to carry that policy by developing independent American sources of secret information . . . resisting all efforts of the British Secret Information [sic] to gobble us up.'[13] He failed. Menzies and SIS were simply too strong and too firmly entrenched for the Americans to make much headway.

Yet Menzies was all too aware of the growing power of the Americans and so was also friendly, courteous and eager to show

willing – especially when the price was not too high. So, when
Churchill agreed, he gave the green light for co-operation on
counter-espionage. Early in 1943 officers from Donovan's X-2
division began to work alongside their British counterparts in
SIS's Section V at St Albans, under Colonel Valentine Vivian, on
the intercepts of Abwehr radio traffic. Even here, however,
Menzies demanded a degree of co-ordination that often amounted
to complete control. 'SIS,' concluded Kermit Roosevelt in his
official history of Donovan's agency, 'never co-operated extensively with OSS, and its security was so effective that it was rarely
possible to determine with assurance where its agents were
located.'[14]

Phillips was not just responsible to Donovan. He was also
reporting regularly to the President. That autumn, as Roosevelt
and Churchill waited anxiously for the launch of the first great
Anglo-American operation of the war in French North Africa,
Eleanor Roosevelt arrived in London on an official visit. 'I confide
my Missus to the care of you and Mrs Churchill,' joked the
President to the Prime Minister. 'I know our better halves will hit
it off beautifully.' Welcomed by the King and Queen and housed
in a private suite in Buckingham Palace, America's first lady
exhausted her hosts in a frenetic tour of factories, army camps,
blitzed cities and Red Cross centres, which matched anything in
energy that she displayed at home. The British press loved her for
it and Churchill enthused to Roosevelt that she had been winning
golden opinions. 'Mrs Roosevelt proceeds indefatigably,' he
noted.[15]

But the press and Churchill were not the only sources of opinion for the President on his wife's timely contribution to
Anglo-American relations. SIS chief Stewart Menzies had his own
enthusiastic comments to add. Taking Phillips aside one day, he
told him that she had made a deep and lasting impression everywhere she went. Phillips immediately ensured that Roosevelt heard
of it. 'Even "C", the invisible Brigadier, tells me that people here
have enthused to him about her speeches,' he told Roosevelt, thus
ensuring that if he wasn't already the President now became fully
familiar with the role Menzies played in the circles that counted in
London.[16] Six days later Churchill delivered his Mansion House

promise about preserving the British Empire. That, too, as well as an assessment of where individual British Cabinet members stood on the issue, Phillips ensured went direct to Roosevelt.

Roosevelt's call for Phillips to go to India as his personal representative with the rank of ambassador came abruptly during Eleanor's British tour. By now American troops were pouring into India, heading for the province of Assam and Burma from where military supplies were being air ferried over 'the hump' into China to help Chiang Kai-shek and his nationalists carry on the fight against the Japanese. Vast assembling and repair centres had been established in Karachi and other cities to the east. The prospect of nationalist-inspired violence and sabotage was becoming an ever bigger nightmare to Roosevelt. Phillips' mission, explained the President, was to talk in a friendly but blunt and earnest spirit to British officials in India in the hope that some sort of settlement with the nationalists might emerge. But Roosevelt, still keeping to his bargain with Churchill, told Phillips he was not to bring any pressure to bear or even to hint at any American intervention or initiative.

That this was mission impossible took some time to dawn on the indefatigable Phillips. His first step was to see Churchill. Like Roosevelt, he had encountered the British Prime Minister once before, as a young and rising politician in London before the First World War. And like the President he had not been impressed. The occasion had been a house party thrown by Lord and Lady Stanley during the investiture of the Prince of Wales (the future King Edward VIII) at Carnarvon Castle after the coronation of King George V and Queen Mary. One of Phillips' fellow guests was a man about his own age. 'I disliked his manners,' recalled Phillips. 'He had little to say to the other guests and apparently did not wish to join in the spirit of the occasion.' Puzzled, the American asked a friend who he was. Winston Churchill, she replied, but then added that he should pay no notice as he was often like that.[17]

Yet when he lunched with Churchill at 10 Downing Street a week before his departure for New Delhi, the Prime Minister was in a friendly and boisterous mood. Dressed in his famous 'siren', or zipper, suit, he struck Phillips as positively cherubic and even admitted that 'much might come' of the mission. But most of the lunch was consumed by a torrent of praise for Roosevelt balanced by a tirade against Wendell Wilkie for his remarks about India. Wilkie, he said, was not to be trusted, reminding him of 'a Newfoundland dog in a small parlour which had wiped its paws on a young lady's blouse and swept off the teacups with its tail'.

By contrast, Roosevelt was the greatest spirit alive in the world and he would follow him in everything he had done in North Africa – an oblique reference to the controversial 'Deal with Darlan' for which Churchill was absorbing much of the heat. As for Stalin, Churchill told Phillips, he had stood up boldly to the Soviet dictator on his recent trip to Moscow to break the news of delays to the second front in Europe. Stalin had no understanding of the problems of transporting whole army divisions across water, he said. All *he* had to do was move his men across his own country.

Phillips left London two days before Christmas – and three days before Darlan's sudden demise in Algiers – buoyed up by his chat with Churchill and by a gracious gesture by the Prime Minister in sending him a rather tattered copy of a small book entitled *Twenty-One Days in India*, given to Churchill by an old family friend when he went out to Bangalore in 1886 as a subaltern in the British Army. 'It is a book famous in a small circle,' noted Churchill, 'and supposed to give very briefly a sweeping glance at a vast, marvellous scene.'

But the huge panorama of Indian politics that lay ahead promised far more than twenty-one days' work. 'It is a very big job,' Phillips confessed to Donovan on the eve of his departure, 'and one which cannot be done speedily.' To help him, however, was one of Donovan's brightest recruits from his own law firm. A graduate of Princeton and Columbia Law School, Dick Heppner was soon to be OSS chief for the whole of south-east Asia and, later, under the post-war Eisenhower administration, Deputy Assistant Secretary of Defense: 'A rare combination,' praised Phillips, 'of enthusiasm, good judgement, and niceness of feeling.' For Phillips was not just going to India for Roosevelt. He also had a mission for Donovan – to repeat his London success and establish in New Delhi an office for OSS.[18]

Technically speaking Donovan's agency already had a presence there. This was Detachment 101, a special operations unit based in Assam under the command of Carl Eifler, one of the first American trainees to pass through SOE's Camp X in Canada. But its exclusive target was the Japanese, and its field of action Burma. By contrast, an OSS base in New Delhi would be targeting India as well as British political and economic intentions in south-east Asia.

Predictably, Phillips was soon encountering gentlemanly but stubborn resistance from his British host. The flight to India was itself an endurance test. A Pan-American passenger flight took him from Ireland to Lisbon from where, after a night's rest, he flew on to Liberia. Here he boarded an American army plane fitted with iron bucket seats for a two-day flight across Central Africa to Khartoum, with another overnight stop in Kano. He eventually reached Cairo in a sandstorm where the plane, running danger-ously short of fuel, had to put down on an emergency landing strip. After providing an advance photo-opportunity for the Indian press by reviewing Sikh troops in the city, he flew on via Basra in Iraq to Karachi, where the legendary American commander of the China–Burma–India theatre, Joseph 'Vinegar Joe' Stilwell, lent his personal plane – nicknamed 'Uncle Joe's Chariot' – to take him on to New Delhi.

Here Linlithgow welcomed him warmly and threw a magnifi-cent dinner for thirty-eight people in his honour. As Phillips entered the dining room, footmen dressed in crimson and gold lined both sides of the long table, one for every two guests. Halfway through the dinner five Indian bagpipers circled the table twice, causing all conversation to cease: 'In recognition of our Scotch host,' mused Phillips. Afterwards, seated on a sofa in the drawing room, he was told that each member of the Indian gov-ernment would be presented for a seven-minute talk. Was he being mistaken for royalty? wondered the awe-struck representative of the President.

He would have been less impressed had he known that behind the scenes Linlithgow was already working vigorously to sabotage his plans for OSS. 'My experience of peripatetic Americans,' Linlithgow privately told Churchill before Phillips even arrived, 'is that their zeal in teaching us our business is in inverse ratio to their understanding of even the most elementary of the problems with which we have to deal.'[19] Phillips he seemed to like, but his presence he found intolerable. Donovan's agency, he complained bitterly to intelligence chiefs in London, was 'intent on conducting secret operations' in India and digging into the country with a view to American commercial penetration after the war. He also suspected that US Naval Intelligence in Bombay was pursuing similar goals and stonewalled every request on the OSS front. In London, the Secretary of State for India, Leo Amery, urged Churchill to raise the issue with Roosevelt as the real problem, he felt, lay with the White House itself.[20]

This meant that even before Phillips left India London had refused permission for an OSS office in the capital of the Raj. Donovan was furious. 'If you won't let us come in the door,' he stormed before Brigadier Cawthorn, the nay-saying head of Indian Army Intelligence, 'we'll come through the transom.'[21] Refusing to take no for an answer, he tried again, this time by approaching Lord Halifax in Washington. Linlithgow countered with an offer to integrate all British and American intelligence and clandestine efforts in India under British control, one that was clearly designed to be refused. Donovan predictably obliged. Domination disguised as co-ordination was not on his agenda.

The Indian press had virtually predicted the outcome. On Phillips' arrival at New Delhi an eager Indian correspondent had asked him his impressions of the country. He'd been flying high, responded the diplomatic Phillips, but the little he'd seen had impressed him. Soon after, a cartoon appeared in the Hindu press showing Phillips looking down over India from a plane. But spread below him, concealing the ground, was a cloud held in place by two winged cherubs. One was Linlithgow; the other Amery.[22]

Phillips' mission failed in two other respects. The 67-year-old American tirelessly toured India meeting British and Indian officials, visiting the princely rulers of Indian states such as the fabulously wealthy Nizam of Hyderabad, talking with Hindus and Muslims, and hearing the views of nationalists and journalists. He even had a three-and-a-half-hour exchange of views with Dr Muhammad Ali Jinnah, the head of the Muslim League, who was demanding the creation of an independent state of Pakistan. Yet one goal eluded Phillips – that of a meeting with Gandhi.

The nationalist leader did not make things easier by launching his hunger strike shortly after Phillips arrived in the country. Amid the speculation that Gandhi might die, he came under mounting pressure for help. 'I have been literally besieged by callers,' he cabled Roosevelt, and asked Linlithgow if he could visit the prisoner. But the Viceroy held firm, insisting that what India needed was a strong hand that refused to waver before such threats. It was certainly not a time for him to meet Gandhi. Linlithgow, Phillips reported to Roosevelt, 'is certainly a man of determination. Perhaps he is a chip off the old block that Americans knew something about in 1776.' If Linlithgow was a diehard, so was Churchill, who behind the scenes robustly supported the veto.[23]

Phillips tried again after Gandhi completed his fast. Choosing his moment carefully, he waited until the Viceroy invited him to the Viceregal Lodge at Dhera Dun for a tiger hunt. Setting off into the jungle at dawn with Linlithgow on the back of an elephant, Phillips earnestly discussed the Indian situation for three hours with the amiable but unbudging Viceroy. No, he could not see Gandhi, repeated Linlithgow. But yes, he conceded reluctantly, he could say publicly that he had asked and been refused. 'My visit to Dhera Dun had been a hunt for Gandhi,' concluded a wistful Phillips. 'I had failed in my principal objective.'[24]

He also failed to shift Roosevelt. Conditions in India were even worse than Phillips expected, and he became increasingly sympathetic to the nationalist cause, pressing the President harder and harder for a White House declaration that America was ready to do more than simply offer bland and meaningless assurances of friendship. He even resuscitated Roosevelt's own idea of a constitutional convention chaired by an American. 'Amazingly radical for a man like Bill,' commented Roosevelt, 'but he has his feet on the ground.' Nonetheless, he declined to rise to the bait and the State Department even refused to support Phillips' request to see Gandhi. He was on his own. Roosevelt had again kept his pact with Churchill not to rock the boat of friendship. He would go so far, but no further, in his support for the nationalists.[25]

The day after his return to Washington Phillips had an unsatisfactory meeting at the White House. The President was in a garrulous mood and did most of the talking. So Phillips put his thoughts in writing and produced a passionate denunciation of the British belief that India was none of America's business; how could this be so, Phillips asked, when America was bearing the brunt of the fighting against Japan?

Again, Roosevelt ducked the issue. By this time Churchill was once more in Washington, this time for the Trident talks. Phillips should go and report directly to the Prime Minister at the British Embassy, said the President.

'I was aware at once that he was not pleased to see me,' noted Phillips of his second wartime encounter with Churchill. Argument was hopeless. 'My answer to you,' spluttered the Prime Minister to Phillips' proposal for immediate reform, 'is: take India if that is what you want! Take it by all means!' By now he was excitedly pacing up and down the room as he warmed to his familiar theme. 'But I warn you that if I open the door a crack there will be the greatest bloodbath in all history; yes, bloodbath in all history. Mark my words,' he concluded, shaking his finger at Phillips. 'I prophesied the present war, and I prophesy the bloodbath.'

Phillips returned straight to the White House. 'Badly' was all he could mutter when Eleanor asked how it had gone.[26] British intelligence kept an eye on him, however, and subsequently reported back to New Delhi that he was doing the rounds in Washington bad-mouthing the Raj.

Despite his undisguised anger with Phillips ('a well-meaning ass') and his frequently expressed irritation with Roosevelt, Churchill in reality was pleased with his ally's compliance on India and even persuaded him to issue a 'stop order' on sending any more American intelligence officers to India until the entire matter had been thrashed out by the Combined Chiefs of Staff. 'The President has been very good to me about India,' he told Halifax later, 'and has respected my clearly expressed resolve not to admit external interference in our affairs.'

A sure sign of Roosevelt's backing-off came after the 1943 Quebec conference, when he threw a lunch for Churchill at the White House. The guest was Mrs Helen Ogden Mills Reid, a vice-

president of the *New York Herald Tribune* and hostile critic of
British rule in India. As they sat on the White House verandah
after lunch the topic of Indians came up. 'Before we proceed any
further,' Churchill said firmly, 'let us get one thing clear. Are we
talking about the brown Indians of India, who have multiplied
alarmingly under benevolent British rule? Or are we speaking of
the red Indians in America who, I understand, are almost extinct?'
Taken aback, Mrs Reid instantly dropped the topic. As for
Roosevelt, he laughed so much that Churchill's aide, Commander
Thompson, thought he might have a seizure. By the end of the
war India and its problems had largely vanished from American
headlines. Independence came in 1947. A bloodbath duly
followed.[27]

Yet this was not the end of the story for OSS in India. Donovan
still refused to take no for an answer and in July 1943 flew to
London to renegotiate the spheres of influence deal of a year
before over special operations. Hard and fast notions of spheres of
control were abandoned and liaison missions encouraged. So far as
India was concerned, the British were now forced to acknowledge
the growing power of OSS and let them set up an office. Phillips'
bright young assistant of only a few months before, Dick Heppner,
opened the OSS office soon after. Later, after Donovan visited
India at the end of the year, it moved to one of the plusher neighbourhoods of New Delhi. Appropriately enough, the sign outside
read 'Dr. L. L. Smith, American Dentist'. The American intelligence foothold in India had been a concession extracted with no
little pain from a deeply suspicious Raj. Relations with the British,
noted Heppner, were 'far from cordial'.[28] It was by no means the
final episode of a story that saw Roosevelt and Churchill sparring
over imperial issues. But from now on, Roosevelt focused his zeal
on other parts of Asia.

16

—⟫◦⟪—

HOUSE GUESTS

In May 1943 Roosevelt and Churchill were together again. This time the summit, held in Washington and codenamed 'Trident', was precipitated by Churchill's sudden crisis of confidence in his ally's commitment to Europe once the North African campaign was over. His fears that serious Anglo-American divergences lurked beneath the surface were echoed by Clementine. 'I'm so afraid the Americans will think that a Pacific slant is to be given to the next phase of the war,' she wrote to him in Washington. '*Surely* the liberation of Europe *must* come first.'[1]

Roosevelt was as affable and hospitable as ever, putting him up in the White House, laying on a dinner hosted by his daughter Anna, and taking him for the weekend to Shangri-La. Churchill watched fascinated as he stuck stamps in his album, and the two of them went fishing for trout in a nearby stream. *En route*, with Eleanor Roosevelt and Harry Hopkins sharing the presidential automobile, they had passed through Frederick, Maryland, where Churchill recited from memory John Greenleaf Whittier's poem 'Barbara Frietchie' about the woman who hung out her Union flag as the Confederate army marched by. Afterwards he regaled his hosts with a review of the battle of Gettysburg and the respective merits of 'Stonewall' Jackson and Robert E. Lee. Even the normally reticent Eleanor warmed to his bounce and charm.

This personal camaraderie provided essential oil for ruffled strategic waters. Although Roosevelt allayed Churchill's fears and stuck to the doctrine of 'Europe First', in reality the Pacific war was absorbing much of America's energies, and there were contentious issues to sort out. Over the ten strenuous days that followed the two men hammered out a target date of 1 May 1944 for the cross-Channel invasion, and agreed that after Sicily their target would be knocking Italy out of the war. They also gave renewed impetus to the joint production of an atomic bomb, co-operation on which had been suspended for over a year because of mutual bureaucratic suspicion.

The upbeat mood was lightened by the final surrender of German forces in North Africa, when church bells were again rung across Britain, as they had been after El Alamein. Churchill left the American capital glowing with the warmth of it all. 'My friendship with the President was vastly stimulated,' he confided to Clementine in a letter dictated on the plane taking him to Gibraltar and Algiers for talks on future Mediterranean plans. 'We could not have been on easier terms.' He concluded on an enigmatic note: 'I must try to make my exceedingly complicated and highly sensitive hen lay a few more eggs.'[2]

This was an apparent reference to his high-grade intercepts from Bletchley Park. For two very good reasons Ultra was much on his mind in Washington. It had continued to throw penetrating light on Wehrmacht activities on the Russian front, and if the second front was impossible that year, then at least the West could help Stalin by passing on to Moscow Ultra's rich harvest. Even as Roosevelt and Churchill met, Hitler was massing his forces for a major offensive against the Kursk salient. It took only a brief discussion in the Oval Office for the two men to agree to send the cryptographers' evidence to Stalin.[3]

More momentous in the long run, however, was that behind the scenes in Washington a crucial Anglo-American intelligence agreement had been hammered out. Earlier that spring the American codebreaking genius William Friedman had headed a US Army delegation to London and a personal welcome by Stewart Menzies for extensive briefings on British codebreaking victories. A few weeks later, among the large British retinue that crossed the

Atlantic aboard the *Queen Mary* with Churchill, was Sir Edward Travis, the head of Bletchley Park. As Churchill was preparing his address to Congress, Travis sat down to place his signature alongside that of George V. Strong, the head of US Army intelligence, on a far-reaching Anglo-American codebreaking and intelligence-sharing agreement so secret that only in the 1990s was it released by the Americans in Washington.

Generally known by its acronym Brusa (Britain/United States), it saw American and British codebreakers agree to a complete exchange of all information about the detection, identification and interception of military and air force signals, including also Abwehr messages, of the Axis powers, with the Americans focusing on the Japanese and the British on the Germans and Italians. Considerable detail was discussed about Ultra's distribution, its exchange between London and Washington, and its security. Non-service enemy and neutral sources were dealt with by later accords, and the two navies already had a separate treaty.[4]

This historic Brusa agreement, which later formed the foundation for all Cold War Sigint co-operation, was only one of several advances in Anglo-American intelligence co-operation that spring. After much hemming and hawing Stewart Menzies had agreed to sign a joint operating agreement on counter-intelligence with Donovan, and soon afterwards four American counter-intelligence officers arrived in Britain to work with the Secret Intelligence Service. One of them, soon to become head of a group that rapidly expanded to over three hundred, was Norman Holmes Pearson, an Oxford-educated English literature lecturer from Yale who was fully indoctrinated into Ultra's secrets and became an *ex officio* member of the 'Double-Cross' committee. This way, Pearson reported, OSS learned the priceless 'fruits of many decades of counter-espionage experience' and was treated as 'an independent equal'. James Jesus Angleton, the post-war CIA counter-intelligence chief who turned the agency upside-down in the 1960s with his quest for Soviet moles, was a colleague.[5] Later that year, Donovan also signed a deal with MI5.

Allied co-operation had advanced on the special operations front, too. On Christmas Eve 1942 Donovan sent his special operations chief, Ellery C. Huntington, on a three-month tour of

Europe, Africa and the Middle East to move from planning into the practical building of behind-the-lines activities. These, he insisted, should not be 'an adjunct' of SOE and must remain independent of the British. After discussions in Baker Street, Huntington and Sir Charles Hambro agreed they should function separately but collaborate closely in pooling resources and facilities. OSS, Huntington told Donovan when he got back to Washington at the end of March 1943, should have 'singleness of purpose, seasoned judgement, a smattering of diplomacy, unquestioned authority, and unity of command. It is one these principles,' he concluded, 'that General Gubbins has done so fine a job in the field for SOE. It will be a harder task for us – since we are starting late in the day – but it can be done.'[6]

Taken together, these various talks and agreements bound Britain and the United States into the closest intelligence alliance history has ever seen.[7] Inevitably, this meant the closest possible co-ordination on security, for enemy penetration of one partner would quickly subvert both. 'If the highest degree of security is to be maintained,' noted the Brusa text, 'it is essential that the same methods should be pursued by both countries at every level and in every area concerned, since a leakage at any one point would jeopardise intelligence from these sources not in one area only but in all theaters of war and for all services.'

Churchill quickly grasped the idea and anxiously kept a careful watch on his allies and their intelligence security. At this critical stage of the war even British security, particularly over Ultra, was causing him nightmares. In the interlude between Casablanca and Washington the Tunisian campaign had given him ample cause for worry, with two major scares that the Germans had learned about Ultra. 'You will, I am sure, guard our precious secret,' he urged General Montgomery. 'Tell even your most trusted commanders only the minimum necessary.' He also demanded a drastic clampdown on Ultra's circulation.[8]

Inevitably he worried about American handling of Ultra. The year before, the *Chicago Tribune* had strongly hinted that America owed its victory at Midway to triumphs in signals intelligence, and in North Africa German penetration of ciphers used by the American military attaché in Cairo had provided Rommel with an open window on much British planning. Many of the American Special Security Officers responsible for explaining and interpreting Ultra intelligence were considerably junior to the commanders they briefed. Churchill could only too easily imagine that some 'cowboy' general would simply ignore their strictures about security. Privately, he ordered the discreet monitoring of the Americans' handling of Ultra and remained vigilant across a broad front. Security breaches by top American officials in Washington about Allied deception campaigns even forced him to take up the issue personally with Roosevelt.[9]

Publicity surrounding Donovan's expanding empire also worried the British. Everyone knew about it, including the Germans, Italians and Russians. American newspapermen had no Official Secrets Act to worry about and Drew Pearson, the crusading Washington columnist, frequently targeted Donovan's agency. It was, he said in a typical volley, 'one of the fanciest groups of dilettante diplomats, Wall Street bankers, and amateur detectives ever seen in Washington'. Such attacks horrified the British and they tried vainly to pressure Donovan to have legislation passed that would prohibit public discussion. But Donovan never even tried. His domestic enemies were simply too powerful. Quite apart from rivals such as J. Edgar Hoover and George Strong, Donovan had to face Congressional critics, such as Senator Burton K. Wheeler, who stridently denounced the 'Gestapo' he had created. So precarious was Donovan's bureaucratic position that early in 1943 an exasperated Roosevelt came close to getting rid of the OSS altogether. All this fuelled the Washington rumour mill and further upset Churchill.[10]

A few weeks after Trident, the *New Yorker* published a lengthy two-part personality profile under the title 'House-Guest'.[11] Its subject was Harry Hopkins. By now, the 52-year-old Iowan – looking, the *New Yorker* said, like 'an animated piece of Shredded Wheat' – was a fixture in the White House. The year before, in a ceremony in the President's study, he had married his third wife, Louise Macy, the vivacious former Paris editor of *Harper's Bazaar*. His new status made no difference at all to his living arrangements. Roosevelt asked him to stay on in the White House and after a few adjustments to his suite Louise moved in with Hopkins and his young daughter Diana. He continued to dine with the President almost every evening.

Washington feasted on speculation about Hopkins' power and influence. In addition to being Roosevelt's special adviser and assistant, he was also the supervisor of Lend-Lease, Chairman of the Munitions Assignment Board, and a member of the seven-man War Mobilisation Committee. Next to the President, he had been the nation's first really influential appreciator of the importance of support for the Soviet Union's war effort and hadn't wavered in his view. 'Hopkins still thinks,' reported the *New Yorker*, 'that the Russian Front is the most important one.'[12]

Admirers respected his loyalty to Roosevelt and his selfless devotion to duty, a view that was later embodied in Robert Sherwood's hefty post-war study of Hopkins' White House years. But detractors, many of whom were Roosevelt-haters, seized on Hopkins as a convenient symbol of all they loathed and resented about the New Deal. By mid-1943 criticisms were becoming virulent and personal, with wild Republican allegations in Congress, such as that Louise Hopkins had accepted a gift of emeralds worth half a million dollars and that Hopkins feasted on caviar and *pâté de foie gras* while demanding sacrifice from the American people. The nadir came when the *Chicago Tribune* likened the former social worker and WPA Administrator to the sinister Russian mystic Rasputin, whose influence over the last of the Czars had been so mysterious and malevolent.[13]

Even some Democrats joined in, jealous of Hopkins' access to the President. Ernest Cuneo, for one, claimed that at Democratic Party headquarters he was 'anathema', adding that he was widely regarded as 'a bootlegging namby-pamby, a sycophant . . . door-mat-in-residence . . . whipping boy . . . spiritual menial [and] hanger-on'. It was obvious that the critics included Cuneo himself. Sam Rosenman, presidential speechwriter and loyalist that he was, conceded that Hopkins sometimes let personal feelings restrict access to Roosevelt.[14]

Yet Cuneo had two more weighty indictments to make. Hopkins' standard *modus operandi* in his scramble to power and influence, he claimed, was first to manoeuvre his target into a defensive position, then to ride to his rescue; and Churchill, claimed Cuneo, was his most prominent victim. On his first visit to Britain Hopkins painted a sombre picture of Roosevelt's attitude to the Prime Minister, then promised that *he*, Hopkins, could change the President's mind. 'Churchill, desperate and on the ropes,' argued Cuneo, 'practically sued for Hopkins' favour. As per ploy Hopkins granted it, acted handsomely in doing it, and in the doing thereof actually convinced Churchill that he had convinced Hopkins to be his "friend at court" and that Hopkins would actually advise him on how to handle Roosevelt without notifying the President.'[15]

Is this extraordinary picture of Hopkins duping a gullible Churchill plausible? Beyond question, Churchill treasured him as a close and intimate friend. Hopkins fuelled his trust – the previous year he had told him before anyone else the secret of his engagement to Louise Macy. The complex 'Trident' discussions confirmed Churchill's belief. In an extraordinary tribute to Hopkins' contribution, he described his efforts as 'priceless'.[16]

Churchill's personal wartime archive also bulges with evidence of his place in the Prime Minister's mind. Notable among the more than 300 messages by, about or to Hopkins is the genuine sympathy and personal grief he showed when Hopkins' son Stephen was killed in action in the Pacific early in 1944. 'Your son, my lord, has paid a soldier's debt,' Churchill inscribed on a scroll he sent to Hopkins, quoting from Shakespeare. Soon after, Hopkins was admitted to hospital with a recurrence of stomach problems. 'He is an indomitable spirit,' Churchill told Roosevelt on hearing the news. 'I cannot help feeling very anxious about his frail body and another operation. I should always be grateful for any news about him, for I rate him highly among the Paladins.'[17] Almost daily, for the next three months, the diplomatic wires hummed with messages between Lord Halifax and London keeping an anxious Prime Minister informed of progress. In turn, Churchill shared the news with Clementine, as though Hopkins were a family member. 'I am always your constant friend,' a relieved Churchill told the convalescent Hopkins in a heartfelt message at the end of the year.[18]

One of the most telling examples of Churchill's dependence on

Hopkins was his reaction early in 1945 to Hopkins' suggestion that he might be appointed United States ambassador in London. The Prime Minister was appalled at the prospect of losing his contact in the White House. 'His war post is in Washington,' he insisted to Halifax – and in the end it came to nothing.[19]

But does all this mean that Cuneo is right and that Hopkins 'conned' Churchill into regarding him as more his friend at court than he really was? Cuneo's description of Hopkins' *modus operandi* is, after all, little more than the technique of all fixers and mediators in any dialogue between two prima donnas. Churchill was certainly susceptible to Hopkins' charm, genuinely liked him, and may occasionally have gazed through rose-coloured glasses on Anglo-American affairs.

Yet he was too old and practised a political hand to fall into the trap suggested by Cuneo. Even when most desperate for American help, and most charmed by Hopkins, as he was during the winter of 1940–41, he deliberately withheld Ultra intelligence about the postponement of Hitler's invasion plans in order to heighten American anxiety and bolster his case for Roosevelt's support. And he resolutely failed to budge in the face of constant pressure from Roosevelt over imperial affairs.

But what about Cuneo's second indictment of Hopkins? This, far more sensitive and sensational, is that Hopkins increasingly interposed himself in 'Big Three' decisions and that during the last two years of the war American grand strategy was essentially pro-Russian. 'Everything about it,' declared Cuneo, 'bore the spoor of Harry the Hop.'[20] Cuneo stopped short of claiming openly that Hopkins had fallen under Soviet or Communist influence, although in the post-war years he joined the legion of Americans who believed that too many 'Reds' had gathered around the wartime White House. He may well have had Hopkins in mind when he alleged that there was a Soviet mole high in the American government, a friend of Roosevelt himself.[21]

More dramatic and explicit charges have recently surfaced that Hopkins was nothing less than a Soviet agent. This time the evidence comes from the Trident conference itself. Could it possibly be true that the man who waited at the Staten Island pier to greet Churchill and the *Queen Mary*, sat in on the military discussions, squeezed into the limousine that took the President and Prime Minister up to Shangri-La, and ironed out problems over the atomic bomb accord, could actually have been Moscow's man? If any one person apart from the two principals had a comprehensive overview of Trident, it was Harry Hopkins.

In 1996 the American National Security Agency carried out the first declassification of post-war intelligence files – the so-called 'Venona' documents. Long the subject of rumours and legend, this was a collection of several thousand cables exchanged between Soviet intelligence agents in New York, Washington and other cities around the world and Moscow throughout the 1940s – including the Second World War. Intercepted and laboriously deciphered by American codebreakers, Venona documents provide an intimate look at Soviet intelligence operations and the long-hidden clue to American successes in breaking such notorious espionage cases as those of the Rosenbergs and the 'Cambridge Comintern' in Britain.

One of the messages in the Venona series, containing information from an agent identified only by the number '19', is dated New York, 29 May 1943, three days after the end of the Trident conference. The sender, codenamed 'Victor', was one of the KGB's leading 'illegal' (deep penetration) officers in the United States. His real name was Iskhak Abdulovich Akhmerov. This dark, stocky and affable man had lived there for several years under varying names and was married to a niece of the American Communist Party leader, Earl Browder. Two of the agents he is known to have controlled in the United States are Alger Hiss and Elizabeth Bentley – the man who defiantly denied it all to the grave, and the woman whose confessions helped uncover Soviet networks in America at the start of the Cold War.

The message contains material given to Akhmerov from '19' about the Trident meeting and Roosevelt's and Churchill's decision over the timetable for the second front in Europe, with its crucial proof for Stalin that a cross-Channel attack was now delayed until 1944. '19' claims to have been personally present at crucial meetings of the two leaders. The message contains cryptonyms easily identified: 'Kapitan' ('Captain') for Roosevelt and 'Kaban' ('Boar') for Churchill. Another, 'Zamestitel' ('Deputy') was first identified by Venona decrypters as meaning Vice-President Henry Wallace, Roosevelt's literal deputy; but it could also have meant Hopkins, who was more truly Roosevelt's right-hand man. But the true identity of '19' remained a mystery for as long as the Venona file remained operational, well into the 1970s.

However, recent analysis of the Venona series, combined with close scrutiny of the timetable of Trident meetings, confirms 'Zamestitel' as Henry Wallace – and thus '19' as Hopkins. This also fits in with Akhmerov's later boastings. In a post-war lecture to fellow KGB officers at the Lubianka in Moscow, he made the extraordinary claim that Hopkins had been the most important of all Soviet wartime agents in the United States. One of those in the audience was the KGB officer Oleg Gordievsky, who later defected to the West, became a British double agent, and in the late 1980s sparked off a heated and acrimonious debate with his revelations about Akhmerov's boastings about Hopkins.[22]

Yet it is a long step indeed from identifying '19' as Harry Hopkins to concluding that he was either wittingly or unwittingly some kind of Soviet agent. It is clear from the text of Akhmerov's message that he is passing on information obtained by someone else, most probably from a source within the Soviet Purchasing Commission in Washington. Hopkins, as Chairman of the Munitions Board, was a frequent legitimate visitor there, and indeed three days before Akhmerov's message had spent two and a half hours with Admiral Akulin and a Mr A. A. Rostarchuk, two of its officials.

That their conversation with Hopkins formed the kernel of the report is supported by the use of the cryptonym '19'. While the KGB never used numerical cryptonyms in its messages from Washington, this was common practice for the GRU, Soviet military intelligence – and Hopkins' contacts at the Soviet Purchasing Commission were military officers who would report through the GRU; and in this case, such an important topic as the timing of the second front would override the normal KGB–GRU rivalry and permit one Soviet intelligence agency, the GRU, to pass on information to another, the KGB.

So, Hopkins told someone at the Soviet Purchasing Commission about the second front. What was it he told them? From

Akhmerov's message it appears that no operational information was given either about the target date or the number of divisions to be assigned to the invasion of France. Rather, the thrust of his comment was that Churchill was mainly responsible for delaying the operation until 1944.

This suggests a radically different interpretation than that of Hopkins as 'Soviet agent'. Quite the contrary, in fact. It points, instead, to Roosevelt using Hopkins as a 'back-channel' to Moscow in order to safeguard his own position with Stalin.

Long before Trident Roosevelt had been hoping for a face-to-face meeting with Stalin that would exclude Churchill. His purpose was both to assure his Soviet ally that the Anglo-American duo were not ganging up on the Soviet dictator, and that he, Roosevelt, did not share identical views with the veteran anti-Bolshevik Churchill. Only three weeks before Akhmerov's message, and on the eve of the British Prime Minister's eager arrival in Washington, Roosevelt told Stalin in a private letter that, 'You and I ought to meet this summer . . . [we] would talk informally and get what we call a meeting of minds.' He added that Churchill would not be invited, suggested that military staffs should be excluded, and proposed either side of the Bering Strait as a convenient rendezvous.[23]

Stalin replied positively the day after Trident ended. By this time Roosevelt was now more anxious than ever to distance himself from any suspicion in Soviet minds that *he* was responsible for the delay to the second front. He knew full well that the Trident news would anger Stalin – and, indeed, when officially informed early in June the Soviet dictator fell into acrimonious argument with his allies.

In being 'indiscreet' with the Soviets and subtly pointing a finger at Churchill, Hopkins was thus reflecting the official, if undercover, White House line. Far from being a Soviet agent of influence, he was a profoundly loyal servant of Franklin D. Roosevelt, his only master.

At no point during the war did Hopkins reveal or harbour sympathies for the principle or practice of the Soviet state. Only days before Hitler's attack on the Soviet Union he had urged a crack-down on Communist efforts to sabotage American war production.

'They are just as much a potential enemy as the Germans,' he declared in urging that troublemakers be prosecuted to the fullest limits of the law. 'I've got away from the notions that I once had about a socialist state,' Hopkins frankly admitted to the *New Yorker* in August 1943. 'I think it can be done under a capitalist economy.' And even his accuser Oleg Gordievsky was forced to accept that at the very worst Hopkins could only be accused of being an 'unconscious' agent of influence, a concept so vague and elastic that it loses precision and meaning. Akhmerov was simply boasting about Hopkins to boost his prestige at home. He would not be the first intelligence officer to follow this well-established practice. Hopkins as Soviet mole is, truly, a red herring.[24]

If anyone should have worried about Hopkins it was Churchill. Roosevelt had not told his ally about his invitation to Stalin and when he learned of it he protested vigorously. Roosevelt replied with a direct lie, denying that he had ever invited Stalin to meet him alone.[25] Had Churchill known about Hopkins as well, he would have been doubly distressed. 'Except for the President,' concluded the *New Yorker*, 'Hopkins admires [Churchill] more than anyone else in the world.' And that was the point. In any choice between the two, Roosevelt came first for the man once described as 'a pilot fish for a shark'. In the rapidly changing balance of power between the Big Three, Churchill was losing out.[26]

Anglo-American military co-operation was prospering, as exemplified in the Brusa accord. Politically, and beyond Europe, harmony was in shorter supply. At Casablanca Averell Harriman had noted that on many issues 'Roosevelt and Churchill did not march to the same drumbeat'.[27] Now they were even more out of step. Stalingrad and the Allies' triumphs in Africa were turning minds to victory and the shape of peace. Roosevelt's views, embodying American dreams and ambitions, increasingly diverged from those of Churchill.

The Prime Minister was all too aware of this. In Pendar's villa at Marrakesh, after Roosevelt had left, he had talked expansively of a rosy Anglo-American future of co-operation and even fusion. Picking up a pencil, on the back of a scrap of paper he drew the symbol of the pound sterling with a dollar sign superimposed upon it. 'This,' he told Pendar, 'is as I see it – the money of the future, the dollar sterling.' At Trident he even talked of hopes for a common citizenship.[28]

Such talk has often been misunderstood as revealing Churchill's naïve optimism and illusions about Anglo-American relations. Yet in reality it emerged most strongly at the very time he began to question their future. Such hopes and visions masked deeper fears about Anglo-American relations brought dramatically to the fore since the Darlan episode. During Trident he reminded Congress that while no one had doubted the Union victory after Gettysburg, far more blood was spilled after it than before. 'War is full of mysteries and surprises,' he warned. 'A false step, an error in strategy, discord or lassitude among the Allies, might soon give the enemy power to confront us with new and hideous facts . . . we must beware of every topic however attractive . . . which turns our minds and energies from [victory].'

To the British Parliament he repeated the warning. 'All sorts of divergences, all sorts of differences of outlook and all sorts of awkward little jars necessarily occur as we roll ponderously forward together along the rough and broken road of war.' Above all, the next presidential election, in 1944, was already casting a shadow across his mind. If Roosevelt chose not to run, or were defeated, it would be a disaster of the first magnitude. There was no one to replace him, and, he confessed to his wife, 'all my hopes for the Anglo-American future would be withered for the lifetime of the present generation – probably for the present century'.[29] A common currency and common citizenship were devices to cement the alliance before it began to crumble and thus reflected anxiety, not optimism, about his relations with Roosevelt and the United States. In the hothouse world of intelligence, affairs in the Balkans, India, China and south-east Asia were to provide graphic examples of Anglo-American discord.

17

<hr />

'ALMOST HOMOSEXUAL'

The two months following Trident were difficult for Roosevelt. A national miners' strike and race riots in Alabama and Detroit troubled the home front and dented the image of a democratic nation united in war. Finally, at the end of July 1943, the President sat down before the microphone to deliver another of his fireside chats.

Despite the problems, his tone was upbeat. Even as Sam Rosenman and Robert Sherwood fine-tuned his speech, news came in that the Italian dictator Mussolini had been toppled from power. 'The first crack in the Axis has come,' began the President. 'The criminal, corrupt fascist regime in Italy is going to pieces.' He went on: 'The massed, angered forces of common humanity are on the march. They are going forward – on the Russian front, in the vast Pacific area, and into Europe – converging upon their ultimate objectives, Berlin and Tokyo.'[1]

The tide of war had decisively turned at last. On the Russian front Hitler's forces had been held at Kursk and the Red Army now held the initiative. In the Pacific, American and Allied forces had recaptured the Solomon Sea and the Japanese were in fighting retreat. In the Atlantic fortune had deserted the U-boats, and over Germany 'firestorm' entered the vocabulary after a massive bombing raid on Hamburg destroyed eight square miles of the city and left over 40,000 dead. In Sicily the Axis forces were in disarray. Indeed, only the day after his broadcast, Roosevelt talked with Churchill over the transatlantic telephone about possible armistice terms with an Italy now anxious to leave the war. Ironically, given the post-Brusa emphasis on security, their conversation was intercepted and unscrambled by German intelligence. Fortunately, it did little more than confirm what Hitler already knew.[2]

In any case, transatlantic telephone calls became redundant when Churchill arrived yet again in North America for talks with the President that spanned an entire four weeks. As before, he arranged for a constant stream of top-grade intelligence. 'I must have good "C" stuff,' he ordered his staff. On 5 August he left Britain on the *Queen Mary*, and after reaching Halifax travelled by train to Quebec city to meet with the Canadian and Quebecois Cabinets. Twenty-four hours later he was relaxing at Hyde Park for a long weekend with the President. Eleanor was there, as was the inevitable Harry Hopkins. So was Mary, Churchill's youngest daughter; her mother, Clementine, exhausted by the sea journey, had stayed in Quebec.

In the scorching heat there was swimming in the outside pool and barbecues with hot dogs, hamburgers, corn on the cob, and watermelon slices. The two leaders also talked business. After reading a bundle of intercepts revealing German atrocities in Yugoslavia, Churchill urged increased support for the guerrillas through supplies and agents. By contrast, Roosevelt's priority was to secure Churchill's wholehearted commitment to the cross-Channel attack. Henry Stimson, who had just returned from London and his own talks with the Prime Minister, urged him to take a tough line. The shadows of Passchendaele and Dunkirk hung too strongly over Churchill. 'We cannot rationally . . . come to grips with our German enemy,' he told Roosevelt, 'under a British commander.'[3] Harry Hopkins also complained that Churchill's foot-dragging over the second front had already prolonged the war.[4] Forced to yield, Churchill agreed to Eisenhower as Supreme Allied Commander for Europe and had to 'dis-invite' Brooke, to whom he had earlier promised the job. By way of balance Mountbatten was given the newly created South-East Asia Command (SEAC). The two leaders also decided to invite Stalin for a tripartite meeting in Alaska, and at last put their signatures to a written agreement about the Manhattan Project, first discussed in June 1942.

At dinner on the final evening Churchill reverted again to his favourite theme of post-war Anglo-American association. Only one of those at the table openly demurred. Significantly, it was Eleanor, who feared it could undermine the concept of a United Nations. Perhaps she was reflecting the views of her diplomatically – and unusually – silent husband.

The two leaders then travelled up to Quebec for several days' talks with their military staffs. By now Sicily had been captured and secret talks begun about Italy joining the Allies after surrender. The talks broke little fresh ground but dispelled some mutual suspicion, and it was agreed to recognise the French Committee of National Liberation headed jointly by Generals De Gaulle and Giraud. Afterwards Churchill went south again, this time to familiar hospitality and a welcome air-conditioned room in the White House. Here he and the President received news of the landings on mainland Italy, the surrender of the Italians, and Stalin's agreement to meet them both – but at a site of his choosing, Tehran. In between Churchill found time to visit Hopkins, laid up by illness again at the Bethesda Naval Hospital, while the President gave him a personally guided tour of Mount Vernon and Williamsburg.[5]

Churchill's occupancy of the White House was almost as disruptive as that of rampaging British troops in 1812. As usual, he kept Roosevelt up well after midnight while taking afternoon naps and roaming the corridors by day in his dressing-gown. It was all too much for the President. 'Winston,' he said with a nice touch of irony after deciding to flee back to Hyde Park, 'please treat the White House as your home. Invite anyone you like for meals and do not hesitate to summon any of my advisers with whom you wish to confer at any time.' Churchill eagerly seized the offer, and in what he later termed 'an event in Anglo-American history', summoned the Joint Chiefs of Staff and their British opposite numbers to the Council Room for an overview of progress in the Italian and Pacific theatres.[6]

In mid-stay, Churchill travelled to Boston to receive an honorary degree from Harvard University, where to the assembled students

he harked again on Anglo-American harmony. Several ideas about
future world security were in play, he said, referring to schemes for
a United Nations, but nothing, he told them in one of his most elo-
quent speeches, would work soundly or for long without the united
effort of the British and American peoples, who were bound by ties
of blood and history and shared common conceptions of what was
right and decent. 'Naturally,' he added, 'I, a child of both worlds,
am conscious of these.'[7] He had already proposed to Roosevelt
that the Combined Chiefs of Staff should continue in existence for
a decade after the war, and the President had seemed to agree.
'Americans have a high respect for us now,' he purred.

Before finally returning home, he dropped in to Hyde Park
again, where they all celebrated the Churchills' thirty-fifth wedding
anniversary. On the train taking him back to Quebec, Churchill
wrote his host a letter of thanks. Breaking from his habit of
addressing him as Mr President, he called him 'Franklin'. It was
a fulsome and appreciative letter of thanks. 'You know,' he wrote,
'how I treasure the friendship with which you have honoured me
and how profoundly I feel that we might together do something
really fine and lasting for our two countries and through them, for
the future of all.'[8]

Churchill's faith in his friendship with Roosevelt and an Anglo-
American future, which reached its peak on this visit, has been
condemned as a naïve and damaging illusion that precipitated 'the
end of glory' and an unhealthy British dependence on the United
States.[9] Yet, even during the war, Churchill's obsession and apparent identity with the American President sparked anxiety among
close colleagues. Anthony Eden, the Foreign Secretary, was one.
For him, it was a diplomatic issue. The energy Churchill expended
on the White House could better be directed, he felt, on the
future of Europe.

But an astonishingly personalised attack along similar lines was
launched behind closed doors only two weeks before Churchill set
sail for Quebec. And it came from within the inner circle of
Churchill's closest personal advisers, indeed from his closest ally
during the wilderness years of the 1930s who had joined him in
Downing Street in 1940 as personal intelligence adviser with an
office next to the Cabinet Room: Major Desmond Morton.

Morton made no secret after the war that he felt used and abandoned by Churchill. 'I have no chip on my shoulder about him,' he confessed in 1960, five years before Churchill's death, 'but I do not care if I never see him again and certainly would not wish to attend his funeral, though I would pray most heartedly for his soul.'[10] Nor, indeed, did he disguise his view that Churchill had been blinded to Roosevelt's 'aim to overthrow the British Empire'.[11]

Now, from an extraordinary inside source, it emerges that even during the war he had turned against the Prime Minister. In a remarkable case of personal disloyalty he delivered his onslaught, not in the privacy of his home, nor in some personal letter or idle moment of exasperation, but in the War Cabinet Offices themselves. And the recipient was none other than the Secret Intelligence Service officer whom he knew to enjoy Churchill's personal trust: Major Gerald Wilkinson.

Since returning from the Pacific Wilkinson had been kicking his heels in London waiting to leave for the United States, taking a specialist SIS course on military, naval and air identifications devised for agents behind enemy lines, and discussing his past and future missions with officials in Whitehall. One of these was Morton.

On Wednesday 21 July 1943 Wilkinson visited the underground War Cabinet Offices on the edge of St James's Park for a forty-five-minute *tour d'horizon* of his work and to thank Morton for the Prime Minister's fruitless efforts to get him back to Australia and MacArthur.

He also seized the chance to repeat his strongly held view – and to reassure Churchill prior to his forthcoming Quebec summit with Roosevelt – that MacArthur was *not* grooming himself as a presidential candidate for 1944. Instead, he assured Morton, MacArthur was aiming to be 'a pan-American hero, the victor of the last battle, Japan, [and] the conqueror of the Philippines with which the lives of his father and himself were so interwoven'. In the absence of an American royalty, Wilkinson argued, MacArthur could fill a popular void 'more historically than [General Ulysses S.] Grant and more emotionally than even Lindbergh'. The risk was not that MacArthur would pit himself against Roosevelt; it was that, because of personal hatred of the President, he would throw in his lot with some Republican candidate, whoever that might be.

Morton absorbed all this carefully, noting only that the practical difficulties of MacArthur seeking the nomination from his base in Australia strengthened Wilkinson's claim. But his major contribution was on another topic altogether – Churchill himself. Praising General de Gaulle as the one French leader whose principles and patriotism had remained unsmirched throughout the war, a strong and unpliable character, unlike Giraud and other 'fuddy-duddys', he explained that this was why Churchill found De Gaulle so hard to deal with. The Prime Minister, first and foremost, was concerned with the future of the Empire – and France and Britain had always quarrelled over imperial affairs. Also, Churchill was a man who depended on personalities to advance his policies, and in De Gaulle he had met a formidable match.

In that sense, Morton went on, Churchill was not primarily a politician. 'He was inclined to conduct his politics according to the personalities available,' recorded Wilkinson afterwards in his notes on Morton's remarks, '[and] to concentrate first upon the selection of personalities and then to act according to the activities or objectives within their range.'

Morton was by now warming to his theme, and went on to contrast Churchill with Roosevelt. The President, he said, was primarily a politician and one of 'far greater ability than Winston, choosing first not the men but the political plan to be followed and then selecting the personalities to fit them'. Then, in an astonishing outburst, he continued: 'For this reason Winston took to Roosevelt, whose general principles so admirably supplemented Winston's imperial ideals, with an enthusiasm and affection that was almost homosexual in its entirety, and that for this reason again Winston attaches enormous importance to the next presidential election.'

On the general subject of American relations Morton added that it was always a first principle of the PM's to give the President anything he wanted.[12]

For Morton to describe Churchill's feelings for Roosevelt as 'almost homosexual' is extraordinary enough. But for the Prime

Minister's intelligence adviser to accuse him of grovelling to the President in every policy issue on the eve of an Anglo–American summit is even more astonishing. What should we make of these astounding claims?

They can best be understood as projections of Morton's feelings of rejection and jealousy. He had met Churchill during the First World War, become a friend in the 1920s, and throughout the 1930s had supplied him with unique inside intelligence about rearmament during regular visits to Chartwell. His influence peaked during the first two years of Churchill's premiership when, ensconced in his office at 10 Downing Street, he controlled intelligence affairs and had access to any secret file he demanded to scrutinise.

British documents only just released reveal how powerful his gatekeeping could be. Early in 1941 Sir Frank Nelson, SOE's first executive head, discovered that Morton had requested an SOE document without his knowledge. Picking up the telephone to protest, he was so shaken by the verbal blast he provoked from Morton that he recorded it in writing for posterity. The gist of Morton's broadside was that 'the Prime Minister hated Dalton, hated Jebb [Gladwyn Jebb, Nelson's chief executive officer], hated me, hated the entire organisation [SOE] and everybody in it, and that . . . if he [Morton] was to be indicted on matters of this description he would . . . cease to help us . . .'.[13] Morton was right about Churchill's view of Dalton, but deliberately misleading about his view of SOE: he was simply conjuring up a hostile picture to bolster his own position as gatekeeper.

By 1943 such threats no longer carried weight and Morton had become much less important to Churchill. With Dalton out of the way and his friend Lord Selborne running SOE, he no longer needed Morton as a shield, while on the secret intelligence and codebreaking side Sir Stewart Menzies, with his daily batch of Ultra, had largely replaced his former friend as principal trusted adviser. Loyalty to the past kept Morton in place, but he was now increasingly on the shelf. 'Little by little,' recorded John Colville, 'he sank into the background.'[14]

After the years of loyalty, often at considerable risk to his career as he leaked intelligence material to his friend, the unmarried

Morton, for whom Chartwell had become a second home, can only have experienced the rejection deeply, one made all the more obvious when he was not included in the party travelling to Quebec. In his outburst to Wilkinson he was almost certainly projecting sentiments about his own relationship with Churchill and his jealousy at Roosevelt's obvious attraction and influence over the Prime Minister.

His remarks certainly can't be taken literally. Morton himself, in calmer post-war mood, said that Churchill was 'psychologically completely male and a textbook example of Freudian maleness in his relations with his parents, children, wife and friends'.[15] Modern parlance would replace the word 'homosexual' with 'homoerotic', or possibly 'homosocial'. Churchill moved and worked in a predominantly male world, imbibing its values, sharing its ethos, and admiring its exemplars such as the dashing young heroes produced by war. Indeed, among the huge personal retinue that travelled with him to Quebec were at least two such men: Orde Wingate, hero of behind-the-lines operations in Burma, and Commander Guy Gibson, leader of the famous Royal Air Force dambuster raids on the Ruhr. Here, Churchill himself was not above projection. 'I knew,' he later wrote, explaining their inclusion, 'how much President Roosevelt liked meeting young, heroic figures.'[16]

Was Morton merely venting personal jealousy when he told Wilkinson that Churchill always gave in to Roosevelt? Or was it more considered and calculating? Perhaps he was giving Wilkinson a warning not to be seduced by Americans – the SIS officer's attraction to MacArthur was all too transparent, and he had leaped at the chance to go to Washington rather than India or Turkey. Was he trying to arm Wilkinson against the Prime Minister himself, in the event that once again he was summoned to brief him? Did he hope that Wilkinson might leak the conversation to Menzies in an effort to ingratiate himself with the SIS chief? Or was he, perhaps, testing Wilkinson's own feelings about Churchill by being deliberately provocative – a tactic that signally failed when Wilkinson adeptly changed the topic back to MacArthur?

In the end, it seems that the simplest explanation is the likeliest. Morton was simply exploding in frustration and using Wilkinson, an SIS man he knew he could trust to keep it secret, as a safety valve. He was, after all, a person who found it notoriously difficult, in John Colville's words, 'to control the flow of his conversation'.[17]

If his outburst also reflected Morton's true views on Churchill and Roosevelt, then he was simply wrong. Only through a profound misunderstanding of Roosevelt could Morton believe that Churchill's imperial views were 'compatible' with those of Roosevelt. Equally misguided was – and still is – the opinion that Churchill gave everything to Roosevelt he wanted. Barely a month after he returned from Quebec he fundamentally challenged his agreements with the President by directing his chiefs of staff to explore, 'in a most secret manner,' whether the commitment about Operation Overlord could be modified to include 'a forward policy in the Balkans'.

What inspired this re-think was growing resistance there to German rule, intelligence reports about partisan activity, and a personal meeting with the principal special operations liaison officer in Greece, Brigadier Eddie Myers. 'God knows where this may lead us with the Americans,' noted Brooke wearily in his diary. They were all soon to find out.[18]

The Balkan guerrillas, boosted by Italy's surrender, were indeed causing problems for the Germans. Since late 1942, when Myers had successfully led a group of partisans to blow up the Gorgopotamos viaduct in Greece, money, arms and agents had been dropped on an increasing scale. Myers arrived at Chequers to report on events soon after Churchill got back from Quebec. Armed with graphic photographs of Italians surrendering and bridges destroyed, Myers had the pleasure of watching as the Prime Minister 'chuckled delightedly' at his tale.[19]

He was likewise entranced by secret operations in Yugoslavia. Only hours after he had left Washington the previous May, one of his former research assistants, the Oxford don William Deakin, parachuted into Yugoslavia as a member of Britain's first official mission to General Tito, leader of the Communist partisans, thus inaugurating a controversial policy that culminated several months later in Britain's abandonment of Tito's rival, the royalist General Mihailovic.[20] Vastly increased supplies to the partisans, and the requisite aircraft, had, Churchill insisted, 'priority even over the bombing of Germany'. On the eve of the Sicily landings he ordered Menzies to provide a special report based on Ultra intelligence, 'showing the heavy fighting and great disorder going on in those regions and assembling also the intelligence about the number of Partisans &c., and of Axis troops involved or contained'. He then sent it to General Alexander in Italy, exhorting him that 'great prizes lie in the Balkan direction'.

Early in July he took a drastic step to increase the standing of the mission with Tito. To the shock and dismay of SOE and the Foreign Office he appointed Fitzroy Maclean as his special emissary to the guerrilla leader. 'What we want,' he told Eden, 'is a daring ambassador–leader with these hardy and hunted guerrillas.'

No better evidence of Churchill's romantic passion for the guerrillas and his belief in behind-the-lines special operations can be found than in his choice of Maclean. A warrior-diplomat of impeccable social pedigree, he had made his name in hit-and-run exploits against the Germans in North Africa, befriended Randolph, Churchill's unruly son, and made a strong impact on Churchill at an embassy dinner in Cairo in August 1942. 'No gentler pirate ever cut a throat or robbed a ship,' wrote Churchill of Maclean, quoting from Byron. Behind Maclean's charismatic charm lay determined ambition.[21]

Summoned to Chequers in July, the 32-year-old Maclean suffered the traditional ritual of staying up late while Churchill watched films and cartoons. Towards midnight a message was brought to Churchill. 'As the squawking of Donald Duck and the baying of Pluto died away,' recalled Maclean, Churchill rose to his feet to announce the dramatic news of the resignation of Mussolini. 'This,' he told Maclean, 'makes your job even more important than ever. The German position in Italy is crumbling. We must now put all the pressure we can on the other side of the Adriatic.' Maclean asked about the political risks of supporting the Communist partisans. His task, Churchill replied, 'was simply to help find out who was killing the most Germans and suggest means by which we could help them kill more'. Two days before Churchill returned from Quebec, Maclean, now a Brigadier and with a mission that included an American major, parachuted into the Yugoslav blackness. 'I fancied myself,' he wrote later, 'as a latter-day Lawrence [of Arabia], blowing up trains and bridges.'[22]

Encoded in all this Lawrentian British swashbuckling, and despite Churchill's claim that he was only interested in killing Germans, was a message to Roosevelt: hands off the Balkans. In Greece Churchill was determined on the post-war return of the monarchy, which he saw as a bulwark against the Communists, who controlled Eam/Elas, the largest of the guerrilla factions – even though this ran counter to the feelings of many Greek expatriates in the United States and the anti-monarchical sentiments of the President himself. In Yugoslavia Churchill's enthusiasm for Tito's Communist partisans outweighed his commitment to the young King Peter, yet here, too, he was determined that Britain should play team captain in Anglo-American intelligence efforts. Fitzroy Maclean might have had an American in his group, but he was under strict instructions to keep him in his place and had communications links kept secret from American eyes.

Donovan chafed bitterly at all this. He had attended the Quebec Conference, grasped the Balkan implications of the Italian surrender, and immediately rushed to Cairo to make hay for OSS. But in this hub of Empire he encountered a wall of British resistance. Frustrated, he appealed to the President. He caught him at a vulnerable moment. He, like Churchill, was fired by prospects of Balkan adventures. 'Jerusalem!' exclaimed Henry Stimson, sick with fear that Churchill's further efforts to delay Overlord would infect the President. '[Roosevelt] is wobbling round again making remarks about the Balkans.' After confronting the President, he extracted a promise that there would be no more such talk until the Russians had advanced so far that American troops could fight side by side with them. 'Remember, no more Balkans,' warned Stimson as he left the White House.[23]

Roosevelt stuck to the Stimson line, but only for regular American forces. Special operations and intelligence were a different matter. In late October 1943 he fired off an urgent message to Churchill proposing Donovan as intelligence supreme in the Balkans, the only man who had any chance of success in uniting the quarrelling partisans. 'I do not believe he can do any harm,' he told Churchill, 'and he might do much good.' Churchill's reply was promptly dismissive and totally predictable. 'I have great admiration for Donovan,' he cabled back, 'but I do not see any centre in the Balkans from which he could grip the situation.'[24]

Roosevelt backed off. Donovan, characteristically, was undeterred. Within weeks he declared that OSS would no longer co-operate with Fitzroy Maclean and would send its own independent missions to both Communist and non-Communist partisans. His subsequent incursions into Balkan resistance laid the seeds of Anglo-American intelligence disputes until the end of the war. Their flavour was captured by an OSS officer who reported after a meeting with Tito's partisans: 'Our cousins [i.e. the British] arranged the meeting, which was held in their shop, but they tactfully withdrew, probably to adjust the microphones in the next room.'

Allied intelligence discord was even stronger in Asia. Here, Gerald Wilkinson's mission vividly demonstrates how a significant subtext consisted of spying on Britain's friends. Arriving in Washington in September, just as Churchill was waxing enthusiastic to Congress about an Anglo-American future, he did the rounds of OSS and the Pentagon exploring the state of American intelligence about China, Japan and the Philippines, and discussing with Stephenson British needs for better Far Eastern intelligence. Late in October he flew back to London to report his findings to Menzies. 'Satisfactory talk,' he noted. '[He] is as quick and helpful as ever.' Then, early in November, he had a revealing meeting with R. Barrington-Ward, the influential editor of *The Times*.

The reason for his visit was highly sensitive. The paper's Far Eastern expert was Ian Morrison, a gifted journalist in his early thirties who had been born in Peking, worked in Japan, and witnessed the British débâcle in south-east Asia. 'If the British ran the rest of their empire as they had run things recently in Singapore,' he argued in *This War Against Japan*, published in 1943, 'then they did not deserve to have an empire at all.' By now he was a toughened war correspondent in New Guinea, living alongside Australian troops, suffering from recurrent malaria, and something of a legend. The American writer Emily Hahn, who had met him in Hong Kong in 1940, described him as 'awfully mysterious and thrilled about his work'. This, and his habit of lying palpably about his job, convinced her that he was a spy. He did, indeed, work for the Far Eastern Bureau, a Singapore-based British propaganda agency, until it was driven out by the Japanese. Only that morning, as Wilkinson paid his visit to Printing House Square, *The Times* had published a special article by Morrison on the behaviour of Australian troops in New Guinea.

This was particularly timely in the light of Wilkinson's visit. New Guinea was part of MacArthur's South-West Pacific Command, from which he had banned both OSS and British intelligence.[25] Wilkinson had his eye on Morrison for a very special mission. Approaching the subject cautiously, he explained to Barrington-Ward – who knew full well that his visitor worked for SIS – that while 'the main business' was espionage against the enemy, more information about conditions and results in certain Allied areas than was obtainable through official channels was necessary.

A particular problem, he explained, was MacArthur's command, which was replete with what he described as 'exaggerations and non-disclosure'. Mountbatten, especially, needed urgently to know more about what was going on there. Stressing that his approach was entirely unofficial and would be disowned if it leaked out, Wilkinson asked *The Times*'s editor if he could use Morrison to report weekly or monthly, or whenever he felt like it, to 'a friend' of Wilkinson's in Australia. Morrison would give the information to Wilkinson, who would then edit and mix it with intelligence from other sources and pass it on. The 'friend' Wilkinson had in mind was Roy Kendall, the SIS chief based in Brisbane.

Barrington-Ward, a close friend of Donovan's former boss in London, Whitney Shephardson, hardly hesitated. First making the ritual disclaimer, that as *The Times* editor he couldn't possibly agree officially to such an idea, he continued that if Morrison wanted to have dinner with Wilkinson and then made certain arrangements that involved him occasionally meeting Wilkinson's 'friend' in Australia, on a purely unofficial basis, then he had no objection. 'We can go ahead,' noted Wilkinson jubilantly afterwards. 'No further reference to *The Times* is necessary or desirable.'[26]

It remains obscure whether Morrison, who was later killed while covering the Korean War, was indeed approached or recruited by

Wilkinson. But what his meeting with Barrington-Ward reveals is that Churchill's 'spy' on MacArthur was still hard at work and that one of his many consumers was Field Marshal Mountbatten, head of South-East Asia Command. Here, as in the Balkans, American and British secret warriors were all too obviously allies at war in more ways than one.

18

'SAME BED,
DIFFERENT DREAMS'

'Don't think for a moment,' Roosevelt had told his son Elliott after Pearl Harbor, 'that Americans would be dying in the Pacific tonight, if it hadn't been for the shortsighted greed of the French and the British and the Dutch. Shall we allow them to do it all, all over again?'[1] The answer was obviously not. Elliott may have exaggerated his father's views, but he did not distort them. The President and Prime Minister shared no common vision of the future for Europe's overseas empires. They were fighting the same enemy, Japan, but that was all. Reluctant to quarrel openly and thus imperil their agreed priority of defeating Hitler, they postponed decisions. But on the ground, issues grew and festered. Nowhere was this more apparent than in south-east Asia and China, especially in the hothouse world of intelligence.

Not surprisingly, given the powerful post-war myth of Anglo-American harmony, neither Washington nor London have been anxious to expose the depths to which rivalry often sank. The British in particular, for whom the 'special relationship' with the United States has become a central tenet of post-war foreign policy, have been protective of a rosy-coloured image of affairs. The five hefty volumes of the official history of British intelligence in the Second World War studiously avoid Asia altogether, while the official historian of SOE in the Far East avoids any reference at all to what is amply documented in the files about serious Anglo-American policy clashes. Here, a conspiracy of amnesia has ruled since 1945.[2]

Even as Churchill and Roosevelt agreed over hot dogs at Hyde Park to appoint Mountbatten as supreme commander of SEAC, in London Donovan was wrapping up his deal with Gubbins over special operations in Asia that abolished strict spheres of influence and made it an open playing field. In Mountbatten Churchill invested hopes of injecting energy into the south-east Asian fighting. But military action had political consequences, especially when working with resistance groups commanded by potential post-war leaders, and he was determined to ensure that Britain's longer-term imperial interests in Malaya and Singapore were neither forgotten nor fell victim to Roosevelt's vision of the post-war world. The South-East Asia Command, in the words of one observer, was essentially a damage-limitation exercise inflicted by the American military presence.[3]

Mountbatten was an enthusiast for special operations. On the eve of his departure for Asia he had intervened forcefully to support SOE in one of its many near-fatal bureaucratic battles in Whitehall. He was thus happy to have it establish a powerful presence in New Delhi – and later at Kandy, Ceylon (now Sri Lanka) to which he moved his advance headquarters in 1944 – in order to plan behind-the-lines missions into such places as Malaya, Thailand and Sumatra.

A 'political' general if ever there was one, this patrician cousin to King George VI was acutely attuned to Churchill's friendship with the American President. Indeed, he and Roosevelt had a special friendly relationship all of their own. As head of Combined Operations, he once sent Roosevelt a cap badge designed for use by both the US Rangers and British Commandos in North Africa. It showed an anchor for the navy, a tommy gun for the army, and an American eagle (astutely replacing the previous albatross) for the air force. 'Dear Dickie,' replied Roosevelt, 'it is a perfect symbol for our joint operations.'[4]

Such White House amiability accompanied Mountbatten to his new post. 'Dear Dickie,' wrote Roosevelt again after Mountbatten had visited China to smooth over relations between the Chinese nationalist leader Chiang Kai-shek and the American commander of the China–Burma–India theatre, the acerbic Joseph Stilwell, 'I am really thrilled . . . that for the first time in two years I have confidence in the personality problems in the China and Burma fields – and you are largely responsible . . . Take care of yourself and keep up the good work.'[5]

So when Bill Donovan flew into New Delhi to talk business, Mountbatten was all smiles. He and the American intelligence chief had recently had an extraordinary encounter at Quebec. When Mountbatten returned to his quarters after winning Roosevelt's approval for his appointment he began to jot down all the things he would have to do. Before he'd finished, there was a knock at the door. It was Donovan. 'Let me be the first to congratulate you on being appointed Supreme Allied Commander South-East Asia,' he said. Mountbatten was appalled. It was still top secret. 'I don't know what you're talking about,' he replied. 'You can't fool me,' answered Donovan, 'I've got spies everywhere.' Recognising defeat, Mountbatten asked, 'Well, supposing you're right, why do you come and worry me about it?' Quick as a flash Donovan replied, 'Because I want your permission to operate in south-east Asia.' 'Are you any good?' asked Mountbatten. 'You bet,' came the response. 'Then I'll test you,' said Mountbatten – and asked Donovan to get him the two best seats for *Oklahoma!* a few days later. 'No seats, no operations in southeast Asia.' Donovan obliged, duly impressed by Mountbatten's command. 'If that man had been born Mr Mountbatten,' he remarked, 'he might be the next Prime Minister of England.'[6]

This Anglo-American *bonhomie* quickly faded. Mountbatten soon decided that Donovan's empire was a mystery and tight control should be the order of the day. To achieve it he created a special joint clandestine division ('P' for priorities) with a British chief and American deputy. Rivalry and suspicion quickly developed. In charge of OSS operations was Dick Heppner, remembered warily by the British as William Phillips' assistant in India. He quickly realised what he was up against.

British intelligence throughout the region was to all intents and purposes run by SOE, known here as 'Force 136'. Apart from special operations, it also dominated secret intelligence. Its rival, the

Secret Intelligence Service, had been weak even before the war. With only two officers, one in Shanghai and the other in Hong Kong (known even to taxi drivers as 'the British secret service man'), and no permanent representatives at all in south-east Asia, it was the Cinderella branch of a service already impoverished and under-resourced.[7] Japanese victories administered a virtual death blow. Hiding behind the title 'Inter-Services Liaison Department', it had a presence, but a feeble and often faltering one. Most of any energy it possessed went to providing operational intelligence for the campaign in Burma.

By contrast SOE was new and dynamic. Its head was Colin Mackenzie, an able, energetic and inventive Scot with powerful commercial expertise in the region as a director of J. & P. Coats, a Glasgow textile company, and a personal friend of the Viceroy of India, Lord Linlithgow. At least twice a week he and Mountbatten would talk over missions. 'He wanted to know exactly what we were doing, when and how, and would naturally put forward suggestions,' recalled Mackenzie.[8] Backing him up were Baker Street heavyweights such as George Taylor, an Australian businessman frequently described as ruthless, and John Keswick, a member of the legendary 'taipan' family that ran Jardine Matheson, the huge Shanghai-based British trading company.

They, too, were keenly sensitive to the region's importance for British commerce and the dangers from America competition. Beneath them marched a small army of experts drawn from the colonial ranks – what one expert has described as 'Empire trade in khaki'.[9] Even the weaker SIS fielded similar players – its first overall Director of Far Eastern affairs was Godfrey Denham, a director and later chairman of Anglo-Dutch Plantations Ltd, a rubber concern in Java. Experienced and hard-headed, they were determined to save the region for British post-war influence.

Day to day they were friendly enough to their American cousins, and agents on the ground were usually oblivious of tensions. Secret operations brought out the best in the American and British soldiers, airmen and agents who took part, and the record demonstrates striking success for many. It was backstage manoeuvring, and the operations that did *not* take place, that revealed conflict and caused problems. Mackenzie's team successfully blocked OSS operations into Malaya, Thailand, and, in alliance with the Dutch, Indonesia. Sir Andrew Gilchrist, later British ambassador to Indonesia, worked for SOE's Siam section (as it was called). 'For all practical purposes,' he said of Section P, it 'confined itself to ensuring that since the rival firms were not to co-operate, their field operations should be kept reasonably well apart.'[10]

It took only a few weeks at Mountbatten's headquarters for Dick Heppner to vent his frustration to Donovan. 'In all our dealings with SEAC,' he protested, 'we have been faced with an invariably hostile attitude on the part of SOE, whose chief, Mr Mackenzie, is a thoroughly unscrupulous behind-the-scenes manipulator.'[11] It was scarce wonder that Americans soon came to joke that SEAC stood for 'Save England's Asiatic Colonies', or that a caustic American song ran: 'Oh, we're planning combined operations / How we treasure combined operations / The Limeys make policy / Yanks fight for the Japs / And one gets its Empire, and one takes the rap.'

Here, as elsewhere, sensitive files were classified either 'Control' or 'Guard' meaning either not for British or American eyes, respectively.[12] Similar sentiments surfaced in the neighbouring China–Burma–India Command. 'Why should American boys die to re-possess colonies for the British and their French and Dutch allies?' asked John Paton Davies, Stilwell's political adviser. 'Reconquest of Empire is the paramount task in British eyes. The raising of the Union Jack over Singapore is more important to the British than any victory parade through Tokyo.' This was not American paranoia. At the second Quebec summit in September 1944 Churchill declared that the recapture of Singapore was the 'supreme British objective in the whole of the Indian and Far Eastern theatres'.[13]

Critical assessments of British policy formed an important part of American intelligence work, as testified early in 1945 by Heppner's successor. His activities, he told Donovan, 'are not only important in defeating the Japs but [as a] listening post for American interests in Asia. This demands close and cordial relations with our allies, especially when we operate in their sphere of interest.' By operating under Mountbatten, he added, OSS 'could provide information as to the activities of British intelligence agencies'.[14]

Britain was not the only target of Roosevelt's concern. Late in November 1944 he voiced the suspicion about a combined European effort to recover their colonies in the region. Patrick Hurley, his ambassador to China, approached his British opposite number to see if it was true, only to encounter a complete denial that anything of the sort was going on or that Britain, as rumoured, had any territorial claims against Thailand. Hurley was deceived. While no *concerted* European plan existed, the French, Dutch and British all expected to regain their empires, and Churchill himself nourished secret designs on the Kra Isthmus in southern Thailand.[15]

Thailand (which Churchill archaically insisted on calling 'Siam') provides a graphic example of Allied discord. As the only pre-war independent state in south-east Asia, it was at war with Britain but regarded by the United States as an enemy-occupied country under a puppet Japanese government. Guaranteeing Thailand's post-war independence and territorial integrity, the Americans heartily embraced the Free Thai movement, a group that developed in opposition to its dictator, Field Marshal Pibul Songgram, the nationalist who in 1939 officially changed the country's name to Thailand (*thai* meaning 'free').

Britain, by contrast, had different plans, arguing that restoration of independence would depend on meeting certain conditions, and harbouring territorial designs on the south of the country. The heads of both the special operations and secret intelligence sections were men with pre-war commercial interests and colonial outlooks on the country and, while prepared to work with the Free Thais, kept strictly separate from the OSS. In turn, the Americans smuggled agents into the country behind British backs. Here, Donovan kept Roosevelt well informed. 'We now have a channel of entry into Thailand through Indo-China,' he reported in December 1944, adding, 'Our British colleagues are not aware of this mission . . .'[16]

Burma saw similar discord. Joint operations and co-operation fighting the Japanese could not disguise radically different political goals. As the base for the longest campaign of any waged by the

British Army in the Second World War, Burma, a British colony providing the eastern gateway to India, was an issue on which Churchill felt strongly. He was perfectly happy to see behind-the-lines operations using hill tribes such as the Karens and the Kachins, groups long opposed to central Burmese control. But when Force 136 began to supply arms and ammunition to the Burma National Army, the country's largest resistance movement, he baulked. Aung San, its leader, was a left-wing nationalist working for independence from Britain, and early in the war he worked with the Japanese against the British. 'Surely we should not boost these people,' argued Anthony Eden. 'I cordially agree,' replied Churchill.[17] The dispute led him to quarrel bitterly with Sir Reginald Dorman Smith, the Governor-Designate of Burma, who thought a promise of eventual independence would be helpful. Churchill accused him of wanting to break up the British Empire and added that 'in [his] opinion what the Burmese and other orientals needed was not independence but the lash'.

This, at least, was how it was reported in Washington by a Thai diplomat who had been sent by OSS on an intelligence-gathering mission to south-east Asia to learn more about post-war British objectives. His report on Dorman Smith's clash with Churchill was based on an interview he'd had with the Governor-Designate himself in Simla, India.[18] It was hardly surprising that Washington ordered its officials throughout the region to ensure that American political warfare was kept strictly separate from British efforts, and that when it came to clandestine war 'OSS in Burma . . . should not in any circumstances become associated in Burmese minds with SOE'.[19]

Even more explosive was French Indo-China, the heartland of France's Asian empire, consisting of Cambodia, Laos and Vietnam. Rich in food and raw materials such as rice and rubber, it had been occupied by the Japanese even before Pearl Harbor while remaining under French administration and a Governor-General loyal to Vichy. De Gaulle and the Free French were determined to win it back for France, and worked hard to stimulate resistance to the Japanese. But among the local (non-French) population the most effective resistance was the Viet Minh, led by the Communist Ho Chi Minh.

Roosevelt had given way to Churchill over India. But on Indo-China it was Roosevelt who forced Churchill to back off. Here, the President's personal dislike for De Gaulle fused with a profound loathing for French colonialism to veto any Free French involvement in the guerrilla war against the Japanese that might open the door to a return of French colonial rule. 'After a hundred years of French rule in Indo-China,' he once told Stalin, 'the inhabitants are worse off than before.'[20] What he wanted was an international trusteeship leading to independence. Thus he vetoed any moves to strengthen Gaullist hands in Asia, and especially the despatch of a Free French mission to Mountbatten's headquarters or the use of a *corps léger*, a commando-style unit of five hundred men – both moves designed to provide the nucleus of a future operational headquarters for Free French sabotage and guerrilla war behind Japanese lines.

SOE fought hard against Roosevelt's line, but Churchill refused to intervene even when an exasperated Selborne told him bluntly that he was standing in the way of his operations in Indo-China. Why not let the French mission go without telling the Americans? he asked. The Foreign Office also resisted in vain. 'Do not raise this before the presidential election, the war will go on a long time,' Churchill warned in March 1944.[21] This exasperated Eden, who prophesied that if the French were officially frozen out they would simply find another way to make their mark.

Again Churchill refused to intervene. One reason was his own dislike of De Gaulle, but more important were his relations with Roosevelt, who had been more outspoken to him on the evils of French colonialism in Indo-China than on any other subject. It was obvious that Roosevelt's feelings about Indo-China were as visceral and emotional as his own about India, and he was determined to avoid a head-on collision. 'It is hard enough to get on in South-East Asia Command when we have virtually only the Americans to deal with,' he told Eden just days before D-Day in Europe. 'The more the French can get their finger in the pie the more trouble they will be . . . do you really want to go and stir all this up at such a time as this?'[22] He was to maintain his veto on special operations in Indo-China until late in 1944.

So was Roosevelt. Nothing, he ordered in October that year,

should be done in regard to resistance groups or in any other way in relation to Indo-China. By this, he was referring to French-inspired resistance only, because from southern China OSS was already supporting Ho Chi Minh's Viet Minh, a controversial decision that returned to haunt Americans during the Vietnam War. Indeed, local American commanders had been ignoring the President's veto by using the French to gain urgent tactical intelligence for the fight against Japan. Such, for example, was the case with the so-called 'GBT Group', which provided Major-General Claire Chennault's 14th Air Force with outstanding intelligence about Indo-China from sources inside the French colonial regime. None of this rubbed off on Roosevelt. On New Year's Day 1945, he firmly reiterated his stand. 'I do not want to get mixed up in any military effort toward the liberation of Indo-China,' he repeated. 'I made this very clear to Mr Churchill.'[23]

Nor did the President and Prime Minister share dreams about China. Roosevelt, like many Americans, nourished an optimistic view of China's prospects, seeing in Chiang Kai-shek a champion of the 'New Asia', a doughty fighter against Japan, and a Chinese George Washington who would be one of the post-war world's great statesmen – 'the undisputed leader of four hundred million people'. By contrast, Churchill was sceptical. When he met the Generalissimo in Cairo he was impressed by his personality but unmoved by his promise. Chiang's government, based at Chungking in the interior, struggled to maintain its authority over a sprawling land mass marked by Japanese occupation, squabbling warlords and a Communist government-in-embryo in north central China. 'Very over-rated,' was his blunt view of Chiang, denouncing the notion of China as a great power as 'an absolute farce'. While he wouldn't oppose Roosevelt on the issue, he said, he would adopt a 'perfectly negative line'.[24]

So far as Allied commands went, China fell firmly into the American sphere, first under Stilwell and then under his successor, General Albert Wedemeyer. This did not mean that Churchill washed his hands of China, even though by 1944 it was clear that Chiang's regime was weak, corrupt and on the edge of civil war. Britain traditionally had strong commercial interests there and he hoped to reassert them. Above all, he was determined that Hong

Kong should return to British rule. In both areas intelligence agencies had an important role to play. In each, the American and British were rivals as well as allies.

The Chinese intelligence scene was dominated by General Tai Li, Chiang's amiably ruthless director of the 'Bureau of Investigation and Statistics', a combined secret police and intelligence agency penetrating every aspect of Chinese life. Totally loyal to Chiang, Tai Li's brutal reputation earned him the title of 'the Chinese Heinrich Himmler'. Little could be done without him, as Donovan was quickly to learn.

His first attempt at initiating sabotage and intelligence, as he explained it to Roosevelt soon after Pearl Harbor, was to use Koreans in exile against both Japan itself and Japanese-occupied China. This was his first mistake, for the Koreans were hardly more popular in China than the Japanese. His second emerged when he told the President that he had made arrangements with the British for a 'tie-up' with Esson Gale, an American university professor he'd charged with the mission. Gale himself did not help by roaming about Chungking passing out cards that described him as an agent for the 'American Intelligence Office', but the real problem was his known and all-too-obvious links with British contacts such as John Keswick, who headed the SOE-run China Commando Group in Chungking training saboteurs and guerrillas for action behind Japanese lines.

This 'old China hand' and well-known symbol of British colonial rule was anathema to Tai Li. Even worse, his assistant was Petro Pavloski, a Russian who had long lived in China. Apparently unknown to Keswick, but not to Tai Li, Pavloski was also a Comintern agent. To Chiang's intelligence chief, all seemed clear: the British, in league with the Americans, were attempting to link up with the Communists. In April 1942, under pressure from Tai Li, Chiang Kai-shek had Keswick expelled and the China Commando Group dissolved. Keswick's decision to take Pavloski with him to his next post, in Washington, only deepened Tai Li's suspicion. As recently released OSS and Chinese files reveal, he was equally hostile to Donovan's idea of mobilising Europeans from among the large exile community in Shanghai, and decided that Donovan was simply trying to carry out what Keswick had failed to do.[25]

Finally, Donovan had to yield to Tai Li's demand for an end to independent American intelligence efforts. Instead, Roosevelt approved a pact making Tai Li head of a joint OSS–Chinese secret service known as the Sino-American Co-operative Organisation, or SACO. In reality there was nothing joint about it. Tai Li's deputy, Captain Milton ('Mary') Miles, of the US Navy, was totally in thrall to Tai Li and resisted all direction from Washington. SACO turned out to be a straitjacket for American intelligence in China – 'a snare', it has been said, 'that the wily Tai Li had used to bind the Americans hand and foot'.[26]

Donovan soon realised his mistake. In December 1943, after obtaining the President's approval for intelligence operations independent of the Chinese, he flew to Chungking, fired Miles, and denounced Tai Li as a mediocre policeman with medieval ideas of intelligence work. 'General,' he said bluntly, 'I want you to know that I am going to send my men into China whether you like it or not. I know that you can have them murdered one by one, but I want you to know that will not deter me.'[27]

Soon after, a separate OSS contingent based at the Kunming headquarters of Chennault's 14th Air Force made contact with the Chinese Communists led by Mao Tse-tung and Chou En-lai in Yenan, in the north of the country. They proved to be a far more superior source on the Japanese than the nationalists.

By late 1944 American intelligence at Kunming was under the command of Dick Heppner, Donovan's former head at Mountbatten's headquarters, with help from an influx of battle-trained American intelligence officers from recently liberated European countries. They quickly put their collective finger on the dismal truths about Chiang's regime – its corruption, its deals with the warlords, and its preference for fighting the Communists over the Japanese. All too often the trails of suspected Japanese agents led to the highest circles in Chungking and had to be abandoned. Inevitably, Tai Li launched a counter-offensive to discredit and neutralise American intelligence and its 'pro-Communist' leanings. Finally, exasperated by the in-fighting, Wedemeyer insisted on imposing order on the Allied secret services in China. After securing Roosevelt's support, Donovan flew out to Chungking to talk it all over.

It was not just the Tai Li/OSS civil war that was at stake, however. The British had also been dabbling in Chinese waters.

The name of John Keswick dominates any discussion of Britain's
wartime intelligence dealings in China. With a finger in every
Chinese pie, he was at the centre of SOE Far Eastern affairs in
London, Chungking and Washington, as well as at SEAC headquarters, where Mountbatten trusted his views on China over that
of his official Foreign Office adviser.

Keswick also had a personal line to Churchill through the Boer
War veteran and First World War VC, General Adrian Carton de
Wiart, the Prime Minister's personal liaison officer with Chiang
Kai-shek. Churchill regarded De Wiart as an old and valued friend
whose judgement he trusted. In turn, the general leaned heavily on
Keswick for advice. 'He was very knowledgeable,' he said later,
'[and] seemed to have a different attitude from that of the others
who knew China intimately, for they all appeared to shrug their
shoulders, content to explain that "East is East and West is
West".'28

Gerald Wilkinson, briefing himself for his mission to the United
States in the summer of 1943, dropped into SOE's Baker Street
headquarters in London and also found Keswick an invaluable
source on the Chinese intelligence scene. Listing five separate
Chinese secret agencies, Keswick placed Tai Li at the top, describing him as 'uncultured, unscrupulous, cunning and capable [and]
would never hesitate to bump off anybody and is a real blower-
upper'. He was also, added Keswick with feeling, anti-foreigner in
general and anti-British in particular. As for British representation
in China, Keswick gave a bleak view of the SIS representation at
Chungking, where relations with some of Tai Li's staff were good
but ineffective, and suggested that Baker Street's man there could
do a far better job – he had established a fruitful alliance with
Wang Ping-shen, head of another of Chiang's intelligence agencies.

But it was Keswick's revelations about the Americans that most
interested Wilkinson. For apart from OSS, they had another string
to their bow – one that was, he emphasised, most secret, and so far
completely unknown to the Chinese: namely a businessman called
Cornelius V. Starr, pre-war head of a successful insurance

company in Shanghai, the American International Underwriters, and owner of the *Shanghai Evening Post* and *Mercury*. Starr's intelligence, gleaned from his extensive commercial connections throughout China, went straight to Donovan via Stilwell's army communications channels. Keswick was particularly well placed to know this, because he had been best friend to Starr and his British-born wife in pre-war Shanghai. Based in New York, Starr had then regarded himself as Donovan's 'honorary mentor' on China and had worked out an ambitious intelligence plan using his insurance and newspapers as cover. More recently, however, especially after Donovan's deal with Tai Li, he'd lost his enthusiasm for the Americans and was beginning to turn back to Keswick and the British.[29]

Wilkinson immediately began to toy with the idea of turning Starr from an American into a British intelligence asset, thus boosting SIS's Chinese intelligence output and gaining credibility with London. Shortly after arriving in Washington he took the train to Brewster, Starr's American home in the wooded hills of upper New York state, where Starr talked fully and frankly about his work. Three-quarters of his time, he said, was going on intelligence efforts to help the Americans, but the British might be able to help with cipher communications. More meetings followed, and by the end of the year Wilkinson was actively recruiting one of Starr's principal agents for work with SIS.[30]

Wilkinson was also behind another Chinese intelligence project with undercurrents of rivalry with the Americans. Its major player was Konrad Hsu, an SIS agent in the United States with a legendary passion for eating steamed clams. Not surprisingly shellfish and seafood inspired the codename of the project – 'Oyster' – with Hsu naturally being 'Clam'. With Hsu using family and business connections in China, and the Canadian government providing a communications network to throw Tai Li and the Japanese off the scent, the project slowly got under way.

At his first meeting with Hsu, a lunch at New York's St Regis Hotel shortly before Christmas 1943, Wilkinson noted that he 'gave repeated evidence of [a] pro-British and anti-American attitude' and spoke favourably of British accomplishments in India. Although wary that Hsu might be doing this deliberately to court his favour, Wilkinson decided he was worth pursuing. After an ebullient and liquid dinner at a Chinese restaurant in Manhattan, Hsu's knees finally buckled after drinking too many ryes at a gulp and Wilkinson had to take him home. 'He is friendly and funny when tight,' he noted, 'and is rather a good Chinese.' In the end, however, Wilkinson had to fall back on Donovan's largesse to finance the operation, which he kept largely separate and secret from his other ventures into China.

SIS did better in China than elsewhere in Asia, and in particular delivered high-quality political intelligence on negotiations between the Communists and Chiang Kai-shek held at Chungking early in 1945. The reason was simple, if startling. Chou En-lai, Mao Tse-tung's right-hand man, was personally keeping British intelligence informed.[31]

But finding 'good' Chinese was not always easy, as SOE found out. Despite Keswick's plaudits, it accomplished little before 1944, its main task being the recruitment of Chinese for sabotage and guerrilla work in Thailand, Burma and Malaya. Two major operations – to cripple the Hong Kong dockyards and make them unusable by the Japanese, and to land a sabotage party on the south China coast – came to nothing. The first, codenamed 'Nonchalant', was abandoned in early 1945. The second, 'Oblivion', ran into Wedemeyer's veto on any British operations in his sphere of control.

Mutual British–American suspicion lingered until the end. In the very month that Roosevelt died, Heppner told Donovan that he had uncovered incontrovertible evidence that the British were trying 'to penetrate, for counter-espionage purposes, OSS and American army and air force units'.[32] They certainly were, with Churchill's vociferous support, trying to accomplish yet another project to be kept secret from the Americans – the capture and liberation of Hong Kong.

The recovery of Hong Kong, jewel of Britain's Far Eastern empire, was vital to Churchill. But how could it best be guaranteed? In 1944 Force 136 concocted a plan for a Sino-British Resistance Group of some 30,000 guerrillas commanded by British officers who would help recapture the colony. But by this time Lord Selborne, the minister in charge of SOE in London, felt his resources were so stretched that he cared little whether it was involved or not. British intelligence chiefs cautioned that the plan would only win Wedemeyer's and Chiang's approval if they were kept in the dark about its ultimate objective. In the end, it was abandoned as unworkable.

Nonetheless, alternative ways existed of easing Britain's return to Hong Kong. SOE's main achievement in China was Operation Remorse, a huge black-market smuggling exercise to acquire Chinese currency – the biggest black market in history, run by a man, Walter Fletcher, whom even his Baker Street masters described as 'a thug with good commercial contacts'.[33] To help protect it from Tai Li's predations, the 'Chinese Himmler' was guaranteed a fifteenth of its profits. These were enormous, and helped fund many of Britain's secret operations. 'Remorse' was at first kept secret from the Americans, not least because some of the proceeds went to bribe warlords in southern China not to block the British return to Hong Kong – a sure sore spot with Roosevelt and Donovan. Indeed, at Yalta in February 1945 Roosevelt told Stalin that he hoped Hong Kong would revert to China and become an internationalised free port.

As for Donovan, he had by this time become anathema to Churchill. When yet another dispute over SOE's role in China blew up with the Americans, in the very week that Roosevelt died, Churchill angrily threw in the towel. 'On the whole,' he told Eden, 'I incline against another SOE–OSS duel, on ground too favourable for that dirty Donovan.'[34] In the end, Hong Kong returned to British rule when its Japanese occupiers formally surrendered following the atom bomb attacks on Hiroshima and Nagasaki. SOE returned also, on the backs of the British Army Aid Group, a rescue and intelligence behind-the-lines organisation that had operated successfully on the mainland provinces adjacent to Hong Kong. Its commander, Colonel Lindsay Ride, knew well where his loyalties, and rivals, lay. 'I was violently anti the major American 1945 policy in China,' he wrote after the war, 'which appeared to us to be China for the Americans . . . and to hell with everyone else.'[35] The British flag was to fly above the colony until 1997.

19

FRIENDS APART

After dark on Armistice Day 1943, Roosevelt drove from the White House to Quantico, Virginia, with Harry Hopkins, 'Pa' Watson, Admiral Leahy and a couple of other aides. The *Potomac* was waiting and from this, early next dawn, they boarded the battleship *Iowa* five miles offshore. Eleven days later, after a stopover to visit Eisenhower in North Africa, the President arrived in Cairo. Churchill was already there to greet him, having himself sailed from Britain in the Royal Navy battleship *Renown*.

The next day the Prime Minister bounded into Roosevelt's room to announce a desert visit to the Pyramids and the Sphinx. Enthused, the President seemed about to rise from his seat, but then sank back when he remembered his legs were powerless. 'We'll wait for you in the car,' Churchill said. Outside, his eyes bright with tears, he turned to his daughter Sarah and said simply, 'I love that man.' Three days later, on American Thanksgiving, Sarah danced with Elliott Roosevelt and Harry Hopkins' son, Robert. Churchill, determined to join in, had to make do with 'Pa' Watson. Roosevelt's contribution to the evening was to carve two huge turkeys for the twenty people at the table. Afterwards he offered a toast. 'Large families are usually more united than small ones,' he said, 'and so, this year, with the people of the United Kingdom in our family, we are a large family, and more united than ever before. I propose a toast to this unity, and may it long continue.' Churchill wrote later that he had never seen the President more cheerful. Yet the next twelve months were to witness some of the most acerbic exchanges of their entire relationship.[1]

Dancing with Watson notwithstanding, Churchill found the Cairo encounter frustrating. Roosevelt had invited along Chiang Kai-shek, whose slogan 'Asia for the Asians' the British Prime Minister found hardly congenial, and about whom he was far less sure than Roosevelt that he would even survive as leader of China. But Chiang and his wife dominated the political and social proceedings, including a multitude of photo-calls, and the Prime Minister had to confess forlornly to his wife that he had failed to get a grip on affairs.[2]

A far weightier figure cast its shadow at the Tehran Conference a few days later. Stalin, whether physically present or not, had already altered the dynamics of the Anglo–American relationship. Roosevelt, keen to build a personal rapport with him, sidestepped private talks with Churchill and at his own meeting with the Soviet leader joined happily in a colonial-bashing session that included his ritual denunciation of the French in Indo-China. As if further to emphasise the shift, he and his entourage moved from the American Legation into the Soviet Embassy after an assassination-plot scare that was adeptly exploited by the NKVD. If the Americans had not been bugged by listening devices before, they certainly were now.

Although Roosevelt was far from seeking the Soviets as a substitute for the British, Churchill felt his subordination keenly. After dinner on the first night he seemed depressed, and when asked what Roosevelt had said could only reply that Harry Hopkins had thought the President was inept and had given the wrong answers to a lot of questions.[3] So he insisted on hosting a 'Big Three' dinner on the night of his sixty-ninth birthday, 30 November. Yet the alcohol-induced conviviality of this and other events could not disguise the truth. 'Atmosphere most cordial but triangular problems difficult,' he reported to Clementine.[4]

Apart from a brief and unnecessary second meeting at Cairo immediately after Tehran, Churchill and Roosevelt were not to

meet again until the second Quebec Conference, codenamed
'Octagon', of September 1944. By then the basic contours of the
war had dramatically shifted. In June Allied forces stormed ashore
in Normandy, Rome was liberated, and American troops stood
poised to enter the Reich. In the east, the triumphant Red Army
had crossed the Romanian and Bulgarian borders and these two
satellite states of Hitler had surrendered. In the Pacific, Guam had
been recaptured, American forces were approaching the
Philippines, and at Pearl Harbor Roosevelt had met with
MacArthur and his other Pacific commanders to sharpen the thrust
against Japan.

These military victories brought their own discords. Still firmly
united in their determination to destroy Hitler and Nazism,
Roosevelt and Churchill disagreed passionately over how to do it.
'The honeymoon is over,' noted Harold Macmillan, Churchill's
political adviser in the Mediterranean. Churchill saw vistas opening up from Italy that Roosevelt dismissed as mere chimeras or
simply irrelevant. For the British Prime Minister, Italy led to the
Balkans and eastern Mediterranean, where British historical and
post-war interests lay exposed. To Roosevelt this was a diversion
from the central thrust against German forces in France.

Ironically, Ultra intelligence, which since the Brusa accords had
been a joint Anglo–American product of their combined codebreaking teams, only entrenched each leader in his own separate
position. Three weeks after D-Day Bletchley Park codebreakers
cracked a German message revealing that Hitler had ordered the
Apennines in Italy to be a 'final blocking line'. That Italy was
where the Nazi dictator felt most vulnerable confirmed Churchill
in his passionate conviction that the projected 'Anvil' landings in
the south of France, which meant removing five divisions from
General Alexander in Italy, were a profound mistake. Urgently, he
penned a plea to Roosevelt that no troops or landing craft should
be withdrawn from Italy and simultaneously ordered Stewart
Menzies to send a copy of the intercept through his own top-secret
channels to the White House.

But the President flatly rejected the idea, wanting no diversions
from Eisenhower's efforts in France. Churchill, incensed, ordered
an aircraft to fly him to Washington to confront his ally, and even

threatened to resign. Eventually he accepted that no amount of arguing would change Roosevelt's mind and instead told the President that his decision was 'the first major strategic and political error for which we have to be responsible'. If only they had been able to meet, he argued, they would have reached 'a happy agreement'. In the biggest strategic argument of the war between the two men, Roosevelt had won.[5]

Churchill also had to yield that August over the Warsaw Uprising. He pleaded for Allied planes to drop supplies to the city, which rose in revolt against the Germans as the Red Army neared, and then halted at, its gates. Stalin denounced the uprising's Home Army resistance leaders as 'power-seeking criminals' and declined permission for Allied planes to land and refuel behind Soviet lines. For fear of jeopardising longer-term military co-operation, such as the use of Soviet air bases for the bombing of Japan, Roosevelt refused to challenge Stalin or act without him.

To these differences were added contentious post-war commercial issues over oil and civil aviation – in both cases with the United States attempting to muscle in on British interests – not to mention their continuing differences over Asia. On top of all this loomed the spectre of British national bankruptcy. 'England is broke,' Churchill told Henry Morgenthau that summer in London. When the Secretary of the Treasury reported this to Roosevelt, the President quipped back: 'Very interesting . . . I will go over there and make a couple of talks and take over the British Empire.' It was the sort of joke that did not amuse Churchill.[6]

They finally got together in September, their sixth meeting since the summer of 1941 and their last important bilateral one. It was, Churchill told Clementine, the most necessary one he had made since the very beginning, with 'delicate and serious' matters to be handled between friends in careful and patient personal discussion. Around the globe, in western Europe, the Mediterranean and Asia, two-thirds of British forces were being 'misemployed' for American ends. Life, he confessed, was 'not very easy', and he hoped she would come with him to Canada – an invitation she accepted.[7]

On board the *Queen Mary* for the transatlantic crossing to Halifax he exuded pessimism. 'Old England was in for dark days ahead,' he moaned. 'Materially and financially the prospects were black.' As for the war, he totally rejected a euphoric assessment by his intelligence chiefs that Germany would collapse that winter, and had a major row with his advisers about it. Throughout the journey he insisted on what had recently become a favourite theme – the 'extreme importance on grounds of high policy of our having a stake in central and southern Europe and not allowing everything to pass into Soviet hands'. As for the Far East, the aim should be to engage the Japanese with maximum force while simultaneously regaining British territory – Singapore, he insisted, was Britain's supreme objective, the only prize that would restore Britain's prestige in the region. Significantly, he also confessed that as soon as operations against Germany were over he wanted to see British forces brought back under independent command.[8]

Roosevelt, too, was suffering bouts of depression. To the darkening shadows of approaching peace were added clear intimations of his own mortality. Since Tehran he had lost weight, the hollows under his eyes had darkened, and he suffered frequent headaches. In March, medical tests had revealed congestive heart failure, a diagnosis kept strictly secret from the public and not even revealed to the patient. Yet he suspected enough to be worried. That summer he asked his daughter Anna, now his constant companion, to invite his mistress of thirty years before, Lucy Mercer, to dinners at the White House when Eleanor was away. The affair had almost destroyed his marriage and he had promised never to see her again. Yet he had, secretly, from time to time since the war began, and he glowed in her presence. Now a widow herself, Lucy spent more and more time with him over the last few months of his life – a reminder of his happy youth as his future visibly and rapidly drained away. A personal comfort, she also listened in on the phone to his transatlantic calls to Churchill.[9]

Yet political mortality hardly bothered him, and he had decided to run again for the presidency in the November elections. The decision came as a relief to Churchill after the earlier scares about a challenge from MacArthur. Still, all the predictions as the two men travelled to Quebec were for a close race. The press, picking up clues, made an issue of Roosevelt's health. 'Let's not be squeamish,' declared the *New York Sun*. 'Six Presidents have died in office.'[10]

Perhaps relieved that his ally had not grown horns during the nine months since they last met, Churchill was delighted to see him waiting in Quebec, and he cabled the War Cabinet that the conference had opened 'with a blaze of friendship'. Certainly, events had a family feel about them. Eleanor had accompanied her husband, and Sir Hastings Ismay, Churchill's personal chief of staff, described the scene as 'more like the reunion of a happy family starting on a holiday than the gathering of sedate Allied war leaders for an important conference'.

But Eleanor sniffed, not for the first time, that Churchill had something 'boyish' about him that explained his success as a war leader, while the Prime Minister in turn ribbed her ceaselessly about the old sore point between them, Spain. Clementine, overwhelmed by social engagements, succumbed one day to 'a filthy temper'. For some enigmatic reason of his own Roosevelt one night selected a film on Woodrow Wilson that followed in detail the First World War President's descent into illness, rejection and death. Churchill abruptly walked out halfway through. Worried about his ally's health, he asked Dr McIntyre, the President's personal physician, if it was all right. McIntyre, as usual, pretended that all was just fine. 'With all my heart I hope so,' replied Churchill. 'We cannot have anything happen to that man.'[11]

Later, when he and the President were presented with honorary degrees from McGill University in Montreal, he spoke warmly of their friendship having grown 'under the hammer blows of war'. There was no substitute, he went on, for personal face-to-face meetings. Telegrams, however long and speedy, were simply 'dead, blank walls compared to personal contacts'.[12]

Another personal link was bothering him. To his considerable distress he had learned that Harry Hopkins, who had so often facilitated personal meetings between the two leaders, had temporarily fallen out of Roosevelt's favour. Following his marriage, he had left the White House in December 1943, was himself now very ill, and had not even been invited to join them. Echoing her husband's fears, Clementine felt that his absence was a disadvantage to Anglo-American relations. Hopkins finally turned up afterwards, at

Hyde Park, to which Churchill and the President retreated when the formal conference was concluded.

Even here his old healing magic seemed lost. Lunch on the second day was dominated by exchanges between Churchill and Eleanor about how to keep the peace once the war was won. Eleanor argued that peace could best be preserved by improving living conditions throughout the world, while Churchill insisted that its best guarantee would be the sanction of Anglo-American military enforcement. The President himself remained mostly silent.[13]

Quebec witnessed the best and worst of times in relations between the two men. On the one hand, although it was quickly abandoned, they agreed on the controversial Morgenthau Plan for the de-industrialisation of Germany, and signed an historic Aide Memoire on the joint military and commercial development of atomic power after the war. On the other hand Churchill had to swallow the bitter pill that Britain was now almost wholly financially dependent on Washington. Roosevelt was generous, agreeing to extend Lend-Lease after Germany was defeated, but he demanded a full accounting and asked probing questions. As the haggling went on, Churchill's patience finally snapped. 'What do you want me to do, stand up and beg like Fala [Roosevelt's dog]?'[14]

This volatile mix of friendship, rivalry and resentment between the two national leaders was amply reflected in the intelligence war in Europe. Dramatic evidence of Churchill's continuing faith in clandestine war surfaced early in 1944 with the arrival in London of a formidable figure from the French resistance: Emmanuel d'Astier de la Vigerie, whose brothers had been deeply implicated in the Darlan assassination and who himself headed the resistance movement Libération as well as being General de Gaulle's Minister of the Interior.

For Churchill his meeting with d'Astier was an electric encounter. The Frenchman was a charismatic figure, he enthused to Roosevelt, 'a man of the Scarlet Pimpernel type', while to his Defence Committee he declared that 'brave and desperate men could cause the most acute embarrassment to the enemy', and Britain should do all in its power to foster and stimulate such a valuable aid to Allied strategy.[15] With sufficient aid, he hoped, the

whole of south-eastern France could be turned into a second
Yugoslavia; unspoken, almost certainly, was the thought that such
an uprising could also make redundant the American 'Anvil' landings in southern France he strongly opposed.

After seeing d'Astier, and then a British secret agent recently
returned from France, Churchill ordered extra supply drops to the
Maquis. 'Even if fairly successful,' he told his special operations
experts, 'the February programme is not enough. Pray start at once
on a programme for the March moon.'[16] Typically, his enthusiasm
caused temporary chaos, and in the end drops to the French
resistance had to yield to the programmes and priorities of Allied
headquarters and General Eisenhower.[17]

Here, British and American secret forces both collaborated and
kept apart, as symbolised by the 'Jedburgh' and 'Sussex' projects.
The former were teams of three, formed by one American agent,
one British agent, and a member of the French resistance, who
were dropped with a radio operator to fight with small resistance
groups in support of the D-Day invasion. By contrast, the 'Sussex'
project was a joint SIS/OSS plan to provide military intelligence
from the invasion area by dropping specially trained pairs of
agents into France in advance of D-Day. Teams would be either
American or British, not joint – although working to a co-
ordinated plan.

All too familiar friction quickly developed. British intelligence
chiefs, citing security, decreed that American intelligence in
London was forbidden from carrying out any operations apart
from 'Sussex', and even the official history of British intelligence,
normally reticent on such touchy issues, accepts there were problems. The Secret Intelligence Service, it acknowledges, insisted on
no independent OSS operational units into Europe without fuller
consultations, rigorously controlled the supply of aircraft for the
dropping of agents, and resisted any American liaison with
foreign intelligence services based in London.[18] 'Our work,' complained the head of the American 'Sussex' groups to Donovan, 'is
carried out under the friendly sufferance of Broadway
[SIS Headquarters], which means that we are liable . . . in some
instances to be kept in a position of subservience.'[19]

Friction was more dramatically obvious in the Balkans. At

Tehran the 'Big Three' had agreed to pour support to Tito's partisans and within weeks, convinced of General Mihailovic's
collaboration with the enemy, Churchill ordered supplies to the
royalist general halted, putting his faith instead in Fitzroy
Maclean's mission with Tito. Soon after, Donovan arrived for
talks with Churchill at Chequers, where his appearance seemed to
presage well for British–American intelligence co-operation in the
battles ahead.

Yet the reality was complex and troubled. So long as he
remained alive, Fitzroy Maclean resolutely denied any Anglo-
American rift in Yugoslavia, a line also reflected in the official
history of British intelligence. But since his death in 1996, and the
opening of OSS and SOE archives, it has become clear that
throughout the Balkans a growing Anglo-American intelligence
rift was casting its shadow. Donovan was trying hard to assert
American influence, as his efforts before Tehran to become Allied
intelligence supremo had already revealed. He had also given the
go-ahead for an OSS mission, codenamed 'Audrey' under Major
Louis Huot, to infiltrate Yugoslavia from Bari in southern Italy
and thus break the British stranglehold on communications from
Cairo. Huot, 'a whirling dervish in his efforts to get guns to Tito',
quickly ran foul of Maclean – especially after he met secretly on
his own with Tito. Maclean protested so forcibly that Donovan
had to ship the unfortunate Huot out of the Balkans altogether.[20]

Matters came to a head with Churchill's decision to abandon
Mihailovic. Many Americans thought that this was a bad mistake.
'If we follow too closely the lead being taken by our British
cousins,' complained the head of American intelligence in Bari, 'we
are letting go by default a force very well disposed to the United
States.' Senior OSS officers in the field told Donovan much the
same, and he insisted that if his agents were to operate with
Maclean the mission should come under the joint command of the
Combined Chiefs of Staff in Washington – and, by obvious impli-
cation, not that of Churchill.[21]

Simultaneously, Churchill was alerted by the Cabinet Secretary
that the Americans were attempting to penetrate British ciphers, an
extraordinary and alarming breach of the self-denying ordinance
that he and the President had reached after Pearl Harbor not to

spy on each other – and an incident still wrapped in secrecy. His first reaction was to consider approaching Roosevelt directly, but in the end he avoided confrontation by ordering that particularly sensitive messages to the British mission in Washington should pass through specially secure channels provided by SIS. He also ordered that his personal communications with Fitzroy Maclean should be kept firmly out of American hands. Donovan, he complained bitterly, 'is shoving his nose in everywhere. We are hardly allowed to breathe'. In a Most Secret cipher telegram sent to General Wilson, Supreme Commander in the Mediterranean, he asked anxiously: 'Are you sure that my telegrams to you through this channel never pass through American hands and are kept strictly secret?'[22]

Donovan had no problems with the Tehran decision to increase supplies to Tito. What he insisted on was the right to keep an *independent* American intelligence mission with Mihailovic, indeed anywhere he liked throughout the Balkans or elsewhere in the world. Gerald Wilkinson, now hard at work in the United States launching his secret 'Oyster' operation into China, visited Donovan shortly after the American intelligence chief returned to Washington after his journeyings to Chungking, Tehran, Cairo and London. 'What an attractive, agreeable and shrewd character Big B is,' recorded Churchill's former 'spy' on MacArthur. 'His conclusion . . . is that we, the British, are having a bit of a revival of our Elizabethan spirit, which he thinks is an excellent thing . . .' But, Wilkinson noted, Donovan had gone on to make one point clear: 'Great as is his desire to co-operate, he is not going to get pushed about . . .'[23]

This was the point Donovan made himself to Churchill at Chequers, and Roosevelt endorsed it. 'Dear Bill,' he wrote, 'I completely approve of the plan . . . to obtain intelligence from [Mihailovic] by sending in a new group . . . it should be made clear to the British that . . . we intend to exercise this freedom of action for obtaining independent American secret intelligence.'[24]

SOE Cairo learned of this in early April 1944, immediately informed London, and Churchill demanded that Roosevelt veto the mission. To be doubly sure he secretly instructed Cairo to delay any arrangement to fly the Americans into Yugoslavia. By all means be courteous, he told them, but be sure to deny them transport. He need not have worried. Roosevelt backed down and ordered Donovan to cancel the mission. 'The hatchet men had done their job at the highest level,' came the bitter complaint from American intelligence officers in Cairo.[25]

But the British hatchet men underestimated Donovan. He convinced the President that it was a difficult task 'to turn off and on intelligence work' and won his consent to a smaller mission. Aware that this would infuriate London, Donovan kept its planning strictly secret. Chosen to head mission 'Ranger' was Lieutenant-Colonel Robert H. McDowell, a US Army intelligence officer who had worked with British intelligence during the First World War. After several unsuccessful attempts his team finally parachuted into Serbia in late August 1944, only two weeks before the Red Army crossed the Yugoslav frontier and just days before Mihailovic ordered a general mobilisation of his Chetnik forces against 'all enemies'. The final battle for Yugoslavia was joined. McDowell, a sympathetic witness on the Chetnik side, began reporting that the partisans were waging a civil war.

News of the Ranger mission quickly reached Tito, who protested bitterly to Maclean. He in turn alerted Churchill, who once again confronted Roosevelt. General Donovan, he protested, was running a Mihailovic lobby. If OSS continued, he warned, 'we lay the scene for a fine civil war'. Claiming that he had made a mistake, Roosevelt ordered McDowell withdrawn. Churchill had once again forced Roosevelt to change course in the shadow war.[26]

Churchill felt just as strongly about Greece, where the left-wing guerrillas of Eam/Elas earned his bitter contempt. 'There is no comparison between them and the bands of Marshal Tito,' he declared. 'They are a mere scourge on the population, and are feared by the Greek villagers more than the Germans.' But many of Donovan's agents, like the President himself, were hostile to the Greek monarchy whose restoration Churchill demanded. Even those who were not often held little truck for Churchill. 'The British,' claimed one OSS officer in Cairo, 'were not interested in Greek liberation . . . but in naked imperial interest.'

The recent avalanche of OSS and SOE files reveals starkly that most American intelligence officers thoroughly disapproved of

British policy towards Greek resistance. This came as no surprise to SOE. Conflict with the Americans had been predicted early on. Even as the joint Brusa codebreaking agreement was being signed in Washington in May 1943, Lord Glenconner, then running special operations out of Cairo, predicted that Anglo-American harmony would quickly break down. 'Personally,' he told the British ambassador to the Greek government-in-exile, 'I think . . . that as soon as [the Americans] have got their personnel, schools, equipment for War Stations, W/T sets and aircraft etc. they will throw off [our] control and do just what they like. If so, the result in the Balkans will be chaotic.'[27]

The Communists were not the only players in the Greek drama to receive a tongue-lashing from Churchill. Donovan also suffered. The cause, once again, was the American chief's resentment at Churchill's attempt to keep secret operations in British hands. In preparation for a showdown with the Communists, British liaison officers had been withdrawn from the guerrillas, and London asked Donovan to do the same. Stephen Penrose, who ran American intelligence into Greece, told Donovan that the move would endanger his men and plunge organised resistance to the Nazis into chaos. Donovan protested to Secretary of State Cordell Hull that the British were interfering with his intelligence operations and again dictating American policy in the Balkans. Hull agreed that intelligence missions should continue but told Donovan that his men should stay out of Greek politics.

To expect that OSS officers, among whom were many passionate Greek–Americans, could stay neutral in what was rapidly descending into civil war was asking the impossible. 'Cynically opportunist' was how the head of the Greek desk in the OSS Research and Analysis division in Cairo bitterly described British policy. The protests leaked back to Washington and surfaced dramatically in the *Washington Post* with a damning critique of Churchill and his policy in Greece by the columnist Drew Pearson.

What Churchill found particularly galling about Pearson's attack was that only two days before, Roosevelt had agreed to the British plans for Operation Manna. To have won the President's rare consent for a vital political battle only to see it resisted by Donovan was particularly intolerable. Churchill vented his anger about

Pearson to Harry Hopkins. 'Is this not the man,' he asked, 'the President described the other day as being America's greatest liar or words to that effect?' Could nothing be done to correct his crude assertions about British policy towards Greece? If nothing could be done, he had 'half a mind' to try his own hand in the matter. It was clear, he observed bitterly, that Pearson's article was part of the campaign against the British in Egypt being waged by Donovan's agency.

Letting off steam to Hopkins was not enough. Still fuming, he sent an unprecedented message to Donovan himself. Marked 'Private and Personal' and 'Off the Record', it angrily warned that attempts to obstruct British policy towards the Greek resistance could cause formidable trouble for the Americans. He hoped not to have to bring the issue before Roosevelt and thus make it an official quarrel between London and Washington. But unless Donovan could smoothe the waters he would have no other choice. Two days later, in an appeasing gesture, Roosevelt offered American planes to help ferry British troops into Greece. To Churchill it might have appeared as another victory in his increasingly acrimonious relations with Donovan's intelligence empire. Yet, even as the President poured oil on troubled waters, Donovan decreed that after the Germans left Greece purely intelligence operations would be carried out independently of any joint Anglo–American control. It was little wonder that a British intelligence officer in Washington reported soon after that at a private dinner he attended, Donovan 'went for Winston and his intolerance and dictatorship proclivities'.[28]

Roosevelt and Churchill were not the only players in the intelligence game. On the eve of the Quebec Conference the Soviet factor was increasingly helping shape the Anglo–American future.

Immediately Hitler launched Operation Barbarossa in 1941, Churchill had ordered the sending of selected items of Ultra to Moscow and approved the creation of SOE and NKVD liaison missions in Moscow and London. With help from SOE, several Soviet agents were dropped behind enemy lines into western Europe and the Balkans.

Donovan was keen to follow Churchill's lead and late in 1943 flew into Moscow to see what he could do. On Christmas Day Stalin's Foreign Minister, Vyacheslav Molotov, gave the idea his blessing, and two days later Roosevelt's intelligence chief had an amiable meeting with Soviet intelligence chiefs at NKVD headquarters to work out details. Then, in March 1944, Roosevelt vetoed the idea. Behind him stood the ever-vigilant FBI chief, J. Edgar Hoover, who denounced as 'highly dangerous' any idea of having an NKVD mission set up base in the American capital. Afraid of the domestic row that would follow the inevitable leaks if he went ahead with Donovan's plan – especially in an election year – Roosevelt opted for safety first.

This did not prevent the NKVD or GRU from operating inside the United States, nor did it halt American or British intelligence exchanges with Moscow. Over the next few crucial months up to and after D-Day intensive intelligence-trading took place between the British and Americans and Stalin in various European capitals. But eventually, and inevitably, it ran into trouble. The sore spot, predictably, was Romania – an oil-rich Hitler satellite bordering the Soviet Union, a long-time happy hunting-ground for Western intelligence agents, and ripe, in Stalin's view, for Soviet plucking. If there was to be trouble between him and the West, it would surface here early. The signs were quick to emerge.

In April 1944 Moscow was officially told that OSS and SOE planned to send six parties into Romania, three American and three British, to organise guerrilla resistance in the event of a German takeover. Would the Russians like to join in? The question was asked diplomatically, but half-heartedly: Donovan was determined to keep his teams independent, and SOE believed that including Russians could mean 'betrayal and even murder'. In the event, to everyone's relief, Moscow declined the offer.[29]

However, the Soviets seized the moment to embarrass the British. Molotov, claiming he had only learned after the fact of a previous secret British mission to Romania, violently accused Churchill of plotting with the Romanian dictator General Ion Antonescu behind Moscow's back. The charge was untrue, a smokescreen deliberately designed to obscure the fact that Moscow itself was involved in secret talks with the Romanians. Nonetheless, the row – later remembered as 'Molotov's little bombshell' – had significant effects: Churchill blamed SOE for the ruckus and from now on took an increasingly cautious view of plans for its post-war future. 'It is a very dangerous thing,' he thundered, 'that the relations of two mighty forces like the British Empire and the USSR should be disturbed by obscure persons playing the fool far below the surface.'

The incident also opened his eyes to the possibility of 'trading' Romania for Greece and laid the seeds of his deal with Stalin at the Moscow Conference that October; and in delaying British plans for secret missions to Romania, it opened the door for Donovan to assert a separate American presence.

'We should carry on as an independent mission,' Donovan ordered in the wake of the Churchill–Molotov row, insisting that OSS operations into Romania would be confined to purely intelligence-gathering tasks.[30] On the eve of D-Day he arrived in London, where he had a lengthy meeting with Sir Alexander Cadogan, the head of the Foreign Office, about intelligence matters – a meeting whose very existence is omitted from the published version of Cadogan's diaries: British sources have rarely welcomed revelations about Anglo-American intelligence links.[31]

The Donovan–Cadogan talks covered both general and specific issues at the heart of the special relationship. On the broad issue, Roosevelt's intelligence chief insisted that the Americans 'must have freedom to ship intelligence units into any area where their presence could appear to be to our advantage'. On Romania, he stressed that the Americans would, of course, keep the British and Russians informed; it was no part of American intent to intensify hard feelings between allies. Cadogan, noted Donovan, was 'exceedingly amiable and understood our position completely'.

But to head off any British second thoughts he decided to provide cover by emphasising a secondary aspect of the missions: their role in helping rescue downed American pilots from bombing missions over the Ploesti oilfields now stranded in Romania – an essentially humanitarian issue that he believed neither the Russians nor the British could oppose. And to wrap up the deal, he confirmed it personally with Churchill. The Prime Minister's several meetings with the American intelligence chief during the Second World War have, like Cadogan's meeting with Donovan, been largely airbrushed from the public record, and are also curiously absent from the otherwise encyclopaedic official Churchill biography.

But on 29 May 1944, just a week before D-Day, Churchill gave his blessing to Donovan's plan for Romania. So did the Secret Intelligence Service, which earlier that month had sent in a mission of its own despite the Molotov bombshell. General Sir Henry Maitland Wilson, the British commander of the Mediterranean, also accepted that the Americans had 'an inherent right' to send in a mission. It was a triumph for Donovan, and on his return to Washington the President gave it his warm approval.[32]

Over the summer Donovan assembled the teams whose ostensible mission was to collect bombing targets, German Order of Battle intelligence, and escape information for the US Air Force. Secretly, however, they now had an additional target. In Romania events had rapidly moved on since the spring. In August King Michael arrested Antonescu, installed a new, pro-Allied government, and on 12 September, the day after Churchill and Roosevelt met up at Quebec, signed an armistice with the Russians. Draconian in its terms, it guaranteed that over the next few months the country was to slip slowly but inexorably under Soviet control.

As elsewhere, the recent wholescale release of American intelligence material throws a sanitising light on the festering growth of intelligence legends and mythologies. Of all eastern European countries, Romania was reconnoitred longest by Donovan's intelligence experts, and it was here that Frank Wisner, one of the CIA's legendary Cold War veterans, began his rise to the top of post-war American intelligence. It was in Romania, claims one of Donovan's biographers, that OSS scored a major early Cold War triumph through the so-called 'Bishop' traffic that exposed Soviet and Communist intentions not just in Romania but throughout eastern and central Europe. By contrast, a history of Donovan's agency, anxious to puncture claims for Donovan as a prescient Cold War warrior, argued that any significant intelligence his agents gathered in Romania was exclusively the result of Soviet help – and hence not anti-Soviet.[33]

Both claims, it is now clear, overstate their case. The Bishop traffic, which relied heavily on sources deep inside Romanian counter-intelligence, was more sensational than accurate. Nonetheless, its efforts, as with much else of Donovan's campaign, were unmistakeably targeted at Soviet and Communist intentions and behaviour rather than military and strategic information relevant to the continuing war against Germany. And even while they eagerly gathered intelligence about the Russians, Donovan's secret warriors were rubbing their hands at beating the British to the target.

A week before Churchill set sail for Quebec, an OSS party landed at Bucharest in two B-17 bombers from Bari in Italy. Their mission was to evacuate over a thousand American bomber aircrew downed in attacks on the Ploesti oilfields and released by the new Romanian government, and to examine damage to the oil installations and collect other intelligence for the 15th US Air Force. Its achievement was phenomenal. In only five days all the American aircrew had been evacuated safely back to Italy, and by the time that Roosevelt and Churchill actually met in Quebec over a ton of invaluable documents on oil and the German Air Force had also been taken out.

Simultaneously with the main OSS mission Wisner arrived direct from Istanbul under strict instructions to gather intelligence on Moscow's intentions towards Romania, economic intelligence relevant to future American business enterprise in the country, and data about the Red Army. 'This place is wild with information and Wisner is in his glory,' reported a colleague from Bucharest. Wisner's reports on Soviet behaviour before and after the Romanian armistice quickly found their way back to Washington and to Roosevelt in Quebec. Even as he and Churchill discussed the Morgenthau Plan, Donovan hurried the first details of the armistice to him.

Wisner's reports – in reality more political reporting than secret intelligence – combined with other information pouring in from the Balkans, led Donovan to tell the President firmly by the end of that month that the Russians clearly intended to dominate the entire area.[34] All this went hand in hand with co-operation with the Soviets on German Order of Battle and other military and strategic intelligence – it was another six months before Hitler's armies were finally defeated. 'I want to express my appreciation,' Donovan told General Fitin, the head of Soviet foreign intelligence, that October, 'for the spirit of friendly co-operation you have shown us. We have tried to reciprocate.'[35]

Anglo-American intelligence relations were likewise delicately balanced. Donovan's insistence on running his own show was still ruffling feathers. Harold Macmillan, the British political adviser in the Mediterranean, was distinctly annoyed that the Americans had not included any British agents in the mission flown into Bucharest, a fact that gave distinct pleasure to Americans on the scene. Even as Churchill stepped ashore in Quebec to embrace Roosevelt, the head of Donovan's agency in the Mediterranean reported gleefully to his boss that 'our cousins are green with envy at our having gotten [to Romania] "the fastest with the mostest" . . . this has been an excellent "dry run" for what we will have to go through in Sofia, Belgrade, Budapest and Vienna'.[36] Both at the summit and below the Americans and the British remained rivals and competitors as well as allies.

20

◆◆◆

ALLIES AT WAR

Churchill knew by now that despite the rhetoric of Anglo-American unity Roosevelt was reluctant to move either in the direction or at the speed he wished. A mere eleven days after returning from Quebec, he flew to Moscow to sign with Stalin his controversial 'percentages deal' over eastern Europe that assigned Romania and Greece to Russian and British spheres of influence respectively, with Hungary, Bulgaria and Yugoslavia marooned in some no-man's-land in between. 'Britain,' Churchill insisted to the Soviet leader, 'must be the leading Mediterranean power.' For this reason, too, he kept an eagle eye on political affairs in Italy.

Roosevelt was far from keen on this Moscow visit, and asked Averell Harriman to sit in as an observer on his ally's talks with Stalin. 'I can tell you quite frankly,' he told him, 'but for you only and not to be communicated under any circumstances to the British or the Russians, that I would have very much preferred to have the next conference between the three of us [i.e., himself, Churchill and Stalin].'[1] It made no difference. Churchill welcomed Harriman but excluded him from his political deal with Stalin. He also concluded a bargain over Asia by agreeing that the Soviet Union should have post-war rights at Port Arthur in China; implicitly, Britain would keep Hong Kong as a trade-off.[2]

Protection of future vital British interests was now paramount to Churchill, and if this meant quarrelling with the Americans, that was too bad. Astonishingly, one recent British critic of Churchill has denounced him as an appeaser during this period for the concessions he made to Roosevelt.[3] On the contrary – he fought vigorously to assert British interests, especially in Italy and Greece, while Roosevelt often gave way. In the former, Churchill's mistrust of a leading Italian politician, Count Sforza, stimulated some terse transatlantic exchanges, while in Greece his absolute determination to pursue British interests led to the deployment of British troops against the Communists that climaxed in open civil war that Christmas – and provoked fierce and often vitriolic criticism in the American press.

Churchill greeted the election result in November that gave Roosevelt an unprecedented fourth term with undisguised elation. 'I always said that a great people could be trusted to stand by the pilot who weathered the storm,' he told Roosevelt on 8 November 1944. 'It is an indescribable relief to me that our comradeship will continue and will help to bring the world out of misery.' And to remind his ally of the message he had sent him before the previous presidential election of 1940, which Roosevelt had failed to acknowledge, he sent him a copy.[4]

The two men's loyalty to each other remained a powerful link. In the row over Greece Roosevelt was unprepared to support Churchill publicly, but he backed him behind the scenes. 'I regard my role,' he assured him from Warm Springs, Georgia, where he was unwinding after the election with Lucy Mercer, 'as that of a loyal friend . . . nothing can in any way shake the unity and association between our two countries'. So saying, he forcefully slapped down Admiral King, who had vetoed American ships from ferrying British forces to Greece. That Christmas, in one of their by now traditional gestures of friendship, he sent Churchill a tree for his family celebrations. Revealingly, his ally was not even there to enjoy it. On Christmas Eve, to the despair of Clementine, he flew off to Athens to see for himself that the Communists were firmly put in their place.[5]

As for Roosevelt, he too had not abandoned any of his views about the post-war world and his nation's interests. 'The British and the French,' he told his new Secretary of State, Edward R. Stettinius Jr, early in the New Year, 'but more particularly the British, [are] working to undermine our whole policy in regard to China . . . and still cling to the idea of white supremacy in Asia.' Simultaneously he spoke of the need for island bases in the Pacific and Africa, of his desire to help sort out the growing crisis in relations between Arabs and Jews over Palestine, of the need to strip Italy and France of colonial territory in east Africa, and of his unrelenting opposition to the return of the Free French to Indo-China. To Congressional leaders he explained how he had already urged Churchill to return Hong Kong to China – and of Churchill's opposition.[6]

The two men enjoyed their final meetings at encounters surrounding the Yalta Conference in February 1945. Three days before the President left Washington, his Secretary of Labour, Frances Perkins, noted with distress that he had 'the pallor, the deep gray color of a man who had long been ill'. The journey to the Crimea did nothing to help, and despite Churchill's breezy assurance that his friend was in the best of health, no one else allowed themselves to be fooled, and Harry Hopkins seriously doubted whether Roosevelt took in more than half of what went on around the table. Official photographs from Yalta tell the story: Roosevelt is gaunt, dark-eyed and shrunken, a blanket around his shoulders. Beside him the older and undoubtedly weary Churchill seemed positively bouncy. Still, despite his usual manoeuvre in evading bilateral talks with the Prime Minister, Roosevelt buoyed Churchill's hopes that Anglo-American relations would endure after the war. The Americans were resolved to see them through, he reported to the War Cabinet.[7]

After it was all over, the two leaders met for the final time aboard the USS *Quincy* at Alexandria. It was almost like old times, with Harry Hopkins back again at Roosevelt's side and the Prime Minister and President agreeing easily on a proposal for the development of atomic bomb research in Britain after the war. After lunch, Churchill took his leave. 'I felt [Roosevelt] had a slender contact with life,' he wrote later. Hopkins' health was little better. So ill did he feel that three days later he left the *Quincy* and flew back to Washington to avoid the long sea journey home. His departure angered Roosevelt, who felt abandoned. 'Why did Harry have to get sick on me?' he asked petulantly, refusing even to say goodbye to the man who had served him so faithfully for so long. They never met again. Two days later, Edwin 'Pa' Watson, his trusted military aide, died on board after a cerebral haemorrhage, plunging the President deeper into depression. Watson's rugged and buoyant figure had been both his guide and anchor throughout the war. It was a 'sorry ship' that took the President back home, recalled Sam Rosenman.[8]

The President had only six weeks to live. Yet, even as his life ebbed away, he remained eager to apply the Atlantic Charter principles to the post-war world. Immediately after Yalta he met in Egypt with the country's King Farouk, Ethiopia's Emperor Haile Selassie, and Ibn Saud, the ruler of Saudi Arabia, setting off British alarm bells about wild American promises of freedom and independence. In mid-Atlantic, soon after Watson's death, he told the three White House press correspondents on board that he hoped other governments would follow the American example in the Philippines and grant self-government to their colonies. Inevitably, talk turned to Britain. Was it Churchill's idea to have everything back just the way it was? asked one of the journalists. 'Yes,' replied Roosevelt, 'he is mid-Victorian in all things like that . . . Dear old Winston will never learn on that point. He has made his speciality on that point. This is, of course, off the record,' he added.

Later, drafting his report for Congress on the Yalta talks, he confided to Rosenman that, for all his affection for 'dear old Winston', he and the Prime Minister were going to have deepseated differences of opinion now that victory was so close.[9] One of these disagreements was on confronting the Soviets. In the weeks after Yalta Churchill repeatedly pushed him to confront Stalin on a number of issues, but the President consistently refused on the grounds that Yalta should be given time to work. To the bitter end, he clung to hopes of keeping the alliance together when peace came. Only the day before he died he drafted a short message to the Prime Minister. 'I would minimize the general Soviet problem as much as possible because most of the problems, in one form or another, seem to arise every day and most of them straighten out . . . We must be firm, however, and our course thus far is correct.'[10]

This picture, of allies at war with their common enemy, but also fighting with each other while constantly groping to feel the shape of the peace ahead, was reflected vividly in the world of their shadow warriors.

'Dear Dickie,' Roosevelt had breezily told Mountbatten in a cheery letter from Warm Springs shortly before Christmas 1944, acknowledging an update on affairs from the supreme commander in south-east Asia, 'it was mightily nice to get [your letter] . . . keep up the good work!'[11] Recent intelligence releases reveal that Donovan was far less delighted at the treatment British intelligence was dishing out to American operatives as they struggled against the Japanese.

To cut through the tangled underbrush of Anglo-American clandestine rivalries, he flew into Mountbatten's headquarters in Ceylon in January 1945 for face-to-face talks with the supreme commander himself. Already he'd complained personally in Washington to Baker Street's London heavyweight, George Taylor, that 'by fair means and foul' the British were restricting American secret operations, especially in Malaya, to a minimum. Smoothly, Taylor assured him that the problem was caused by 'independent competitive planning' and that earlier and better voluntary co-operation in the planning of missions behind enemy lines would iron out the wrinkles. Yet Taylor secretly believed that to pre-empt the Americans Britain should intensify its secret operations in Siam, Indo-China and Hong Kong.[12]

Flanked by their respective regional intelligence experts, Donovan and Mountbatten straightened out several tangled lines of responsibility and command that had been generating friction in their affairs, and agreed to set up new joint machinery for the early planning of secret missions. Soon after, Donovan flew to Kunming, headquarters of the American military command in China, and held a similar meeting, this time including the sinister Tai Li, to sort out matters for the China theatre.[13]

This useful clearing of the air gave added impetus to operations against the Japanese. It did not, however, alter longer-term thinking or bring the American and British much closer together. As one newly surfaced British document on SOE's relations with their American cousins in Asia stresses, it was firm doctrine in London that it should remain the senior partner in relation to resistance movements in British territories, and that in China 'we should try to reserve primarily to ourselves the Hong Kong and adjacent areas'. Moreover, in the wake of the Donovan–Mountbatten meeting, the Americans had been forced to give way to British insistence on control of all secret operations into Malaya.

Donovan's shadow warriors also clung to their national perspectives. OSS was important not just for defeating the Japanese, Roosevelt's intelligence chief was briefed for his meeting with Mountbatten by his senior regional commander, Colonel John Coughlin, but it also provided a 'listening post for American interests in Asia'. Part of his mandate, he reminded Donovan, was to provide information to Washington on the activities of British intelligence services.[14]

None of this was openly stated at the meeting in Ceylon – except for one issue where Roosevelt felt especially strongly and had actively intervened: Thailand. To the President, policy towards this country that had escaped Western colonialism provided a touchstone for the post-war world. Not surprisingly, the Americans resisted British proposals for a joint mission to the country and dealt separately with Pridi Phanomyong, the Free Thai leader and Regent in Bangkok. Pridi played astutely to Roosevelt's sympathies. Early in 1945 he met secretly with two American agents infiltrated into the country by seaplane, pledged himself in support of the United Nations, and gave them a gold cigarette case as a personal gift for Roosevelt. It had special significance, Donovan told the President when it reached Washington, 'because of the affixed Royal Siamese Crown and the inscribed Royal Siamese initials'. So delighted was Roosevelt that he demanded full operational details of the mission involved.[15]

Anglo-American tension and the serious prospect of a Roosevelt–Churchill clash remained highest, however, over Indo-China. The flashpoint remained the issue of involving the Free French in clandestine operations and Roosevelt's adamant resistance to De Gaulle and any French return to its colonial fiefdom.

Churchill deliberately refused to raise the issue with Roosevelt until 1945, although after their Quebec encounter, when he increasingly took an independent line, he connived at getting round the President's veto and authorised Mountbatten to permit a Free French mission at Kandy. Soon after, a Special Duties flight landed an emissary from General de Gaulle to the Hanoi French Command at a landing strip at Dien Bien Phu. Over the next few months an intensive supply effort by Force 136 dropped W/T sets, agents and weapons to create a Gaullist resistance force that would ensure the future of Indo-China for France.

Officially, however, the British were not helping the Free French, and this helped precipitate one of the low points of Anglo-American relations in south-east Asia. In January 1945 fighters of the US 14th Air Force shot down three British bombers on an intelligence mission into Indo-China. Rumours instantly flew of a blatant and deliberate attack, although it was almost certainly a genuine error caused by American pilots mistaking the planes for Japanese aircraft. Whatever the truth, fingers could still be pointed at serious Anglo-American rivalry, for the Royal Air Force liaison officer with the 14th Air Force in Kunming had deliberately been kept in the dark about the flights because of the political storm this could create. Not surprisingly, the British decided that 'sealed lips' were in everyone's best interests and that no official enquiry should be launched.[16]

In March 1945, in the wake of this incident and after open fighting broke out between the Japanese and French forces formerly loyal to Vichy, Churchill finally broached the issue directly with his White House friend. Even then, he refused to share his deepest feelings, which he reserved for the head of the British military mission in the American capital. It would look very bad in history if they were to let the French forces in Indo-China be cut to pieces by the Japanese through shortage of arms if there was anything they could do to save them, he confessed. He remained reluctant to bring the issue into the open. 'I feel a little shy of overburdening the President at the moment,' he noted less than two weeks before his ally died. 'I hear he is very hard pressed and I like to keep him as much as possible for the big things.' But before he died, Roosevelt effectively agreed that Mountbatten should be allowed to conduct intelligence and guerrilla activities in Indo-China – and thereby acquiesced indirectly in Indo-China's return to France.[17]

As for Europe, once D-Day was successful and the Allies were firmly back on the continent, co-ordination of British and American special operations and intelligence, other than their joint codebreaking efforts at Bletchley Park and elsewhere, rapidly disintegrated. As soon as he could, Donovan shifted his European headquarters from London to Paris, withdrew his liaison officers from SOE's German section in London, and started his own operations into Hitler's heartland.

It was a sign of changing times that the move was not unwelcome in London, where British intelligence chiefs nurtured their own yearnings for independence and echoed Churchill's own increasingly separatist line. 'The great Bill Donovan shows sense,' confessed SOE's Sir Colin Gubbins at the time of Churchill's Quebec visit, 'and of course he is absolutely right, as it is the postwar [world] that we must now think of and our show must be British and not integrated . . . I am encouraging him on these lines.'[18] Sir Stewart Menzies felt much the same way. In January 1945 Eisenhower's headquarters proposed subordinating SIS operations to joint Anglo-American clandestine planning. Menzies firmly refused on the grounds that its intelligence operations should be 'entirely under British command for policy'. He took a similar robust line in the Middle East.[19]

The Soviet spectre had already focused Churchill's mind on the future of special operations. Within a week of returning from Moscow in October he turned his gaze again to SOE. Britain's shadow warriors still had a vital role to play. But now it was less a case of setting Europe ablaze than of dousing the left-wing and nationalist fires that threatened Britain's long-term interests. In northern Italy, where the partisans were severely harrying the Germans, SOE in August alone had infiltrated over sixty officers. But only small arms were supplied, armed groups were kept to the absolute minimum, and careful plans were laid for the disarming of partisans as soon as the Germans retreated. There was to be no repeat of the Eam/Elas crisis in Greece, and Italy was to remain firmly anchored to the West. Similar concerns shaped secret operations in countries yet to be liberated such as Austria, Denmark and Norway.[20]

Yet, so far as SOE's post-war future was concerned, Churchill put off any decision. Although he had fathered the agency and defended it robustly against Whitehall predators, its political dabblings had increasingly bothered him. The Romanian affair in April 1944 provoked severe doubts. 'The part your naughty deeds in war play,' he chided Selborne, 'in peace cannot at all be considered at the present time.' And to Harold Macmillan, who was keen to see subversive war continued into the peace, he pronounced that SOE in the Middle East should be dealt with firmly. 'They are a fertile sprout of mischief and overstaffing,' he declared.[21]

Throughout the late summer and autumn, as he met Roosevelt at Quebec and Stalin in Moscow, competing Whitehall mandarins lobbied the Prime Minister over the peacetime continuation and control of special operations. One growing concern was rivalry with their transatlantic ally. 'It would be foolish to ignore the strength of OSS,' declared Sir Colin Gubbins after returning from a visit to Washington. 'It embraces so many facets of secret work that it can be likened to the NKVD . . . of the Big Three, is Great Britain going to be the only one without such an instrument?'[22] Selborne argued likewise. Any government that neglected special operations in the post-war world, he told Churchill, would be 'like an admiral who said he did not require submarines'. Churchill agreed, but faced with a fight between the military and a Foreign Office desperate to wrench special operations back under SIS control, he postponed a decision.

There was another factor, too – his coalition partner, Clement Attlee. The Labour leader had been a sympathetic midwife at the birth of SOE, when Britain had its back to the wall and heady talk of 'people's war' was in vogue. It was radically different now. The war was all but won, the coalition's days were numbered, and, provoked by events in Greece, Labour voices bitterly denounced Britain for opposing the forces throughout Europe that had been 'the backbone of the resistance'. It all made Attlee cautious of anything resembling 'a British Comintern'.[23]

The future of the spycatchers at home proved even more

contentious. Churchill had become profoundly uneasy about the wartime increase in their powers, but attempts to rein in MI5 and the Security Panel had been sabotaged from within. In the meantime professional rivalries between SIS and MI5 inevitably surfaced as they jostled for post-war advantage, and Stewart Menzies referred ominously to the dangers of an 'internal Gestapo'. As rumours spread in late 1944 of a major review of the British intelligence community, voices in MI5 began to express dread about the impact of Churchill and claimed that he and his friends 'snooped around' too much in its work. Even Sir Alan Brooke felt there was a 'grave danger of [MI5] falling into the clutches of unscrupulous political hands of which there are too many at present'. Here again Churchill refused to tackle the issue so long as the war waged on.[24]

Why, after all, meddle with an agency so brilliantly successful in the double-cross game against the Germans? Yet MI5 dismally failed in rooting out some major Soviet spies in Britain. Despite eventually turning their suspicious eye on Communists in government service, British spycatchers failed to detect the high-level espionage of the infamous 'Cambridge Five' of Kim Philby, Donald Maclean, Guy Burgess, Anthony Blunt and John Cairncross. Four of them managed to penetrate the intelligence services, and through them all many British wartime secrets, including information about Bletchley Park codebreaking and atomic collaboration with the United States, reached Moscow. On the former, of course, Churchill himself had personally ensured that Stalin receive Ultra material of significance, but on the latter he and Roosevelt agreed to keep Moscow in the dark. This was anathema to some of the scientists involved, most notably the German refugee Klaus Fuchs, who began to pass Anglo-American secrets to the Soviets in 1941 and continued after he reached Los Alamos two years later.

In the United States Soviet intelligence worked hard and successfully to extract atomic secrets, as the well-known events climaxing in the post-war Rosenberg trial revealed. They also had agents elsewhere, some of them high up in Washington. The most infamous of these was Alger Hiss, the State Department's Deputy Director of Special Political Affairs, who attended the Yalta

Conference as a member of the official American delegation. There was also Harry Dexter White, of the Treasury, an adviser of Henry Morgenthau, who played a major part in post-war American financial planning. These agents, undetected by American or British counter-intelligence, were a useful asset to Stalin in his negotiations with Roosevelt and Churchill.[25]

Roosevelt faced similar demands as Churchill for a post-war life for his shadow warriors. Donovan began his campaign even before D-Day. As early as the Salerno landings in Italy he called for the creation of a 'Fourth Arm' of warfare to be headed by a civilian appointed by the President, but it was rapidly emerging problems with the Soviets in the Balkans and eastern Europe a year later that added urgency to the project. Shortly after Churchill's Moscow talks with Stalin, and his first discussions with Selborne over the future of Britain's shadow warriors, Donovan proposed to Roosevelt an American post-war centralised intelligence service in charge of all secret activity including secret intelligence, counter-espionage, cryptanalysis and subversive operations. Not surprisingly, he argued there was no need for a new organisation, as it already existed in the OSS.[26]

Roosevelt invited his intelligence chief to develop a full-scale proposal. By mid-November, ten days after Roosevelt's re-election, Donovan had a draft presidential directive creating a 'central intelligence agency' on the President's desk. 'There are common-sense reasons,' he told him, with growing conflicts with Moscow in mind, 'why you may desire to lay the keel of the ship at once.'

Yet not just anti-Soviet motives were at play. Also potent was the persistent rivalry with Britain, where thinking mirrored that of Sir Colin Gubbins in London. A post-war agency would, the draft directive's author promised, enable the United States to free itself from 'our present national dependence upon British intelligence'. Rivalry with Britain underlay other clandestine schemes cooked up by Donovan. Early in 1944 he had asked one of his veterans, the British-trained Carleton S. Coon, a Harvard anthropologist who'd headed a secret mission in North Africa, to develop a long-term plan for intelligence in Arabia and the Muslim world to enhance American interests in oil, air bases and markets. Having had close dealings with both SOE and SIS, Coon reported that to succeed such a scheme would have to be totally 'sealed off' from existing American agencies that were too easily penetrable by America's allies – meaning primarily Britain.

Similar schemes were penned for the Far East and the fostering of American commercial, industrial and political needs where the potential targets were also the European colonial powers. Even John Franklin Carter, who'd run his personal networks for the President earlier in the war, highlighted the rivalry with Britain in a plan he developed that would see him once again reporting direct to the White House. The British had penetrated Donovan's agency, he warned Roosevelt, and 'since they will be pursuing their own ends, which are not necessarily either hostile to or synonymous with our own ends, reliance should be placed on the alternative method . . .'[27]

Predictably, bureaucratic warfare broke out in Washington as rival agencies such as the FBI and army intelligence tried to capture, mutilate or kill off the idea. This campaign was given heart by Roosevelt himself on the eve of Yalta, when he told Secretary of State Stettinius that while foreign intelligence should undoubtedly be consolidated, he thought it should be confined to military and related subjects – thereby excluding much of the political and economic dimension being pushed by Donovan.

He was also reluctant to send too provocative a signal to Moscow, hopeful as he remained that not all chances of post-war co-operation with Stalin were doomed. He offered graphic illustration of this in his extraordinary reaction to a considerable intelligence coup delivered by Donovan shortly before Christmas 1944.

After weeks of clandestine talks in Stockholm, Donovan's office in the Swedish capital purchased from Finnish sources 1,500 pages of Soviet material captured during the Finnish–Soviet war that included a partially charred NKVD codebook – a prize of inestimable value. But far from congratulating Donovan, the President ordered him to inform the Russians and hand the codebook back. This, reluctantly, America's intelligence chief did – but not before secretly copying it and hence holding on to a weapon that later proved of crucial importance in identifying Soviet agents at work in the West.[28]

The debate over OSS's future erupted sensationally into the public arena while the President was in the Crimea. On 9 February 1945 the Washington *Times-Herald*, the *New York Daily News* and the *Chicago Tribune*, all anti-Roosevelt papers owned by the McCormick–Patterson press empire, came out with dramatic headlines: 'DONOVAN PROPOSES SUPER SPY SYSTEM FOR POST-WAR NEW DEAL; WOULD TAKE OVER FBI, SECRET SERVICE, ONI AND G-2 PROJECT FOR U.S.; SUPER SPIES DISCLOSED IN SECRET MEMO; NEW DEAL PLANS SUPER SPY SYSTEM; SLEUTHS WOULD SNOOP ON U.S. AND THE WORLD; ORDER CREATING IT ALREADY DRAFTED; NEW DEAL PLANS TO SPY ON WORLD AND HOME FOLKS; SUPER GESTAPO AGENCY IS UNDER CREATION.'

The author was a journalist, Walter Trohan, a man close to J. Edgar Hoover, and it was obvious he had seen the full text of the draft directive. After quoting extensively from it, he claimed that the new Donovan agency would have an independent budget and what he called 'secret funds for spy work along the lines of bribing and luxury living described in the novels of E. Phillips Oppenheim'. In the national uproar that followed, Congressional voices were raised denouncing the scheme as a 'New Deal OGPU' and, more frequently, as a 'Gestapo'. Amid the clamour, more moderate observers dismissed comparisons with the Nazi and Soviet secret police to defend the idea. The veteran CBS reporter Ed Murrow pointed out that after the fighting ended the United States would need intelligence of a high order if it were not to be handicapped in its relations with other powers, while the *Washington Post* argued the proposal should be judged on its merits as a serious contribution to the debate over national security.

The controversy also sparked comment overseas. In London, *The Economist* mocked the Americans for being unable to keep even the most basic secrets secret. 'How many water mains are to be pierced before the United States Congress passes an Official Secrets Act to protect itself and its Allies? Is freedom to blab essential to democracy?' it asked scathingly. On both sides of the Atlantic, 'Gestapo' jibes entered the debate over the future of the intelligence services. Churchill, unwisely, even introduced it into his election campaign, and paid the price. Nor did Hitler's propaganda boss, Joseph Goebbels, stand aside. 'A NET OF JEWISH

INFORMERS THROUGHOUT THE WORLD' shouted the headline in the Nazi *Tagepost*, as it went on to claim that Donovan's agency would work alongside the Soviet NKVD 'to envelop and dominate the whole world'.[29]

Such sensational exposure effectively sabotaged Donovan's plan. Remarkably, throughout the controversy, the White House lifted not a finger to help him despite his protests that the leak struck at the very heart of military security. Yet there may be a good reason for this. Trohan later claimed that he had been summoned one day by Steve Early, the President's press secretary, given the Donovan plan, and told that the President wanted the story out. If true, this was either to test the waters of public opinion, or else kill off the idea entirely. Some of Roosevelt's closest advisers certainly wanted to avoid any Congressional hearings about a new agency that would endanger America's best sources of intelligence in Ultra and Magic. The war, after all, had yet to be won. The President himself had earlier commissioned a separate report on OSS that recommended it be broken up to avoid the prospect of a 'post-war Gestapo'.[30]

In any event, a month later Roosevelt re-opened the issue by asking Donovan to collect the opinions of top foreign intelligence and internal security agencies. 'They should all be asked,' he instructed, 'to contribute their suggestions to the proposed centralised intelligence service.' One of the first to respond was Henry Morgenthau. 'I am sceptical as to the necessity or propriety of establishing such an agency,' he told Donovan. 'Why couldn't the purpose be achieved by a better liaison between departments and agencies?' Besides, he added, 'The burdens on the President are now monumental. We shouldn't add to them if we can avoid them.' His reply was dated 12 April. By the time it was despatched, Roosevelt was already dead and Donovan had lost his strongest friend in Washington.[31]

So long as the war was still to be won Churchill kept a close eye on Ultra. The failure in December of Britain's Joint Intelligence Committee to warn of Hitler's counter-offensive in the Ardennes only confirmed his belief that he should see the raw material himself. As usual, he paid special attention to items he found useful for his own political or strategic agenda. One such item surfaced in mid–March 1945.

By this time British and American forces were poised for their major offensive across the Rhine and the Red Army was within fifty miles of Berlin. Churchill again flew off for an eyewitness view. At Eisenhower's HQ he crossed the Rhine in a launch and was only narrowly dissuaded from making himself a target for snipers. He described the whole affair as 'a jolly day'. Typically Churchillian, it obscured his genuine distress at the strained faces of German civilians which intensified his fears about Soviet intentions. Dismemberment of Germany, so loosely ratified at Yalta, now seemed unwise.

On the eve of his departure he received an intercept from 'C'.[32] It was a Magic message from Berne to Tokyo referring to Nazi plans for a last-ditch stand in southern Germany. Intelligence reports from Eisenhower's HQ talked darkly of a 'German Maquis-to-be'. In reality, they originated with a German deception, strongly promoted by Goebbels and swallowed by the OSS in Switzerland, to deter the Allies from insisting on total victory. Churchill asked the Joint Intelligence Committee for its opinion. On the one hand, continued Wehrmacht resistance at Lake Balaton in Hungary and in Italy seemed consistent with such a plan; on the other, there might be nothing in the rumours at all. JIC agreed with his scepticism and dismissed reports from agents about the construction of underground buildings. Military intelligence separately pointed out that German plans for the dispersal of military staffs from Berlin revealed by Ultra referred exclusively to Thuringia.

Churchill quickly grasped the assessment's significance. If there was to be no southern redoubt, then Anglo-American forces could focus on reaching Berlin. He bombarded Roosevelt and Eisenhower with messages stressing the political significance of occupying the German capital and safeguarding the country's future. But Eisenhower's intelligence continued to warn of a last-ditch Nazi stand in the mountains of the south. Determined to pre-empt it, he shifted the axis of his advance further south than originally planned. This had the effect of leaving Berlin to the Russians. Churchill could only warn and plead. 'I moved among cheering crowds,' he wrote later of these closing days of the battle for Germany, 'with an aching heart and a mind oppressed by foreboding.'[33] But he had no choice but reluctantly to accept Eisenhower's decision. It was one shared and supported by Roosevelt.

The President and Eleanor retreated to Hyde Park in the last week of March. Here, in the familiar surroundings of the family home, and with spring already apparent in the woods around them, he said he wanted her to travel with him in April to San Francisco for the opening session of the United Nations and then, in May, to London. Here they would stay with the King and Queen at Buckingham Palace, drive through the streets of London, address Parliament, and spend time with Churchill and his family at Chequers before crossing to Holland, visiting the troops, and ending up in Paris.

Churchill was enthusiastic about the trip. 'He is going to get from the British people the greatest reception ever accorded to any human being since Lord Nelson made his triumphant return to London,' he told Sam Rosenman, who was staying at Chequers for the weekend, while to Roosevelt himself that same week he declared that, 'Our friendship is the rock on which I build for the future so long as I am one of the builders.'

After returning from Hyde Park Roosevelt travelled to Warm Springs, Georgia, for a two-week rest. Eleanor stayed behind, and after a few days Lucy Mercer joined him. His old friend Henry Morgenthau dropped by and was shocked by Roosevelt's aged and haggard appearance, noting that his hands shook so much that he couldn't even pour cocktails. The next day, 12 April 1945, as he sat with Lucy and the butler was preparing lunch, Roosevelt suffered a severe cerebral haemorrhage and died two hours later.

In London, Churchill was dining at The Other Club with his old American friend Bernard Baruch, after which he returned to the Annexe to 10 Downing Street, above the Cabinet War Rooms, to work on papers. Here, shortly after midnight, he heard the news from Warm Springs. Immediately he began to make plans for flying to America for the funeral. But late the next day he changed his mind. Too many government ministers were already abroad, too much urgent political business was crowding in as the wartime coalition neared its end, and events in Europe were moving too quickly – that day the Red Army entered Vienna and British and American forces liberated the concentration camps of Belsen and Buchenwald.

Suggestions that he declined to attend the funeral out of dis-illusionment with Roosevelt run counter to the evidence of his first, spontaneous, reaction, indeed to his very character. 'I have lost a dear and cherished friendship which was forged in the fire of war,' he told Eleanor, and to Harry Hopkins he confessed that he felt a painful personal loss quite apart from the ties of public action that had bound them together. 'I had a true affection for Franklin,' he said. To Parliament, after leaving the memorial serv-ice for the President at St Paul's Cathedral, he delivered a more fulsome tribute to his friend and ally. Seventeen hundred messages had passed between them, and in nine meetings and several con-ferences they had spent a hundred and twenty days of close personal contact together. As a result he had conceived an admir-ation for Roosevelt as statesman, man of affairs and war leader, and felt confidence in his character and outlook and a personal regard – 'affection, I must say' – for the President. Yet it was surely sig-nificant that in surveying their wartime relations he spent most time on Roosevelt's help in the years before Pearl Harbor and then, covering the next three years in a paragraph, moved to Yalta and evidence of Roosevelt's frailty. 'Often,' said Churchill, 'there was a faraway look in his eyes.' Then, having stressed Roosevelt's love for his country, he concluded: 'In Franklin Roosevelt there died the greatest American friend we have ever known and the greatest champion of freedom who has ever brought help and comfort from the new world to the old.'[34]

Eleanor Roosevelt described her husband's relationship with Churchill as 'a fortunate friendship'. Churchill himself painted it romantically as the literal personification of the 'special relation-ship' between Britain and America – a term he coined himself.

Few in Britain dared challenge this view until after his death. Then, in 1972, Corelli Barnett launched a broadside against Churchill. In *The Collapse of British Power*, a lament for the loss of national glory, he argued that by fooling himself that America was a friend and not a rival Churchill had merely replaced Berlin with Washington as the focus of British appeasement. 'From 1940 to the end of the Second World War and after,' he wrote, 'it was America, not Russia, which was to constitute the lurking menace to British interests which Churchill, in his passionate obsession with defeating Germany, failed to perceive.'[35] Other critics followed. Churchill was completely blind, John Grigg argued, in failing to appreciate Roosevelt's hostility to the British Empire. 'Though he was Britain's loyal ally in the war against Hitler,' wrote Grigg, 'he was no friend at all to Britain's interests in the world . . . It was the ultimate self-deception on Churchill's part to imagine that he could call in the New World to make the British Empire viable and respectable.' More recently, historian John Charmley has pushed this theme even further by suggesting that a compromise peace with Hitler in 1940 could have protected British interests better than Churchill's alliance with the United States and the Soviet Union. Instead, Britain became an American puppet.[36] Pre-war echoes could be detected in much of this criticism. Churchill was a controversial figure in British politics before the war. Many Tories only begrudgingly, and temporarily, forgave his maverick behaviour under Neville Chamberlain, and few forgot his early desertion of the party and his pre-First World War flirtation with radical liberalism.

In the United States, Roosevelt's reputation has also taken severe knocks. Here, too, he carried the burden of pre-war controversies, especially the visceral dislike among Republicans for his radical New Deal. Like Churchill, he was seen by many as a turncoat, a man of wealth who had abandoned his 'natural' party. In the United States it was 'business as usual' during the war, and his critics remained vocal. Why, many asked even before it was over, did he drag his heels in the 1930s in the face of the Nazi threat? Why did he fail to anticipate Pearl Harbor – or, worse, deliberately manoeuvre events to allow it to happen? Why was he so naïve about Stalin that he signed the Yalta accord that betrayed eastern Europe and imprisoned it behind the Iron Curtain? And, more recently, why did he fail to rescue the Jews of Europe? Even a highly sympathetic biographer such as James MacGregor Burns, who characterises him as 'The Soldier of Freedom', describes

Roosevelt as a deeply divided man whose strategy was flawed by contradictions that poisoned relations with the Soviet Union and Asia.

It is easy to scoff at Churchill's rosy view of his relations with Roosevelt, although this too frequently confuses purposeful rhetoric with reality and ignores how often he fought with his friend over imperial issues: his public enthusiasm for Anglo-American union peaked precisely when he became anxious about Roosevelt's growing muscle within the alliance and the divergence of their strategic thinking and longer-term political goals. It is also not hard to demonstrate how Roosevelt's actions often failed to match his vision, how he curtailed civil liberties, and how he paved the way for the post-war 'imperial presidency'. There is little point, too, in denying that Britain was financially weakened by the war and became a junior partner to the United States. Few historians would now accept uncritically the essentially propagandist view of his relations with Roosevelt promoted by Churchill. 'By the time of Roosevelt's death,' writes the distinguished American scholar, Warren Kimball, editor of their voluminous correspondence, 'the Churchill–Roosevelt relationship had become routine – more than a façade, but less than the personal, near friendship that it had been.' Similarly, Keith Sainsbury, a British historian, has described them recently as 'uneasy partners'.[37] The person who knew this better than anyone was Churchill himself.

Fantasies about the durability of the British Empire, and finger-pointing at Roosevelt over its decline, resemble debates in the United States about 'the loss' of China. Such illusions, themselves fuelled by national dreams of glory, are curiously blind to the tides of nationalism that destroyed the British – and American – empires after the Second World War, as though the rest of the world had no history of its own.

Sixty years on, with personal memories of the Second World War rapidly fading, the real challenge is to demonstrate that despite their differences and rivalries Roosevelt and Churchill built and kept together a coalition that helped deliver victory and formed the backbone of Western defence in the Cold War that followed. Now it is over, we can appreciate how extraordinary it was that the United States enjoyed access to British facilities and bases around the world, and how in turn Britain enjoyed the fruits of American power, technology and expertise.

At the heart of this Cold War alliance lay an unbreakable thread of intelligence co-operation, a hidden dimension whose history is only now being written. With roots stretching back before the First World War, it came to fruition with Roosevelt and Churchill – even if, in the case of the President, the work was completed by his successors.

There are no friendly secret services, it is said, only the secret services of friendly powers. Secret intelligence provides a particularly sensitive touchstone of trust between nations. Here the evidence strongly contradicts the simplistic view of Churchill weakly yielding to Roosevelt. The two men, as has been seen, shared a fascination for the 'secret world' that led both to a far more direct participation in clandestine operations than their biographers, or historians of intelligence, have ever acknowledged. And even when not involved directly in operations, they set the trend, pace and direction for their intelligence bureaucracies. It is one thing to show how secret agencies have grown and relate to each other, another to demonstrate how their political masters have encouraged and used them.

Roosevelt lent discreet but powerful support to British intelligence before Pearl Harbor, both in its security, secret propaganda and counter-espionage campaigns on American soil as well as foreign operations such as the Juan March bribery scheme in Spain. Churchill was duly grateful, and when he let Roosevelt into the secret of British codebreaking triumphs during his stay at the White House over Christmas 1941, he demonstrated extraordinary faith in his new ally. This reached its zenith in the shared codebreaking operations that delivered such rewards as Magic and Ultra.

But this did not happen immediately, nor did Churchill unilaterally show his hand. The record shows that he was an extremely tough bargainer, unwilling to give anything away he did not have to. In 1940–41 he deliberately withheld intelligence from Roosevelt about the abandonment of German invasion plans in order to keep up the pressure for American help, and only in 1943, when American forces were actively engaged in the ground war in

Europe, did Bletchley Park fully open its doors to American cryptographers. American cryptographers revealed similar pragmatic caution.

The glamour and excitement of codebreaking – that unseen window on to the unsuspecting target – should not obscure the fact that many other forms of intelligence co-operation took place, such as in the realms of special operations and human secret intelligence. Here, if either of the two powers was dependent, it was the United States. After learning as much as he could from the British, Roosevelt's intelligence chief, 'Wild Bill' Donovan, spent much of the war fighting to free himself from domination by Britain's Special Operations Executive and Secret Intelligence Service, striving instead for co-operation between equals. Backed by Roosevelt, he encountered fierce opposition from the British secret services, supported by Churchill, who were determined to preserve British primacy in key areas such as the Balkans, the Middle East and south-east Asia. Yet, by confining such differences to their secret services, the two men skilfully avoided open personal confrontation.

In his determination to build an American intelligence effort independent of the British, combined with the anti-colonial sentiments he shared with the President, Donovan often appeared anti-British. Churchill, as we have seen, was frequently exasperated by him. But from an American perspective the British could be equally difficult. Having failed to control American intelligence through integration, the British also opted for a policy of independence.

The 'hidden dimension' of the Roosevelt–Churchill relationship contained both co-operation and conflict. Where they agreed, it cemented the alliance and was a potent weapon that helped shorten the conflict. Where they fought and bickered, it provided a safety valve for tensions that could have disastrously split their partnership. Roosevelt realised this over India, Churchill over Indo-China. Each, in the end, respected the other's position on a highly emotive issue.

Yet increasingly in 1944–45 they came to share a common perception of a new threat. Well before Yalta, Donovan was sounding the alarm about Soviet behaviour in Europe. In Asia, he and his subordinates sang an anti-colonial tune. Yet in the weeks before Roosevelt's death American shadow warriors were rapidly changing tack. Only a few days before the President died, Donovan sent him thoughts on the post-war world that were startling in their rejection of much earlier thinking. If the United States stood aside, he argued, the Soviets would dominate post-war Europe and Asia. 'The United States should realise its interest in the maintenance of the British, French and Dutch colonial empires,' he declared. Schemes of trusteeship, or of otherwise weakening colonial rule, should be abandoned, and instead the United States should encourage the liberalisation of colonial regimes in order to maintain them and check Soviet influence. Sent to Roosevelt only ten days before he died, we have no way of knowing what he made of it.[38] Churchill would certainly have endorsed it.

However uneasy, however difficult, this was a rich and complex partnership that survived the greatest and most terrible conflict in history. To win it, they were willing to trust each other with their closest secrets while remaining firmly attached to their distinct national interests. Within a year of Roosevelt's death American and British codebreakers signed an agreement that extended their wartime co-operation into the Cold War that followed. Many of those who had tracked U-boats together, eavesdropped on the Wehrmacht, or intercepted diplomatic messages of many hostile, neutral, or even friendly states, now worked hand in glove in the signals intelligence war against the Soviet Union and its satellites. Roosevelt's successor, President Harry Truman, abolished the Office of Strategic Services. But within months a central intelligence agency was being reconstructed and the CIA, formally created in 1947, built rapidly and extensively on the expertise created by Donovan with Roosevelt's support. The core of the CIA, and many of its most outstanding officers, were drawn from former members of the OSS. In Britain, SOE was also disbanded. But its functions were assumed – or taken back – by the Secret Intelligence Service, which in the Cold War years enjoyed far greater resources and prestige than it had ever done during Hitler's rise to power.

In any final assessment of Western victory during the fifty years of hot and cold war that began in 1939 and ended in the rubble of the Berlin Wall, the ties of Anglo-American intelligence must play a significant part. Roosevelt and Churchill, both men of secrets, threw their enthusiastic weight behind those links. For that reason alone, their place on that London bench should remain secure.

NOTES

ABBREVIATIONS

CAC   Churchill Archives Centre, Churchill College, Cambridge
FDRL   Franklin D. Roosevelt Library, Hyde Park, New York
HI   Hoover Institution, Stanford, California
IWM   Imperial War Museum, London
NA   National Archives, Washington DC
PRO   Public Record Office, Kew

Further publication details can be found in the Bibliography.

PROLOGUE

1. Roosevelt to Churchill, 14 December 1942, in Warren F. Kimball (ed.), *Churchill and Roosevelt: The Complete Correspondence*, Vol. II, p. 73.
2. John Charmley, *Churchill's Grand Alliance, passim.*
3. Joseph P. Kennedy, unpublished diplomatic memoir, quoted in Michael Beschloss, *Kennedy and Roosevelt*, pp. 198–200.
4. David Reynolds, *The Creation of the Anglo-American Alliance*, pp. 24–5.
5. Churchill to Clementine Churchill, 14 February 1921, in CHAR 2/14, CAC.
6. Brian McKercher, 'Churchill, the European Balance of Power, and the USA'.

7. Ted Morgan, *FDR: A Biography*, p. 165; Kimball, *Forged in War*, p. 36; Reynolds, op. cit., p. 24.
8. David Stafford, *The Silent Game*, pp. 160–74.
9. Christopher Hitchens, *Blood, Class, and Nostalgia*, pp. 319–39; Robin Edmonds, *The Big Three*, p. 393.
10. Kimball, *The Juggler*, p. 7.
11. Report of the Political Warfare Executive, 'Political Warfare in the US', quoted in Richard Aldrich, 'American Intelligence and the British Raj: The OSS, the SSU and India, 1942–1947'.
12. Richard Breitman's *Official Secrets: What the Nazis Planned, What the British and Americans Knew* (London and New York, 1998) is a good start.

1: MEN OF SECRETS

1. Quoted in Fred F. Manget, 'Presidential Powers and Foreign Intelligence Operations'. For an overview of American Presidents' use of intelligence, see Christopher Andrew, *For the President's Eyes Only*, *passim*.
2. James R. Leutze, *Bargaining for Supremacy*, p. 42.
3. A. G. Gardiner, *Pillars of Society*, pp. 55–63.
4. Jeffery M. Dorwart, *The Office of Naval Intelligence*, pp. 104–12; Dorwart, *Conflict of Duty*, pp. 162–71; Rhodri Jeffreys-Jones, *American Espionage*, p. 24.
5. G. J. A. O'Toole, *Honorable Treachery*, pp. 289–90.
6. Ibid., pp. 286–7.
7. Sir Guy Gaunt, *The Yield of the Years*, *passim*; Dorwart, *The Office of Naval Intelligence*, p. 129; Patrick Beesly, *Room 40*, p. 228; O'Toole, op. cit., p. 239.
8. Dorwart, op. cit., p. 125.
9. Ibid., p. 123.
10. Barbara Tuchman, *The Zimmerman Telegram*, *passim*; Beesly, op. cit., pp. 204–24; Andrew, *Secret Service*, pp. 108–14.
11. On Bell, see Beesly, op. cit., pp. 225–50.
12. Geoffrey Ward, *A First-Class Temperament*, p. 392.
13. Ted Morgan, *FDR: A Biography*, pp. 194–5; Andrew, *For the President's Eyes Only*, pp. 78–9; John Ferris, 'Whitehall's Black Chamber: British Cryptology and the Government Code and Cypher School, 1919–29'; Alastair Denniston, 'Account of the Origins and Work of the Government Code and Cypher School', 1944, Denniston Papers, 1/4, CAC; Clarke Papers 3, 'GC and CS: Its Foundation and Development With Special Reference to the Naval Side', CAC.

14. Morgan, op. cit., pp. 234–45.
15. Robert E. Angevine, '"Gentlemen Do Read Each Other's Mail": American Intelligence in the Interwar Era'. Cf. Nathan Miller, *Spying for America, passim*.
16. Leutze, op. cit., p. 20.
17. Ibid., pp. 11–42; Richard A. Harrison, 'Testing the Water: A Secret Probe Towards Anglo-American Military Co-operation in 1936'.
18. Richard Dunlop, *Donovan, America's Master Spy*, p. 421.
19. O'Toole, op. cit., pp. 356–7; Brian R. Sullivan, '"A Highly Commendable Action": William J. Donovan's Intelligence Mission for Mussolini and Roosevelt, December 1935–February 1936'.
20. Hayden B. Peake, 'OSS and the Venona Decrypts'; for Roosevelt and Hoover, see Richard Gid Powers, *Secrecy and Power, passim* and Athan Theoharis and John Stuart Cox, *The Boss, passim*.
21. William Corson, *The Armies of Ignorance*, p. 95.
22. Peake, 'Soviet Espionage and the Office of Strategic Services'. Peake depends heavily here on Allen Weinstein, *Perjury: The Hiss–Chambers Case* (New York, 1978), and adds that while Berle did not mention the meeting with Roosevelt in his diary, the writer Isaac Don Levine claims that Berle told the President.
23. Peake, op. cit.; Christopher Andrew and Oleg Gordievsky, *KGB*, pp. 182–5, 226–7; O'Toole, *Honorable Treachery*, pp. 323–5.
24. Warren F. Kimball, *The Juggler*, p. 14.
25. Mark M. Lowenthal, 'Searching for National Intelligence: US Intelligence and Policy Before the Second World War'.
26. David Stafford, *Churchill and Secret Service, passim*.
27. Ibid., p. 27.
28. Ibid., p. 129.

2: EXCHANGING VIEWS

1. Patrick Beesly, *Very Special Admiral*, pp. 172–5; Andrew Lycett, *Ian Fleming, passim*.
2. Jeffery M. Dorwart, *Conflict of Duty*, pp. 138–42.
3. War Cabinet minutes 65/1, 5 October 1939, quoted in Sir Martin Gilbert (ed.), *The Churchill War Papers*, Vol. I, p. 206.
4. War Cabinet: Confidential Annex, CAB 66/3, 5 October 1939, quoted in Gilbert, op. cit., pp. 207–8; Kell Diary, IWM, 5 October 1939.
5. Roosevelt to Churchill, 11 September 1939, in Warren F. Kimball (ed.), *Churchill and Roosevelt: The Complete Correspondence*, Vol. I, pp. 24–5; Joseph P. Lash, *Roosevelt and Churchill*, pp. 21–3.

6. Winston S. Churchill, *Great Contemporaries*, p. 303.
7. Gilbert, op. cit., pp. 209–10; Churchill, op. cit., pp. 371–82.
8. Admiral Fraser, 'Winston Spencer Churchill, Servant of Crown and Commonwealth', pp. 80–1, quoted in Gilbert, op. cit., p. 213.
9. Gilbert, *Winston S. Churchill*, Vol. VI, pp. 52–5.
10. Kimball, op. cit., Vol. I, pp. xx–xxi; Vol. II, pp. 356–7.
11. Robert Fisk, *In Time of War*, pp. 130–1.
12. Ibid., pp. 112–17.
13. Churchill, *The Second World War*, Vol. I, p. 358; Churchill to Sir Dudley Pound, 23 October 1939, in Gilbert, *The Churchill War Papers*, Vol. I, pp. 281, 299–303, 357.
14. Stafford, *Churchill and Secret Service*, pp. 170–1.
15. Ibid., pp. 171–3.
16. Michael Beschloss, *Kennedy and Roosevelt*, p. 191.
17. Lash, op. cit., pp. 21–33.
18. Dorwart, 'The Roosevelt–Astor Espionage Ring'; Dorwart, *Conflict of Duty*, pp. 162–71.
19. Morgenthau Diaries, transcript of conversation between Morgenthau and Purvis, 26 February 1940, Box 240, FDRL; Herbert E. Gaston, Assistant Secretary of the Treasury, to General Watson, Secretary to the President, 6 February 1940; President's Official File 3906, 'Amtorg Trading Company', FDRL.
20. Dorwart, 'The Roosevelt–Astor Espionage Ring'.
21. O'Toole, op. cit., p. 349.

3: KNOWING FRIENDS

1. Robert E. Sherwood, *Roosevelt and Hopkins*, *passim*; Matthew B. Wills, *Wartime Missions of Harry L. Hopkins*, pp. x–xi; George McJimsey, *Harry Hopkins*, *passim*.
2. David Dimbleby and David Reynolds, *An Ocean Apart*, p. 125.
3. Doris Kearns Goodwin, *No Ordinary Time*, pp. 13–39.
4. Sir Martin Gilbert, *Winston S. Churchill*, Vol. VI, pp. 285–326.
5. John Colville, *The Churchillians*, p. 53.
6. Ronald Lewin, *Ultra Goes to War*, p. 183; Gilbert, op. cit., pp. 609–13; F. H. Hinsley *et al.*, *British Intelligence in the Second World War*, Vol. I, *passim*.
7. Hinsley, op. cit., Vol. I, pp. 267–98; Vol. II, pp. 3–39.
8. Anthony Cave Brown, *'C': The Life of Sir Stewart Menzies*, pp. 317–18.
9. Morton to 'C', 27 September 1940, HW1/1 (Government Code and Cypher School: Signals Intelligence passed to the Prime Minister,

Messages and Correspondence), PRO; Hinsley, 'Churchill and the Use of Special Intelligence' in Robert Blake and Wm. Roger Louis (eds), *Churchill*, pp. 407–26.

10. Lewin, op. cit., p. 67; Robert Cecil, '"C"'s War', *Intelligence and National Security*, Vol. I, No. 2, May 1986, pp. 170–88; Cave Brown, op. cit., *passim*.

11. Kathryn Brown, 'Intelligence and the Decision to Collect It: Churchill's Wartime Diplomatic Signals Intelligence'; Robin Denniston, 'Diplomatic Eavesdropping, 1922–1944: A New Source Discovered', pp. 423–48; Denniston, *Churchill's Secret War*, pp. 19–32; Eunan O'Halpin, '"According to the Irish Minister in Rome . . .": British Decrypts and Irish Diplomacy in the Second World War', *Irish Studies in International Affairs*, Vol. 6, 1995, pp. 95–105. I am grateful to Dr O'Halpin for kindly providing me with a copy of this article.

12. Gilbert, *Winston S. Churchill*, Vol. VI, p. 1154.

13. Hugh Dalton, *The Fateful Years, 1931–1945*; David Stafford, *Britain and European Resistance, 1940–45*, pp. 10–27; M. R. D. Foot, *SOE in France*, pp. 1–10; for the SOE 'Charter', see WP (40) 271 in ADM 223/480, PRO.

14. Quoted in Stafford, *Camp X*, p. 16.

15. Thomas F. Troy, *Wild Bill and Intrepid*, *passim*; Stafford, *Camp X*, *passim*; H. Montgomery Hyde, *The Quiet Canadian*, p. 99; Stafford, 'A Myth Called Intrepid'; Timothy Naftali, 'Intrepid's Last Deception: Documenting the Career of Sir William Stephenson'.

16. Jeffery M. Dorwart, *The Office of Naval Intelligence*, pp. 166–9; Dorwart, *New York History*, pp. 318–22.

17. Bradley F. Smith, *The Shadow Warriors*, pp. 30–9.

18. Joseph P. Lash, *Roosevelt and Churchill*, pp. 138–9.

19. Gilbert, *Winston S. Churchill*, Vol. VI, pp. 326, 389, 492–3; Sam Rosenman, *Working With Roosevelt*, p. 189.

20. R. Bearse and A. Read, *Conspirator*, *passim*; Brian Simpson, *In the Highest Degree Odious: Detention Without Trial in Wartime Britain*, pp. 112–52, 431–3; Joan Miller, *One Girl's War*, pp. 16–32; Anthony Masters, *The Man Who Was 'M'*, pp. 147–9; Peter and Lily Gillman, *Collar the Lot*, pp. 115–29; Andrew Lownie, 'Tyler Kent: Isolationist or Spy?', in Rhodri Jeffreys-Jones and Andrew Lownie (eds), *North American Spies*, pp. 49–78; Eric Homberger, '"Uncle Max" and His Thrillers', *Intelligence and National Security*, Vol. 3, No. 2, April 1988, pp. 312–21; Simpson, op. cit., *passim*; Gillman and Gillman, op. cit., *passim*; Gilbert, *Winston S. Churchill*, Vol. VI, p. 459ff; Angus Calder, *The People's War*, pp. 118–36; Hinsley, op. cit., pp. 47–76; Paul Addison, *Churchill on the Home Front*, pp. 341–3; PREM 7/2, PRO.

21. Lash, op. cit., pp. 138–9.

22. Gilbert, *The Churchill War Papers*, Vol. II, pp. xxi–xxiii.
23. Troy, op. cit., p. 59.
24. Bradley F. Smith, *The Ultra–Magic Deals*, pp. 43–55. But for a corrective, see Ralph Erskine, 'Churchill and the Start of the Ultra–Magic Deals'.
25. Gilbert, *Winston S. Churchill*, Vol. VI, p. 672.
26. Kathryn Brown, op. cit.

4: MAKING CONTACT

1. Doris Kearns Goodwin, *No Ordinary Time*, pp. 188–9.
2. Sir Martin Gilbert, *Winston S. Churchill*, Vol. VI, p. 889.
3. Goodwin, *No Ordinary Time*, p. 194–6; David Reynolds, *The Creation of the Anglo-American Alliance*, pp. 147–61; Gilbert, op. cit., p. 974; Robert E. Sherwood, *Roosevelt and Hopkins*, pp. 221–9.
4. Reynolds, op. cit., p. 159; Joseph P. Lash, *Roosevelt and Churchill*, pp. 271–3.
5. Sherwood, op. cit., pp. 229–63.
6. Ibid., p. 238.
7. Sherwood, *The White House Papers of Harry L. Hopkins*, *passim*; Gilbert, op. cit., pp. 981–1000.
8. Sherwood, *Roosevelt and Hopkins*, pp. 240–2, 277.
9. Gilbert, op. cit., p. 992.
10. Lash, op. cit., p. 281.
11. Brian McKercher, 'Churchill, the European Balance of Power, and the USA', pp. 42–64.
12. Churchill to Roosevelt, 26 October 1940, in Gilbert, op. cit., p. 869. For Churchill's management of intelligence, see Michael Handel, 'The Politics of Intelligence', *Intelligence and National Security*, Vol. 2, No. 4, October 1987, especially pp. 8–10.
13. Roosevelt to Churchill, 16 January 1941, in Warren F. Kimball (ed.), *Churchill and Roosevelt: The Complete Correspondence*, Vol. I, p. 129.
14. Gilbert, op. cit., p. 996.
15. Ibid., pp. 986, 993–4, 996; Sherwood, op. cit., pp. 256–7.
16. Sherwood, op. cit., pp. 248–50.
17. FBI File, 'Winston S. Churchill', Freedom of Information Request, File Number 417132/HO-1271428, dated 21 December 1998.
18. Anthony Cave Brown, *The Last Hero*, p. 153.
19. 'Personal and Most Secret from Former Naval Person for President', 10 March 1941, in Warren F. Kimball (ed.), *Churchill and Roosevelt: The Complete Correspondence*, Vol. I, p. 145.

20. Bradley F. Smith, *The Shadow Warriors*, pp. 42–3.
21. Smith, *The Ultra–Magic Deals*, pp. 54–63.
22. Prescott Currier, 'My "Purple" Trip to England in 1941'.
23. Gilbert, op. cit., pp. 1008–10.
24. Ibid., p. 1016.
25. 'C' to Churchill, C/5906, 26 February 1941, C/506, and Churchill's reply, 27 February 1941; A. G. Denniston to Menzies, 3 March 1941, HW 1/2, PRO. Author's underlining. Also Ralph Erskine, 'Churchill and the Start of the Ultra–Magic Deals', p. 57.
26. 'Captain Joe Baker-Cresswell', captain of the *Bulldog*, obituary, *Daily Telegraph*, 7 March 1997; David Kahn, *Seizing the Enigma*, pp. 1–13, 161–9; Hinsley and Stripp, *Codebreakers*, pp. 79–80; Hinsley *et al.*, *British Intelligence in the Second World War*, Vol. I, pp. 337–9; Vol. II, pp. 163–76; Beesly, *Very Special Intelligence*, pp. 71–2.
27. 'C' to Prime Minister, C/6863, 24 June 1941, in HW 1/6, PRO; see also Hinsley, op. cit., Vol. II, p. 55.
28. Ibid.
29. Thomas F. Troy, *Donovan and the CIA*, p. 40.
30. Ibid.; Smith, *The Shadow Warriors*, pp. 55–68; Lash, op. cit., p. 283.
31. Beesly, *Very Special Admiral*, pp. 181–2.
32. Smith, 'Admiral Godfrey's Mission to America, June/July 1941', pp. 441–50.
33. Alex Danchev, *Establishing the Anglo-American Alliance*, pp. 24–65; Christopher Andrew, *For the President's Eyes Only*, p. 101.
34. Danchev, op. cit., pp. 24–5.

5: UNDECLARED WAR

1. HW 1/6, C/6863, 24 June 1941, PRO.
2. Theodore A. Wilson, *The First Summit*, pp. 1–7; Joseph P. Lash, *Roosevelt and Churchill*, p. 393.
3. H. V. Morton, *Atlantic Meeting*, p. 5.
4. Sir Martin Gilbert, *Winston S. Churchill*, Vol. VI, p. 1155; Lash, op. cit., pp. 596–7; Churchill's own account is in *The Second World War*, Vol. II, pp. 354–80.
5. Gilbert, op. cit., p. 1154.
6. Morton, op. cit., p. 67.
7. Wilson, op. cit., p. 72; Robert E. Sherwood, *The White House Papers of Harry L. Hopkins*, Vol. I, p. 351.
8. Doris Kearns Goodwin, *No Ordinary Time*, p. 264.
9. Churchill, op. cit., Vol. III, p. 364.

10. Elliott Roosevelt, *As He Saw It*, p. 24.
11. Churchill, op. cit., p. 365; Goodwin, op. cit., p. 267; Gilbert, op. cit., p. 1159; Wilson, op. cit., p. 111.
12. Dalton to Churchill, 12 February 1941, HS 1/350; FO 371/27924-9, PRO; Dalton Diary, 10 February 1941 and subsequent entries, British Library of Political and Economic Science.
13. Warren F. Kimball (ed.), *Churchill and Roosevelt: The Complete Correspondence*, Vol. I, pp. 135–6.
14. HS 1/350, PRO.
15. For the Foreign Office files on the affair, see FO 371/27924-27929, PRO.
16. Jürgen Rohwer, 'The Wireless War', in Stephen Howarth and Derek Law (eds), *The Battle of the Atlantic, 1939–1945*, Annapolis, MD, 1994.
17. F. H. Hinsley *et al.*, *British Intelligence in the Second World War*, Vol. II, pp. 747–8, Appendix 19, 'The Breaking of the U-Boat Enigma'; Bradley F. Smith, *The Ultra–Magic Deals*, pp. 86–90.
18. J. L. Granatstein and David Stafford, *Spy Wars*, pp. 31–4.
19. Smith, *The Shadow Warriors*, pp. 58–60; William L. Langer and S. Gleason, *The Undeclared War*, p. 379; President's Secretary's File, Box 74, FDRL; *Foreign Relations of the United States*, 1941, Vol. I, p. 350.
20. Smith, op. cit., pp. 86–93.
21. Roosevelt to Biddle, 17 November 1941, *FDR Correspondence*, p. 1241.
22. Ted Morgan, *FDR: A Biography*, pp. 599–603.
23. David Stafford, '"Intrepid": Myth and Reality'; Stafford, *Camp X*, pp. 271–92; Granatstein and Stafford, *Spy Wars*, pp. 76–87; Nigel West, *Unreliable Witness*, pp. 127–38; Timothy Naftali, 'Intrepid's Last Deception: Documenting the Career of Sir William Stephenson'.
24. Francis MacDonnell, 'The Search for a Second Zimmerman Telegram: FDR, BSC, and the Latin American Front', *International Journal of Intelligence and Counter-Intelligence*, Vol. 4, No. 4, pp. 487–8. The same author's *Insidious Foes: The Axis Fifth Column and the American Home Front* deals perceptively and at length with Roosevelt's policies in this area.
25. H. Montgomery Hyde, *Secret Intelligence Agent*, pp. 153–9. For Hyde's biography of Stephenson, see *The Quiet Canadian* (*Room 3603* in the US).
26. Hoover to Watson, 10 July 1941, in Macdonnell, op. cit., p. 493.
27. Ivar Bryce, *You Only Live Once: Memories of Ian Fleming, passim*; John Bratzel and Leslie Rout, 'FDR and the "Secret Map"', in *The Wilson Quarterly*, Vol. 9, No. 1, January 1985.
28. 'Britain's War in America', *Washington Post*, 17 September 1989, quoted in Naftali, op. cit., p. 72.

29. See for example the books by Hyde and Bryce, and William Stephenson, *A Man Called Intrepid, passim*; also Christopher Andrew, *For the President's Eyes Only*, p. 103.
30. MacDonnell, op. cit., p. 490.
31. For the 11 May meeting, see 'CD [Sir Frank Nelson] to 4800 [Stephenson]', 17 May 1941, America File 122, SOE Archive, kindly made available to the author by the SOE Adviser, Duncan Stuart, CMG, in a letter dated 11 December 1998. For Dalton's reaction, see Ben Pimlott (ed.), *The Wartime Diary of Hugh Dalton*, p. 216.
32. See 'AD/Z [Colonel F. T. 'Tommy' Davies] Personally from 4800 [Stephenson]', 23 August 1941, America File 122, SOE Archive, with thanks to the SOE Adviser, Duncan Stuart, CMG, letter to author, 11 December 1998. For the BSC report on Vichy, see *British Security Coordination*, pp. 188–99.

6: THE LAST PIRATE OF THE MEDITERRANEAN

1. Rhodri Jeffreys-Jones, 'United States Secret Service' in *The Greenwood Encyclopaedia of American Institutions: Government Agencies* (editor-in-chief: Donald R. Whitman), Westport, 1983.
2. *Webster's American Biographies*, p. 738; John Morton Blum, *Roosevelt and Morgenthau*, p. 25; James MacGregor Burns, *Roosevelt: The Soldier of Freedom*, p. 8.
3. John Morton Blum, *From the Morgenthau Diaries*, Vol. II, pp. 338–9.
4. Simon to Morgenthau, 19 July 1940, Morgenthau Diaries, Vol. 284, FDRL.
5. Halifax to Morgenthau, 1 November 1941, and Memorandum for the Secretary's Diary, 5 November 1941, Morgenthau Diaries, Book 466, 27–30 November 1941, Microfilm Reel 130, FDRL. I am grateful to Raymond Teichmann and Robert Parks of the Franklin Delano Roosevelt Library for helping me locate this and related material. For Gilbert, see *Winston S. Churchill*, Vol. VI, p. 585.
6. Alan Hillgarth, dedication in *The War Maker*; Denis Smyth, 'Alan Hillgarth', *Dictionary of National Biography, 1971–1980*, pp. 409–10; Bradley F. Smith, *Diplomacy and Strategy of Survival, passim*; PREM 3/409/7; PREM 4/21/2A, 4/32/7, 7/4; FO 371/26890-26907; ADM 223/409, 479–81 and /805 (all PRO) also contain much about Hillgarth and Spain; see also Churchill, *The Second World War*, Vol. II, p. 443; Gilbert, op. cit., pp. 585, 678, and Vol. VII, p. 456; Lord Templewood, *Ambassador on Special Leave*, pp. 132–3; Patrick Beesly, *Very Special Admiral, passim*; Andrew Lycett, *Ian Fleming*, pp. 109–10,

125–45. I am grateful to Mr Lycett for drawing my attention to the ADM 223 files.

7. Kim Philby, *My Silent War*, p. 39.
8. Denis Smyth, '"Les Chevaliers de Saint-George": La Grande-Bretagne et la corruption des généraux espagnoles', pp. 29–54. I am grateful to Professor Smyth for this and other information about Hillgarth, as well as to Alan Hillgarth's son, Dr Jocelyn Hillgarth.
9. J. G. Beevor, *SOE*, p. 31; Donald McLachlan, *Room 39: Naval Intelligence in Action, 1939–45, passim*. McLachlan draws heavily on a lengthy memorandum written by Hillgarth on his experience as naval attaché in Madrid.
10. John Brooks, 'Annals of Finance', Parts 1 and 2, *New Yorker*, 21 and 28 May 1979.
11. Ibid., 21 May 1979.
12. Paul Preston, *The Coming of the Spanish Civil War*, p. 49.
13. For brief biographical sketches of March, see: Robert W. Kern, *Historical Dictionary of Modern Spain, 1700–1988*, pp. 320–1, and Robert H. Wheatley in James Cortado (ed.), *Historical Dictionary of the Spanish Civil War*, pp. 318–19. For March and the Spanish Civil War, see Paul Preston, *Franco*, p. 135; Preston, *The Coming of the Spanish Civil War*, *passim*; and Hugh Thomas, *The Spanish Civil War*, pp. 203–4.
14. David Stafford, *The Silent Game*, pp. 73–77.
15. Basil Thomson, *The Scene Changes*, p. 294, entry for 26 June 1916.
16. Churchill to the Director of Naval Intelligence, 26 September 1939: 'Juan March: Some Notes About the Man'; John Godfrey, 'Interview with Mr Juan March, 23 September 1939'; and memo to Churchill, 17 December 1939, all in ADM 223/490, PRO.
17. Alan Hillgarth, 'Notes on Conversation with Don Juan March at 18.30 on 27th September 1939' and 'Notes Dictated by Naval Attaché, Madrid, 15.12.39', in ADM 223/490, PRO.
18. Hillgarth to Churchill, handwritten letter of 19 January 1940; Ian Fleming to Godfrey, 17 February 1940; Godfrey to Seal, 18 February 1940, all in ADM 223/490, PRO; and Andrew Lycett, op. cit., p. 110.
19. Gilbert, *Winston S. Churchill*, Vol. VI, p. 443.
20. Kenneth Benton, 'The ISOS Years: Madrid, 1941–43', *Journal of Contemporary History*, Vol. 30, 1995, pp. 359–410.
21. Preston, *Franco*, pp. 431–3.
22. Denis Smyth, *Diplomacy and Strategy of Survival*, p. 226.
23. See 'SOE Shipping Co. in Spain', Vol. 1, April–December 1941, HS 6/975, PRO.
24. Weddell to Washington, 1 March 1941, *Foreign Relations of the United States*, 1941, Vol. II, pp. 881–5.

25. Preston, op. cit., p. 427.
26. I. C. B. Dear (ed.), *The Oxford Companion to the Second World War*, pp. 487–8.
27. See 'The Ambassador in Spain [Weddell] to the Secretary of State [Cordell Hull]', 1 March 1941, in *Foreign Relations of the United States, 1941*, Vol. II, pp. 881–5; Alex Danchev, *Establishing the Anglo-American Alliance*, p. 62; Lycett, op. cit., pp. 125, 131.
28. Lycett, op. cit., pp. 124–5; Smyth, *Diplomacy and Strategy of Survival*, pp. 163–4; David Stafford, *Britain and European Resistance*, p. 55.
29. Roosevelt to Churchill, 31 December 1940, in Warren F. Kimball (ed.), *Churchill and Roosevelt: The Complete Correspondence*, Vol. I, pp. 117–18; Churchill to Roosevelt, 29 May 1941, ibid., p. 201; Smyth, *Diplomacy and Strategy of Survival*, pp. 230–1.
30. *Foreign Relations of the United States, 1941*, Vol. I, pp. 356–7. 'Pilgrim' was later abandoned.
31. Churchill to Kingsley Wood and Anthony Eden, 25 September 1941, PREM 4/32/7, PRO.

7: THE CAVALRY OF ST GEORGE

1. Adam LeBor, *Hitler's Secret Bankers, passim*.
2. Minutes of Treasury Group Meeting, 11.15 A.M., 4 November 1941, Morgenthau Diary, Vol. 457, pp. 97–105; Morgenthau to Roosevelt, 14 November 1941, President's Secretary's File, Box 80, FDRL. See also Foley to Morgenthau, 2 June 1942, for details of Treasury investigations into Swiss Banks and their German connections. Morgenthau Diary, Book 535, Microfilm Reel 155, FDRL. See also LeBor, op. cit., pp. 93–5.
3. 'Memorandum for the Secretary's Diary', 5 November 1941, Morgenthau Diary, Book 466, 27–30 November 1941, Microfilm Reel 130, FDRL.
4. PREM 4/32/7, PRO.
5. See entry for 2.06 P.M., 28 November 1941, Morgenthau Diary, Book 466, Microfilm Reel 130, FDRL.
6. See 'SOE Shipping Co. in Spain', Vol. 1, April–December 1941, HS 6/975, PRO.
7. John Brooks, 'Annals of Finance', *New Yorker*, 21 May 1979.
8. For Solborg, see R. Harris Smith, *OSS*, pp. 27, 41; Bradley F. Smith, *The Shadow Warriors*, pp. 58–9; *Foreign Relations of the United States, 1941*, Vol. II, especially pp. 420–3, and 1942, Vol. II, *passim*; Anthony Cave Brown, *The Last Hero*, pp. 217–34.

9. Solborg to Donovan, 4 March 1942, Donovan Papers, CAC.
10. Solborg to Preston Goodfellow, 21 March 1942, Goodfellow Papers, HI.
11. See for example Solborg's report No. 1191, 27 March 1942, including 'Anglo-Portuguese Talks, Allied Plans for the Defence of Portuguese Possessions, and British Secret Organisation'. The source and reliability of this report is described as 'British: Good' – Donovan Papers, Microfilm Reel 92, CAC; also, for Beevor, see 'HB to Caesar through AD', 28 September 1942, HS 6/986, PRO.
12. Solborg to Lee, 17 April 1942, in Donovan Papers, CAC.
13. J. G. Beevor, *SOE*, p. 64.
14. Sir Stafford Cripps to the Prime Minister, undated, 1941, PREM 3/409/7, PRO; cf. Brown, op. cit., pp. 225–6.
15. Chiefs of Staff to Britman Washington, 8 August 1942; JSM Washington to Chiefs of Staff, 8 August 1942, and Minute by Bridges to Mr Martin, 10 August 1942, PREM 3/409/7, PRO.
16. Solborg to Lee, 17 April 1942, Donovan Papers, Microfilm Reel 93, CAC. Anthony Cave Brown, in *The Last Hero*, p. 225, quotes what appears to be an almost identical letter from Solborg to Donovan, dated 15 April 1942, commenting that the worth of the report is difficult to assess. Obviously, it was accurate. Curiously, Solborg tells Lee in his letter of 17 April that he is *not* writing to Donovan because he has heard he has had an accident and he does not wish to risk his letter falling into the hands of anyone else. He is leaving it 'entirely to your judgement as to how to deal with this intelligence', he tells Lee. For the Aranda approach to the US Embassy in March 1942, see Gregory Thomas to Colonel Donovan, 23 February 1943, Donovan Papers, CAC.
17. Robin Winks, *Cloak and Gown*, p. 152.
18. Carleton J. Hayes, *Wartime Mission in Spain, 1942–1945*, pp. 7, 11.
19. Winks, op. cit., p. 173; Brown, op. cit., pp. 226–30; Christopher Hitchens, *Blood, Class, and Nostalgia*, pp. 327–35.
20. 'Affidavit de M. Hillgarth du 3 mai 1968', Case of the Barcelona Traction Company, Annexe No. 33, Document No. 1, International Court of Justice, The Hague.
21. See, especially, the argument of Mr Francis Mann QC, counsel for the Belgian government, in the International Court of Justice *Pleadings* on the case, Vol. VIII, pp. 89–95.
22. Smyth, '"Les Chevaliers de Saint-George"; La Grande-Bretagne et la corruption des généraux espagnoles', p. 47.
23. Doris Kearns Goodwin, *No Ordinary Time*, p. 382.
24. Hillgarth to Churchill, 28 July 1943, PREM 4/21/2, PRO.
25. Stafford, *Churchill and Secret Service*, pp. 319–27.
26. International Court of Justice, *Pleadings*, 1958–61, then ten volumes,

1962–70 (The Hague). See also ICJ, *Report of Judgement*, 1970. Mann's reference to the British Secret Service is in ICJ, *Pleadings*, Vol. X, pp. 52–3.
27. 'Affidavit de M. Hillgarth du 3 mai 1968', op. cit.
28. Hillgarth to Sir Herbert Brittain, KBE, CB, 23 November 1951, in *Affaire relative à la Barcelona Traction, Light & Power Company Ltd (Nouvelle Requête, 1962), Red Book No. 1, Documents déposés en février 1966 et juillet 1968 par le gouvernement espagnol*, pp. 333–5. I am grateful to Lawrence Collins QC and the Librarian of the British Institute of International and Comparative Law for making this and other related documents available.
29. Beevor, op. cit., p. 42.
30. Brooks, op. cit., p. 48.

8: INTERCEPT MAGIC

1. David Stafford, *Camp X*, pp. 17–24.
2. Winston S. Churchill, Jr, *His Father's Son: The Life of Randolph Churchill*, p. 197.
3. Testimony by Schulz before the Joint Committee on the Investigation into Pearl Harbor, quoted in Robert E. Sherwood, *The White House Papers of Harry L. Hopkins*, Vol. I, pp. 430–2.
4. Sherwood, op. cit., p. 435. The best study of Roosevelt's handling of Magic is David Kahn, 'Roosevelt, Magic, and Ultra'; Pearl Harbor conspiracies are also clinically despatched by Kahn in 'The Intelligence Failure of Pearl Harbor'; Louis W. Tordella and Edwin C. Fischel, 'A New Pearl Harbor Villain: Churchill' (a dissection of Eric Nave and James Rusbridger's *Betrayal at Pearl Harbor: How Churchill Lured Roosevelt into World War II*). Likewise, see Richard Aldrich, 'Conspiracy or Confusion? Churchill, Roosevelt and Pearl Harbor', *Intelligence and National Security*, Vol. 7, No. 3, July 1992.
5. Doris Kearns Goodwin, *No Ordinary Time*, pp. 289–90.
6. John G. Winant, *A Letter from Grosvenor Square: An Account of a Stewardship*, pp. 196–9, quoted in Sir Martin Gilbert, *Winston S. Churchill*, Vol. VI, p. 1266.
7. HW/303, PRO.
8. John Ferris, 'From Broadway House to Bletchley Park: The Diary of Captain Malcolm D. Kennedy, 1934–1946'.
9. Gilbert, op. cit., pp. 1267–8; Winston S. Churchill, *The Second World War*, Vol. III, pp. 509–12.
10. Frederick D. Parker, 'The Unsolved Messages of Pearl Harbor', pp. 295–313.

11. Christopher Andrew, *For the President's Eyes Only*, pp. 103–11.
12. Kahn, 'Roosevelt, Magic, and Ultra'.
13. Ibid.
14. Andrew, op. cit., p. 108.
15. Kahn, op. cit.
16. Andrew, op. cit., p. 108.
17. Kahn, op. cit.
18. Ibid.
19. Ibid.
20. Stafford, *Churchill and Secret Service*, pp. 230–1.
21. Anthony Cave Brown, *The Last Hero*, pp. 6–7.
22. Goodwin, op. cit., pp. 294–5.
23. Gerald Pawle, *The War and Colonel Warden*, p. 147.

9: THE TIES THAT BIND

1. For accounts of the Washington visit, see: Winston S. Churchill, *The Grand Alliance*, pp. 522–99; Sir Martin Gilbert, *Winston S. Churchill*, Vol. VII, pp. 23–44; Doris Kearns Goodwin, *No Ordinary Time*, pp. 300–13; Robert E. Sherwood, *The White House Papers of Harry L. Hopkins*, Vol. I, pp. 446–91; Robert H. Pilpel, *Churchill in America*, pp. 136–60; Elliott Roosevelt (ed.), *FDR: His Personal Letters*, p. 1260; Gerald Pawle, *The War and Colonel Warden*, pp. 147–54.
2. Goodwin, op. cit., pp. 307–11; Mary Soames, *Clementine Churchill*, pp. 320–9.
3. Ted Morgan, *FDR: A Biography*, p. 632.
4. Goodwin, op. cit., pp. 310–11.
5. Roosevelt to Churchill, 31 January 1942, and Churchill to Roosevelt, 1 February 1942, in Warren F. Kimball (ed.), *Churchill and Roosevelt: The Complete Correspondence*, Vol. I, pp. 338–9.
6. Gilbert, op. cit., p. 44; Morgan, op. cit., p. 27.
7. Sherwood, op. cit., Vol. I, p. 446; Gilbert, op. cit., p. 28.
8. Gilbert, op. cit., pp. 30–1.
9. For background to the Saint-Pierre-et-Miquelon case, see John Bryden, *Best-Kept Secret*, pp. 198–203. For State Department and Roosevelt's reactions, see *Foreign Relations of the United States*, 1941, Vol. II, pp. 540–71, and Roosevelt memo of 1 January 1942, in Elliott Roosevelt, op. cit., p. 1268.
10. Churchill to Roosevelt, 25 February 1942, in Kimball, op. cit., p. 371. Obviously, FDR did not burn the letter.
11. Ibid.; Joint Intelligence Committee (41) 40th, 30 December 1941, in

CAB 81/88, PRO; Bradley F. Smith, *The Ultra–Magic Deals*, p. 94; Roosevelt to Cordell Hull, 9 January 1942, in Elliott Roosevelt, op. cit., pp. 1270–1.

12. F. H. Hinsley *et al.*, *British Intelligence in the Second World War*, Vol. II, p. 179; Churchill to Roosevelt, 5 March 1942, in Kimball, op. cit., p. 381.
13. Gilbert, op. cit., pp. 69–73.
14. Roosevelt to Churchill, 18 March 1942, in Kimball, op. cit., pp. 420–2.
15. HW 1/431, PRO.
16. Gilbert, op. cit., pp. 80–3.
17. Carl Boyd, *Hitler's Japanese Confidant*, pp. 8, 18.
18. Ibid., p. 65.
19. Ibid., pp. 117–22, 185–91.

10: FIFTH COLUMNS

1. Arthur Bryant, *The Turn of the Tide*, p. 332.
2. Ibid., p. 334.
3. Gerald Pawle, *The War and Colonel Warden*, p. 174.
4. Doris Kearns Goodwin, *No Ordinary Time*, p. 346.
5. Quoted in Bryant, op. cit., p. 335.
6. Quoted in Goodwin, op. cit., p. 347.
7. Warren F. Kimball, *Forged in War*, p. 150; Goodwin, op. cit., p. 348.
8. Bradley F. Smith, *The Ultra–Magic Deals*, pp. 125–72.
9. Christopher Andrew, *For the President's Eyes Only*, p. 136; John Bryden, *Best-Kept Secret*, pp. 180–2.
10. F. H. Hinsley *et al.*, *British Intelligence in the Second World War*, Vol. II, pp. 58–61; Churchill/'C' exchanges, June 1941, HW 1/8, PRO.
11. 'C' to Prime Minister, 28 September 1941, HW 1/95, PRO.
12. Smith, *Sharing Secrets With Stalin*, pp. 231–2.
13. PREM 3, 418/5, PRO; W. P. Crozier, *Off the Record: Political Interviews, 1933–1943*, p. 138; Brian Simpson, *In the Highest Degree Odious*, pp. 248–50, 389–91.
14. Sam Rosenman, *Working With Roosevelt*, pp. 297–8.
15. Smith, *The Shadow Warriors*, pp. 98–9.
16. Ted Morgan, *FDR: A Biography*, p. 627.
17. Robert Dallek, *Franklin D. Roosevelt and American Foreign Policy*, pp. 334–5; Morgan, op. cit., pp. 628–9; Goodwin, op. cit., pp. 321–2.
18. For the weekend's events at Shangri-La, see the detailed notes kept by Mrs Rosenman, along with his own recollections, in Sam Rosenman, *Working With Roosevelt*, pp. 322–7. Details about the disposal of the

saboteurs' bodies can be found in a memorandum written for Roosevelt by Brigadier-General S. U. Marietta of the Walter Reed General Hospital, 14 August 1942, President's Secretary's File, Box 5, FDRL. For Roosevelt's earlier involvement and exchanges with his officials, see Francis Biddle, 'Memorandum for the President', 19 June 1942, President's Secretary's File, Box 56, FDRL; J. Edgar Hoover to Marvin H. McIntyre, Secretary to the President, 22 June 1942, Official File 10b, Box 16, FDRL.

19. Roosevelt to Biddle, 30 June 1942, President's Secretary's File, 'Justice, 1940–44', Box 56, FDRL.
20. See various letters from the public, President's Official Files, 'Nazi Spies, 1942–45', Box 5036, FDRL.
21. See Biddle, 'Memorandum for the President', 1 July 1942, President's Official Files, 'Nazi Spies, 1942–45', Box 5036, FDRL. The transcripts of the trial, in eighteen volumes, and related documents, are in Map Room files, Boxes 198–201. For FDR's execution order, see document dated 'White House, 12 noon, 7 August 1942', Map Room, Box 200, FDRL.

11: ACTION STATIONS

1. Bradley F. Smith, *The Shadow Warriors*, pp. 102, 115.
2. Roosevelt to Churchill, 22 March 1942, in Warren F. Kimball (ed.), *Churchill and Roosevelt: The Complete Correspondence*, Vol. I, p. 427.
3. Anthony Cave Brown, *The Last Hero*, p. 218; Roosevelt to Donovan, 13 April 1942, President's Personal File 6558, FDRL.
4. 'Former Naval Person to President. Personal and Secret', 7 February 1942, in Kimball, op. cit., pp. 349–51.
5. For the 1942 SOE/OSS agreement, see Record Group 218, CCS 385, NA; David Stafford, *Camp X*, pp. 135–8; and Bickham Sweet-Escott, *Baker Street Irregular*, p. 126.
6. *New York Times Book Review*, 30 June 1963.
7. Stafford, '"Intrepid": Myth and Reality', pp. 303–17.
8. For the writing of the BSC History, see Stafford, *Camp X*, pp. 250–7.
9. *British Security Coordination, passim.*
10. 'Report on British Security Co-ordination in the United States of America'. See especially Part III, 'Special Operations'. Copy seen by the author.
11. Berle to Roosevelt, 13 February 1942, FDRL, quoted in Christopher Andrew, *For the President's Eyes Only*, p. 128.
12. David Walker, 'Democracy Goes to War: Politics, Intelligence, and

Decision-making in the United States', in Rhodri Jeffreys-Jones and Andrew Lownie (eds), *North American Spies*, pp. 79–101.

13. Untitled typescript page in Cuneo file marked 'Hopkins A-4-8', Cuneo Papers, Box 131, FDRL.

14. PREM 3/409/4 & 5, *passim*, PRO; F. H. Hinsley *et al.*, *British Intelligence in the Second World War*, Vol. II, pp. 14–15.

15. 'Colonel Bill Hudson', obituary, *Daily Telegraph*, 21 November 1995; Dalton to Churchill, 11 December 1941, PREM 3/409/7, PRO; DO (41) 72nd, 15 December 1941, PRO; Ralph Bennett, *Ultra and the Mediterranean Strategy*, pp. 324–31; Mark Wheeler, *Britain and the War for Yugoslavia, 1940–1943*, p. 117.

16. John Steinbeck, *The Moon is Down*, p. 118. See also Donald Coers, *John Steinbeck as Propagandist: 'The Moon is Down' Goes to War*; Jay Parini, *John Steinbeck: A Biography*; Stafford, 'Churchill, SOE, and Northern Europe', in *La Résistance et les européens du nord/Het Verzet En Noord-Europa*, Brussels, 1994, pp. 143–55.

17. Stafford, *Britain and European Resistance, 1940–1945*, p. 100.

18. HS 4/18, 19, 22, 24, PRO; see also Callum MacDonald, *The Killing of SS Obergruppenführer Reinhard Heydrich*, *passim*.

19. Hesketh Prichard, 'Operation Autonomous', 22 January 1942, HS 4/39, PRO.

20. Peter Wilkinson and Joan Bright Astley, *Gubbins and SOE*, pp. 107–8; Wilkinson to author, personal communication; Gubbins to Moravec, 30 May 1942, HS 4/39, PRO; Selborne, SOE quarterly report March–June 1942, PREM 3/409/5, PRO.

21. See Nelson D. Langford (ed.), *OSS Against the Reich: The World War II Diaries of Colonel David K. E. Bruce*, *passim*.

22. Roosevelt to Churchill, 24 October 1941, in Kimball, op. cit., pp. 263–4; Brown, *'C': The Secret Life of Sir Stewart Menzies*, p. 364.

23. Smith, *The Shadow Warriors*, p. 189; Peter Grose, *Gentleman Spy: The Life of Allen Dulles*, pp. 148–256.

24. Churchill to C.-in-C. Middle East, 23 September 1942 and related correspondence, PREM 3/117, PRO; Michael Howard, *British Intelligence in the Second World War*, Vol. V, *Strategic Deception*, pp. ix–xiii, 3–44; Michael Handel, *Strategic and Operational Deception in the Second World War*, pp. 1–91; Ronald Lewin, *Ultra Goes to War*, pp. 299–301.

25. Brown, *Bodyguard of Lies*, p. 270.

26. Katherine L. Herbig, 'American Strategic Deception in the Pacific, 1942–44', in Handel, op. cit., pp. 260–99.

12: OUR MAN IN MANILA

1. Transcript, coast-to-coast broadcast by NBC on 19 April 1942, in Wilkinson Papers 3/2/3, CAC.
2. Churchill to Roosevelt, 13 June 1942, in Warren F. Kimball (ed.), *Churchill and Roosevelt: The Complete Correspondence*, Vol. I, p. 510; Mountbatten to Roosevelt, 15 June 1942, Hopkins Papers, Box 194, FDRL.
3. Wilkinson Papers, op. cit.
4. Some of what follows is from Christopher Thorne, 'MacArthur, Australia and the British, 1942–1943: The Secret Journal of MacArthur's British Liaison Officer'. Other material has been extracted from the papers that still remain open at Churchill College, including an account by Wilkinson of his experiences in the Philippines during and after the Japanese invasion. Additional items have been gleaned from various previously published sources, including David Day, *Reluctant Nation* and *The Pearl Harbor Hearings*.
5. Edwin P. Hoyt's *Davies: The Inside Story of a British–American Family in the Pacific and Its Business Enterprises* tells the company's story. For family details, I am indebted to Rupert Wilkinson, Mary June Pettyfer and Mariana Barry.
6. *Philippines Herald*, obituary of Wilkinson, 5 July 1965.
7. Henry Clausen and Bruce Lee, *Final Judgement*, pp. 115–16, 401; Peter Elphick, *Far Eastern File*, pp. 293–5. Both draw from the report on Pearl Harbor written by Clausen in 1945 for Henry Stimson included in the official *Pearl Harbor Hearings*.
8. William Manchester, *The American Caesar*, pp. 3–4.
9. Eric Larrabee, *Commander-in-Chief*, pp. 305–8.

13: 'JUST A ROMANTIC LIMEY'

1. Edward J. Drea, *MacArthur's Ultra*, pp. 19–21.
2. Wilkinson Diary 1/1, September 1942–February 1943, *passim*.
3. Eric Larrabee, *Commander-in-Chief*, p. 329.
4. Christopher Thorne, *Allies of a Kind*, p. 157.
5. Wilkinson Diary, 13 February 1943.
6. Ibid., 26 January 1943.
7. David Day, *Reluctant Nation*, p. 90; Halifax to Churchill, 22 February 1943, CHAR 20/107/10, CAC.
8. *Evening News*, 14 August 1943; Wilkinson, 3/1.
9. Larrabee, op. cit., p. 330.

10. Churchill to MacArthur, 1 April 1943, CHAR 20/107/10, CAC.
11. D. M. Horner, *High Command*, p. 367.
12. Top-secret appendix to affidavit dated 8 May 1945 by Major-General C. A. Willoughby, Clausen Report, *Pearl Harbor Hearings*. For Willoughby, see Frank Kluckhohn, 'Heidelberg to Manila – The Story of General Willoughby', *The Reporter*, 19 August 1952, p. 26.
13. Wilkinson Diary, 30 June 1943.
14. But see Richard Aldrich, 'Imperial Rivalry: British and American Intelligence in Asia, 1942–46', published before the ban was imposed; also Bradley F. Smith, *The Shadow Warriors*, p. 258, likewise.
15. Churchill to MacArthur, 2 October 1943, CHAR 20/119/86, CAC; MacArthur to Churchill, 6 October 1943, CHAR 20/120/22, CAC.
16. Quoted in Thorne, 'MacArthur, Australia and the British 1942–1943: The Secret Journal of MacArthur's British Liaison Officer', p. 206.
17. D. M. Horner, *High Command*, p. 312; Ismay to Churchill, 21 April 1944, PREM 3 63/13, PRO.
18. *Honolulu Advertiser*, 15 February 1946.

14: 'I LOVE THESE AMERICANS'

1. James MacGregor Burns, *Roosevelt: The Soldier of Freedom*, p. 286.
2. Winston S. Churchill, *The Second World War*, Vol. IV, p. 560; Sir Martin Gilbert, *Winston S. Churchill*, Vol. VII, p. 283; Anthony Verrier, *Assassination in Algiers*, *passim*; Arthur L. Funk, *The Politics of Torch*, Appendix B; Francis Brooks Richards, *Secret Flotillas: The Clandestine Sea Lines to France and French North Africa, 1940–1944*, pp. 582–610; Charles Williams, *The Last Great Frenchman*, pp. 195–205.
3. CAB 69/4, Defence Committee, 29 December 1942, DO (42) 20th, PRO.
4. Anthony Cave Brown, *'C': The Life of Sir Stewart Menzies*, pp. 447–53.
5. David Stafford, *Camp X*, p. 3.
6. For the assassination of Darlan, see Verrier, op. cit., *passim*; Williams, op. cit., pp. 195–206; Richards, op. cit., pp. 582–610; Funk, op. cit.
7. Peter Wilkinson and Joan Bright Astley, *Gubbins and SOE*, p. 118.
8. Sam Rosenman, *Working With Roosevelt*, pp. 335–6.
9. Churchill to Roosevelt, 31 October 1942, in Warren F. Kimball (ed.), *Churchill and Roosevelt: The Complete Correspondence*, Vol. I, pp. 648–51.
10. Roosevelt to King George VI, from Casablanca, 24 January 1943, in Elliott Roosevelt (ed.), *FDR: His Personal Letters*, p. 1394. For his insightful essay on the conference, I am indebted to Warren Kimball's essay in his book, *The Juggler*, pp. 63–81.

11. Averell Harriman, *Special Envoy*, p. 180.
12. Alex Danchev, *Establishing the Anglo-American Alliance*, p. 1.
13. Churchill, op. cit., p. 157.
14. Kenneth Pendar, *Adventure in Diplomacy*, pp. 1, 12.
15. Ibid., p. 146.
16. Lord Moran, *Churchill*, p. 90.
17. Churchill, op. cit., p. 604.
18. Pendar, op. cit., pp. 151–2.
19. Elliott Roosevelt, *As He Saw It*, p. 71.
20. Churchill to Roosevelt, 1 January 1943, in Kimball, op. cit., pp. 101–2.
21. Edwin T. Layton, *'And I Was There': Pearl Harbor and Midway – Breaking the Secrets*, pp. 474–6.

15: MISSION IMPOSSIBLE

1. See Roger W. Louis, *Imperialism at Bay*; Christopher Thorne, *Allies of a Kind*, *passim*; also David Reynolds, *Rich Relations*, *passim*.
2. Patrick French, *Liberty or Death*, pp. 132–3, 177; Lawrence James, *Raj*, p. 556.
3. French, op. cit., p. 161.
4. 'Report on British Security Co-ordination in the United States of America', 17 March 1943. Copy seen by author.
5. Robert E. Sherwood, *The White House Papers of Harry L. Hopkins*, Vol. II, pp. 534–7; Winston S. Churchill, *The Second World War*, Vol. IV, pp. 190–1; Warren F. Kimball (ed.), *Churchill and Roosevelt: The Complete Correspondence*, pp. 446–9, 501.
6. Sherwood, op. cit., Vol. II, p. 516.
7. Donovan to Roosevelt, 20 April 1942, quoted in Richard Aldrich, 'American Intelligence and the British Raj: The OSS, the SSU and India, 1942–1947'.
8. Gary Hess, *America Encounters India*, pp. 94–5.
9. William Phillips, *Ventures in Diplomacy*, p. 69; Hess, op. cit., pp. 89–112; Donald C. Watt, *Succeeding John Bull*, p. 236.
10. Phillips to Roosevelt, 24 June 1942, and Roosevelt's reply, 29 June, President's Secretary's File, Box 552, FDRL.
11. 'Record of Discussions Held With Colonel Donovan in Mr Phillips' Office on 12th September 1942', Donovan Papers, Microfilm Reel 85, CAC.
12. Whitney Shephardson to Phillips, 19 November 1942, Donovan Papers, Microfilm Reel 85, CAC.
13. Phillips, op. cit., p. 334.

56

14. F. H. Hinsley *et al.*, *British Intelligence in the Second World War*, Vol. IV, p. 187; Bradley F. Smith, *The Shadow Warriors*, p. 173; Nigel West, *MI6*, p. 215.
15. Doris Kearns Goodwin, *No Ordinary Time*, p. 382.
16. Phillips to Roosevelt, 4 November 1942, President's Secretary's File, Box 38, FDRL.
17. Phillips, op. cit., pp. 54–5.
18. Phillips to Donovan, 22 December 1942, Donovan Papers, Microfilm Reel 83, CAC.
19. French, op. cit., p. 143.
20. Amery to Linlithgow, 19 February 1943, in Mansergh, *The Transfer of Power*, Vol. III, p. 699.
21. Linlithgow to Amery, 19 February and 2 March 1943, in Mansergh, op. cit., pp. 690, 748–9; Marshall Windmiller, 'A Tumultuous Time: OSS and Army Intelligence in India, 1942–46'; Aldrich, 'Imperial Rivalry: British and American Intelligence in Asia, 1942–46'; Aldrich, 'American Intelligence and the British Raj: The OSS, the SSU and India, 1942–1947'; Smith, op. cit., pp. 255–7.
22. Ellery C. Huntington, Jr, to Brigadier-General William J. Donovan, 12 April 1943; Merrell to Phillips, 18 May 1943; Phillips to Donovan, 18 May 1943: Donovan Papers, Microfilm Reel 40, CAC; Phillips, op. cit., p. 349.
23. Mansergh, op. cit., p. 783.
24. Phillips, op. cit., p. 383.
25. Roosevelt to Hopkins, 19 March 1943, in Elliott Roosevelt (ed.), *FDR: His Personal Letters*, p. 1414.
26. Phillips, op. cit., pp. 389–90.
27. William D. Leahy to Donovan, 5 June 1943, and subsequent correspondence, Donovan Papers, Microfilm Reel 40, CAC; French, op. cit., p. 183; Gerald Pawle, *The War and Colonel Warden*, pp. 249–51.
28. 'Intelligence and Quasi-Intelligence Activities in India', Combined Chiefs of Staff 196/4, 4 September 1943, Donovan Papers, Microfilm Reel 40; Marshall Windmiller, op. cit.

16: HOUSE GUESTS

1. Clementine Churchill to Winston Churchill, 13 May 1943, in Mary Soames (ed.), *Speaking for Themselves*, pp. 479–80.
2. Ibid., pp. 483–4.
3. T. P. Mulligan, 'Spies, Ciphers, and "Zitadelle"', *Journal of*

Contemporary History, Vol. 22, 1987, pp. 246–50; F. H. Hinsley *et al.*, *British Intelligence in the Second World War*, Vol. II, pp. 624–7.

4. An abridged text, with some security deletions, can be found in Carl Boyd, *Hitler's Japanese Confidant*; the full text is in NARA RG 457, Historic Collection No. 4632. I am grateful to Ralph Erskine for letting me see a copy.

5. John Costello, *Mask of Treachery*, pp. 424–5.

6. Colonel Ellery C. Huntington to General William J. Donovan, 'Report on European Trip – December 24, 1942 to March 21, 1943', Donovan Papers, Microfilm Reel 40, CAC.

7. Bradley F. Smith, *The Ultra–Magic Deals*, pp. 131–72.

8. Sir Martin Gilbert, *Winston S. Churchill*, Vol. VII, pp. 295, 360–1, 366; Churchill/Sir Edward Bridges exchanges, May 1943, PREM 4/68/6A, PRO; Hinsley, op. cit., pp. 596–7.

9. 'Deception: Indiscretions by Members of the US Administration and High Officials', and personal minute by the Prime Minister, July 1943, PREM 3/117, PRO; also Ronald Lewin, *Ultra Goes to War*, p. 253.

10. Anthony Cave Brown, *The Last Hero*, pp. 301–45.

11. Geoffrey T. Hellman, 'House Guest', *New Yorker*, 7 and 14 August 1943.

12. Ibid., Part 1, p. 26.

13. Doris Kearns Goodwin, *No Ordinary Time*, pp. 458–9.

14. Ernest Cuneo, undated typescript entitled 'Hopkins', pp. 1–2, in Hopkins File, Cuneo Papers, Box 131, FDRL; Sam Rosenman, *Working With Roosevelt*, p. 218.

15. Cuneo, op. cit.

16. Gilbert, op. cit., p. 410.

17. Churchill to Roosevelt, 13 February 1944, CHAR 20/156, CAC.

18. Churchill to Hopkins, 30 November 1944, CHAR 20/176/29, CAC.

19. Churchill to Halifax, 11 January 1945, CHAR 20/210/87, CAC.

20. Cuneo, op. cit.

21. See Hayden B. Peake, 'Soviet Espionage and the Office of Strategic Services' in Warren F. Kimball (ed.), *America Unbound*, p. 132.

22. Eduard Mark, 'Venona's Source 19 and the "Trident" Conference of 1943: Diplomacy or Espionage?'; Christopher Andrew and Oleg Gordievsky, *KGB*, pp. 232–6.

23. Roosevelt to Stalin, 5 May 1943, delivered by hand of Joseph E. Davies in Moscow, in Elliott Roosevelt (ed.), *FDR: His Personal Letters*, pp. 1422–3.

24. George McJimsey, *Harry Hopkins*, p. 197; Hellman, op. cit., Part 2, p. 35.

25. Robin Edmonds, *The Big Three*, p. 329.

26. Alex Danchev, *Very Special Relationship*, p. 18.

27. Averell Harriman, *Special Envoy*, p. 191.

28. Kenneth Pendar, *Adventure in Diplomacy*, p. 153.

29. Winston Churchill to Clementine, 28 May 1943, in Soames, op. cit., p. 482.

17: 'ALMOST HOMOSEXUAL'

1. Doris Kearns Goodwin, *No Ordinary Time*, p. 449; Sir Martin Gilbert, *Winston S. Churchill*, Vol. VII, p. 447.

2. Warren F. Kimball (ed.), *Churchill and Roosevelt: The Complete Correspondence*, Vol. II, pp. 356–7.

3. James MacGregor Burns, *Roosevelt: The Soldier of Freedom*, p. 392.

4. Lord Moran, *Churchill*, p. 117.

5. Gerald Pawle, *The War and Colonel Warden*, p. 249; Mary Soames, *Clementine Churchill*, p. 340.

6. Winston S. Churchill, *The Second World War*, Vol. V, p. 119.

7. Robert Rhodes James, *Churchill Speaks, 1897–1963*, pp. 815–17.

8. Kimball, op. cit., p. 447.

9. John Charmley, *Churchill: The End of Glory* and *Churchill's Grand Alliance, passim.*

10. Sir Desmond Morton to R. W. Thompson, 20 August 1960, in Thompson, *Churchill and Morton*, p. 81.

11. Thompson, op. cit., p. 30.

12. Gerald Wilkinson, diary entry for Wednesday 21 July 1943: 'Major Desmond Morton'. In private hands.

13. Sir Frank Nelson, file memo, 17 February 1941, in HS 6/309, Vol. 2, No. 1, PRO.

14. John Colville, *The Churchillians*, p. 206.

15. Thompson, op. cit., p. 78.

16. Churchill, op. cit., p. 59.

17. Colville, op. cit., p. 205.

18. Gilbert, op. cit., pp. 532–3.

19. Brigadier E. C. W. Myers, 'The Andarte Delegation to Cairo: August 1943', in Phyllis Auty and Richard Clogg (eds), *British Policy Towards Wartime Resistance in Yugoslavia and Greece*, p. 160. See also Morton to Churchill, 1 December 1942, PREM 3/409/7, PRO; C. M. Woodhouse, *Something Ventured*, pp. 21–51.

20. Ralph Bennett, *Ultra and the Mediterranean Strategy*, p. 345; F. H. Hinsley *et al., British Intelligence in the Second World War*, Vol. III, pp. 137–62.

21. Frank McLynn, *Fitzroy Maclean, passim*; Fitzroy Maclean, *Eastern Approaches*, pp. 303–533; Gilbert, op. cit., pp. 435, 440, 448, 454; Elizabeth Barker, 'Some Factors in British Decision-making Over Yugoslavia', in Auty and Clogg, op. cit., pp. 22–58.
22. Maclean, op. cit., pp. 280–1; McLynn, op. cit., pp. 120–37, 138–56.
23. Morgan, *FDR: A Biography*, p. 689.
24. Roosevelt to Churchill, 22 October 1943; Churchill to Roosevelt, 23 October 1943, in Kimball, op. cit., pp. 548–9, 553–4.
25. For Morrison as war correspondent, see Phillip Knightley, *The First Casualty*, pp. 286–7, 339–40. He was later killed while reporting on the Korean War; see also Peter Elphick, *Far Eastern File*, pp. 80, 199; Bradley F. Smith, *The Shadow Warriors*, p. 255.
26. Wilkinson Diary, 2 November 1943.

18: 'SAME BED, DIFFERENT DREAMS'

1. Quoted in Gary Hess, *The United States' Emergence as a Southeast Asia Power*, p. 48.
2. F. H. Hinsley *et al.*, *British Intelligence in the Second World War, passim*; Charles Cruickshank, *SOE in the Far East, passim*.
3. Richard Aldrich, 'Imperial Rivalry: British and American Intelligence in Asia, 1942–46', p. 9.
4. Roosevelt to Mountbatten, 3 December 1942, in Elliott Roosevelt (ed.), *FDR: His Personal Letters*, p. 1375.
5. Roosevelt to Mountbatten, 8 November 1943, op. cit., p. 1468.
6. Richard Hough, *Mountbatten*, pp. 166–7; R. Harris Smith, *OSS*, p. 286.
7. Aldrich, 'Britain's Secret Intelligence Service in Asia During the Second World War'.
8. Mackenzie interview, 1986, *The Special Operations Executive: Sound Archive and Oral History Recordings*, No. 9471, p. 153, IWM.
9. Aldrich, op. cit.
10. Andrew Gilchrist, *Bangkok Top Secret*, p. 189.
11. Heppner to Donovan, 12 November 1943, quoted in Marshall Windmiller, 'A Tumultuous Time: OSS and Army Intelligence in India, 1942–46'.
12. Smith, op. cit., p. 287; Aldrich, op. cit.
13. Sir Martin Gilbert, *Winston S. Churchill*, Vol. VII, p. 955; Aldrich, op. cit.; also Christopher Thorne, *Allies of a Kind, passim*; Donald C. Watt, *Succeeding John Bull, passim*.
14. Aldrich, op. cit., p. 14.

15. Ibid., p. 21; Thorne, op. cit., p. 594.
16. Aldrich, 'Imperial Rivalry: British and American Intelligence in Asia, 1942–46', pp. 24–6; Aldrich, *The Key to the South*, p. 375; Donovan to Roosevelt, 15 December 1941, PSF/OSS Reports, Box 151, FDRL.
17. Thorne, op. cit., p. 611.
18. Aldrich, op. cit., p. 20.
19. Thorne, op. cit., p. 591.
20. Roosevelt to Hull, 24 January 1944, in Elliott Roosevelt, op. cit., p. 1489.
21. Aldrich, op. cit., p. 7.
22. Churchill to Eden, 21 May 1944, CHAR 20/160, CAC; Cruickshank, op. cit., pp. 123–4; Watt, op. cit., p. 206.
23. Ronald Spector, 'Allied Intelligence and Indo-China, 1943–1945', *Pacific Historical Review*, Vol. 51, p. 82. See also Halifax to Stettinius, 23 November 1944, and Roosevelt to Stettinius, President's Secretary's File, Box 39, FDRL.
24. Thorne, op. cit., pp. 174, 421.
25. Maochun Yu, *OSS in China*, pp. 20–3, 92–4.
26. Ibid., pp. 31–2; Bradley F. Smith, *The Shadow Warriors*, p. 198.
27. Edmond Taylor, *Awakening from History*, p. 275.
28. Adrian Carton de Wiart, *Happy Odyssey*, p. 238, and Foreword by Churchill, p. 7.
29. Yu, op. cit., pp. 60–2, 102–6; Wilkinson Diary, 'Talk with JK at Baker Street', 31 July 1943; Bradley F. Smith, op. cit., p. 133.
30. See for example Wilkinson's Diary, 14 and 15 December 1943.
31. Aldrich, 'Britain's Secret Intelligence Service in Asia During the Second World War', p. 210.
32. Aldrich, 'Imperial Rivalry: British and American Intelligence in Asia, 1942–46', p. 27.
33. M. R. D. Foot, *SOE*, p. 243.
34. Aldrich, op. cit., p. 5.
35. Edwin Ride, *BAAG Hong Kong Resistance*, p. viii.

19: FRIENDS APART

1. Sarah Churchill, *A Thread in the Tapestry*, p. 63; Burns, *The Soldier of Freedom*, p. 405; Churchill, *The Second World War*, Vol. V, p. 290.
2. Churchill to Clementine, 26 November 1943, in Mary Soames (ed.) *Speaking for Themselves*, pp. 487–8.
3. James MacGregor Burns, *Roosevelt: The Soldier of Freedom*, p. 409.

4. 'Colonel Warden to Mrs Warden', 29 November 1943, in Soames, op. cit., p. 489.

5. Roosevelt–Churchill exchanges, 28 June–1 July 1944, in Warren F. Kimball (ed.), *Churchill and Roosevelt: The Complete Correspondence*, Vol. III, pp. 214–29.

6. John Morton Blum (ed.), *From the Morgenthau Diaries*, Vol. III, pp. 308–9.

7. Churchill to Clementine, 17 August 1944, in Soames, op. cit., pp. 500–2.

8. Sir Martin Gilbert, *Winston S. Churchill*, Vol. VII, pp. 949, 951, 955.

9. Burns, op. cit., pp. 448–51; Doris Kearns Goodwin, *No Ordinary Time*, pp. 500, 542.

10. Goodwin, op. cit., p. 549.

11. Ibid., p. 545.

12. Gilbert, op. cit., p. 968.

13. Burns, op. cit., p. 521.

14. Blum, *Roosevelt and Morgenthau*, pp. 598–9.

15. War Cabinet, 27 January 1944, CAB 80/78, PRO; PREM 3/185/1, PRO.

16. Churchill minute, 2 February 1944, PREM 7/5, PRO.

17. M. R. D. Foot, *SOE in France*, p. 355.

18. F. H. Hinsley *et al.*, *British Intelligence in the Second World War*, Vol. III, p. 464.

19. Anthony Cave Brown, *'C': The Secret Life of Sir Stewart Menzies*, p. 547.

20. See Deane to Donovan, 7 September 1943, Donovan Papers, Microfilm Reel 122, CAC; Frank McLynn, *Fitzroy Maclean*, pp. 167–9; Kirk Ford Jr, *OSS and the Yugoslav Resistance, 1943–1945*, pp. 24–6; Hinsley, op. cit., p. 463; R. Harris Smith, *OSS*, *passim*.

21. Wilkinson and Astley, *Gubbins of SOE*, p. 143; McLynn, op. cit., pp. 188–90; Gilbert, op. cit., p. 690; Ford, op. cit., pp. 60–1; Macmillan to Churchill, 22 January 1944, CHAR 20/155, CAC; Brown, *The Last Hero*, p. 457.

22. Churchill to Bridges, 27 January 1944, CHAR 20/152, CAC; Churchill to Eden, 12 February and 8 March 1944, loc. cit.; Churchill to Wilson, 6 March 1944, loc. cit.

23. Wilkinson Diary, 3 March 1944.

24. Brown, op. cit., p. 453.

25. Churchill to Roosevelt, 6 April 1944; Roosevelt to Churchill, 8 April 1944, in Kimball, op. cit., pp. 80–82; Ford, op. cit., pp. 39–41.

26. Ford, op. cit., pp. 119–21.

27. Glenconner to Leeper, 18 May 1943, in HS 5/587, PRO. For recent OSS material, I am grateful to Professor Richard Clogg for letting me read his unpublished article, 'Distant Cousins: The Special Operations Executive and the Office of Strategic Services at Odds Over Greece'.

28. Churchill to Hopkins, 24 August 1944, CHAR 20/180, CAC; Brown, op. cit., pp. 595–609; Wilson to Toulmin, 30 August 1944, Donovan Papers, Microfilm Reel 120, CAC.

29. Elizabeth Barker, *British Policy in South-East Europe*, p. 234.

30. See Glavin for Toulmin from 109 (Donovan), 12 May 1944, in Donovan Papers, CAC.

31. David Dilks (ed.), *The Diaries of Sir Alexander Cadogan*, *passim*.

32. Donovan to Magruder, 18 May 1944; 109 (Donovan) to 106 (Buxton), 30 May 1944; Toulmin to Donovan, 21 June 1944; Donovan to JCS, 3 August 1944, Donovan Papers, CAC.

33. Brown, op. cit., pp. 679–81; Bradley F. Smith, *The Shadow Warriors*, p. 351. For a review and analysis of recent OSS/Romanian releases, see Edouard Mark, 'The OSS in Romania, 1944–45: An Intelligence Operation of the Early Cold War'.

34. Washington to Istanbul, 26 August 1944; Ross to Green, 2 September 1944, Donovan Papers, Microfilm Reel 122, CAC; Mark, op. cit., p. 321; Charles S. Cheston, Memorandum for the President, 15 September 1944, Donovan Papers, loc. cit.; Donovan to Roosevelt, 29 September 1944, cited in Smith, op. cit., p. 352.

35. Donovan to Fitin, 10 October 1944, Donovan Papers, Microfilm Reel 121, CAC.

36. Colonel Edward J. Glavin to Donovan, 9 September 1944, and ibid., 'OSS Activities in Romania', 11 September 1944, Donovan Papers, Microfilm Reel 122, CAC.

20: ALLIES AT WAR

1. Roosevelt to Harriman, 4 October 1944, Hopkins Papers, Box 335, FDRL; Roosevelt to Churchill, 4 October 1944, in Warren F. Kimball (ed.), *Churchill and Roosevelt: The Complete Correspondence*, Vol. III, p. 344.

2. Kimball, *Forged in War*, pp. 286–7; Sir Martin Gilbert, *Winston S. Churchill*, Vol. VII, p. 1039.

3. John Charmley, *Churchill: The End of Glory*, *passim*.

4. Churchill to Roosevelt, 8 November 1944, in Kimball, *Churchill and Roosevelt: The Complete Correspondence*, Vol. III, p. 383.

5. Roosevelt to Churchill, 13 December 1944, in Kimball, op. cit., pp. 455–6; see also James MacGregor Burns, *Roosevelt: The Soldier of Freedom*, pp. 538–9.
6. Thomas Campbell and George Herring (eds), *The Diaries of Edward R. Stettinius Jr*, pp. 207–15.
7. Doris Kearns Goodwin, *No Ordinary Time*, p. 570; Gilbert, op. cit., pp. 1175, 1195.
8. Goodwin, op. cit., pp. 583–4.
9. Sam Rosenman, *Working With Roosevelt*, pp. 478–80.
10. Kimball, *Forged in War*, pp. 322–3, 335.
11. Roosevelt to Mountbatten, December 1944, in Elliott Roosevelt (ed.), *FDR: His Personal Letters*, p. 1560.
12. See 'Rocket Tribe B.B. 100 from A.D., repeated London for C.D., New York to Delhi', 18 November 1944, and related correspondence, in HS1/307, PRO.
13. Rear Headquarters SEAC, Meeting with Major-General Donovan, 'Clandestine Organisations', 14 January 1945, HS 1/229, PRO; 'Minutes of Conference on Clandestine and Quasi-Military Activities, HQ US Forces, China Theater', 24 January 1945, HS 1/323, PRO; Meeting Between Heads and Representatives of Clandestine Services of Great Britain and the United States of America, Held in Hut 10, SEAC, 29 January 1945, HS 1/229, PRO.
14. Memorandum by Colonel John Coughlin, 'The Relations of OSS to the SEAC and India–Burma Theater', 15 January 1945 (one copy only, for the personal use of General Donovan), quoted in Richard Aldrich, 'American Intelligence and the British Raj: The OSS, the SSU and India, 1942–1947', pp. 140–1.
15. Donovan to Roosevelt, 5 March 1945, and related correspondence, President's Secretary's File, OSS Reports, 3 March–9 September 1945, Box 151, FDRL.
16. See ADCOS (A), 27 February 1945, to Sec/SAC Top Secret, WO 203/4331, PRO; Kenneth A. Merrick, *Flights of the Forgotten*, p. 280; also AIR 27/1765 Operations Record Book, No. 358 Squadron, PRO; Wilson to Chiefs of Staff, reporting on converation with Wedermeyer, 9 March 1945, HS 1/169, PRO.
17. Donald C. Watt, *Succeeding John Bull*, pp. 194–219, 239; Churchill to Roosevelt, 17 March 1945, Roosevelt to Churchill, 22 March 1945, in Kimball, *Churchill and Roosevelt: The Complete Correspondence*, Vol. III, pp. 111, 572–3, 582–3; Ronald Spector, 'Allied Intelligence and Indo-China, 1943–1945', *Pacific Historical Review*, pp. 51, 82; Charles Cruickshank, *SOE in the Far East*, pp. 124–5.
18. Peter Wilkinson and Joan Bright Astley, *Gubbins and SOE*, pp. 211–12.

19. Richard Aldrich, 'Britain's Secret Intelligence Service in Asia During the Second World War', p. 216.
20. Stafford, *Britain and European Resistance*, pp. 144–98.
21. Stafford, op. cit., pp. 177–8; Ivor Porter, *Operation Autonomous: With SOE in Wartime Romania*, pp. 99–164; Churchill to Eden, 22 May 1944, CHAR 20/152, CAC.
22. Wilkinson and Astley, op. cit., p. 216.
23. Paul Addison, *The Road to 1945*, p. 255.
24. F. H. Hinsley *et al.*, *British Intelligence in the Second World War*, Vol. IV, p. 177; Aldrich, 'Secret Intelligence for a Post-war World: Reshaping the British Intelligence Community', in Aldrich (ed.), *British Intelligence, Strategy, and the Cold War*, pp. 15–49.
25. See Christopher Andrew and Oleg Gordievsky, *KGB*, passim.
26. Donovan to Roosevelt, 18 November 1944, in Morgenthau Papers, Microfilm Reel 242, FDRL; Bradley F. Smith, *The Shadow Warriors*, pp. 394–5; Anthony Cave Brown, *The Last Hero*, p. 625.
27. Aldrich, op. cit., pp. 155–6; Brown, op. cit., p. 625; John Franklin Carter to Roosevelt, 26 October 1944, President's Secretary's File, Box 153, FDRL.
28. Smith, op. cit., pp. 353–5; Andrew, *For the President's Eyes Only*, pp. 145–6.
29. Brown, op. cit., pp. 627–33.
30. Aldrich, 'Imperial Rivalry: British and American Intelligence in Asia, 1942–46', p. 153; Andrew, op. cit., pp. 156–7.
31. Roosevelt to Donovan, 5 April 1945, and Morgenthau to Donovan, 12 April 1945, Morgenthau Papers, Box 836, Microfilm Reel 242, FDRL.
32. Hinsley, op. cit., Vol. III, pp. 714–18.
33. Churchill, *The Second World War*, Vol. VI, p. 391.
34. Gilbert, op. cit., pp. 1291–301; Goodwin, *No Ordinary Time*, pp. 595–615; Churchill, op. cit., pp. 403–15; *Hansard*, 17 April 1945, Vol. 410, Cols 73–8.
35. Corelli Barnett, *The Collapse of British Power*, p. 589.
36. John Grigg, *1943: The Victory That Never Was*, pp. 123–5; Charmley, *Churchill: The End of Glory* and *Churchill's Grand Alliance*, passim.
37. Kimball, *Forged in War*, p. 331; Keith Sainsbury, *Churchill and Roosevelt at War*, p. 1.
38. OSS memorandum, 'Problems and Objectives of US Policy', 2 April 1945, quoted in Aldrich, op. cit., pp. 45–46.

BIBLIOGRAPHY

BOOKS

Aldrich, Richard, *The Key to the South: Britain, the United States and Thailand During the Approach of the Pacific War, 1929–1942*, Kuala Lumpur, 1993

Alexander, Martin (ed.), *Knowing Your Friends: Intelligence Inside Alliances and Coalitions from 1914 to the Cold War*, London, 1998

Alldritt, Keith, *The Greatest of Friends: Franklin D. Roosevelt and Winston Churchill, 1941–1945*, London, 1995

Andrew, Christopher, *Secret Service: The Making of the British Intelligence Community*, London, 1985

——, with Oleg Gordievsky, *KGB*, London, 1990

——, *For The President's Eyes Only*, London, 1995

Bearse, R., and Read, A., *Conspirator: The Untold Story of Churchill, Roosevelt and Tyler Kent, Spy*, London, 1991

Beesly, Patrick, *Very Special Intelligence: The Story of the Admiralty's Operational Intelligence Centre, 1939–1945*, London, 1977

——, *Very Special Admiral: The Life of J. H. Godfrey*, London, 1980

——, *Room 40: British Naval Intelligence, 1914–1918*, London, 1982

Beevor, J. G., *SOE: Recollections and Reflections, 1940–1945*, London, 1981

Berle, Beatrice Bishop, and Jacobs, Travis Beal, *Navigating the Rapids, 1918–1971: From the Papers of Adolf A. Berle*, New York, 1973

Beschloss, Michael, *Kennedy and Roosevelt: The Uneasy Alliance*, New York, 1980

Blum, John Morton, *From the Morgenthau Diaries:* Vol. II, *Years of Urgency, 1938–1941*; and Vol. III, *Years of War, 1941–1945*, Boston, MA, 1965, 1967

——, *Roosevelt and Morgenthau*, Boston, MA, 1970

Boyd, Carl, *Hitler's Japanese Confidant: General Oshima Hiroshi and MAGIC Intelligence, 1941–1945*, Wichita, KS, 1993

British Security Coordination, *British Security Coordination: The Secret History of British Intelligence in the Americas, 1940–45*, London, 1998

Brown, Anthony Cave (ed.), *The Secret War Report of the OSS*, New York, 1976

Brown, Anthony Cave, *The Last Hero: Wild Bill Donovan*, London, 1982

——, *'C': The Secret Life of Sir Stewart Menzies*, London, 1987

Bryden, John, *Best-Kept Secret: Canadian Secret Intelligence in the Second World War*, Toronto, 1993

Burns, James MacGregor, *Roosevelt: The Soldier of Freedom, 1940–1945*, New York, 1970

Campbell, Thomas, and Herring, George (eds), *The Diaries of Edward R. Stettinius, Jr, 1943–1946*, New York, 1975

Charmley, John, *Churchill: The End of Glory*, London, 1993

——, *Churchill's Grand Alliance: The Anglo-American Special Relationship, 1940–1957*, London, 1995

Churchill, Winston S., *The Second World War*, six volumes, London, 1948–54

Churchill, Winston S., Jr, *His Father's Son: The Life of Randolph Churchill*, London, 1997

Clausen, Henry, and Lee, Bruce, *Pearl Harbor: Final Judgement*, London, 1993

Colville, John, *The Churchillians*, London, 1981

Corson, William, *The Armies of Ignorance*, New York, 1977

Cortada, James (ed.) *Historical Dictionary of the Spanish Civil War, 1936–1939*, New Haven, CT, 1982

Cruickshank, Charles, *SOE in the Far East*, Oxford, 1983

Cull, Nicholas, *Selling War*, London, 1995

Dallek, Robert, *Franklin D. Roosevelt and American Foreign Policy 1932–1945*, New York, 1995

——, *Franklin D. Roosevelt as World Leader: An Inaugural Lecture Delivered Before the University of Oxford on 16 May 1995*, Oxford, 1995

Danchev, Alex, *Very Special Relationship: Field Marshal Sir John Dill and the Anglo-American Alliance, 1941–44*, London, 1986

——, *Establishing the Anglo-American Alliance: The Second World War Diaries of Brigadier Vivian Dykes*, London, 1990

Day, David, *Reluctant Nation: Australia and the Allied Defeat of Japan, 1941–1945*, Melbourne, 1985

Dear, I. C. B., *The Oxford Companion to the Second World War*, Oxford, 1995

Dennett, Laurie, *Slaughter & May: A Century in the City*, London, 1989

Department of State, *Foreign Relations of the United States*, 1939–1945

de Wiart, Sir Adrian Carton, *Happy Odyssey*, London, 1950

Dilks, David (ed.), *The Diaries of Sir Alexander Cadogan, 1938–45*, London, 1971

Dimbleby, David, and Reynolds, David, *An Ocean Apart: The Relationship Between Britain and America in the Twentieth Century*, London, 1988

Dorwart, Jeffery M., *The Office of Naval Intelligence: The Birth of America's First Intelligence Agency, 1865–1918*, Annapolis, MD, 1979

——, *Conflict of Duty: The US Navy's Intelligence Dilemma, 1919–1945*, Annapolis, MD, 1983

Drea, Edward J., *MacArthur's Ultra: Codebreaking and the War Against Japan, 1942–1945*, Wichita, KS, 1992

Dunlop, Richard, *Donovan: America's Master Spy*, New York, 1982

Edmonds, Robin, *The Big Three: Churchill, Roosevelt and Stalin in Peace and War*, London, 1991

Eisenhower, John S. D., *Allies: Pearl Harbor to D-Day*, New York, 1982

Elphick, Peter, *Far Eastern File: The Intelligence War in the Far East, 1930–1945*, London, 1998

Eubank, Keith, *Summit at Teheran*, New York, 1985

Fisk, Robert, *In Time of War: Ireland, Ulster and the Price of Neutrality*, London, 1983

Foot, M. R. D., *SOE: An Outline History of the Special Operations Executive, 1940–46*, London, 1984

Franklin, Jay [John Franklin Carter], *The Catoctin Conversation*, New York, 1947

French, Patrick, *Liberty or Death: India's Journey to Independence and Division*, London, 1998

Gaunt, Sir Guy, *The Yield of the Years: A Story of Adventure Afloat and Ashore*, London, 1940

Gilbert, Sir Martin (ed.), *The Churchill War Papers:* Vol. I, *At the Admiralty, September 1939–May 1940*; and Vol. II, *Never Surrender, May 1940–December 1940*, London, 1994, 1996

——, and Churchill, Randolph, *Winston S. Churchill*, Vols I–VIII, London, 1966–88

Gilchrist, Andrew, *Bangkok Top Secret*, London, 1970

Glendevon, John, *The Viceroy at Bay: Lord Linlithgow in India, 1936–1943*, London, 1971

Goodwin, Doris Kearns, *No Ordinary Time: Franklin and Eleanor Roosevelt – The Home Front in World War II*, New York, 1995

Granatstein, J. L., and Stafford, David, *Spy Wars: Espionage and Canada from Gouzenko to Glasnost*, Toronto, 1989

Grose, Peter, *Gentleman Spy: The Life of Allen Dulles*, London, 1995

Handel, Michael (ed.), *Strategic and Operational Deception in the Second World War*, London, 1987

Harriman, W. Averell, and Abel, Elie, *Special Envoy to Churchill and Stalin, 1941–1946*, New York, 1975

Hess, Gary, *America Encounters India, 1941–1947*, Baltimore, MD, 1971

——, *The United States' Emergence as a Southeast Asian Power, 1940–1950*, New York, 1987

Hitchens, Christopher, *Blood, Class, and Nostalgia: Anglo-American Ironies*, New York, 1990

Horner, D. M., *High Command: Australia and Allied Strategy, 1939–1945*, Canberra, 1982

Hough, Richard, *Mountbatten: Hero of Our Time*, London, 1980

Hoyt, Edwin P., *The Inside Story of a British–American Family in the Pacific and Its Business Enterprises*, Honolulu, 1983

Hyde, H. Montgomery, *The Quiet Canadian*, London, 1962

——, *Secret Intelligence Agent*, London, 1982

James, D. Clayton, *The Years of MacArthur*, Vol. II, *1941–1945*, Boston, MA, 1975

James, Lawrence, *Raj: The Making and Unmaking of British India*, London, 1997

Jeffreys-Jones, Rhodri, *American Espionage: From Secret Service to CIA*, New York, 1977

——, *Eagle Against Empire: American Opposition to European Imperialism, 1914–1982*, Aix-en-Provence, 1983

——, *The CIA and American Democracy*, New Haven, CT, 1989

——, and Andrew, Christopher, *Eternal Vigilance? Fifty Years of the CIA*, London, 1997

——, and Lownie, Andrew, *North American Spies*, Edinburgh, 1991

Johns, Philip, *Within Two Cloaks*, London, 1979

Kahn, David, *Seizing the Enigma*, London, 1991

Kern, Robert W., *Historical Dictionary of Modern Spain, 1700–1988*, New Haven, CT, 1988

Kimball, Warren F., *The Juggler: Franklin Roosevelt as Wartime Statesman*, Princeton, NJ, 1991

——, *The Most Unsordid Act: Lend-Lease, 1939–1941*, Baltimore, MD, 1969

——, *Forged in War: Churchill, Roosevelt and the Second World War*, London, 1997

—— (ed.), *Churchill and Roosevelt: The Complete Correspondence*, three volumes, Princeton, NJ, 1984

—— (ed.), *Unbound: World War II and the Making of a Superpower*, New York, 1992

Langer, William L., and Gleason, S., *The Undeclared War, 1940–1941*, London, 1953

Langford, Nelson D. (ed.), *OSS Against the Reich: The World War II Diaries of Colonel David K. E. Bruce*, Kent, OH, 1991

Larrabee, Eric, *Commander-in-Chief: Franklin Delano Roosevelt, His Lieutenants, and Their War*, New York, 1987

Lash, Joseph P., *Roosevelt and Churchill, 1939–1941: The Partnership That Saved the West*, London, 1977

LeBor, Adam, *Hitler's Secret Bankers: The Myth of Swiss Neutrality During the Holocaust*, Secaucus, NJ, 1997

Leutze, James R., *Bargaining for Supremacy: Anglo-American Naval Collaboration, 1937–1941*, Chapel Hill, NC, 1977

Lewin, Ronald, *Ultra Goes to War*, London, 1981

——, *The American Magic*, New York, 1982

Louis, Wm. Roger, *Imperialism at Bay: The United States and the Decolonization of the British Empire*, Oxford, 1977

Lycett, Andrew, *Ian Fleming*, London, 1995

MacArthur, Douglas, *Reminiscences*, New York, 1964

MacDonnell, Francis, *Insidious Foes: The Axis Fifth Column and the American Home Front*, New York, 1995

McJimsey, George, *Harry Hopkins: Ally of the Poor and Defender of Democracy*, Cambridge, MA, 1987

McNeill, William Hardy, *America, Britain and Russia: Their Co-Operation and Conflict, 1941–1946*, London, 1953

Mahl, Thomas E., *Desperate Deception: British Covert Operations in the United States, 1939–44*, Washington, DC, 1998

Manchester, William, *The American Caesar: Douglas MacArthur, 1880–1964*, London, 1979

Mansergh, Nicholas (ed.), *Constitutional Relations Between Britain and India: The Transfer of Power, 1942–1947*, Vol. III, London, 1971

Merrick, Kenneth A., *Flights of the Forgotten: Special Duties Operations in World War Two*, London, 1989

Miller, Nathan, *Spying for America: The Hidden History of US Intelligence*, New York, 1989

Moran, Lord, *Churchill: Taken from the Diaries*, Boston, MA, 1966

Morgan, Ted, *FDR: A Biography*, London, 1986

O'Toole, G. J. A., *Honorable Treachery: A History of US Intelligence, Espionage, and Covert Action from the American Revolution to the CIA*, New York, 1991

Parker, R. A. C. (ed.), *Winston Churchill: Studies in Statesmanship*, London, 1995

Pawle, Gerald, *The War and Colonel Warden*, London, 1963

Pendar, Kenneth, *Adventure in Diplomacy*, London, 1966

Philby, Kim, *My Silent War*, London, 1968

Phillips, William, *Ventures in Diplomacy*, Portland, OR, 1952

Pilpel, Robert H., *Churchill in America, 1895–1961: An Affectionate Portrait*, New York, 1976

Pimlott, Ben, *Hugh Dalton*, London, 1985

—— (ed.), *The Second World War Diary of Hugh Dalton, 1940–45*, London, 1986

Powers, Richard Gid, *Secrecy and Power: The Life of J. Edgar Hoover*, New York, 1987

Prados, John, *Combined Fleet Decoded: The Secret History of American Intelligence and the Japanese Navy in World War II*, New York, 1995

Preston, Paul, *The Coming of the Spanish Civil War*, London, 1978

——, *Franco*, London, 1993

Reynolds, David, *The Creation of the Anglo-American Alliance, 1937–41: A Study in Competitive Co-Operation*, London, 1981

——, *Rich Relations: The American Occupation of Britain, 1942–1945*, London, 1996

Richards, Brooks, *Secret Flotillas*, London, 1996

Ride, Edwin, *BAAG Hong Kong Resistance, 1942–1945*, Hong Kong, 1981

Robertson, K. G. (ed.), *British and American Approaches to Intelligence*, Basingstoke, 1987

Roosevelt, Archie, *For Lust of Knowing: Memoirs of an Intelligence Officer*, Boston, 1988

Roosevelt, Elliott, *As He Saw It*, New York, 1946

—— (cd.), *FDR: His Personal Letters, 1928–1945*, New York, 1950

Rosenman, Sam, *Working With Roosevelt*, London, 1952

Sainsbury, Keith, *Churchill and Roosevelt at War*, London, 1996

Sherwood, Robert E., *The White House Papers of Harry L. Hopkins*, two volumes, London, 1948, 1949

——, *Roosevelt and Hopkins: An Intimate History*, New York, 1950

Smith, Bradley F., *The Shadow Warriors: OSS and the Origins of the CIA*, London, 1983

——, *The Ultra–Magic Deals and the Most Secret Special Relationship, 1940–1946*, London, 1993

——, *Sharing Secrets With Stalin: How the Allies Traded Intelligence, 1941–1945*, Lawrence, KS, 1996

Smith, R. Harris, *OSS: The Secret History of America's First Central Intelligence Agency*, Berkeley, CA, 1972

Smyth, Denis, *Diplomacy and Strategy of Survival: British Policy and Franco's Spain*, Cambridge, 1986

Soames, Mary, *Clementine Churchill*, London, 1979
—— (ed.), *Speaking for Themselves*, London, 1998
Stafford, David, *Britain and European Resistance, 1940–45*, London, 1980
——, *Camp X: SOE and the American Connection*, London, 1987
——, *The Silent Game*, London, 1987
——, *Churchill and Secret Service*, London, 1997
Steinbeck, John, *The Moon is Down*, London, 1942
Sweet-Escott, Bickham, *Baker Street Irregular*, London, 1965
Taylor, Edmond, *Awakening from History*, London, 1971
Theoharis, Athan, and Cox, John Stuart, *The Boss: J. Edgar Hoover and the Great American Inquisition*, Philadelphia, PA, 1988
Thomas, Hugh, *The Spanish Civil War*, London, 1977
Thomson, Sir Basil, *The Scene Changes*, London, 1939
Thorne, Christopher, *Allies of a Kind: The United States, Britain and the War Against Japan, 1941–1945*, London, 1978
Troy, Thomas F., *Wild Bill and Intrepid: Donovan, Stephenson, and the Origins of the CIA*, New Haven, CT, 1996
Tuchman, Barbara, *The Zimmerman Telegram*, London, 1959
Ward, Geoffrey C., *A First-Class Temperament: The Emergence of Franklin Roosevelt*, New York, 1998
Wasserstein, Bernard, *Secret War in Shanghai: Treachery, Subversion and Collaboration in the Second World War*, London, 1998
Watt, Donald, *Succeeding John Bull: America in Britain's Place, 1900–75*, London, 1984
West, Nigel, *MI6: British Secret Intelligence Service Operations, 1909–45*, London, 1983
——, *Secret War: The Story of SOE*, London, 1992
Williams, Charles, *The Last Great Frenchman: A Life of General de Gaulle*, London, 1993
Wills, Matthew B., *Wartime Missions of Harry L. Hopkins*, Ralegh, NC, 1997
Wilson, Theodore A., *The First Summit: Roosevelt and Churchill at Placentia Bay, 1941*, London, 1969
Winks, Robin, *Cloak and Gown: Scholars in the Secret War, 1939–1961*, New York, 1987
Winterbotham, F. W., *The Ultra Secret*, London, 1974
Yu, Maochun, *OSS in China: Prelude to Cold War*, New Haven, CT, 1996
Ziegler, Philip, *Mountbatten: The Official Biography*, London, 1985

ARTICLES AND CHAPTERS

Addison, Paul, 'Churchill and the Price of Victory: 1939–1945', in Nick

Tiratsoo (ed.), *From Blitz to Blair: A New History of Britain Since 1939*, London, 1997

Aldrich, Richard, 'Imperial Rivalry: British and American Intelligence in Asia, 1942–46', *Intelligence and National Security*, Vol. 3, No. 1, January 1988

——, 'American Intelligence and the British Raj: The OSS, the SSU and India, 1942–1947', *Intelligence and National Security*, Vol. 13, No. 1, Spring 1998

——, 'Britain's Secret Intelligence Service in Asia During the Second World War', *Modern Asian Studies*, Vol. 32, No. 1, February 1998

Angevine, Robert E., '"Gentlemen Do Read Each Other's Mail": American Intelligence in the Interwar Era', *Intelligence and National Security*, Vol. 7, No. 2, April 1992

Brown, Kathryn, 'Intelligence and the Decision to Collect It: Churchill's Wartime Diplomatic Signals Intelligence', *Intelligence and National Security*, Vol. 10, No. 3, July 1995

Currier, Prescott, 'My "Purple Trip" to England in 1941', *Cryptologia*, Vol. XX, No. 3, July 1996

Denniston, Robin, 'Diplomatic Eavesdropping, 1922–1944: A New Source Discovered', *Intelligence and National Security*, Vol. 10, No. 3, July 1995

Dorwart, Jeffery M., 'The Roosevelt–Astor Espionage Ring', *New York History*, Vol. LXII, No. 3, July 1981

Erskine, Ralph, 'Churchill and the Start of the Ultra–Magic Deals', *International Journal of Intelligence and Counter-Intelligence*, Vol. 10, No. 1, January 1997

Ferris, John, 'Whitehall's Black Chamber: British Cryptology and the Government Code and Cypher School, 1919–29', *Intelligence and National Security*, Vol. 2, No. 2, January 1987

——, 'From Broadway House to Bletchley Park: The Diary of Captain Malcolm D. Kennedy, 1934–1946', *Intelligence and National Security*, Vol. 4, No. 3, July 1989

Foot, M. R. D., 'A Comparison of SOE and OSS', in K. G. Robertson (ed.), *British and American Approaches to Intelligence*

Harrison, Richard A., 'Testing the Water: A Secret Probe Towards Anglo-American Military Co-operation in 1936', *International History Review*, Vol. VII, No. 2, May 1985

Handel, Michael, 'The Politics of Intelligence', *Intelligence and National Security*, Vol. 2, No. 4, October 1987

Kahn, David, 'The Intelligence Failure of Pearl Harbor', *Foreign Affairs*, Vol. 70, No. 5, Winter 1991–92

——, 'Roosevelt, Magic, and Ultra', *Cryptologia*, Vol. XVI, No. 4, October 1992

Kruh, Louis, 'British–American Cryptanalytic Co-operation and an Unprecedented Admission by Winston Churchill', *Cryptologia*, Vol. XIII, No. 2, April 1989

Lowenthal, Mark M., 'Searching for National Intelligence: US Intelligence and Policy Before the Second World War', *Intelligence and National Security*, Vol. 6, No. 4, October 1991

McKercher, Brian, 'Churchill, the European Balance of Power and the USA', in R. A. C. Parker (ed.), *Winston Churchill: Studies in Statesmanship*

Manget, Fred F., 'Presidential Powers and Foreign Intelligence Operations', *Journal of Intelligence and Counter-Intelligence*, Vol. 5, No. 2, Summer 1992

Mark, Eduard, 'The OSS in Romania, 1944–45: An Intelligence Operation of the Early Cold War', *Intelligence and National Security*, Vol. 9, No. 2, April 1994

——, 'Venona's Source 19 and the "Trident" Conference of 1943: Diplomacy or Espionage?', *Intelligence and National Security*, Vol. 13, No. 2, Summer 1998

Naftali, Timothy, 'Intrepid's Last Deception: Documenting the Career of Sir William Stephenson', *Intelligence and National Security*, Vol. 8, No. 3, July 1993

Parker, Frederick D., 'The Unsolved Messages of Pearl Harbor', *Cryptologia*, Vol. XV, No. 4, October 1991

Peake, Hayden B., 'Soviet Espionage and the Office of Strategic Services', in Warren F. Kimball (ed.), *Unbound: World War II and the Making of a Superpower*

——, 'OSS and the Venona Decrypts', *Intelligence and National Security*, Vol. 12, No. 3, July 1997

Smith, Bradley F., 'Admiral Godfrey's Mission to America, June/July 1941', *Intelligence and National Security*, Vol. 1, No. 3, September 1986

Smyth, Denis, '"Les Chevaliers de Saint-George": La Grande-Bretagne et la corruption des généraux espagnoles', *Guerre Mondiales*, No. 162, 1991.

Stafford, David, '"Intrepid": Myth and Reality', *Journal of Contemporary History*, Vol. 22, No. 1, April 1987

Sullivan, Brian R., '"A Highly Commendable Action": William J. Donovan's Intelligence Mission for Mussolini and Roosevelt, December 1935–February 1936', *Intelligence and National Security*, Vol. 6, No. 2, April 1991

Thorne, Christopher, 'MacArthur, Australia and the British, 1942–1943: The Secret Journal of MacArthur's British Liaison Officer', *The Australian Outlook*, Vol. 29, Nos 1 and 2, 1975

Windmiller, Marshall, 'A Tumultuous Time: OSS and Army Intelligence in India, 1942–1946', *International Journal of Intelligence and Counter-Intelligence*, Vol. 8, No. 1, Spring 1995

INDEX